KEYNES'S ECONOMICS
AND THE THEORY
OF VALUE AND

KEYNES'S ECONOMICS AND THE THEORY OF VALUE AND DISTRIBUTION

edited by

John Eatwell & Murray Milgate

Duckworth

First published in 1983 by
Gerald Duckworth & Co. Ltd.
The Old Piano Factory
43 Gloucester Crescent, London NW1

ISBN 0 7156 1688 9 (cased)
ISBN 0 7156 1749 4 (paper)

British Library Cataloguing in Publication Data

Keynes's economics and the theory of value and
distribution.
1. Keynes, John Maynard 2. Keynesian economics
I. Eatwell, John II. Milgate, Murray
330.15'6 HB99.7

ISBN 0-7156-1688-9
ISBN 0-7156-1749-4 Pbk

Photoset in North Wales by
Derek Doyle & Associates, Mold, Clwyd
and printed in Great Britain by
Ebenezer Baylis and Son Ltd, Worcester

Contents

Preface

In an article first published in Italian in 1964, which appears here in the English translation of 1978 (Chapter 2), Pierangelo Garegnani changed the perspective of the debate on theories of output and employment by focussing on the relationship between theories of value and distribution and the associated theories of output and employment. He identified the analytical unity of the neoclassical theories of value and distribution and of output and employment as a central issue, and deployed the critique of the former, which derives from the inadequacy of the treatment of capital, as an equally conclusive critique of the latter. Garegnani's emphasis on the role of the theory of value threw open a wide variety of questions: What is the relationship between the classical theory of value and distribution, recently revivified by Sraffa, and the analysis of employment? To what extent have orthodox theorists evaded the difficulties inherent in their theory of value by locating their analyses of employment in the short run (an issue tackled by Garegnani in Chapter 7)? Can capital theoretic results be used to re-assess Keynes's theory of investment which Garegnani identifies as the Achilles' heel (or should it be the Trojan horse?) of the system presented in the *General Theory*? What is meant by a long-run theory of output and employment? What is the relationship between monetary policy and the distribution of income? What role, if any, is played by uncertainty and expectations?

Many of the papers in this book derive from attempts to tackle these questions.[1] The authors are, in general, in agreement with the broad lines of the approach presented by Garegnani, but this does not mean that they would all agree on the details. The issues are of such theoretical novelty that several are still the subject of considerable debate. Probably the most difficult of these issues involves the problems which surround the characterisation of a long-run theory of employment. A long-run position is that in which the structure of capacity has been adjusted to the structure of demand, and hence in which there is a uniform rate of profit in each line of production. This requires that the markets for produced commodities 'clear', but whether there is full

[1] The chapters by Peter Kenway, Richard Kahn and Bertram Schefold have different origins, but their approach is similar to that of the rest of the collection.

employment of labour is quite another question. The neoclassical theory of value and distribution associates the determination of long-run positions with 'clearing' of the labour market. The classical theory, however, does not; the question of the overall level of activity being left open in the classical analysis of value and distribution, in which the size and composition of output is taken as 'given'. But then does Keynes's principle of effective demand provide a new long-run theory of output, i.e. a theory of the determination of that level of output in which the structure of capacity is adjusted to demand, or is it simply a theory of capacity utilisation?[2]

Whatever the controversy concerning the way forward, we hope that the essays collected in this volume will help to clarify the content of current debates on theories of employment and on employment policy. The confusion precipitated by the neoclassical synthesis and by later developments of orthodox theory has seriously distorted both empirical analysis and the formulation of economic policy, and has been a major factor behind the apparent weakness of the theoretical opposition to monetarism. This collection is intended to dispel that confusion.

We wish to thank the Cambridge Political Economy Society and Academic Press for permission to reprint Chapters 2, 3, 4, 5, 8, 9 and 12 from the *Cambridge Journal of Economics*; the editors of the *Review of Economic Studies* for permission to reprint the addendum to Chapter 2; *Thames Papers in Political Economy* and *Annali della Facolta di Economia e Commercio*, Perugia, for permission to reprint Chapter 6; and North-Holland Publishing Company for permission to reprint Chapter 7. The other chapters have not been published before.

Cambridge
May 1983

J.E.
M.M.

[2] In a letter to the editors Garegnani has argued that 'The meaning of "long run" cannot but be partly different when used in connection with a theory of aggregate output than when it is used for the theory of relative output. While the meaning of given plant or productive capacity remains, what is relevant for Marshall is the lack of congruence between relative capacity and relative demand in the several industries. What is relevant for a theory of aggregate output like that of Keynes is the lack of congruence between aggregate capacity and aggregate demand (see above p.24n). When this distinction is made it should be clear that Keynes is concerned with a short period analysis of aggregate output (the determination of the level of capacity utilisation) and that a long period analysis of aggregate output, *i.e.* an analysis of the reciprocal adaptation of aggregate supply and aggregate demand is one and the same thing as a theory of accumulation. This is absent in Keynes apart from some hints we find in the first two sections of chapter 24 of the *General Theory*.' The editors are not in agreement with this argument, but to thrash out the whole issue will require another book!

Contributors

J. Eatwell	Trinity College, Cambridge
P. Garegnani	University of Rome
R.F. Kahn	King's College, Cambridge
P. Kenway	Trinity College, Cambridge
M. Magnani	Bank of Italy
M. Milgate	Sometime Fellow of St Catherine's College, Cambridge, and University of Sydney
C. Panico	Queens' College, Cambridge and University of Naples
J. Robinson	Newnham College, Cambridge
B. Schefold	J.-W. Goethe University, Frankfurt

1

Introduction

John Eatwell and Murray Milgate

The key issues in any consideration of the relationship between the theory of output and the theory of value and distribution can be revealed by the answers given to two questions:

1. Does the determination of relative prices in a market economy also involve the determination of the size and composition of output and, in particular, is the level of output such that labour is fully employed (in the sense that at the going wage all workers willing to offer labour would be able to find employment)?

2. Are variations in relative prices associated with variations in output such that the economy tends towards a level of output compatible with the full employment of labour?

Each of these questions can be supplemented with a further question: if not, why not?

The significance of these questions can be illustrated in terms of the most elementary piece of orthodox neoclassical analysis. This involves the argument that the price of a commodity is determined by the relationship between demand and supply. According to this account, 'equilibrium', determined at the point of intersection of a function relating price to quantity demanded and another relating price to quantity supplied, is defined as market clearing. When this view of price determination is extended to the economic system as a whole, the equilibrium position of the economy is characterised by a set of market-clearing prices, with associated quantities (levels of commodity output and levels of 'factor' utilisation), such that the markets for all commodities and all 'factors of production' clear. In particular, the labour market clears at the equilibrium level of the wage (relative to the associated set of equilibrium prices).

In terms of this familiar approach to the analysis of price formation the answer to the first question is obvious. Equilibrium prices and equilibrium quantities are determined simultaneously. The theory of value, based on demand and supply, is one and the same thing as the theory of output. If there exists an equilibrium set of prices then there exists an equilibrium set of outputs – equilibrium in the sense of market clearing, including the full employment of labour, as defined above. Furthermore, this theory of the simultaneous determination of prices and quantities is typically presented in such a way – by juxtaposing demand and supply functions – that the idea that prices adjust automatically so as to clear markets, thus tending to push the economic system towards a full-employment level of output, seems to follow as a self-evident corollary of the theory. (It does not in fact follow as readily as might appear at first sight, since the stability of an equilibrium is less easily demonstrated than its existence; but we will leave these difficulties to one side for the moment.[1])

Here, then, one has the demand-and-supply (neoclassical) analysis of prices and quantities in a nutshell: the equilibrium set of outputs (and levels of 'factor' utilisation) is determined simultaneously with the equilibrium set of prices (of commodities and 'factors of production'); variations in relative prices, sparked off by an imbalance between demand and supply, will be associated with variations in quantities in a direction which ensures that both prices and quantities tend towards their equilibrium levels. Neoclassical analysis, therefore, answers the first two questions posed above in the affirmative.

An analysis of unemployment may then be derived directly from these relationships between prices and quantities. Any inhibition to the tendency of prices and quantities to find their equilibrium (market-clearing) levels will leave the economic system in disequilibrium with, perhaps, either an excess demand for labour or an excess supply of labour (i.e. unemployment). An

[1] The fact that neoclassical theory lacks adequate stability properties highlights a major weakness of the demand-and-supply approach. Even in the best of all possible worlds, in which all of the most abstract assumptions on preferences and technology required by this theory are satisfied, it is not possible to prove, without resort to additional assumptions devoid of acceptable economic content (like weak gross-substitutability between all commodities), that demand and supply functions yield stable equilibria – let alone to show that these equilibria may sensibly be regarded as 'centres of gravitation' which underlie the necessarily complex day-to-day behaviour that the economic system will exhibit. (On the notion of 'centres of gravitation', see below, pp.8-12.) In fact, the difficulties associated with the proof of stability raise serious doubts about the usefulness of the whole demand-and-supply approach to the question of existence of equilibrium. If one is to have any faith in the notion that the mutual interaction of demand and supply captures the persistent and systematic forces at work in a market economy, then it would not be too much to expect that these 'systematic' forces would be strong enough in themselves to re-establish 'equilibrium' in the face of a one-off disturbance from equilibrium and in the absence of any market imperfections. Since this is the very question that neoclassical stability analysis addresses and fails to answer adequately, one is naturally led to doubt the appropriateness of isolating the forces of demand and supply as the supposedly dominant factors at work. An 'equilibrium' which cannot be shown to be the point towards which the economy would, *ceteris paribus*, tend, cannot be said to capture the systematic forces determining either the 'equilibrium' of the system or its direction of movement.

enormous variety of analyses of unemployment are constructed in this way.

The general tenor of the neoclassical analysis of the causes of unemployment is that while the economy *would* be self-regulating in the best of all possible worlds (i.e. the implicit tendency towards the full employment of labour would be realised) – the market is *inhibited* from fulfilling this task by the presence of certain 'frictions' or 'rigidities'. In the literature on the problem of unemployment, examples of such inhibitions are legion. They include:

'sticky' prices (particularly 'sticky' or even rigidly fixed wages and/or 'sticky' interest rates);

institutional barriers to the efficacy of the price mechanism, such as monopoly pricing (by firms or individual groups of workers);

inefficiencies introduced into the working of the 'real' economy by the operations of the monetary system;

the failure of individual agents to respond appropriately to price signals because of disbelief in those signals, the disbelief being derived from uncertainty about the current or future state of the market, or from incorrect expectations concerning future movements in relative prices, or from false 'conjectures' about the actual state of the market.

Indeed, examples of 'frictions' and 'rigidities' can be multiplied at will – any factor which causes the market to work *imperfectly* will do. It will be convenient, therefore, to group all the authors of the myriad of arguments of this kind together under the general heading of 'imperfectionists'.[2] (For a more detailed discussion of the basis for, and content of, this classification, see Chapter 15.)

From what has already been said, the usefulness of such a classification should be obvious. For although this kind of argument comes in many varieties, each is no more than a particular species of the larger genus. Underlying them is a fundamental similarity: that if the particular aspect (or aspects) of the economic system which gives rise to the breakdown of the market mechanism were to be absent, then the system would tend towards the full employment of labour (and other 'factors of production'). Thus, in all cases, the analysis of unemployment is viewed as no more than an aspect of the neoclassical theory of value and distribution. According to this approach, whether a relatively 'optimistic' or 'pessimistic' stance is taken with respect to the efficacy of the market mechanism in promoting full employment, the analysis of output and employment is part and parcel of the theory of relative

[2] It should be noted that by referring to this kind of analysis as 'imperfectionist' we do not intend to imply that the envisaged failure of the market mechanism to operate in the way depicted by the underlying demand-and-supply theory *necessarily* derives from imperfections of competition.

price determination. This is so even in the case of those imperfectionists who feel that the essential workings of the theory are distorted gravely in the real world.

In marked contrast to the analyses outlined above are those theories of employment which propose no particular functional relationship between prices and quantities. The central proposition of neoclassical analysis, that the theory of value and distribution is also the theory of output, is rejected, together with the connected notion that appropriate variations in relative prices will promote variations in quantities, so moving the economic system in the direction of a full-employment equilibrium.

Unfortunately, this rejection of the neoclassical theory of value and distribution – of the entire apparatus of demand-and-supply analysis – has not always been backed up by rigorous analytical arguments; so much so that it has sometimes been confused with an imperfectionist position. A striking example of this is the rejection by a number of writers of the neoclassical theory of value, and their advocacy of the idea that relative prices, far from being determined by demand and supply, are determined by a mark-up over normal prime cost where this mark-up is insensitive to variations in the conditions of demand (see, for example, Kalecki, 1939; Neild, 1963; Godley and Nordhaus, 1972). Quite apart from the obvious shortcomings of 'mark-up' analysis as a theory of price formation – it is in essence a proposition about the stability of the ratio between prices and costs rather than a theory about the determination of either of those magnitudes, or even of the size of the ratio – this attempt to separate the study of relative price determination from the analysis of output may readily be confused with an imperfectionist argument based on 'sticky' prices arising from the presence of monopolistic or oligopolistic influences in commodity markets.[3] Moreover, the bald assertion that prices and quantities do not bear the well-defined functional relationship to one another that is postulated in neoclassical theory does not provide a satisfactory analytical basis upon which to build up a critique of the neoclassical position.

Yet the requisite critique does exist, and a prominent theme of this book is that this critique is to be found in the outcome of the debate over the neoclassical theory of distribution and, in particular, over its treatment of 'capital' as a 'factor of production' on a par, so to speak, with land and labour. While this debate is seen by many as a rather esoteric controversy in the more abstract realms of economic theory, its implications are more far-reaching than has hitherto been appreciated. The central conclusion of the debate may be summed up, in broad terms, as follows: when applied to the analysis of a capitalistic economy (that is, an economic system where some of the means of production are reproducible), the neoclassical theory is logically incapable of determining the long-run equilibrium of the economy

[3] Thus Malinvaud (1977) cites the results of Godley and Nordhaus (1972) in support of his orthodox imperfectionist position.

and the associated general rate of profit whenever capital consists of more than one reproducible commodity. Since, in equilibrium, relative prices may be expressed as functions of the general rate of profit, the neoclassical proposition that equilibrium prices are determined by demand and supply (or, more generally, by the competitive resolution of individual utility maximisation subject to constraint) is also deprived of its logical foundation (see Garegnani, 1970; the final section of this paper is printed as an addendum to Chapter 2).

The relevance of this critique of the neoclassical theory of value and distribution to the problem of the missing critique of the neoclassical theory of output and employment should be apparent from what has already been said. Because the neoclassical analysis of the determination of prices and the determination of quantities is one and the same theory (that of the mutual interaction of demand and supply), the critique of the neoclassical theory of value is simultaneously a critique of the neoclassical theory of output and employment. Therefore, the first of the two questions that were posed at the very outset of this discussion must, on the grounds of the requirement of logical consistency alone, be answered in the negative. The second question, from which neoclassical theory derives the idea that under the operation of the market mechanism there is a long-run tendency towards a determinate full-employment equilibrium, is rendered superfluous.

But this is not all. If the general (or long-run) case of the neoclassical model has been shown to be logically deficient, then all imperfectionist arguments – which are derived by examining the implications of the introduction of particular (or short-run) modifications into the general case – are incapable of providing a satisfactory analysis of the problem of unemployment. This is not to say that many of the features of the economic system cited by the imperfectionists will have no role to play in a theory of employment based on quite different foundations to those adopted by the neoclassicals. After all, much of the credibility of imperfectionist arguments derives from their pragmatic objections to the direct applicability of the assumptions of the more abstract versions of demand-and-supply theory. But pragmatism is not enough. The implications of more realistic hypotheses must be explored in the context of the general theoretical framework within which they are applied. Since the account of a self-regulating market mechanism which operates according to the theory of demand and supply is unacceptable on the grounds that it is logically inconsistent, any analysis of unemployment which in turn derives its rationale from that very model is also unsatisfactory. The mechanisms of demand-and-supply theory are just not there.[4,5]

[4] The spectacle of professional economists crossing swords in the daily newspapers over whether governments should be advised to adopt those economic policy measures which are suggested by the general neoclassical model or whether they should be more sensible and adopt those policies suggested by a more 'realistic' modification of that model while conceding that, at a general theoretical level at least, they are all on the same side of the fence, is rivalled only by the remarkable propensity of orthodox economic theorists to ignore, or interpret as confirmation

The question that immediately arises is this: if the neoclassical theory of value, distribution, output and employment must be rejected, then what approach to the study of these questions are we to adopt? On this question, the papers collected in this volume are largely of one mind; the gap may be filled by a return to the approach to the study of value and distribution developed by the old classical economists and Marx, and rehabilitated more recently by Piero Sraffa (1960) (but we should note the reservations expressed by Joan Robinson). According to this theory, the size and composition of output is taken as a datum in the determination of relative prices – hence no functional relationship between prices and quantities is involved (on this point, see Eatwell, 1977). From the perspective of the classical characterisation of the workings of a market economy, the analysis of value and distribution is conducted separately from the analysis of output. Of course, in adopting this theoretical stance, neither the old classical economists and Marx nor their modern counterparts would deny that all aspects of the market system (prices, distribution and output) act and react upon one another. Their argument is rather that the analysis of the determination of relative prices is conducted assuming the size and composition of output to be given (i.e. without taking into account, at this stage, the implications of changes in output). Likewise, the analysis of output is conducted assuming prices and distribution as given. Once the explanation of the determination of these variables has been accomplished satisfactorily, their interactions may then be examined in a more complex narrative; but this additional investigation leaves the process of determination of the relevant variables unaltered. These *separable* explanations of the forces which determine relative prices, distribution and output, and the *subsequent* consideration of the interactions between them, is the hallmark of the classical approach to economic theory. It should not be confused with the necessary simultaneous determination of these magnitudes that neoclassical theory entails.

Thus we arrive at the basic conclusions concerning the relationship between theories of output and theories of value to which the attempt to answer our two initial questions has led. Alternative analyses of unemployment can be distinguished on the basis of whether the study of the factors determining output (and employment) is separable from the study of value and distribution or whether the analysis of output and employment is treated as an aspect of the theory of value and distribution. The discredited neoclassical theory *and* its imperfectionist variants fall into the latter category; the classical theory of value falls into the former.

---

of the presence of 'frictions' or 'rigidities', the steadily accumulating literature of applied economics that has failed to find evidence that any of the neoclassical mechanisms are actually present in real market economies.

[5] The *theory* that states that the equilibrium position is determined by supply and demand should be carefully distinguished from the proposition that competition (sometimes called the 'law' of supply and demand) tends to *establish* normal prices, the magnitude of which is determined by forces captured in a different theory altogether (see Eatwell, 1982).

Moreover, since the study of value and distribution along classical lines leaves 'open' the question concerning the determination of the normal levels of output and employment (as shown by Garegnani in Chapter 2), the development of the classical alternative leads directly to the requirement of providing a satisfactory theory of output which is not essentially connected with the analysis of value. The interesting new idea that emerges from the general line of enquiry pursued in this book is that Keynes's theory of effective demand provides just such an analysis of output and employment.

The proposition that the level of activity is determined by the level of expenditure, and that the volume of savings is maintained (in the long run) in equality with the amount of investment by variations in the aggregate level of output, does not rely for its general validity upon any theory concerning the joint determination of equilibrium relative prices and quantities such as that provided by the neoclassicals. Indeed, precisely the reverse is true: the theory of effective demand when applied to the long-period analysis of output and employment is incompatible with such joint determination of prices and quantities. Keynes's use of the propensity to consume as the link between investment, output and saving replaces the neoclassical mechanism of adjustment which is supposed to operate via variations in relative prices (and, in particular, the rate of interest). The theory of effective demand thus establishes a normal level of output which is not necessarily that which ensures the full employment of labour. The neoclassical presumption that there will always be forces at work (however 'weak' the imperfectionists may assert their influence to be) tending to push output towards the full-employment level has no place in Keynes's economics.

This, of course, refers only to Keynes's original contribution in the *General Theory* of a theory of output and employment based on the principle of effective demand. Unfortunately, however, Keynes detracted from the strength of his own argument by re-introducing elements of the neoclassical theory of value and distribution in his discussions of the determinants of the volume of investment. By proposing a functional link between distribution (the rate of interest) and the amount of investment in the form of the marginal efficiency of capital schedule, the possibility re-emerged that appropriate variations in the rate of interest will initiate changes in the level of investment that would tend to push the economic system towards full employment. To obviate this possibility, Keynes was led to defer to the liquidity-preference theory of the rate of interest, and so to the role of uncertainty and expectations, which ensure a 'stickiness' in the rate of interest – i.e. to an essentially imperfectionist argument.[6] This is exactly the kind of argument that, for almost fifty years, mainstream writers, ignoring the radical implications that Keynes himself felt would follow from the application of the principle of effective demand to

[6] An alternative imperfectionist argument, which has less textual basis in the *General Theory*, invokes the idea of a relatively inelastic investment demand function so that even if the rate of interest were 'free' to vary, the volume of investment would be 'unresponsive' to such variations.

the determination of the normal levels of output and employment, have asserted to be the only appropriate interpretation of Keynes. Thus, paradoxically, we have witnessed the spectacle of a supposedly 'Keynesian alternative' that rests upon just the sort of imperfectionist arguments that are everywhere apparent in the writings of Marshall and Pigou, Keynes's arch theoretical adversaries.

The presence of both radical and orthodox elements in the *General Theory* calls for two observations. The first concerns the problem of the interpretation of that book. A careful examination of Keynes's central arguments in the constructive parts of the *General Theory* reveals that an interpretation which emphasises the radical, as opposed to the orthodox strands of thought therein is more consistent with the substance of Keynes's positive arguments as well as being more in line with Keynes's own views on the significance of his contribution (see Chapters 5 and 10). Moreover, on Keynes's own authority, the orthodox elements are not essential to his main thesis. The second observation relates to the theoretical consistency of those orthodox elements themselves. For it turns out that the critique of the neoclassical theory of value and distribution is also a critique of the idea that there exists an inverse relationship between the amount of investment and the rate of interest (i.e. Keynes's marginal efficiency of capital schedule) (see Chapter 2). When taken together, these two facts imply that the marginal-efficiency-of-capital theory of investment must be dropped, and that only the principle of effective demand can be retained. But in the reconstruction of a more consistent approach to the study of value, distribution and output, this is a positive step – for it is the principle of effective demand that provides the basis for an analysis of output which does not involve the simultaneous determination of prices and quantities and which is, at the same time, perfectly compatible with the classical theory of value and distribution.

Thus we arrive at the major theme that emerges from the contributions assembled in this volume. The relationship between Keynes's theory of output and employment is addressed from the perspective of whether the analysis of output is one and the same thing as the analysis of value and distribution or whether it is *separable* (in the sense defined above, p. 6) from the analysis of value and distribution.

However, this straightforward perspective may be obscured by a number of issues which must be dealt with before we can proceed: the relationship between the long run and the short run in the analysis of output and employment, the change in the notion of equilibrium in modern neoclassical general equilibrium theory, the treatment of uncertainty and expectations, and the separation of 'macro-economics' from 'micro-economics'.

Long run and short run

In orthodox neoclassical circles, Keynes's economics is typically characterised as consisting essentially of a 'short-run theory of output'.

Although the definition of the 'short run' is sometimes left unstated, there can be little doubt that it is thought to be analogous to Marshall's famous distinction between the short-run and long-run equilibrium of the firm. Such interpretations of Keynes's economics as a short-run theory usually cite in support of their case Keynes's own usage of the term in the *General Theory*. Yet a careful examination of the context within which Keynes adopts this concept reveals that he is using it in an altogether different sense than did Marshall.

For Marshall, the short run and the long run both refer to the same given set of circumstances. The short run is that state of the economy in which the system has not yet fully adjusted itself to an equilibrium between demand and supply that is consistent with the given set of circumstances (firms, for example, may have not yet adjusted the level and composition of their production to the composition and level of demand). The long run, on the other hand, is that state of the economy where full adjustment has taken place. Borrowing the terminology of Adam Smith, Marshall regarded these long-period 'normal' positions as centres of gravitation of the system; that is, positions toward which the economy would tend to be pushed under the influence of the more systematic and persistent forces which characterise its operation.

The significance of this distinction between long-run and short-run analysis when it is applied within the context of neoclassical demand and supply theory is readily apparent. For although the conclusions of the long-run version of this theory imply the full employment of labour (and other 'factors of production'), in any short-run situation in which complete adjustment has not occurred, there will be no guarantee that the long-run conclusions apply. In particular, there may well be unemployment in the short run. Of course, there is still the presumption that there will be a tendency for such short-run unemployment to be eliminated as the operation of the price mechanism sets in motion forces which drive the economic system towards its long-run, full employment position. Thus, since short-run analysis is derived directly from long-run analysis, it can have no meaning independently of that long-run analysis. The conclusions of short-run neoclassical theory temporarily modify, but do not overturn, the validity of the conclusions of the long-run theory – they stand in relation to long-run conclusions in the same way as the particular case stands in relation to the general case. Whatever theory is offered for the determination of long-run variables, it is not left behind by moving to a consideration of a short-run deviations. When one seeks to discover the theoretical foundations of any short-run analysis, one must look to its basis in the associated long-run theory.

From this essentially simple perspective, it becomes apparent that many imperfectionist analyses of unemployment are no more than examples of short-run neoclassical theory where, for example, full adjustment is inhibited by relatively 'sticky' prices. The label of 'Keynesian' is then often misleadingly applied to such arguments by drawing on one or other of the more memorable of Keynes's pre-*General Theory* statements such as 'we are always in the short run' or 'in the long run we are all dead'. The problem is that while such an argument was undoubtedly at the bottom of the discussion in Keynes's early writings, in particular the *Tract on Monetary Reform* and the *Treatise on Money*,[7] the idea that such an analysis underlies the central propositions of the *General Theory* is seriously to be questioned.

In the *General Theory*, Keynes's 'short-run' analysis is quite different in content from anything that is to be found in Marshall. For while this Keynesian short run refers to a set of circumstances where 'we take as given the existing skill and quantity of available labour, the existing quality and quantity of available equipment, and the existing technique' (Keynes, 1936, p. 245), it is invoked not in order to establish the possibility that complete adjustment to a long-run full employment equilibrium of the neoclassical kind will not occur. but rather in order to abstract from those more slowly working secular changes due to accumulation, technological progress and population growth or decline. This procedure, by allowing Keynes to focus upon the persistent and systematic forces that act to determine the levels of output and employment, is more directly analogous to that traditionally adopted for the construction of a long-period theory – the important difference being that the determining circumstances offered by Keynes (i.e. the theory of employment and output based on the principle of effective demand) are not those of 'demand and supply' that form the basis of the conventional neoclassical wisdom.

The change in the concept of equilibrium

The debate over the issues covered by the articles collected in this book has been made rather more difficult than it might have been by the change in the concept of equilibrium used by neoclassical economists. This change, the origins of which may be traced to the inter-war period (Milgate, 1979), has been shown by Garegnani (Chapter 7) to be a reaction to the logical deficiencies of the neoclassical analysis of value and distribution; deficiencies which were fully exposed in the capital theory debate.

The change in the concept of equilibrium has involved the abandonment of the notion of the equilibrium of the economy as the centre of gravitation towards which the competitive decisions of profit-maximising entrepreneurs would tend to push the system – a centre of gravitation consequently characterised by a *uniform* rate of profit on the cost of production of the capital used in each particular line. Modern neoclassical economists have replaced this traditional notion of equilibrium by a concept of equilibrium as a position in which all markets clear, including markets for an *arbitrary* stock

[7] Indeed, it is from the former of these two works, dating from 1923, that Keynes's more celebrated estimates of the 'length' of the short run are drawn – not from the *General Theory* at all.

of capital goods, where there is *no* presumption that the rate of profit on the reproduction cost of capital goods will be uniform. Since this type of equilibrium is typically presented as a temporal sequence of instantaneously cleared markets, it may be called an 'intertemporal equilibrium'. There are a number of versions of such 'intertemporal' equilibria, ranging from Hicks's 'temporary equilibrium' to the Arrow-Debreu 'full intertemporal equilibrium'. However, all versions suffer from the same fundamental deficiencies. Since they are positions of the economy in which the rate of profit is not uniform, they are positions from which profit-maximising entrepreneurs would tend to move away. Hence they cannot be characterised as centres of gravitation: as positions to which the economy would tend. (This argument is presented in greater detail in Eatwell, 1982.)

None the less, this unsatisfactory concept of equilibrium has been adopted as the new object for neoclassical demand-and-supply theory. Incapable of providing a logically coherent explanation of the determination of *long-run* equilibrium, the same theoretical apparatus is now applied to the new conception of equilibrium. And imperfectionist arguments are likewise transmuted to the new environment. Since the essence of the imperfectionist position is the inability of the economy to achieve market-clearing equilibrium, the same analysis applies whether the (logically unsuccessful) attempt is made to characterise the long-period position as market-clearing, or whether the analysis is applied to the new intertemporal definition of equilibrium. Indeed, the fact that the 'equilibrium' from which the imperfectionist position deviates (and in terms of which it is defined) is not the long-period position of the economy, is typically ignored; formal results on intertemporal models are interpreted *as if* they applied to a model in which the equilibrium was a competitive centre of gravitation.

The development of imperfectionist arguments within the intertemporal general equilibrium setting is, therefore, doubly disingenuous. Disequilibrium arguments are developed in terms of a concept of equilibrium which is itself a 'disequilibrium' in the sense that it is a point from which profit-maximising entrepreneurs would tend to move away. And these arguments are then applied to concrete analyses of wages, unemployment, fiscal and monetary policy etc., presupposing (incorrectly) that the equilibria they define *do* capture the dominant forces of the economy and hence do define a centre of gravitation. Yet there is little point in discussing policy issues if it cannot reasonably be supposed that general tendencies in the economy are captured by the notion of equilibrium which serves as the benchmark for that analysis. Intertemporal equilibrium manifestly fails to meet this requirement.

There are general analytical reasons for rejecting the concept of equilibrium used in modern general equilibrium theory; these are outlined by Garegnani in Chapter 7. When attempts are made, via imperfectionist arguments, to derive results which might be used to interpret the actual behaviour of the economy, the sterility of the underlying concept of equilibrium is starkly revealed (some examples of this are highlighted by Kahn in his criticisms of Malinvaud in Chapter 12).

It is important to stress that our arguments should not be mistaken for the advocacy of what has been referred to above as 'long-period analysis' to the exclusion of everything else. The true point is rather different – it is that if one wishes to conduct an adequate 'disequilibrium' analysis one must first be satisfied that the 'equilibrium' analysis from which the disequilibrium is *necessarily* derived is acceptable in terms of two connected and minimal conditions: that the 'equilibrium' *theory* satisfies the requirement of logical consistency and that the notion of equilibrium (which expresses the *object* that the theory is to explain) captures the persistent and systematic forces that work through competition towards equalisation of the rate of profit on the supply-price of capital. Early neoclassical theory, which chose as its object the long-period positions of the system, clearly met the second condition but failed, as the capital theory debates of the 1960s manifestly showed, to meet the requirements of logical consistency. Modern neoclassical economics, based on the notion of intertemporal equilibrium, fails to meet the second condition. Imperfectionist arguments (or 'disequilibrium' analysis) derived from either of these two versions of neoclassical economics must therefore be rejected, even if for somewhat different reasons.

Uncertainty and expectations

Much confusion has been introduced into the debate on theories of unemployment by the variety of roles given to uncertainty and expectations. Uncertainty concerning future events is a fact of life, and expectations concerning the likely path of the economy undoubtedly affect economic decisions. But it is not immediately obvious what role these essentially unobservable factors should play in the formulation of economic analysis.

Economic analysis attempts to identify the fundamental causal relationships underlying the working of a market economy. The multiplier, for example, traces the impact of investment on the aggregate level of output. The effects of mistakes made by individuals because of their past uncertainties concerning future events will be revealed by the objective circumstances of today. For example, past uncertainty over the future demand for a given product may have led to its being underproduced, and will clearly be evident by either its market price being above its long-run normal price, or by run-down of stocks, or a lengthening of order-books, or any combination of these. The influence of uncertainty is just one of those multitude of influences which cause the day-to-day circumstances of the economy to deviate from the long-run normal position. Uncertainty and expectations may thus be confined to the category of 'temporary' or non-systematic effects, as distinct from the persistent and systematic forces which act to determine the long-run position.

If, on the other hand, an attempt is made to locate uncertainty and expectations within the class of the persistent, systematic forces characterising the workings of the economy, then the analysis becomes bereft of any definite result – the behaviour of the economy being as arbitrary as the hypothesis made about the formation of expectations.

In fact, a very interesting example of the arbitrary character of assumptions on the formation of expectations is provided by the recent interest in models of so-called 'rational expectations'. The essential proposition of the rational expectations hypothesis is that individuals 'rationally' use the economic information available to them, so that the expected value of their prediction of the future magnitudes of economic variables is equal to the prediction that would be made by the relevant and correct economic theory. Hence the expected value of forecasting error is zero. The position of the economy may only be affected by random events or imperfect information – expectations do not matter. In this way the rational expectations hypothesis removes the role of expectations as far as the determination of the long-run position of the economy is concerned; this is left to be characterised in terms of dominant behavioural relations which are specified independently of uncertainty. In this latter sense, in exposing the true nature of the theory used, rational expectations models are a considerable advance over the imperfectionist models which attempt to analyse unemployment in terms of the arbitrary imperfections introduced into the operation of the price mechanism by erroneous expectations (or, in some cases, by an all-pervasive uncertainty which renders the price mechanism completely impotent).[8]

What is wrong with the rational expectations hypothesis is not that the role of expectations as an element in the general analysis of economic behaviour is reduced – that is a forward step. What is wrong is rather that, first, the model adopted by the rational expectations theorists is the neoclassical theory of value and output, and secondly, that the role of expectations is purged from the system by making manifestly improbable assumptions on the economic behaviour of individuals, rather than by the recognition that such factors have no role to play in an economic analysis which is to have any definite content (this point is discussed in greater detail in Chapter 15).

The treatment of expectations as 'secondary', would seem to sit ill with the obvious point that uncertainty is a fact of economic life and that many economic decisions necessarily involve some estimation of future events. However, the point being made is that economic theory should be confined to those phenomena which may be analysed in terms of the concrete

[8] Unfortunately, some credibility was given to these imperfectionist exercises by Keynes's appeal to the role of uncertainty (notably in Keynes, 1937a); an appeal motivated by the unfortunate consequences attendant upon his reintroduction of the price mechanism into the analysis of output, in the form of the marginal efficiency of capital schedule. This has lead many anti-neoclassical writers erroneously to locate the essential novelty of the *General Theory* in the role attributed to expectations, rather than in the new theory of saving and investment; thus blurring the distinction between a separable analysis of output and an analysis of output which is merely based on imperfectionist arguments (see Chapter 14).

behavioural relations of a market economy, and should eschew those phenomena about which nothing definite can be said. Uncertainty may be a fact of life, but the market economy operates systematically in an uncertain world, and it is those systematic operations which are the proper subject matter of economics. Neoclassical analysis has accustomed economists to placing unreasonable faith in subjective propositions. But when subjective factors are projected from the present into the future what was unreasonable becomes ridiculous.

The confusion introduced by appeals to the role of uncertainty and expectations is particularly clear in the analysis of investment. Investment decisions must be affected in some way by estimations of the future, but there is no reason to suppose that these estimations follow any systematic pattern. Indeed, there is no reason to suppose that investment can be analysed in terms of a simple parametric model. In neoclassical theory investment is reduced to an element within the theory of value and distribution, the function relating investment to the rate of interest being confronted with a function relating saving to the rate of interest in order to determine the equilibrium volume of saving and investment. As the capital theory debates have shown, this view of investment is logically untenable. How then is investment to be analysed?

Investment is accumulation, and the process of accumulation in market economies is a process which varies in character from one historical period to another, indeed from one specific economy to another. Some generalisations can be made – e.g., the rate of investment will probably be positively affected by the rate of growth of demand, by the rate of technological change, even by growth of population. But attempts to construct a general 'model' would seem to be misconceived. There is no general behavioural 'mechanism' determining investment, analogous to the mechanism linking investment and output, or that linking the level of real wages and the rate of profit.

Macroeconomics and microeconomics

Up to this point we have deliberately refrained from commenting on a now customary issue in 'Keynesian' economics: the relationship between macroeconomics and microeconomics. The explanation for this omission is that it would not have been possible to set this distinction in its appropriate analytical context without first having traced the basis of the neoclassical theory of output (and employment) to its foundation in the neoclassical explanation of the determination of relative prices. For the distinction between macroeconomics and microeconomics was introduced into neoclassical economics largely in an attempt to accommodate the seemingly incompatible conclusions drawn on the one hand by Keynes in the *General Theory* concerning the levels of output and employment, and on the other by the orthodox theorists of value and distribution.

Initially, at least, the distinction between macroeconomics and microeconomics became associated in neoclassical literature with the idea that the differences in the conclusions arrived at by Keynes ('macroeconomics') and those arrived at by the theory of value and distribution ('microeconomics') were somehow to be accounted for by the doctrine that 'what is true for the individual producer or consumer (microeconomics) need not be true for these individuals treated in the aggregate (macroeconomics)'. This doctrine, in turn, spawned a more serious and voluminous literature on the 'problem of aggregation' and led eventually to a whole programme of research devoted to unearthing the microfoundations of 'Keynesian' macroeconomics.

It should be clear, however, that this approach to the discussion and development of Keynes's contribution to economic theory is no more than the familiar imperfectionist theme in another guise: the question is merely one of reconciling the possibility of prolonged unemployment with the key implication of the neoclassical theory of value and distribution that there will always be forces at work in a market economy tending to push the system towards a configuration of relative prices compatible with the full employment of 'factors of production' (including labour). Indeed, when the literature on the formal problem of aggregation seemed to be leading only towards successively more perplexing mathematical conundrums – thus leaving 'Keynesian' macroeconomics with apparently no foundation in the neoclassical theory of value and distribution – the problem began explicitly to be tackled in the imperfectionist framework by investigating what modifications could be introduced into the theory of value and distribution (microeconomics) so as to produce 'Keynesian' conclusions.

As we have seen, such attempts to accommodate Keynes in an imperfectionist framework, like the neoclassical theory of value and distribution upon which it is based, have been applied indifferently to the analysis of long-period normal equilibrium *and* to the analysis of intertemporal equilibrium. Similarly, a microeconomic foundation for 'Keynesian' macroeconomics has been sought within both of these systems. In both cases, the argument has been returned to the point from which it began: the necessity of modifying the orthodox view of price formation to deal with an analysis of unemployment. But, given the logical inconsistency of the long-period version of the neoclassical theory of value and distribution (see above, pp. 4-5), together with the fact that the alternative neoclassical approach, couched in terms of the notion of intertemporal equilibrium, does not provide a satisfactory object of analysis (see above, pp.10-12), the attempt to derive 'macroeconomic' conclusions from a microfoundation taken from either of these neoclassical approaches to the theory of value, distribution and output is unacceptable.

In the final analysis, it would seem better to avoid the use of the terms 'macroeconomics' and 'microeconomics' if only because their use obscures the substantive analytical point at issue in the debate over the connection between them, i.e. the relationship between a theory of output and a theory of value and distribution.

Concluding remarks

By now it should be clear that one of the main aims of this book is to smoke out the imperfectionist interpretations of Keynes's theory of output and employment and to reveal them in a clearer analytical perspective. At best these interpretations are no more than an uneasy and misleading compromise between concerned pragmatism and an unwieldy and unsatisfactory theory of value and distribution based on demand and supply. At worst, they represent mystifying apologetics for this discredited economic theory itself.[9]

On the positive side, the essays assembled in this volume provide the essential ingredients of a framework for demonstrating the manner in which the classical theory of value may be regarded as being congruent with Keynes's principle of effective demand. The potential for a reconstruction of economic theory along these lines is not difficult to grasp – some of the new perspectives it entails have been outlined in this introductory essay. Of course, many difficult analytical problems remain to be settled, not the least of which are to be found in the important areas of the theory of money and the theory of capitalist accumulation. Yet it is not too much to hope that, starting from the more appropriate analysis of value, distribution and output which emerges in these essays, a measure of perseverance and consistency of purpose will yield fruitful results in these crucial fields of study.

The implications of this new approach can be summed up in the answers it provides to the two questions posed at the beginning of this chapter:

1. The determination of relative prices in a market economy does not involve the simultaneous determination of the size and composition of output. Prices and quantities are determined by separable, though interacting forces. The level of output associated with long-run normal prices is not necessarily the full-employment level.

2. Variations in relative prices are determined by forces which have no immediate relation to the forces determining the level of output. The economic system will certainly tend towards its centre of gravitation, but that centre is not necessarily a full-employment position.

The simple reason why full employment disappears from the picture is that relative prices just are not determined in accordance with the principles of the neoclassical theory of demand and supply. Instead, the level of employment is determined by the level of effective demand; a magnitude which is

[9] As an example of the latter: 'But of course it is absolutely correct to maintain that every feature of an actual economy which Keynes regarded as important is missing in Debreu .... But it is also true that Debreu and others have made a significant contribution to the understanding of Keynesian economics just by describing so precisely what would have to be the case if there were to be no Keynesian problems' (Hahn, 1973a, p. 34).

not susceptible to systematic variation in the face of changes in relative prices, the wage rate or the rate of profit. When the discussion of economic policy is conducted in the framework provided by these simple propositions, it will acquire a more logically consistent and empirically relevant content.

It is not without interest to recall, in conclusion, some remarks of Keynes which seem not only to capture the general flavour of the arguments presented in this introduction, but also to suggest the particular analytical task that the articles in this book tackle:

> On the one side are those who believe that the existing economic system is, in the long run, a self-adjusting system, though with creaks and groans and jerks, and interrupted by time lags, outside interference and mistakes ...
>
> On the other side of the gulf are those who reject the idea that the existing economic system is, in any significant sense, self-adjusting ...
>
> The strength of the self-adjusting school depends on its having behind it almost the whole body of organised economic thinking and doctrine of the last hundred years. This is a formidable power. It is the product of acute minds and has persuaded and convinced the great majority of the intelligent and disinterested persons who have studied it. It has vast prestige and a more far-reaching influence than is obvious. For it lies behind the education and the habitual modes of thought, not only of economists, but of bankers and business men and civil servants and politicians of all parties ...
>
> Thus, if the heretics on the other side of the gulf are to demolish the forces of nineteenth-century orthodoxy ... they must attack them in their citadel. No successful attack has yet been made ... They have made no impression on the citadel. Indeed, many of them themselves accept the orthodox premises; and it is only because their flair is stronger than their logic that they do not accept its conclusions (Keynes, 1973, vol. 13, pp. 486-9).

PART ONE

Analysis

2

Notes on consumption, investment and effective demand

Pierangelo Garegnani

The purpose of these Notes is to reconsider the theoretical problems raised by the question of the long run influence of consumption on investment.

Current economic theory does not appear to provide a generally accepted answer to this question: its position on the issue is ambiguous and contradictory. Pre-Keynesian theory gave a simple answer: the level of investment is determined by the community's decision to save, allowance always being made for frictions not dissimilar to those admitted in other parts of economic theory. In order to obtain a larger volume of investment, consumption should be discouraged. The criticism by Keynes has shown the weakness of this traditional answer. But while Keynes's different conclusions have been generally accepted for the analysis of trade cycles and other short-period phenomena, the theoretical situation remains uncertain with respect to the long period, which is our primary concern here. With respect to long-period

* Reprinted from *Cambridge Journal of Economics* 1978, **2**, 335-53 and **3**, 63-82. These notes are an abridged version of a paper first published in Italian in *Economia Internazionale,* 1964 and 1965. The translation has been prepared by Jan Kregel, Ian Steedman and the author. The original paper was itself taken from the theoretical part of a study conducted in 1961 for the 'Associazione per lo Sviluppo del Mezzogiorno' (SVIMEZ). The subject of that study was the relationship between consumption and investment in the Italian economy. The theoretical part included, besides the material of this article, an analysis of how the independence of investment from the capacity to save may assert itself in the course of a process of accumulation. This was done with particular regard to economies with a large reserve of labour which either is unemployed or utilises traditional methods of production. The theoretical part was followed by an empirical part in which a comparison between unutilised capacity and the additional outputs required, directly and indirectly, by hypothetical additional investment (for 1955-60), specified in volume and composition, seemed to suggest that the limit to investment in Italy in that period was set by the incentive to invest and not by the level of consumption, contrary to what was then often argued. The results of the study are available as a mimeographed volume from SVIMEZ (via di Porta Pinciana, 6, Rome), which I thank for permission to publish the part contained in these Notes. I also wish to thank Claudio Napoleoni, Sergio Steve, Paolo Sylos-Labini and Volrico Travaglini for their comments on the manuscripts of this work.

analysis some discussions of Keynes's theory, conducted on the assumption of flexible wages and prices – or, more realistically, on the assumption of a flexible monetary policy – have, in fact, created a climate of professional opinion by no means hostile to a reaffirmation, in less rigid terms, of the traditional theory – though they have not succeeded in restoring to that theory the confidence it once enjoyed.

Our consideration of the problem has seemed useful because the terms in which the question has been discussed so far may be significantly modified, in the present writer's view, by the recent criticisms of the notion of 'capital' as a factor of production.

The traditional doctrine, in which planned investment adjusts to planned savings, appears to be centred on the idea of an investment demand function elastic with respect to the rate of interest. This idea has not been disputed in the course of the Keynesian controversy, at least with respect to long-run conditions. Keynes himself adopted it in the form of the 'marginal efficiency of capital' and focused his criticism on the notion that the rate of interest would be flexible enough to be the equilibrator of saving and investment decisions. This particular course, followed by the Keynesian controversy, is important, we believe, for an explanation of the present theoretical uncertainty concerning problems of capital accumulation. The notion of a demand function for investible resources has, in fact, provided the main basis for attempts to confine to short-period conditions the obstacles which impede the equilibrating role of the rate of interest and has thus favoured the persistence, in part of the literature, of a confidence in the traditional theory of accumulation.

We shall argue in these Notes that this notion of an interest-elastic investment demand function has its basis in the conception of capital as a factor employable in production in proportions which will increase, relative to other factors, as the rate of interest decreases. It follows that the recent criticism of this conception of capital has an important bearing on the question of the influence of consumption on investment. We shall indeed argue that such criticism provides a firmer ground for the rejection of the long-period dependence of investment on decisions to save.

These Notes will consist of two parts. In Part I we shall investigate the premises from which traditional theory derived the assertion that there exists a tendency for effective demand to adapt to productive capacity. We shall see in section 1.1 how this is the question which lies behind the problem of the relation between consumption and investment. The analysis will begin, in section 1.2, by distinguishing between two theoretical approaches which Keynes included in what he called the 'classical school': that of Ricardo and the 'classical school' proper, on the one hand, and, on the other, that of the later marginalist theories to which Keynes was in fact referring. In sections 1.3-1.6 we shall then proceed to argue that it is in these latter theories only that we can find premises supporting the traditional thesis. In section 1.7 we shall then discuss the validity of these premises, and conclude that, even if we remain within the limits of an analysis conducted in 'real' and 'static' terms – abstracting, that is, from the obstacles which the monetary system and the state of expectations may raise for an equilibrating process – economic theory does not seem to provide a sufficient basis for the idea that market forces can ensure the adjustment of decisions to invest to decisions to save in the long period.

In Part II the question will be taken up in the context of monetary theory, within which Keynes conducted his criticism of traditional theory. We shall then examine the subsequent attempts to support the traditional doctrine by means of an analysis founded on the hypothesis of flexible money wages, or, alternatively, a flexible monetary policy. We shall seek to show that these attempts rest crucially on the hypothesis of a high interest elasticity of investment. At this point we shall refer back to the result of the analysis in 'real' terms conducted in Part I and conclude that even in long periods and in normal situations, investment will be independent of saving decisions, at least below the limit set by the community's saving in conditions of full utilisation of productive capacity and constancy of the level of prices.

Part I: 'Real' analysis

1.1. The tendency to a full utilisation of productive capacity

As is well known, the position of traditional theory on the relation between consumption and investment derives from the idea that the aggregate demand for output tends to the level which ensures the full utilisation of the available productive capacity. Let us in fact assume a rise in the relevant part of the curve representing the community's propensity to consume. If productive capacity always tended to be fully utilised, the increased output of consumption goods could only be obtained by decreasing the output of capital goods, i.e. by decreasing investment.[1] Traditional theories did not, of course, ignore the possibility of 'frictions' capable of delaying the achievement of full utilisation of productive capacity; it was in terms of these 'frictions' that trade cycles were explained. But this admission did not alter the conclusion that the volume of investment, taken as an average over a normal succession of periods of prosperity and depression, would be determined by the community's decisions to save.

However, when we admit, as Keynes did, the possibility of equilibria with partial utilisation of productive capacity, the traditional thesis can no longer be maintained. An upward shift of the schedule of the propensity to consume might in fact result in an increased utilisation of productive capacity and might therefore result in a constant, or even an increased, volume of investment. The question of the effect on investment thus remains open: invest-

[1] A closed economy will be assumed; we shall also abstract from all state economic activity other than monetary policy.

ment might decrease if production is close to the limit of productive capacity, but the opposite effect is also possible – and indeed probable if there are margins of unutilised productive capacity, whether they be large or small.

In the following sections we shall examine the premises from which traditional theory derived the doctrine that market forces lead to the full utilisation of productive capacity. Before proceeding to this examination, however, an observation must be made. By productive capacity we have so far meant the equipment of capital goods[2] in existence in the economy in a given situation, together with only that part of the total supply of labour which is required for the full utilisation of this equipment. By this definition we have departed from the terms in which the controversy between Keynes and traditional theory was conducted. It was there assumed that a full utilisation of the existing capital equipment would allow for the employment of the entire labour force.

The more general notion of productive capacity we have so far used would seem to be the appropriate one in discussing long period tendencies, where unemployment of labour from below-capacity utilisation of equipment may itself generate so-called 'structural' unemployment unless it is quickly corrected; indeed this notion of capacity has been that on which the traditional thesis of the alternative between consumption and investment had to be based in order to apply it to economies with 'structural' unemployment. A difficulty however would be raised by using the general notion in the rest of this paper, for the assumptions by which such 'structural' unemployment has been reconciled with traditional theory (i.e., fundamentally, the existence of circumstances imposing a real wage higher than that which competition would enforce, and the lack of a sufficient variability in the proportions between capital and labour) would interfere with an examination of the Keynesian controversy in its own terms. We have accordingly decided to separate the two issues: our examination of the Keynesian controversy will be carried out under the assumption that existing equipment suffices to employ the entire supply of labour, whereas the applicability of our conclusions to an economy with 'structural' unemployment will be considered later, at the end of Part II of these Notes.

1.2. Ricardo and 'Say's Law'

As soon as we consider the question of the premises from which the traditional theories drew the conclusion about the tendency to 'full employment', it becomes necessary to distinguish clearly between the two

[2] As usual, productive equipment is assumed to be appropriate to the composition of aggregate demand at its full employment level, so as to abstract from problems of disproportions among industries. In what follows the concept of 'productive equipment' will refer only to fixed capital goods; it may be supposed that circulating capital (stocks and goods in process) can adapt rapidly to changes in the level of activity.

types of theories which Keynes included in what he called the 'classical school'. According to Keynes that school included Ricardo and 'the *followers* of Ricardo ... who adopted and perfected the theory of the Ricardian economics, including (for example) J.S. Mill, Marshall, Edgeworth and Professor Pigou' (Keynes, 1936, p. 3). Now, the theory of Ricardo, on the one hand, and the theories of Marshall and Pigou (and more generally the theories developed in the last quarter of the past century) on the other, differ radically on the principle of full employment. While this is not the place to deal with the question at all exhaustively, we have to consider it because we shall find that we must confine our attention to the second group of theories alone.

Apart from Marshall's tendency to present his own doctrines as a continuation of Ricardian theory, what more specifically led Keynes to identify Ricardo's position with that of Marshall and Pigou in this respect, was a particular interpretation of the famous controversy between Ricardo and Malthus on the possibility of a 'general glut of commodities'. On closer examination, this interpretation appears to have been seriously misleading.

Malthus held that an accumulation of capital at the expense of 'unproductive consumption' (the consumption of classes other than the workers) would cause a rapid fall of the rate of profit and would thus eliminate the incentive to further accumulation. This fall would result from the decrease in prices due to the difficulty of finding outlets for the increased production. In Malthus's words:

> under a rapid accumulation of capital ... the demand, compared with the supply of material products, would prematurely fail, and the motive to further accumulation be checked, ... It follows that ... it is necessary that a country with great powers of production should possess a body of consumers who are not themselves engaged in production (Malthus, 1958, p. 398).

Ricardo, for his part, rejected the idea that accumulation would be limited by a lack of outlets for the increasing output, asserting that 'demand is only limited by production' (Ricardo, 1951, p. 290).

The question under discussion between Malthus and Ricardo thus exhibits undoubted similarities with that which was under discussion, more than a century later, between Keynes and Pigou. These similarities may be expressed by saying that Malthus, like Keynes (and numerous authors who were Malthus's contemporaries or predecessors), recognised the possibility that demand could set a limit to aggregate production, whereas Ricardo, like the 'orthodox' contemporaries of Keynes, denied that possibility. But it would be an error to move from acknowledging a similarity in the *question* under discussion to asserting a similarity in the *analysis* of that question. In particular, it would be an error to attribute to Malthus and Ricardo something akin to the theoretical core of the controversy between Keynes and the orthodox economists, i.e. the question whether the rate of interest can ensure that decisions to invest will adjust to decisions to save.[3]

The most evident deficiency of such an attribution is that both Malthus and Ricardo always identified decisions to save with decisions to invest:[4] there could therefore be no disagreement between them concerning the existence of factors capable of equilibrating decisions to invest and decisions to save. In Ricardo and Malthus, as in Smith before them, the question of a possible divergence between the two magnitudes had not been posed. They took it as a *fact* that anyone who had saved would have used his savings to employ productive labourers, or would have lent it to others who would have so used it.[5]

When we consider the position of the classical economists in this light, it should not come as a surprise that we cannot find in Ricardo the idea that the rate of interest would be the 'balancing factor which brings the demand for saving in the shape of new investment ... into equality with the supply of saving' (Keynes, 1936, p. 165), which Keynes attributed to the 'classical school'. The rate of interest appears in Ricardo only as a phenomenon subordinate to the rate of profits and governed by the latter. No particular role is attributed to it, apart from that of distributing profits between those who lend money and those who bear the 'risk and trouble' of employing capital in production (see, for example, Ricardo, 1951a, pp. 296-8 and 363-4).

It seems that a more correct interpretation of the controversy between Ricardo and Malthus should begin by recognising that the question under discussion concerned the circumstances determining the rate of profits. Ricardo's theory of profits was being advanced against the vaguer dominant theory, which had its origins in Adam Smith and which Malthus adopted with some particular emphasis. Smith had asserted:

> When the stocks of many rich merchants are turned into the same trade, their

[3] Keynes advanced this interpretation in his essay on Malthus written in 1933: see in particular the phrases 'Malthus's complete comprehension of the effects of excess saving on output' (Keynes, 1951, p. 118); or 'The whole problem of the balance between Saving and Investment had been posed in the Preface [to the *Principles* of Malthus]' (p. 122). This interpretation is again taken up in the *General Theory*, where Ricardo is considered as the originator of the 'classical theory' and, in particular, of the 'classical theory of interest' (Keynes, 1936, ch. 14, especially pp. 190-2). This interpretation, which remains flexible in Keynes, becomes more rigid in some Keynesian literature (cf., e.g., Klein, 1950, pp. 125-30).

[4] See, e.g., Malthus's acceptance of Ricardo's assertion that an increase of £10,000 in the income of an individual would bring about an increase in the demand for commodities of the same value, whether this increase were saved or consumed (Malthus, 1958, pp. 322-3). The fact that Malthus, like the other classical economists, tended to identify savings and investment, has been noted by R.L. Meek (1950-51, p. 156, n. ii); L. Robbins (1958, p. 248) and J.A. Schumpeter (1954, p. 641), and has been used by B.A. Corry (1959) for a more general criticism of the prevailing idea that Malthus was a precursor of Keynes.

[5] Nor can we find in these authors an analysis of the possible changes in the intervals of time elapsing between the acts of purchase and sale; an analysis which would have led, by another route, to the admission of a possible divergence between planned savings and investment as they are defined today. A few decades after Ricardo's *Principles*, this kind of analysis brought Marx to reject 'Say's law' and the Ricardian position on the subject (cf., e.g., Marx, 1969, pp. 493-9).

> mutual competition naturally tends to lower its profit; and when there is a like increase of stock in all the different trades carried on in the same society, the same competition must produce the same effect in them all (Smith, 1904, p. 89; cf. also pp. 352-3).

thus seeming to suppose that the limit which the market poses to the expansion of output in a single industry also exists for the expansion of aggregate output. It was from this theory of Smith that Malthus started in his defence, against Ricardo, of 'unproductive' consumption which, he argued, was essential in order to give a profitable outlet to production. In his words, unproductive consumption constituted 'a means to increase the exchange value of the entire product' and hence the rate of profits (Malthus, 1958, p. 398).

Ricardo opposed these views on profits (see Sraffa's introduction to Ricardo, 1951a; pp. xxxi-xxxiii). Arguing from the premise that, in the long run, the wage would be determined by the level of subsistence, he drew the logically consistent conclusion that the rate of profits could fall in the process of accumulation only as a result of the diminished productivity of the labour employed, on progressively less fertile lands, to produce the subsistence of an increasing population (Ricardo, 1951a, p. 292). No room was left for any permanent influence of demand on profits. Smith's argument concerning the influence of 'competition' on the rate of profits, on the other hand, consisted simply of an illegitimate extension, to an increase of aggregate output, of a proposition applicable to an increase in the output of a particular commodity. In the case of a single commodity, a part of the income generated by the additional production will be used for buying other commodities and will therefore not be available for absorbing the increased output of the commodity at an unchanged price. But this is clearly not so when a simultaneous expansion of all outputs occurs in the appropriate proportions. Since Malthus appears to have failed to add anything clear and consistent to Smith's argument,[6] their ideas on profits must have appeared to Ricardo to be the result of overlooking the necessary connection between production and income. Since Ricardo identified decisions to save with decisions to invest, to recognise the connection between production and income was the same as admitting Say's principle, that 'demand is only limited by production'.[7]

[6] In Malthus's *Principles* (1st ed., 1820) it is stated that the productivity of labour on the least fertile land under cultivation does not determine the rate of profits, but only establishes a maximum above which profits cannot rise. Below this limit profits would be determined by the circumstances to which Malthus variously refers as 'principles of competition', 'principles of demand and supply', 'demand' sometimes specified by the adjectives 'effectual' or 'effective', etc. (Malthus, 1958, ch. 5). Malthus expressly refers to Smith for his ideas on the subject: 'We can know little of the laws which determine profits, unless, ... [we] have recourse to that very principle of competition brought forward by Adam Smith, which Mr Ricardo expressly rejects ...' (Ricardo, 1951b, p. 269).

[7] The question is dealt with in ch. 21 of the *Principles*, in the form of a criticism of Smith's theory (cf. in particular pp. 289-96). Also in the 3rd edition of the *Principles* (1821), published after Malthus's *Principles*, Ricardo does not explicitly refer to Malthus's ideas on the subject. He

It therefore seems possible to conclude that in Ricardo 'Say's law' was not the result of an analysis of the investment-saving process but rather the result of the *lack* of any such analysis.

It would perhaps be possible to go further and assert that, in this respect, Ricardo's theory of distribution is *open*, in the sense that it *neither* provides premises capable of justifying the tendency of investment to adjust to saving, *nor* depends on the existence of such a tendency.[8] This 'open' character sharply distinguishes the Ricardian theory from the subsequent marginalist theories, which saw distribution as the result of forces of demand for and supply of 'factors of production'. As we shall argue presently, these theories provide the premises from which the role of the rate of interest as the equilibrator of decisions to invest and decisions to save was originally derived. At the same time, by determining distribution in terms of the equality between demand for and supply of factors of production, these theories depend for their validity on the absence of any long-run limits to aggregate production stemming from demand.

The absence from Ricardo's work of the notion of demands for the factors, elastic with respect to their prices, deserves to be stressed here, because it makes clear how little Keynes's 'Classical school' has in common with Ricardo. We have seen that the 'Classical' proposition criticised by Keynes concerned the existence of forces leading to the full employment of labour. But 'Say's law' did not lead Ricardo to any such proposition; it only led him to deny that demand could prevent the system from achieving that level of employment which was compatible with past accumulation, whether this level allowed for the employment of the entire labour force or only a part of it. Thus Ricardo admitted the possibility of the unemployment of labour and thought that it could only be eliminated by further accumulation of capital, or by a decrease in the population. Lower wage rates could therefore reduce unemployment only through higher profits and faster accumulation, or through a slower increase of population – and not, as marginalist theories were later to maintain, by causing such changes in the methods of production, or in the relative outputs of consumption goods, as would permit the employment of the entire labour force with an unchanged 'quantity of capital'.[9]

---

seems to have thought that the criticism of Smith in ch. 21 was sufficient. In his letters to Malthus and in his *Notes on Malthus* (1820), his arguments keep close to those of ch. 21, except when Malthus's ambiguities lead him to believe that Malthus's statements might coincide with his own (cf. Ricardo, 1951b, n. 201, p. 311).

[8] Thus Marx had no difficulty in rejecting 'Say's law' while sharing the basic elements of Ricardo's theory of value and distribution (cf. n. 5 above). The Ricardian theory of distribution, while it excludes the possibility of permanent effects of aggregate demand on the rate of profits, is not incompatible with effects of that demand on aggregate output or the speed of accumulation.

[9] Of the numerous relevant passages of the *Principles*, the following, which summarises the conclusion of his famous ch. 31 'On Machinery', may suffice here: 'the discovery and use of machinery may be attended with a diminution of gross produce; and whenever that is the case,

1.3. The marginalist theories

The search for premises capable of supporting the principle of a tendency to full utilisation of productive capacity must therefore turn to the theories developed in the final quarter of the last century around the twin concepts of marginal utility and marginal productivity. These theories determine the relative prices of commodities and the distribution of the social product by means of three groups of data: (a) consumers' preferences; (b) technical conditions of production; (c) the quantities of 'factors of production' available in the community. In equilibrium the relative prices of the commodities and of the services of factors of production would be such that the quantities of commodities demanded would be equal to the quantities produced and, at the same time, the quantities of factors' services required in production would be equal to the respective quantities supplied.[10] It is in *this* equality between demand for and supply of factors' services – and not in Ricardo's theory – that we find Keynes's 'classical' principle of the tendency to 'full employment' of labour and other factors.

The premises from which the marginalist authors derived – or, in Keynes's opinion, believed they could derive – the principle of a tendency to the full employment of factors are well known. They can be traced back to a particular conception of the social process of production. In this conception the elements required for production are treated as 'factors of production' which can be employed in the economic system in proportions which vary as the relative prices of their services vary. This is, in turn, the result of two characteristics of the economic system as envisaged in the marginalist theories. On the one hand, we have the 'substitutability' in consumption between goods which will generally require different proportions of the factors for their production. On the other hand we have, for any given level of technical knowledge, the possibility of producing any commodity with different proportions of the same factors; under the assumption of continuous variability of factor proportions, this leads to the well known conditions of profit maximisation in terms of the 'marginal products' of the factors. By either route we arrive at an inverse relation between the price of the service of

it will be injurious to the labouring class, as some of their number will be thrown out of employment, and population will become redundant, compared with the funds which are to employ it' and, a few lines above, 'But with every *increase* of capital he would employ more labourers; and, therefore, a portion of the people thrown out of work in the first instance, would be subsequently employed' (Ricardo, 1951a, p. 390; our italics). An interesting expression of the contrast between the Ricardian and the marginalist theories on the employment of labour is provided by Wicksell's criticism of Ricardo's thesis on the effects of the introduction of machinery. Wicksell argues that production will not decrease because 'as soon as a number of labourers have been made superfluous by these changes, and wages have accordingly fallen, then, as Ricardo failed to see, [other] methods of production ... will become more profitable ... and absorb the surplus of idle labourers' (Wicksell, 1934, p. 137).

[10] This is true under the assumption that the factor is scarce, i.e. that the quantity available does not exceed the quantity which entrepreneurs would demand at a price of zero.

the factor and the quantity in which the factor would be employed in equilibrium, given the quantities employed of the other factors.[11]

The way is then open for a second proposition according to which competition among the owners of a factor will modify the price of its service until the entire supply will be employed. With this second proposition, the inverse relation between the employment of a factor and the price of its service can be legitimately envisaged as a 'demand function' which, in conjunction with a 'supply function' of the same service, will give rise to the competitive tendency to an 'equilibrium' between such demand and supply.

The reasoning leading to a negatively elastic demand for the factor was conducted on the assumption that the quantity employed of the other factors remained constant, or more generally, remained equal to their supply (assumed not to fall drastically as their remuneration rises). But this assumption can now be seen to have been justified, for the same process which is at work in the market for the variable factor, assuming an equality between the quantity demanded and supplied of the other factors, will be at work in the market for the latter factors and will secure that very equality.

These, in summary, were the forces which would lead the economic system towards the full employment of all factors. Thus Pigou in his *Theory of Unemployment*, to which Keynes would later refer as his primary example of the 'classical' analysis, stated, not without reference to the unemployment afflicting England in the period between the wars, that

> With perfectly free competition among work people and labour perfectly mobile ... there will always be at work a strong tendency for wage rates to be so related to demand that everybody is employed (Pigou, 1933, p. 252).

The basis of this statement was fundamentally an application to labour, and to short-period conditions, of the basic argument that the quantities demanded and supplied of the factors would tend to equality by means of changes in the relative prices of their services.

1.4 Savings, investment and the marginalist theory of interest

But were the above premises regarding the productive process in fact adequate for the derivation of a tendency of the economic system to the full employment of labour and of the other productive resources? As is well known, Keynes denied this.

[11] The changes in the distribution of the social product which correspond to changes of the relative prices of productive services may themselves influence the quantities of the services demanded. Thus, a preference by workers for labour-intensive goods would tend to decrease the quantity of labour demanded as the wage decreases, and would therefore act in a direction contrary to the 'substitution effect' considered in the text. We have, however, ignored, here and elsewhere in the text, the circumstances which may cause an instability of the (non-monetary) equilibrium of exchange and production: we have therefore supposed that, as is usually assumed, such causes of instability do not generally raise serious difficulties in factor markets (cf. Hicks, 1946, p. 104).

In the *General Theory* he starts from an examination of the idea that changes in the wage rate would lead to full employment and he distinguishes two 'postulates'. He accepts the first, according to which the wage must be equal to the marginal product of labour, *given the level of employment*. In doing so, he accepts the conception of the productive process found in traditional theory. However, he rejects the second 'postulate', which states that 'the utility of the wage when a given volume of labour is employed is equal to the marginal disutility of that amount of employment' (Keynes, 1936, p. 5). Market forces, that is, would not succeed in equalising the quantity demanded and supplied of labour.

The argument which Keynes uses to deny that the flexibility of the wage would lead to the full employment of labour is founded on the premise that market forces cannot ensure that investment will adjust to savings. Given that premise, one must conclude that decreases in the money wage rate – the only wage rate on which the competition of unemployed workers can act directly – cannot ensure a tendency to the full employment of labour. In fact, if entrepreneurs reacted to the decrease in wages by increasing employment, the level of real national income would rise and savings would then exceed investment.[12] Since the latter would not adjust to the former, aggregate demand would be insufficient to absorb the increased production at its 'supply price' and output would be decreased. Indeed, if the fall of money wages should leave the level of investment unaffected, the employment of labour would have to return to its previous level, the only one at which saving is in equilibrium with investment. The only effect of the fall of the money wage would be a proportionate fall of the price level, leaving both the real wage and the amount of employment unchanged.

A detailed consideration of Keynes's position on the effects of a fall in wages must be postponed until Part II of these Notes. We have referred to the problem here only in order to bring to light the conclusion that the marginalist notion of a demand for labour elastic with respect to the real wage rate does not suffice to support the conclusion that competition among workers will lead to full employment. The *further* condition that investment adjusts to the changes in savings consequent on changes in employment is also required.

This second condition, concerning the dependence of investment on saving, is that which was referred to above when we discussed Ricardo and Malthus. The marginalist context is, however, very different from that of

[12] The concepts of national income, investment and saving used in the text are the generally accepted ones of gross national income, investment and saving. With regard to the well known ambiguity implicit in the use of the terms 'investment' and 'saving', it is sufficient to recall here that, while *realised* investment and saving are equal by definition, investment and saving may differ when we consider the quantities that would result from individual decisions *under hypothetical circumstances*, e.g. the amount of saving at a given level of real income, distributed in a *given* way, with a *given* system of relative prices, etc. The expressions 'decisions to invest' and 'decisions to save' or, alternatively, 'planned investment' and 'planned savings', will be used in the text to indicate investment and saving in this second sense.

those authors. The identification of decisions to save with decisions to invest, which explained Ricardo's acceptance of 'Say's law', is not to be found here. Instead we find the theory that the rate of interest is 'the factor which brings the demand for investment and the willingness to save into equilibrium with one another'.

Keynes's tendency in the *General Theory* was to consider this theory of interest as a further, unwarranted hypothesis that marginalist authors had introduced alongside the valid hypothesis concerning the variability of the proportions of factors of production in the productive process. It appears, however, that the theory of interest is in fact strictly dependent on those marginalist hypotheses.

In order to clarify this dependence, it is convenient to start by distinguishing two propositions in that theory of interest. The first concerns the possibility of establishing an inverse relation between the volume of planned investment and the rate of interest. The second proposition concerns the possibility of supposing that the interest rate is sufficiently sensitive to divergences between investment decisions and full employment saving to ensure its equilibrating role.

It is to the first of these two propositions that we must now turn our attention. The proposition is essential to the traditional theory, particularly when we admit, as is generally done, that, given the level of real national income, the dependence of decisions to save on the rate of interest is uncertain in both direction and intensity. If we could not suppose that – on average and under normal conditions – a decrease in the rate of interest would bring about an increase in the volume of investment, we could not suppose that there would be a rate of interest at which planned investment would be equal to full employment saving. No ground would then be left for the second proposition above (on which Keynes was to focus his criticism), concerning the tendency of the rate of interest toward such an 'equilibrium level'.

It is in this relationship between the rate of interest and planned investment that the dependence of the traditional theory of interest on marginalist premises is most clearly manifest. To understand this dependence it will first be necessary to consider why, and in what way, marginalist theorists have to introduce a special 'factor of production' – capital – conceived as the value of the capital goods used in production.

1.5. Capital as a factor of production and the demand function for investible resources

We have seen how the marginalist theory of distribution hinges on the notion of factors of production which may be employed in variable proportions in the economic system. Capital goods have to find a place among these factors. However the application to capital goods of the notion of a factor, or factors, of production raises special problems. Capital goods, like other produced goods, have values which tend to equality with their supply prices. But free competition entails that the share of national income attributed to the owners of such goods, over and above what is necessary for their replacement, tends to be distributed in proportion to the value of those goods, so as to give rise to a uniform rate of return on all kinds of capital goods. If we consider this uniform rate of return from the viewpoint of these theories, in which each rate of remuneration is the price of the service of a factor of production, the various capital goods will *ultimately* have to appear as quantities, measured by their values, of a single factor of production, 'capital'. The net rate of return on capital goods, or rate of interest on 'capital', will then have to be determined by *ultimately* referring, in the forms considered below, to the conditions of demand and supply of this special factor.

We have so far identified a factor of production, 'capital', conceived as an amount of value which may assume the form of the specific capital goods appropriate to the situations considered. But, as an amount of value, 'capital' is not defined until we have specified the standard in which that value is to be measured.[13] Beneath the variety and, at times, the vagueness of the indications given in this respect by the marginalist theorists, there lies a common idea. The capital goods, and hence the quantity of capital they represent, result from investment; since investment is seen as the demand for savings, 'capital' emerges as something which is homogeneous with saving. Its natural unit is therefore the same as we would use for saving, i.e. some composite unit of consumption goods capable of measuring the subjective satisfactions from which (according to these theorists) consumers abstain when they save. 'Capital' thus appears as past savings which are, so to speak, 'incorporated' in the capital goods, existing at a given instant of time. As a result of the productive consumption of those goods, these past savings will periodically re-emerge in a 'free' form and can be re-incorporated in capital goods of the same or of different kinds; alternatively, they can be turned back into consumption.

Marginalist theorists then proceeded to apply the argument described in section 1.3; this special factor, measured in value terms, now being included alongside the others.[14] In particular, they thought it possible to state that, given the quantities employed of the other factors, entrepreneurs would find it profitable to use a larger 'quantity of capital' the lower the rate of interest.

The application of this principle to the theory of distribution has taken two forms, which we shall now distinguish in order to show how either route

[13] In the case of factors of production which can be measured in physical terms, the choice of the unit of measurement is unimportant because a change of unit only implies multiplying the quantities by a *constant*. However, this is no longer true in the case of capital and other value magnitudes since the relative values of the commodities constituting alternative standards of value will themselves be different in different situations (e.g. in the situations to which the different points of the demand functions for a factor of production refer).

[14] Some marginalist theorists, such as J.B. Clark and, ultimately, also Marshall and his school, seem to have thought that the case in which a factor of production, 'capital', is conceived as an amount of value, could be treated similarly to that in which all factors are measurable in physical terms. A more interesting, indirect procedure was that adopted by theorists such as Böhm-Bawerk and Wicksell, who conceived of capital as a 'subsistence fund', used in order to

leads to the idea of a demand function for investment elastic with respect to the rate of interest.

The first approach is that of authors like J.B. Clark, Böhm-Bawerk or Wicksell, who expressly aim at a general solution of the problem of distribution. These authors refer to an equilibrium situation in which the condition of a uniform net rate of return on the various capital goods is realised. Given this condition, it becomes impossible to take the physical capital stock, i.e. the available quantities of the various capital goods, as given.[15] The 'capital' incorporated in such goods, i.e. their value, has instead to be taken as given. Capital is thus allowed to change its 'form' – though not its quantity – in order to acquire the physical compositon compatible with equilibrium conditions. The theory of distribution then follows along the lines already indicated in section 1.3. It may be described in terms of the forces envisaged to be at work in the capital market. We shall have a *total* demand for capital, i.e. for capital *as a stock*, as distinguished from the demand for investment, i.e. for capital *as a flow*. This 'total' demand function gives the quantity of capital which the system would employ at the various rates of interest, assuming that the markets for products and for the other factors are all in the equilibrium corresponding to the rate of interest.[16] Given the amount of capital available, the rate of interest will be determined together with the rest of the system (cf. Clark, 1907, ch. 9; Böhm-Bawerk, 1930; Wicksell, 1934).

'advance' the remuneration to the 'original' factors of production (land and labour) during the time elapsing before completion of the consumption goods produced by them. In any given instant, this 'fund' would be 'embodied' in the capital goods, and it would be measured by their value in terms of consumption goods. As the rate of interest decreased (the wage increased), the 'time structure' of production was supposed to change so as to require a larger 'subsistence fund' in order to employ the same quantities of the 'original factors'. (Cf. the following footnote for Walras's still different approach.)

[15] A demonstration of the inconsistency between a uniform rate of return on the supply price of capital goods and the treatment of the quantities of the various kinds of capital goods as data has been given by the author (Garegnani, 1960, Part II, chs 2, 3 and Appendix G). The problem is there considered as a criticism of Walras's theory of distribution which suffers from this very inconsistency.

[16] Under more general assumptions, the 'demand function' for capital described in the text would result from the following procedure. We take as *data*: (a) the preferences of the consumers; (b) the techniques of production; (c) the available quantites of all factors except capital; (d) the criteria determining the distribution of ownership of capital goods (the quantities of which are among the unknowns of the equations) among the individuals; (e) the criteria determining the age distribution of fixed capital. For any level of the rate of interest – *the independent variable* in this system – the equations concerning the conditions of equilibrium in the markets for the products and for the factors *other than* capital will determine, in addition to the usual unknowns of a general equilibrium system, the physical quantities of the capital goods of the different kinds in use in the assumed equilibrium position. The prices of these capital goods being also determined by the equations, the quantity of capital employed in equilibrium for the given rate of interest can easily be obtained. By repeating this procedure for other rates of interest, we obtain the corresponding points of the demand function for capital. In short, we subtract from the usual equations of general equilibrium the one requiring equality between the quantity of capital employed and the quantity available; the degree of freedom which the system acquires permits the definition of the relationship between the quantity of capital employed and the rate of interest.

We thus find a demand function for capital elastic with respect to the rate of interest, but we do not immediately find a demand function for *investment* elastic with respect to the rate of interest. The latter is, however, implied by the former or, more exactly, the former represents, in the form of a demand for a stock, a time sequence of demands for investment through which alone that stock-demand can be manifested and can determine the rate of interest. In any given instant the available 'capital' will not in fact be a 'fluid' which may quickly assume a form compatible with the conditions corresponding to any point of the demand function for capital. On the contrary, in any given instant 'capital' is incorporated in a given set of capital goods and it can only assume the appropriate physical form *over a period of time* during which most of the capital goods in existence are consumed and the available capital becomes 'free' to be reinvested in capital goods suitable for use with other techniques or in other productive sectors.

This relation between demand for capital as a stock and demand for investment can be seen in its most simple form if it is assumed that, in each industry, production takes place in an annual cycle and all capital is circulating capital (i.e. is entirely used up in the course of one year). If the wage rate and product prices are assumed to adapt without appreciable delay to the equilibrium compatible with the new rate of interest, the investment demand function at the end of each year will be nothing other than the demand function for capital as a stock. When there is fixed capital the analogous relation between demand for investment and demand for capital as a stock will be less simple but no less strict (see Appendix below, pp. 64-5).

The theory implies that such circumstances as delayed adjustments in the markets for labour and products, or irregularity in the age distribution of fixed capital, do not fundamentally alter the terms of the question. As a result, the interest elasticity of the sequence of demands for investment would reflect, on average, the elasticity of the demand for capital as a stock. Hence the significance of a demand for capital as a stock which exhibits, in a clear form, the basic tendencies which must emerge from the multiplicity of forces acting in any given moment of time.

By contrast, this multiplicity of forces is precisely what the second way of approaching the variability of the proportions between 'capital' and labour (and other factors) may seem to be dealing with. This second approach is that of Marshall and the tradition which he originated; it underlies both the controversy between Pigou and Keynes and the subsequent related literature. It is presented, less ambitiously, as a theory of the 'short period' and at times it seems that Marshall declines to claim it as a theory of distribution at all.[17] Unlike the version of Clark and Böhm-Bawerk, it appears

[17] In a well known passage coming after he has given an example to demonstrate why entrepreneurs will invest up to the point where the 'marginal product' of capital is equal to the rate of interest, Marshall says, 'But illustrations of this kind ... cannot be made into a theory of interest, any more than into a theory of wages, without reasoning in a circle' (Marshall, 1920, VI.1.8).

to renounce the attempt to determine an equilibrium situation characterised by a uniform rate of return on the supply prices of the capital goods. It can thus avoid referring to the 'quantity of capital' available in the community as a given magnitude. Instead, it takes as given the productive equipment existing in the various industries, on which a 'quasi rent' is obtained, depending on the level of the wage and the demand for the products. The real wage, on the other hand, is determined by the relation between the supply of and the demand for labour, the latter depending on the available productive equipment. The rate of interest results, finally, from the equilibrium between the current demand for investible resources and the current supply of savings. It is here, in the analysis of the investment-savings market, that the notion of capital as an amount of value appears in this group of theories (cf. the distinction between 'quasi rent on an old investment of capital' and 'interest on free capital', Marshall, 1920, V.9.3; also VI.2.6; VI.6.6).

Indeed, if we were to take literally the claims of these theories, and to confine ourselves to considering the capital goods as physically specified elements of a given productive equipment (modifiable only by means of current investment), it would be difficult to see how we could ever provide any theoretical basis for the notion, plausible as it may seem, of a demand function for investment elastic with respect to the rate of interest. We should be moving on the dubious ground of wages and prices determined according to a short-period analysis of the economy as a whole (for a critique of this particular group of theories, see Kaldor, 1955-56, pp. 90-1). In the course of such an analysis we would be faced by a multiplicity of factors, each of which may influence the demand for investment. We should thus have to take account of the disproportions between available equipment and the level of demand for products in each industry; the age structure of existing equipment and the connected irregular replacement requirements, etc. Above all, the hypothesis of a given productive equipment, whose physical composition in each industry, and distribution among industries, has not adapted to the state of demand for products, would force us to attribute a decisive role to the expectations which the entrepreneurs entertain about future changes in relative prices, demands for products, wage rates and the general level of prices. The attempt to determine the effects on investment of changes in the rate of interest on such indefinite grounds would seem liable to dissolve into casuistry concerning the influence of these changes on the expectations of entrepreneurs. And this influence would differ from situation to situation, thus making impossible any general and unambiguous conclusions concerning direction and intensity of the effects of interest on investment. Moreover, consideration of the influence of the rate of interest on the decisions of entrepreneurs regarding the techniques to be adopted for the new plant, and the product to be obtained from it,[18] would not permit any

[18] Numerous difficulties would be encountered in specifying this influence of the rate of interest. They would result from the short-period assumptions and the consequent

conclusion to be drawn concerning the *amount* of investment involved, if the comparison between techniques and lines of production were conducted in terms of equipments defined in *physical* and not in *value* terms.

It is therefore evident that this cannot in fact be the basis on which the theories here described assert that 'the demand for the loan of capital ... obeys a law similar to that which holds for the sale of commodities ... When the price rises the amount that can be sold diminishes' (Marshall, 1920, VI.1.8). It must then be supposed implicitly that the circumstances characteristic of the short period (the disproportions in the physical composition of the available equipment, and the influence of expectations) are classified with those to which Marshall referred as 'passing events ... and causes whose action is fitful and short lived', so that over a sufficiently long period of time they 'efface one another's influence' and allow the 'persistent causes' to emerge. And these 'persistent causes', to which we are thus referred as the basis for an investment demand elastic with respect to the rate of interest, are ultimately the same as those analysed by the first group of theories: i.e. the substitution between factors (through both alternative techniques of production and consumers' choices) as a result of which a fall in the rate of interest would lead to an equilibrium position such that the proportion in which 'capital' (the value magnitude) is combined with other factors is larger (Marshall, 1920, V.3.7). The different starting point – i.e. the physically specified equipment – and the apparent realism of the second group of theories appears to have obscured but not altered the basis on which the supposed inverse relation between investment and interest, essential for both groups of theories, must rest in the last analysis.

1.6. The premises of marginalist theory and the tendency to the full utilisation of productive resources

Our search for the premises of the traditional thesis that aggregate demand tends to adjust to the level of production thus seems to lead us to the marginalist conception of the process of production. This conception has, in effect, provided the theoretical basis for an inverse relation between the amount of investment and the rate of interest and hence for the first of the

indefiniteness of the effects which the rate of interest will have on real wages and the system of relative prices. On the other hand, with real wages and relative prices expected to remain constant, there is no reason why, assuming perfect competition and a fall in the rate of interest, the tendency to profit maximisation should lead entrepreneurs to change the techniques of production, rather than simply to expand the scale of production to profit from the gap between the rate of profits and the rate of interest. Under the assumptions of the theory, in fact, the individual producer always has the possibility of acquiring additional quantities of labour; the limit set by the available labour force can only influence the entrepreneur's decisions through increases in wages. More generally, investment decisions taken by the entrepreneurs in the expectation that the ruling rate of wages and the relative prices will remain unchanged could hardly be realised, since they would have to be revised as soon as the effects of the change in the rate of interest on prices and wages became perceptible.

two propositions which we distinguished above (p. 32) in the traditional theory of interest.

That relation once admitted, the marginalist approach to the theory of distribution led naturally to the second step: to suppose a sensitivity of the rate of interest to a divergence between planned investment and planned savings sufficient to tend to eliminate that divergence. This step was in fact taken when the rate of interest was considered (sometimes more explicitly, sometimes less so) as the price for the service of 'capital', determined by the conditions of demand for and supply of that factor, simultaneously with the prices for the use of the other factors.[19]

Since the *General Theory*, it has been widely recognised that this second step hid serious and perhaps decisive difficulties for the traditional theory of distribution. As Keynes showed, money in its role as a store of value may deprive the rate of interest of a sensitivity sufficient to adjust decisions to invest to decisions to save. A more powerful equilibrator between the two kinds of decisions can then act: variations in the level of employment of labour. And the controversy concerning the validity of the traditional thesis of the tendency to full employment has in fact been centred principally on problems related to the sensitivity of the rate of interest.

The basic idea of a demand function for investible resources has not been questioned, however. Nor is it surprising that criticism of the full employment thesis took this particular course. When, in the period between the two wars, the contrast between this thesis and the fact of large unemployment in the chief capitalist economies was particularly acute, criticism of the received theory naturally turned to the more empirical and less thoroughly explored monetary side of the theory, rather than to premises of pure theory which had by then acquired unchallenged acceptance. But the question we must now ask ourselves is whether those premises were in fact as solid as Keynes himself seems to have supposed. As we shall see in the next section, this question cannot be answered affirmatively.

It thus becomes possible, and necessary, to criticise the traditional view that interest is the equilibrator between saving and investment, while remaining within the confines of that analysis of 'real forces' in which this view was supposed to have its basis. The remainder of Part I of these Notes will be devoted to this question. The other criticism which Keynes conducted in terms of a monetary economy, and the controversy which ensued from it, will then be discussed in Part II. We shall there see how the uncertainty of

[19] We may note, in this connection, the contrast which Keynes pointed out in these economists, between the general acceptance of the notion that the rate of interest is 'the factor which brings the demand for investment and the willingness to save into equilibrium with one another' and the difficulty of finding a treatment or even an explicit statement of the notion (cf. Keynes, 1936, pp. 175f). These authors rarely conducted a detailed analysis of the process by which savings are turned into increments of the capital stock; they derived their position on the question largely from the idea that the prices of the productive services are determined by the equilibrium between the respective quantities demanded and supplied (cf. e.g., Marshall, 1920, VI.2.4).

the conclusions of that controversy with respect to long-period tendencies will lead us back to the questions of 'real theory' discussed in Part I.

1.7. *The validity of the marginalist postulates and the theory of interest*

We have seen in section 1.5 how the competitive tendency to a uniform rate of profits ultimately brings the marginalist theorists to the notion of a factor of production, 'capital', measured in value terms; we also saw how the corresponding demand function finds concrete expression in a demand function for investible resources, elastic with respect to the rate of interest. What we must now discuss is the validity of these notions.

The difficulties arise from the fact that the introduction of the factor 'capital' is incompatible with the logical basis on which the marginalist schema of factors of production rests. The principle that the proportions in which the factors are employed vary with the prices of their services, so as to give rise to demand functions of these services, can in fact be deduced from the conditions of equilibrium in production only if the quantities of the factors can all be defined independently of the system of prices. But this *cannot* be done when one of the factors is the value of the magnitude 'capital'. As the rate of interest and the wage rate vary, the switch of techniques or the change in the relative outputs of consumption goods might well change the proportions between the two factors in a direction contrary to that asserted in marginalist theory. [See the 'Symposium' in the *Quarterly Journal of Economics*, 1966, and Garegnani, 1970 (the final section of which is printed as an addendum to this chapter) (eds).]

In fact, when we recognise the dependence of the value of capital goods on distribution, it becomes meaningless to compare the proportions of capital to labour required by different techniques, or in different lines of production, in the unqualified way characteristic of traditional theory, and the same applies for any comparison of the proportions in which the two factors are used in the economy at different rates of interest and wages. With respect to the first type of comparison, the *order* in which the techniques for the production of a commodity are placed with reference to their proportions of capital to labour in the economy, the very direction in which this ratio will change with distribution will depend on the commodity in terms of which the value of the capital goods is measured. (The assumed change in the rate of interest may indeed change the relative value of two alternative standards of value in such a way that, when using one standard we have an *increase* in the ratio of capital to labour, whereas the use of the other standard will give a *decrease* in that ratio.)

If the marginalist principle concerning the way in which the proportions of factors change with distribution is incorrect, we may ask what theoretical basis, if any, remains for the notion of demand functions for factors. In section 1.3 we examined the relation between the price of the service of a factor. We then considered how the *negative slope* of that function, and the analogous form of the corresponding relation for the other factor, allowed these relations to be viewed as 'demand functions' capable of determining, in conjunction with the 'supply functions' of the factors, the prices of their services. Let us now follow the same line of argument, assuming that the two factors are 'capital' and labour.

Consider first the relation between the rate of interest and the value of the capital goods in use, assuming a constant quantity of labour employed and equilibrium in the markets for the products.[20] The value of the capital goods employed will vary with the rate of interest for two different reasons, which we must now attempt to distinguish.

In the first place, we have changes in the value of the physical capital employed to which there corresponds no physical change in capital: these changes will be due purely to a change in the value of the capital goods relative to the commodity used as the standard of value.

In the second place, we have those changes in the value of physical capital to which there correspond *physical changes* in capital, which are due either to changes in the techniques adopted for producing the commodities, or to changes in the proportions in which those commodities are produced. The traditional thesis was that these changes in physical capital would ensure a *rise* in the value of the capital goods employed as the rate of interest falls, and *vice versa*. However, we now know that the analysis underlying this conclusion is invalid and that there is no reason why this second kind of change should have one sign rather than the other.

When we combine the two kinds of value changes that we have just considered separately, it seems that little or nothing of general validity can be said concerning the form of the relationship between the value of physical capital and the rate of interest. If we represent the relationship on a diagram, with the rate of interest on the vertical axis, the curve may just as well slope up to the right as down to the right, and it may alternate such slopes any number of times. Moreover, the form of the curve will depend on which commodity is used as the standard of value.

It seems, then, that even if the initial hypothesis of a constancy in the quantity of labour employed were well founded, the form which the relationship between the value of the capital goods and the rate of interest could assume would make it difficult to envisage it as a 'demand function' for capital – i.e. as the basis of a demand function for investible resources, capable of determining, together with a supply function of such resources, the rate of interest.

Yet the considerations which make this true of the relation between the rate of interest and the quantity of capital also undermine the validity of the assumption of constancy in the quantity of labour employed. As we have seen above, the traditional theory assumed a mechanism which equalised the

[20] This relationship between the value of the capital goods and the rate of interest results from the procedure indicated in n.16 above.

quantity demanded and supplied of labour and thus ensured that the quantity employed would remain constant – or that it would change in accordance with the supply function of labour if this had some elasticity. But this equilibrating mechanism of demand and supply can no longer be assumed: the relationship between the real wage and the labour employed with a constant quantity of capital would show the same characteristics as the relationship between the quantity of capital and the rate of interest and hence it could not be interpreted as a demand function, any more than could the first relationship.

What we have attempted to argue here throws doubt on the entire explanation of distribution in terms of demand and supply for factors of production. It does so for reasons altogether independent of any 'Keynesian' argument regarding the obstacles which money or the state of expectations may raise to the tendency towards 'equilibrium' in the markets for labour and investment. The questions in the theory of distribution which are thus opened up are the subject of the current debate on capital, and to these questions we shall have occasion to return in our Part II. Our concern here is only that of showing the weakness of the premises underlying the notion of a demand function for investment elastic with respect to the rate of interest. Thus deprived of its theoretical foundation, that notion cannot, on the other hand, find genuine support on any purely empirical ground.[21]

It therefore seems possible to assert that – even if the rate of interest could be assumed to be sufficiently sensitive to divergences between planned investment and planned savings – there would not be sufficient ground for arguing that the rate of interest could ensure that decisions to invest will adapt to decisions to save: nor would there be sufficient ground for arguing that aggregate demand will adapt to the level of production compatible with the full employment of the productive resources available in the economy. We shall return to these considerations in Part II, after discussing the criticism of the traditional principle of a tendency to the full employment of labour, which Keynes raised on the different ground of monetary analysis.

Part II: Monetary analysis

In Part I we looked for the premises from which traditional theory derived the assertion that aggregate demand would adjust to productive capacity. These premises were found to lie ultimately in the conception of capital as a

[21] The changes in the rate of interest discussed here would imply changes in most of the variables of the system (the relative prices of the products, the levels of output, the labour employed, etc.), each of which may in turn react on the level of investment. It would therefore seem that the question of the influence of interest on investment can only be meaningfully discussed within a theoretical scheme which accounts for the relations between these variables. It seems unlikely that all these interrelationships could be accounted for in an empirical study. As it happens, the results of the numerous empirical investigations concerning the *direct* influence of the rate of interest on entrepreneurs' decisions to invest are known to be negative (cf. Andrews, 1938; Sayers, 1940; Ebersole, 1938-39; Brockie and Grey, 1956).

'factor of production' employable in increasing proportion to other factors as the rate of interest falls – the basis, as we argued, of the idea of a demand schedule for 'saving' determining the rate of interest in conjunction with the supply schedule of full employment saving. The deficiencies of that conception of capital led us to the conclusion that, contrary to what is often argued, an analysis conducted in 'real' and 'static' terms provides no basis for the belief that investment decisions can, in the long period, adjust to decisions to save.

In this second Part of the paper, the problem will be approached in terms of the 'monetary' analysis of Keynes's *General Theory* and the subsequent controversy. In section 2.1, we shall use Wicksell's theory of the price level as an example of how traditional theories would link their 'real' analysis of distribution with their analysis of the money rate of interest. We shall then argue, in section 2.2, that Keynes's different conclusions concerning the effects of deficiencies in aggregate demand are explained by his rejection of the orthodox theory of the interest rate, and not by the assumption of money-wage rigidity. The examination, in section 2.3, of the deficiencies of Keynes's own critique of that theory of interest will then pave the way for a discussion, in section 2.4, of the subsequent attempts to rehabilitate traditional theory. We shall thus finally arrive, in section 2.5, at those questions of 'real' theory to which the differences between the conclusions of Keynes and those of the orthodox economists are ultimately traceable, and we shall conclude the article by referring back to the result of our analysis in Part I.

2.1. An example of the marginalist analysis of the market for loans: Wicksell's monetary theory

While the economic theories prevailing before Keynes's critique assumed a spontaneous tendency to the full employment of productive capacity, they nevertheless had to explain the fact that periods of prosperity alternate with periods of depression, in which there is unemployment and in which production in many sectors falls below productive capacity. The explanation of these phenomena was found in obstacles – not unlike the 'frictions' recognised in other branches of economic theory – which retarded the action of the underlying forces described by the theory, obstacles which were generally attributed to the working of the credit system. The treatment of these problems thus came to be part of a theory of money, separate from the main body of economic theory concerned with distribution and relative prices.

One kind of explanation of the alternation between periods of prosperity and of depression saw its origin in fluctuations of the psychological state of confidence, intensified by the speculative purchasing of commodities financed by bank loans when prices rise, and by the inevitable subsequent sales as soon as a downturn in prices is foreseen. This appears to have been Marshall's position. He saw the sole effective remedy for unemployment due to depression as lying in the greatest possible restriction of 'reckless inflations of credit', which are 'the chief cause of all economic malaise', in that they are followed by liquidations and bankruptcies which shake the 'general state of confidence'. In the subsequent period, marked by lack of confidence, individuals, while having the power to purchase, can choose not to exercise that power; and, in particular, they can choose not to lend capital to new firms. Unemployment results in the industries which produce investment goods; unemployment which then tends to spread to the consumer goods industries as well (Marshall, 1920, VI.13.10; see also Marshall, 1965, VI.3.3, pp. 249-51). Thus, according to Marshall, no real limits to the possibility of employing additional capital in production are involved; the limit consists only in an overestimation of risk, which is bound to disappear as soon as the consequences of the previous wave of optimism have exhausted themselves.

By contrast, an alternative explanation of these phenomena stressed objective factors and, in particular, the discontinuous character of technical progress. This was Wicksell's approach. He wrote: 'The principal and sufficient cause of cyclical fluctuations should rather be sought in the fact that in its very nature technical or commercial advance cannot maintain the same even progress as does, in our days, the increase in needs ... but is sometimes precipitate, sometimes delayed' (Wicksell, 1935, p. 211; see also Wicksell, 1907, pp. 223-39), which results, according to Wicksell, in fluctuations in the profitability of investment, to which the structure of interest rates on money loans adjusts only with a lag, causing price variations meanwhile. Here we meet Wicksell's monetary theory, to which we must now proceed. This theory constitutes perhaps the most important pre-Keynesian attempt to ground by means of a systematic analysis of the money loan market (the market in which the rate of interest is actually observed) the marginalist concept of interest as the supply-and-demand determined price of the productive factor 'capital'. Moreover, Wicksell's analysis is akin to that of the *General Theory*, in that it is focused on the source and the effects of variations in *aggregate* monetary expenditure: it will thus prove useful as a term of comparison below, when we consider the 'real' or 'monetary' nature of the hypotheses underlying the different conclusions reached by Keynes.

Fundamental to Wicksell's theory is the concept of an interest rate referred to as 'natural', 'normal' or 'real': the rate, that is, at which '*the demand for loan capital and the supply of savings* exactly agree' (Wicksell, 1935, p. 193).[22] The 'natural' rate, Wicksell writes, 'more or less corresponds to the expected yield on the newly created capital' or, as he puts it elsewhere, to the return on capital which becomes 'free' in the course of the period considered, and can

[22] Savings, the supply of which is referred to by Wicksell in the above passage, should be understood to be the planned gross savings, given by the difference between gross income and consumption under the assumption of full employment of resources with equilibrium relative prices and distribution. (See n. 25 below, for a discussion of alternative interpretations of these equilibrium prices.)

thus be 'invested' in the most profitable physical form.[23] Since the expected return on 'newly created capital' will tend to coincide, under normal conditions, with the return which will be realised, the 'natural' rate of interest is the rate of interest which Wicksell had related, in the real part of his theory, to the data concerning the available quantities of factors, technical knowledge and the tastes of consumers (cf. Wicksell, 1935, pp. 205-6). It follows that the natural rate of interest is liable to vary as a result of changes in any of these data. The explanation of variations in the price level can then be found, Wicksell argues, in the slowness with which the banks adjust their lending rates of interest to variations in the natural rate.

Before proceeding with Wicksell's argument, let us stop to emphasise two aspects of it which are important for us here. The first is the assertion that the market rate of interest can differ from the 'natural' rate for non-negligible periods of time. The second is that the possibility of this is attributed to the existence of the banking system. Wicksell maintains in fact that if money loans were to take place directly, from person to person, their supply would be largely determined by money savings. The forces of demand for, and supply of savings could then act *directly* on the market for money loans and bring the rate of interest back to the level of the natural rate, as soon as the former began to diverge from the latter. Thus if, for example, there were an increase in the profitability of investment, the increased 'demand for loan capital' would encounter the limit to the supply of loans set by the flow of savings: an increase in the market rate of interest, towards the new level of the 'natural' rate, would result. The situation is quite different when there is

[23] Wicksell's concept of 'free' capital merits closer consideration because it highlights some difficulties which are implicit in the traditional concepts of the demand for and the supply of saving. At the time of *Geldzins und Güterpreise* (1898), Wicksell assumed that money lent to entrepreneurs for investment would, in the final analysis, be spent solely on consumption goods, to be 'advanced' as wages and rents to the 'original' factors (see, e.g., Wicksell, 1965, pp. 102-3); such goods would have constituted a 'free' or 'liquid' capital, which is to be distinguished from 'invested' capital, represented by capital goods. Yet this concept of investment expenditure is invalid, unless one supposes an economy in which the production of consumption goods takes place in annual cycles and starts each year with land and labour unassisted by any capital goods. Under any other assumption, investment expenditure will be largely upon capital goods. Then the consumption goods which the saver has 'forgone' are not produced at all when the investment process develops smoothly; the rôle of such 'forgoing' being only that of freeing for the production of capital goods the resources which would otherwise have been required for the production of the 'forgone' consumption goods. In this case, as Wicksell recognised in the *Lectures* (Wicksell, 1935, p. 192), 'free' capital does not take any *physical* form at all; and the concept merely serves to mark the fact that, in so far as the decisions in question were *correctly foreseen in the past*, the relevant sums of money may be spent on capital goods of any type whatever.

The qualification concerning the necessity that the current saving and investment decisions were correctly foreseen in the past is important: demand for, and supply of saving involve the decisions of *three* groups of people and not just of two, as might appear at first sight. The idea of a 'supply of savings' presupposes the coincidence of the savings decisions of income recipients and the decisions of producers concerning the divisions of aggregate supply between consumption and capital goods. Similarly, the idea of a demand for saving or investment presupposes that the producers of capital goods correctly foresee the physical compositon of the investment demand.

a developed banking system. Indeed, the volume of bank loans is independent of the flow of money savings: 'By the concentration in their hands of private cash holdings ... [the banks] possess a fund for loans which is always elastic and, on certain assumptions, inexhaustible' (Wicksell, 1935, p. 194). Hence the banks can accommodate any variation in the demand for loans without changing their rates of interest and can thus sever the link between the market rate of interest and the 'natural' rate which would otherwise have operated through demand and supply in the loan market.

Yet if this direct link between the two rates is broken, Wicksell continues, another, far less rigid link will nevertheless continue to hold good and will act via the price level. Let us in fact consider an initial situation of real and monetary equilibrium, in which there occurs an increase in the profitability of investment, and suppose that the banks meet the increased demand for loans by an expansion of credit, leaving the rate of interest unchanged. As the loans come to be used for the purchase of means of production, the flow of aggregate money expenditure will increase: to an initially unchanged consumption expenditure there will be added the increased investment expenditure. This increased aggregate expenditure, meeting a virtually unchanged volume of output, will lead to an increase in money prices: the increase will at first be in the prices of investment goods, but then, when the increased money income thus generated permits increases in consumption expenditure, the prices of consumer goods will also increase – and this latter increase may be contributed to by transfers of resources from the production of consumer goods to that of investment goods (see Wicksell, 1935, p. 194).[24] If we assume that the money rates of payment to primary factors tend to increase in the same proportion as prices, the profitability of investments will continue to exceed the market rate of interest and, as long as this condition holds good, the inflationary process will continue (ibid., pp. 195-7). An analogous process will take place, but in the opposite direction, when the 'natural' rate of interest falls and the banks keep the market rate unchanged (ibid., p. 200). But, Wicksell concludes, it will be these very cumulative processes of inflation or deflation which will compel the banks eventually to raise, or lower, the market rate of interest towards its 'natural' level (ibid., p. 201), the only level at which there will be price stability.

The theory briefly set out above brings to light the (often implicit) grounds on which the marginalist theorists maintained that the separation between savings decisions and investment decisions – or the influence of monetary factors in the loan market – could not endanger, other than temporarily, the claimed tendency to the full employment of the factors of production. At the

[24] To the extent that monetary expansion transfers resources from the production of consumption goods to the production of investment goods, real accumulation will be higher than it would have been at the 'natural' rate. To this extent, the 'natural' rate itself would tend to fall and approach the market rate. Wicksell admits this effect, but considers it to be of secondary importance (evidently because of his implicit assumption of a highly elastic demand for capital) (cf. Wicksell, 1935, pp. 198-9).

basis of their argument there lay the postulate of the elasticity of the demand for capital with respect to the rate of interest.[25] This elasticity, it was thought, would make it possible for the rate of interest to adjust planned investment to planned savings through the play of demand and supply in the market for money loans. But if this first demand-and-supply mechanism were seriously hampered by monetary factors, that same elasticity would ensure that changes in the rate of interest would suffice to re-establish equilibrium in the face of variations of aggregate expenditure due to inequality between planned savings and investment. It is Wicksell's merit to provide a systematic and rigorous version of this line of thought; even if, in doing so, he shows that the link between saving and investment decisions must often be the indirect one.[26]

It is not surprising, therefore, that Wicksell did not find, in his analysis of the loan market, any factors which might bring into question the conclusions

[25] In *Geldzins und Güterpreise* Wicksell seems to explain the increase in the demand for 'loan capital' that results from a decrease in the rate of interest in terms of the incentive that the growing difference between the rate of profits obtainable in production (equal to the 'natural' rate of interest) and the market rate of interest gives entrepreneurs to expand the *scale* of aggregate output (cf. Wicksell, 1965, pp. 89-90, and Wicksell, 1935, pp. 195-6).

This explanation brings us to the question hinted at above (n. 22) concerning the relative prices and distribution underlying the schedules of the demand for and supply of saving in traditional theory. Two alternative assumptions are conceivable: (a) that relative prices and factor remunerations are those ruling in the given situation and do not change as we move along the schedules; (b) that wages, the rents of natural resources and the relative product prices are those which would obtain in the equilibrium situation corresponding to the rate of interest assumed for the loan market (see above, n. 16). According to assumption (a), used in *Geldzins*, the rate of profits obtainable in production being given, independently of the assumed rate of interest on loans, the search for maximum profits would lead, not only to changes in production methods adopted (factor proportions), but also to changes in the *scale* of every line of production. This explanation of the demand for investible funds does not, however, appear to be acceptable. Since the traditional theory assumes that labour and natural resources always tend to be fully utilised, the tendency to increase the scale of production in the aggregate could only lead to changes in the real remuneration of labour and natural resources. The investment planned to change the scale of production would thus be countermanded when, as it began to be carried out, distribution and relative prices adapt themselves to the rate of interest ruling in the loan market. The demand for investible funds will then in fact turn out to be determined exclusively by the tendency to change the ratio of capital to 'original' factors, i.e. according to assumption (b), as was assumed in the argument of Part I of these Notes (cf. pp. 35-6). (Similar considerations hold for the supply of savings, which will also be influenced by changes in distribution and relative prices.)

In the *Lectures* Wicksell seems to take account of this and to modify somewhat his earlier position (cf., e.g., the reference in Wicksell, 1935, p. 195, to 'increasing roundaboutness which is undoubtedly invoked by a fall in interest rates'). Wicksell's reluctance to adopt this second point of view exclusively is probably due to the difficulty of admitting a rapid adjustment of distribution and relative prices to the rate of interest on loans or, alternatively, of assuming correct entrepreneurs' forecasts of such effects. But since assumption (a) is even less acceptable, it would seem that this difficulty is inseparable fiom the idea of supply and demand schedules for savings.

[26] Similar suggestions were frequent in other marginalist writers. Consider, e.g., Marshall's argument in *Money, Credit and Commerce* that an influx of precious metals would initially produce a fall in the rates of interest, which would then rise again as a result of the rise in prices that that influx had brought about (Marshall, 1965, VI.2.2, p. 255).

of the 'real' theory on the tendency to full employment of factors: variations of monetary expenditure are seen to have effects on the level of prices, but not on the levels of production and of factor employment. The rationale for this lay in two complementary elements. On the one hand, there was the idea that on the appearance of unemployment of the primary factors, competition would lead to a decrease in their monetary rates of remuneration; this made plausible the hypothesis that prices would fall in step with monetary expenditure, leaving the volume of output virtually unchanged. On the other hand, this hypothesis did not entail admitting an absurd process of unending deflation or inflation of prices: the elasticity of demand for investible funds in fact ensured the existence of a 'natural' rate of interest to which the banks would be able, and eventually compelled, to bring back the money rate of interest. It was thus natural for Wicksell to suppose that any under-utilisation of productive equipment and primary factors could only be temporary and could therefore be neglected in an analysis of value and distribution conducted at the level of general principles.[27]

2.2. Keynes's theory and the rigidity of money wages

What we must now consider is why Keynes, although starting from premises not unlike those of Wicksell, arrives at radically different conclusions.

The picture which Keynes's *General Theory* draws is well known. As in Wicksell, the system of interest rates is proximately determined by monetary factors. Keynes approaches the problem of the rate of interest from the angle of the demand for and supply of the stock of money. The demand for money, or 'liquidity preference', is explained in terms not only of the two traditional 'transactions' and 'precautionary' motives, but also in terms of the 'speculative motive', which expresses the preference for money, as a means of holding wealth, of those who expect falls in the value of bonds (= increases in the rate of interest). According to Keynes, the demand for money due to this third motive must be elastic with respect to the rate of interest, since the lower is that rate, the greater is the risk that it will rise, and the smaller is the compensation for such risk provided by the interest rate (Keynes, 1936, pp. 201-2). The rate of interest is thus the price which will bring into equality, not the demand for and supply of saving, but rather the desire to hold wealth in the form of money and the quantity of money made available by the monetary authorities. It is therefore determined once 'liquidity preference' and the quantity of money are known. Planned investment, on the other hand, depends on the rate of interest in the manner shown by the 'marginal efficiency of capital schedule'. Once the rate of interest is determined, there-

[27] The possibility is mentioned in the *Lectures* that increases in money demand might be satisfied, in part, by increases in output made possible by the presence of previously unemployed productive resources. Such a possibility is judged to be of secondary importance and is ignored in the rest of Wicksell's discussion (Wicksell, 1935, p. 195).

fore, the volume of planned investment is also determined, when expressed in 'real' terms, i.e. in wage units.[28]

There is thus no reason why the amount of investment should coincide with the amount of saving out of full employment income. Yet equilibrium requires equality between planned investment and planned saving; if that equality is not satisfied, aggregate monetary expenditure will tend to change over time.

It is necessary to distinguish, at this point, between the case in which planned investment exceeds full employment savings and the opposite case. In the former, equilibrium would be reached, according to Keynes, via an inflationary process not unlike that found in Wicksell: because of the increase of prices and money wages, the money value of national income (and thus the 'transactions' demand for money) would increase until it caused a rise in the rate of interest great enough to eliminate the cause of the inflation (see, for example, ibid., p. 202). For the analysis of the second case, however, Keynes introduces the 'propensity to consume' and, therewith, the most original part of his analysis. It is assumed that, other things being equal, when employment increases the community will increase aggregate consumption, but by less than income has increased. It is then shown how, when planned investment falls short of planned saving, equality between investment and saving will be achieved through a contraction of the national product. The possibility of 'equilibria' characterised by unemployment of labour and under-capacity working of equipment is thus asserted.[29]

Keynes's conclusions concerning his second case stand in sharp contrast to those which Wicksell had reached for the case in which the rate of interest was initially above the 'natural rate'. The search for the sources of this difference cannot but start from the most obvious difference between the assumptions underlying the two analyses: the high flexibility of money wages assumed by Wicksell but denied by Keynes. As we have seen, Wicksell assumed a tendency for prices and wages to fall in the same proportion as aggregate expenditure; it was precisely this process of price and wage deflation that would eventually oblige the banks to bring the rate of interest down to its 'natural' level. By contrast, Keynes assumes that any shortfall of

[28] Keynes reduces the different qualities of labour to homogeneity by multiplying the quantity of each by the ratio which its wage bears to that of a standard type of labour. These ratios are assumed to be constant (Keynes 1936, p. 41).

[29] On the assumption given above concerning the behaviour of consumption, the aggregate demand function will intersect the aggregate supply function from above and the equilibrium can be supposed to be stable. Thus, if employment happened to be higher than is indicated by the equilibrium point, entrepreneurs would have an incentive to reduce the number of workers employed, since the aggregate expenditure in wage units would be *less* than the 'aggregate supply price' of that output. This would be so *if* this expenditure were that shown by the aggregate demand function, i.e. that which would obtain with a disposable income equal to the supply price; *a fortiori*, expenditure will be less than supply price if, as a result of the failure to realise the full supply price, the disposable income is itself less than the 'supply price'. Similarly, entrepreneurs would have an incentive to increase output whenever employment was initially below the equilibrium level.

planned investment relative to planned saving is followed by decreases in total expenditure *measured in wage-units*: he assumes, that is, that money wages do not fall or, more exactly, do not fall in the same proportion as money expenditure has fallen. Given this assumption, there must be a shrinking of output, since the entrepreneurs will not continue to produce at below normal profits. It must now be asked to what extent Keynes's thesis would remain valid were we to admit, with Wicksell, that competition amongst unemployed workers would give rise to a continuous fall in the money wage. Must we then conclude that under-employment 'equilibria' exist only during the time required for a sufficient fall in money wages?

As is well known, Keynes denied that the novelty of his conclusions turned on the hypothesis of money wage rigidity, and chapter 19 of the *General Theory* is devoted to this question. The argument develops in two stages. Keynes assumes at first that the fall in the money wage rate will cause a shift in neither the consumption function nor the marginal efficiency of capital schedule. He also assumes that it will not affect the rate of interest. In this case, the fall in wages could not lead to permanent increases of employment and real income (Keynes, 1936, pp. 261-2). Thus, Keynes concludes, the fall in wages could affect employment *only* through its effects on the propensity to consume, on the marginal efficiency of capital schedule, and on the rate of interest.

Keynes then proceeds to the second stage of his argument and considers the effects of a fall in wages on the consumption function and on the marginal efficiency of capital schedule. He concludes that, in a closed economy, these effects will be negative, rather than positive, in their implications for employment. He therefore turns to consider the effects on the rate of interest, remarking that it is to these effects alone that reference can be made by those who claim that wage flexibility will lead to full employment. Yet if the available quantity of money contracts in step with money income, 'there is ... nothing to hope in this direction'. If the quantity of money remains approximately constant, however, Keynes continues, there will be effects on the rate of interest analogous to those which the monetary authorities can achieve by purchasing bonds on the 'open market'. In either case the quantity of money increases relative to money income: a greater quantity of money thus becomes available to meet the demand for money deriving from the 'speculative motive' and, given the speculative demand schedule, the interest rate must fall. It follows, says Keynes, that, leaving aside the disadvantages specific to this particular method of increasing the relative supply of money, decreases in money wages encounter limits to their effect on the rate of interst analogous to those specific to open market operations. Just as open market operations can have but a limited influence on long-term rates of interest when the increase in the quantity of money is moderate, whereas they can have unfavourable effects on the state of confidence when the increase is large, so a moderate fall in money wage rates will prove insufficient, whereas a large fall could shatter the state of confidence. Keynes thus concludes by asserting firmly that: 'There is, therefore, no ground for the belief that a flexible wage policy is capable of maintaining a state of continuous full employment – any more than for the belief that an open-market monetary policy is capable, unaided, of achieving this result' (Keynes, 1936, p. 267; but see also p. 27 and our n. 32 below).

We shall have reason to return to this argument of Keynes later on and to discuss its limitations. Here we need only note that the hypothesis of money wage rigidity does not suffice to explain the difference between Keynes's conclusions and those of the traditional economists; the flexibility of prices and wages would lead to the full employment of factors *only if* the resulting decrease in the rate of interest could so affect planned investment as to make it equal to full employment savings. Keynes denied that the rate of interest could play that equilibrating role and it is *here*, in the theory of the rate of interest, that he diverges from Wicksell and the other 'orthodox' economists.

Thus two results begin to emerge from this preliminary discussion of Keynes's analysis.

The first result is to confirm what we maintained in Part I of these Notes (see pp. 31-2): the source of the difference between Keynes and the orthodox economists is to be sought in the theory of the rate of interest.

The second result concerns the precise *nature* of this difference in the theory of the rate of interest. Keynes's conclusions rest, in fact, not so much on the particular theory of the rate of interest which he put forward, as on his rejection of the traditional theory, which determined the rate of interest by the demand for and the supply of savings. An interesting expression of this negative rôle which the theory of the rate of interest plays in the *General Theory* may perhaps be found in a seldom noted passage written by Keynes one year after that book. Referring to his own theory and to its genesis, he says:

> the initial novelty lies in my maintaining that it is not the rate of interest, but the level of incomes which ensures equality between saving and investment. The arguments which lead up to this initial conclusion are independent of my subsequent theory of the rate of interest, and in fact I reached it before I had reached the latter theory. But the result of it was to leave the rate of interest in the air. If the rate of interest is not determined by saving and investment in the same way in which price is determined by supply and demand, how is it determined? ... It was only when [attempts in other directions failed] ... that I hit on what I now think to be the true explanation (Keynes, 1937, p. 250).

It is then in the *critique* of the traditional theory of interest, rather than in the hypothesis of money wage rigidity, that the roots of Keynes's conclusions are to be sought. It is to that critique, contained in chapter 14 of the *General Theory*, that we must now direct our attention. Indeed, if the critique were well founded, the hypothesis of money wage rigidity would appear to be a consequence, and not a premise of the thesis that there exists no tendency to the full employment of factors. To assume wage flexibility, in the absence of a rate of interest capable of adjusting planned investment to full employment saving, would compel us to allow for an absurd process of unending deflation of prices and wages when investment is less than full employment savings.[30]

2.3. Keynes's critique of the traditional theory of interest

Keynes's critique of the traditional theory of interest appears to contain two strands. On the one hand, there is the charge that the theory is indeterminate. To each level of utilisation of productive capacity there corresponds a different real income and hence a different supply of savings schedule: given the marginal efficiency of capital schedule, there are therefore not one but many rates of interest at which planned investment and planned saving are equal – one for each level of real income (Keynes, 1936, pp. 179-82). On the other hand, there is the thesis that the rate of interest constitutes not the price of savings but, rather, the price needed to induce individuals to hold wealth in forms other than money.

The first criticism does not seem to be well founded. Let us begin by accepting, in accord with traditional theory, the following two propositions: (a) that at each level of real income the action, in the loan market, of the demand for savings and the supply forthcoming at that real income, creates a tendency for the rate of interest to move towards the level at which the two schedules intersect;[31] (b) that the money wage is flexible in the presence of unemployment.

We now assume a level of investment insufficient to ensure the full employment of labour; by assumption (b) the money wage will fall. As Keynes admits in his discussion of falls in money wages, one can now suppose that the entrepreneurs react initially by increasing output in the expectation of a demand for their products which is unchanged in money terms. Under our present hypothesis, this expectation could not be entirely disappointed, since, the supply of 'real' savings being shifted to the right, there will, by assumption (a), be a tendency for the rate of interest to fall; the consequent increase in investment will make possible the maintenance, at least in part, of the initial increase in employment. Since, by assumption (b), there will be decreases in the money wage as long as there is unemployment, this process will eventually lead to the achievement of full employment. As a result the full-employment supply schedule of savings is the *only* supply of savings to which the theory under examination need refer in the determination of the equilibrium rate of interest: the dependence of the supply of savings on the level of employment does not warrant the charge of

[30] Keynes's conclusions concerning the effects of money wage decreases on the propensity to consume have been questioned in terms of the so-called 'Pigou effect': the significance of the latter for our argument will be discussed below, n. 39.

[31] If this assumption is not accepted, the critique of the traditional theory will lie in the reasons for which the assumption is rejected and not in any indeterminacy of the theory.

indeterminacy laid by Keynes.[32] (Analogous conclusions would be reached if traditional theory were to maintain, with Wicksell, that the presence of the banking system makes assumption (a) unacceptable, but were to admit, at the same time, the possibility, and eventually the necessity, that the banks should bring the rate of interest to its 'natural' level.)

We may therefore confine our attention to the second strand of Keynes's criticism of the received theory of interest. This may be summarised by saying that the traditional theory of interest ignored the effects deriving from the rôle of money as a store of value. When this rôle is given due weight, Keynes states, one must recognise that the aggregate demand for money depends on the rate of interest, as well as on the total money volume of transactions. For a given money value of output, the demand for money will be greater the lower is the rate of interest: the latter will then have the rôle of bringing about equality between the quantity of money made available by the monetary authorities and the demand for money, not that of equating the demand for and the supply of saving (see, for example, Keynes, 1936, p. 167).

Keynes therefore confines himself, in this second criticism, to counterposing his own theory of interest to the traditional one, and the force of his argument is thus merely that of the theory which he puts forward. The idea that the demand for money depends on the rate of interest – which is quite in accord with marginalist principles when it is presented in terms of equality, at the margin, between the sacrifice of liquidity and the payment therefore – has been generally accepted in subsequent literature. The same has not occurred for the critique of the traditional theory of interest which Keynes wished to base on that idea. Indeed, we shall see in the next section how it has been argued that the rate of interest can equalise *both* the demand for and supply of the stock of money *and* the demand for and supply of savings.

These attempts to reinstate the traditional analysis were undoubtedly encouraged by the feeling that Keynes's theory of interest would not conflict with orthodox theory properly interpreted. As exemplified above by

[32] Keynes himself appears at times to imply that variations in money wages could justify the traditional theory of interest when this refers to a full employment income for defining the supply schedule of saving. Thus he writes, 'the position could only be saved by some complicated assumption providing for an automatic change in the wage-unit of an amount just sufficient in its effect on liquidity-preference to establish a rate of interest which would just offset the supposed shift [of the marginal efficiency of capital], so as to leave output at the same level as before' (Keynes, 1936, pp. 179-80). But in introducing the idea of 'liquidity preference', Keynes here forces his own theory on the traditional one. More relevant to the latter would seem to be another passage: 'If, however, there is a negligible demand for cash from the speculative-motive except for a short transitional interval, an increase in the quantity of money will have to lower the rate of interest almost forthwith, in whatever degree is necessary to raise employment and the wage-unit sufficiently to cause the additional cash to be absorbed by the transactions-motive and the precautionary-motive' (ibid., p. 171). Keynes is here referring to increases in the quantity of money, but the same conclusions hold for reductions in the money wage, given the quantity of money; it is then difficult to see how this position can be reconciled with the assertion that the traditional theory is indeterminate.

reference to Wicksell, the orthodox theory of interest was only meant to refer to long-run tendencies, destined to assert themselves against the short-term obstacles raised by a number of other factors.

When examined from this standpoint, Keynes's theory of interest appears to be unsatisfactory. The quantity of money demanded on account of the speculative motive depends, Keynes says, not on the absolute level of the rate of interest but, rather, on the extent to which that rate lies below the rates which the various holders of wealth expect in the future (see ibid., p. 201). The position of the speculative demand for money schedule, and hence the rate of interest, thus come to depend on expectations about the future course of the latter. However, in the absence of their ulterior explanation, these expectations introduce a serious element of indeterminacy into the theory. Thus if it were assumed that expected rates of interest tend, albeit with a certain lag, to move parallel to the actual rate of interest, the principal reason advanced by Keynes for the interest-elasticity of the speculative demand for money – the growing divergence between expected rates and the current rate when the latter falls – would lapse. This point is reinforced when it is noted that the supply of money which is to satisfy the speculative demand can only change due to *either* changes in the money value of aggregate output *or* the policy of the monetary authorities: and it is difficult to imagine, in either case, that there will not be some effect on expected interest rates. Keynes does in fact recognise this possible instability of the expectations on which the market rate of interest would depend and he takes it into account by admitting the possibility of shifts in the speculative demand for money schedule in the face of, for example, a central bank policy of monetary expansion (see, for example, ibid., pp. 197-8). Yet it is clear that, in so far as it is probable that speculative demand shifts as the supply of money changes, Keynes's analysis loses much of its force: like any other analysis in terms of demand and supply, it presupposes a sufficient mutual independence of the two schedules.

Keynes's theory appears therefore to rest on the assumption of a considerable degree of stability of the expectations concerning the rate of interest: a stability which can only be based on stable views, on the part of the owners of wealth, as to what constitutes a 'normal' level of the interest rate. This seems in fact to be Keynes's rationale for the 'speculative' demand for money. Yet when it is interpreted in this way, the inadequacy of the liquidity preference theory as a long-period analysis of the rate of interest becomes even clearer; the average value, over time, of the rate of interest on long-term loans proves to be largely determined by views about the 'normal' rate of interest, views which the theory does not explain (cf. ibid., p. 201).

This deficiency of Keynes's theory was, for example, the starting point for a more direct defence of the traditional theory than that which we shall consider in the next section; the prevailing views about the normal level of the interest rate were explained by some authors in terms of a substantially correct estimation of the rate of interest needed to adjust investment to the economy's full employment level of saving (taken as an average over the long period).[33] This defence of traditional theory does not appear to be adequately argued, but the very fact that it could be put forward serves to indicate the *lacuna* left by Keynes in his long-period analysis of the rate of interest; a *lacuna* which had to be filled, either by a return to the traditional theory or by its more radical rejection.[34]

2.4. *The attempts to rehabilitate traditional theory*

If the *General Theory* left the theory of interest at this parting of the ways, Keynes's concept of the marginal efficiency of capital made it easy to return to the traditional theory. Keynes had already considered this possibility when he affirmed that those believing in the re-equilibrating tendencies of the economic system must base their argument on the effects which falls in money wages and prices, or open market operations of the central bank, could have in increasing the quantity of money available for meeting the speculative demand. As was seen in section 2.2, Keynes had denied that one could thus reach full employment. However, his arguments to this effect – based principally on the negative effects which significant falls in money wages or increases in the quantity of money would have on the 'state of confidence' – lose much of their force when the issue is, not the recovery of the economy from a situation of cyclical depression, but rather the possibility of keeping the average level of investment sufficiently close to the full employment volume of savings over a long period. In this latter context, once it is admitted (on the basis of marginalist principles) that the marginal efficiency of capital schedule is highly elastic with respect to the rate of interest, the decreases in money wages, or increases in the quantity of money, required to ensure a sufficiently high average level of employment no longer appear drastic, as they can now be spread out over a long period of time. Besides, in the long period, the psychological factors summed up in the 'state of confidence' lose much of their force by comparison with the objective factors on which the real profitability of investment is supposed to depend.

This is in fact the line of argument taken in the attempts to rehabilitate traditional theory, which we referred to in the previous section.[35] The

[33] 'What this seems to point to is that [the normal rate of interest] must be determined by people's estimate of the pressure of outside forces of some kind; and it seems natural to suggest that in a free enterprise economy these forces are none other than our old friends productivity and thrift' (Robertson, 1963, p. 388).

[34] There are hints in this latter direction in the *General Theory*. Keynes, in fact, asserts the 'conventional' character of the rate of interest, and hence the capacity of the monetary authorities to control the average level of the interest rate on long-term loans, if they act with sufficient 'persistence and consistency of purpose' (cf. Keynes, 1936, p. 204). This idea which, if consistently developed, would lead to a theory of value and distribution radically different from the marginalist theory (see below, pp. 62-3) does not seem to have been taken up in the subsequent literature.

[35] Hicks (1937a) seems to have opened up this line of argument by distinguishing between Keynes's 'special theory' and his 'general theory'. In the former, one would not consider the

dominant concern of these authors with long-period tendencies[36] allowed them to ignore the negative psychological effects of falls in wages and prices, or increases in the quantity of money. That same concern explains, in part, a subtle but important shift in the interpretation of the 'speculative' demand for money. This demand is now made to depend not so much on views of what constitutes a normal level of the rate of interest, but rather on the convenience and security deriving from the holding of one's wealth in the form of money; the security in question is relative to those risks of changes in the value of bonds, entirely due to uncertainty, which would exist even when a rise in the rate of interest appeared no more probable than an equal fall.[37] By this change in the interpretation of liquidity preference, a sufficient stability is attributed to the demand for money without having recourse to views about a 'normal' rate of interest, which are not explained within the theory. Moreover, one thereby avoids consideration of the possibility of a high elasticity of the demand for money, with respect to the rate of interest, at rates above the minimum level to which we shall refer below; a possibility to which Keynes had attached considerable importance[38] and which can be explained only in terms of sufficiently unanimous views of wealth holders about what constitutes the normal level of the interest rate.

Given these premises, it is not difficult to conclude that, if unemployment of labour leads to the continuous fall of money wages, one will eventually reach – subject to the exception to be considered shortly – a state of equilibrium. In this equilibrium, the ratio between the money value of output and the available quantity of money permits a level of the interest rate at which investment is equal to full employment savings.

The significance of this argument does not depend on the assumption of a high flexibility of money wages, an assumption generally held to be of doubtful applicability. If the flexibility of money wages would permit the achievement of full employment in the way just described, then the same

---

effect of changes in the money value of output on the demand for money; in the latter, admitting this influence, one would, by contrast, reach 'appreciably more orthodox' conclusions – amongst others, the possibility of increasing employment via money wage reductions, as well as by increases in the quantity of money (Hicks, 1937a, pp. 467-70; and p. 465 for the effects of money wage flexibility). The argument was then taken up and rendered more explicit by Modigliani (1944); Haberler (1939), ch. 8 and (1964), pp. 240-3; by Tobin (1955), etc. The conclusions of this line of argument have provided the theoretical basis of the numerous theories of economic growth on traditional lines (see, e.g., Solow, 1956, pp. 91-3; Swann, 1956, p. 335; Meade, 1961, p. 35).

[36] Thus in Modigliani (1944a, p. 187) the analysis is said to be conducted 'under "static" assumptions', since its object is the 'determinants of equilibrium and not ... the explanation of business cycles'.

[37] On the distinction between these two interpretations of 'liquidity preference', see Robertson (1963), pp. 382-3. For the tendency to adopt the second interpretation of 'liquidity preference' in these rehabilitations, see Hicks (1937a), p. 467, and Modigliani (1944a), p. 193.

[38] Cf. for example, 'opinion about the future of the rate of interest may be so unanimous that a small change in present rates may cause a mass movement into cash' (Keynes, 1936, p. 172; see also p. 203).

result can be obtained with an expansionary monetary policy. As Modigliani puts it, 'It is the fact that money wages are too high relative to the quantity of money that explains why it is unprofitable to expand employment to the "full employment" level'; and the remedy can take the form of *either* a decrease in money wages *or* an increase in the quantity of money, money wages being constant (cf. Modigliani, 1944a, p. 225, and Hicks, 1937a, p. 465 and pp. 473-5).

We referred above to an exception to these conclusions. The authors in question in fact admit only one situation in which money wage flexibility, or an expansionary monetary policy, cannot lead the economy back to full employment. This is the so-called 'Keynesian case': a situation in which the rate of interest required to ensure full employment is negative or, at least, lower than that rate of interest which, in the view of the majority of wealth holders, would be barely sufficient to compensate for the risk and inconvenience of holding any part of their wealth in any form other than money. At this level of the interest rate the elasticity of the demand for money would tend to become infinite (cf. Modigliani, 1944a, p. 222n; Hicks, 1937a, pp. 460-2), and decreases in money wages or increases in the quantity of money could not lead to any further fall in the rate of interest. However, these authors attribute limited importance to this possibility – and here we find, yet again, the basic marginalist idea of a demand for capital which is, under normal conditions, highly elastic with respect to the rate of interest. The inelasticity and position of the schedule of the marginal efficiency of capital which would be needed to explain a full-employment rate of interest lying below that minimum level are held to be possible only in deep depressions, when they would be due to the conditions of uncertainty and over-estimation of risks characteristic of such situations. These authors in fact maintain, agreeing here with Keynes, that a situation in which the preceding accumulation of capital has reduced the actual yield of capital almost to zero has never yet occurred (Modigliani, 1944a, p. 222n; Keynes, 1936, p. 207).

The relevance of the 'Keynesian case' is thus confined to the analysis of short-period phenomena and the same is true for the importance of the psychological factors to which Keynes had referred, in chapter 19 of the *General Theory*, in order to deny the possibility of reaching full employment through falls in money wages or increases in the quantity of money. In the former as in the latter context, the psychological state of lack of confidence characteristic of depressions would, as long as it persisted, constitute the obstacle which prevents a return to the full employment of factors, following an argument not unlike that which had been put forward by Marshall long before.[39]

[39] A different attempt to rehabilitate the principle of the tendency to full employment is that based on the so-called 'Pigou Effect'. When money wages and prices fall, the aggregate net credit of the private sector of the economy – equal to the total net debt of the government and the central bank (banknotes and government stock) in a closed economy – will increase in real

2.5. *Novel and traditional elements in Keynes's theory: the marginal efficiency of capital*

The line of argument considered in the previous section thus leads to a substantial rehabilitation of traditional theory for the long period and, in particular, for accumulation. The scheme of the long run inter-relation between 'real' and monetary forces which that argument presents does not differ essentially from that which Wicksell had presented earlier. In the former, as in the latter, it is admitted that monetary factors can, temporarily, keep the market rate of interest at a level other than the full employment rate[40] – equivalent to the 'natural' rate in Wicksell's theory. In both schemata, however, the full employment – or 'natural' – rate of interest continues to be the equilibrium one towards which the market rate of interest tends to gravitate. The divergence between the two rates would cause inflationary or deflationary tendencies, whether the latter consist principally of falls in prices and wages or mainly of unemployment of labour; these tendencies would then induce the monetary authorities, who are credited, in both arguments, with proximate control over the rate of interest, to adjust the ruling rate to its 'natural', or full employment, level.[41]

When compared with these similarities in the conclusions, the concepts of liquidity preference and of the consumption function – the specifically Keynesian elements of the above rehabilitations of the traditional theory – are of relatively minor importance. These elements are accorded a dominant role only for the analysis of the short period and the trade cycle. In this more limited context, the effects of the rate of interest on the demand for money

---

terms. The propensity to save of wealth-holders will consequently fall until the full employment level of savings equals the level of investment forthcoming in the situation under consideration. (Cf. Pigou, 1947, pp. 249-51; Haberler, 1969, pp. 483-9; Patinkin, 1948, pp. 258-70.) This argument does not support the traditional doctrine that the level of investment is determined by the community's propensity to save and is thus of limited interest to us here. One remark concerning it may however be made. It is reasonable to suppose that the greater part of saving comes from high income recipients and that this group will also hold a large fraction of both the public debt and idle money balances. Thus what the 'Pigou Effect' implies is an increase in wealth of high income recipients (whose incomes will also increase in real terms at the expense of tax payers so long as the state pays a constant rate of interest on its debt) such as to lead them to reduce their savings by the required amount. Now – even admitting that the redistribution of wealth and income against private debtors and the redistribution of income through the government's interest payments do not impede the reduction in the propensity to save – it seems hard not to conclude that long before the community comes to accept such a redistribution of wealth, other methods of solving the problem of unemployment will have become inevitable, which will be of more direct and less uncertain effect.

[40] It is interesting to note how the concept of a full-employment rate of interest, though a consequence of the idea of a marginal-efficiency-of-capital, is given very little prominence in the *General Theory*, where it just crops up here and there almost accidentally (cf., e.g., Keynes, 1936, pp. 202, 236, 375).

[41] The 'spontaneous' tendency to equilibrium in the case of wage flexibility, asserted in these arguments, still requires that the monetary authorities hold the stock of money constant and thus permit the *ratio* of the available quantity of money to the money value of the national product to rise.

highlight an obstacle capable of retarding the action of the 'real forces' on the rate of interest, particularly in the case of deflation. The consumption function then allows a theoretical treatment of the effects on real income and employment of decreases in money expenditure in the presence of rigid money wages. Thus, in Hicks's words, Keynes's theory apears to be 'the Economics of Depression'; and, in this perspective, Keynes's specific contribution consisted of laying 'enormous emphasis' on the qualifications to traditional theory, the need for which had already been admitted by Marshall or by his successors (Hicks, 1937, pp. 472 and 465).

We have clearly moved far from the meaning which Keynes himself attributed to his theory when he contrasted it with the traditional theory, which he held to be applicable only in the 'special case' of full employment. And what is most remarkable is that this reversal of meanings is achieved without rejecting the basic assumptions of the *General Theory*, but on the contrary, by moving within its conceptual framework. This possibility of attributing contrasting meanings to Keynes's theory would therefore seem to arise from within that theory itself, and it will be of interest, at this point in our argument, to seek to identify its source.

To note that the theory had been formulated by Keynes on the basis of short-period assumptions, and thus left open problems concerning long-period tendencies, does not appear to go to the root of the matter. Indeed, it remains to be explained why Keynes restricted to the short period an argument whose implications would, he thought, reach far beyond the theory of cyclical phenomena.[42] Above all, we have to explain why the long-period implications which Keynes thought he could deduce have proved to be open to contradiction within his own theoretical framework.

It seems that the root of this ambivalence must rather be sought in the composite character of Keynes's theory. The *General Theory* might be said to contain two fundamentally heterogeneous strands of thought, the one superimposed on the other. A vision of the mode of operation of the economic system, which is in radical conflict with that of the dominant theory, is imposed, as if by force, upon a conceptual basis which is to a large extent still the traditional one, thus giving rise to an inherently unstable compromise. The novel part of Keynes's theory centres on the thesis that it is principally variations in the level of aggregate output that equilibrate investment and saving in a capitalist economy,[43] a thesis which is suggested directly by an unprejudiced observation of the facts. But this thesis was in conflict with the generally accepted theory of distribution on both the latter's main flanks: that of the labour market – where Keynes had to deny that wages would be determined by the equilibrium between the demand for and supply of labour – and that of the capital market – where Keynes had similarly to deny that

[42] For the long-period consequences that Keynes drew from his theory, consider Keynes (1936), pp. 372-3; see also the passage quoted in n. 49 below, as well as, more generally, the first two sections of ch. 24 of the *General Theory*.

[43] In this connection see the passage from the *General Theory* quoted on p. 50 above.

the rate of interest would be determined by the equilibrium between the demand for and supply of savings. Thus, in order to develop his initial idea and get it accepted, Keynes had to work out a critique of the traditional theory of distribution and it is in the way in which he conducted that critique that the compromise referred to above finds its origin.

As was seen in Part I of these Notes, one can distinguish two successive logical stages in the traditional analysis of distribution (cf. p. 39 above). In the first, from the marginalist premises concerning production and consumption one derives the idea that, given the quantities employed of all factors but one, the quantity employed of this latter factor increases as its real rate of remuneration falls. In the next step, it is maintained that, as a result of competition both amongst the entrepreneurs and amongst the owners of factors, there will be a tendency towards rates of remuneration at which the quantity employed will equal the quantity supplied for each factor. Now, in his critique, Keynes accepts the first stage of the argument: in this way he inherits the traditional part of his theory, which is epitomised by the two schedules of the marginal efficiency of capital and of the marginal product of labour. His critique has then to turn exclusively on the second stage of the argument. And at the second stage – with the conclusions from the first stage having already been admitted – the capacity of traditional theory to resist attack proved to be greater than Keynes had thought.

The traditional strand of Keynes's thought does not, of course, merely represent a remnant of received modes of thought which can readily be separated from the remainder of his theory, leaving the latter unaffected. Indeed, it is the schedules of the marginal product of labour and of the marginal efficiency of capital which determine the level of real wages and the volume of investment within the system. One may perhaps wonder how acceptable these determinations are and, above all, how consistent they are with the other parts of Keynes's theory, as soon as problems which are not strictly confined to the short period have to be confronted.[44] The fact

[44] In Keynes's theory the money rate of interest is made to depend on factors which are largely independent of those affecting the real wage. While this may be admissible in a short-period analysis, in which the distributive variables may be said to diverge from their long-period levels, the same could not be admitted for these latter levels without contradicting the unique, inverse relation which must obtain in the long period between the real wage and the rate of profits (and hence the average long-period rate of interest) (cf., e.g., Sraffa, 1960, section 49). Doubts about Keynes's determination of the wage are strengthened when one considers that the assumption of decreasing returns on which it is based may be questioned as soon as we admit: (a) that the degree of utilisation of the existing productive equipment will generally vary with the quantity of labour employed; and (b) that, in the short period, the quantity employed of some types of labour is constant, or varies less than in proportion to the quantity of output. But if the returns to labour were constant or increasing, up to or near full utilisation of existing equipment, then a real wage equal to the marginal product of labour would imply that gross profits remain constant or fall as the level of activity increases, which is clearly contrary to experience. It will also be clear that this same determination of the wage is of no relevance when we leave a strict short-period analysis and must therefore first explain why the productive equipment is what it is rather than some other.

Keynes's use of the marginal efficiency of capital also presents difficulties. In particular, it is

remains, nevertheless, that it is thanks to this particular conjunction of traditional elements and short-period assumptions that Keynes is able to develop, to some extent, the novel strand of his thought, without having simultaneously to face the fundamental problems of value and distribution.

However, the price which Keynes has to pay for the traditional strand in his thought becomes clear with respect to the schedule of the marginal efficiency of capital.[45] As was seen in section 2.2, the conflict with traditional theory over the tendency to an equilibrium between demand and supply in the labour market is, in effect, reducible to that over the determination of the rate of interest. The critique of the traditional theory of interest becomes then the key to an acceptance of Keynes's arguments – and the concept of the marginal efficiency of capital proves to be the Achilles' heel of that very critique. Keynes sees the rate of interest as determined by monetary factors: but, as Wicksell's earlier analysis had shown, the idea of an investment demand schedule constitutes an obstacle which a monetary theory of interest cannot easily overcome. Indeed, admitting an elastic investment demand schedule leads to maintaining, on the one hand, the existence of a full-employment level of the rate of interest and, on the other, the presence of

not clear in what sense decreasing returns to increases in the stocks of the different capital goods can be assumed, as is done by Keynes (p. 136), when, there being unemployment, additional equipment be used together with additional labour.

These deficiencies regarding the marginal productivity of labour and marginal efficiency of capital may serve to confirm the difficulties Keynes had in reconciling the innovatory and the traditional parts of his thought in the *General Theory*. They can also explain how the desire to bring consistency back into economic theory might have encouraged the attempts to confine the implications of Keynes's theory strictly to short-period analysis.

[45] An opinion about the nature of the 'marginal efficiency of capital' different from that in the text – and from that of Keynes, who saw his notion as a version of the traditional one (cf., e.g., Keynes, 1936, pp. 139-40) – is advanced by L. Pasinetti, when he writes that such a Keynesian concept reveals a 'different origin' than marginal economic analysis (1974, p. 43). Pasinetti assumes in fact that the prospective yields of capital assets are *independent* of the rate of interest ruling in the loan market (cf., e.g., p. 37). The investment projects could then be always ordered according to a decreasing rate of profitability, independent of the interest rate, thus ensuring the existence of a decreasing relation between the interest rate and the volume of investment.

We have, however, seen in n. 25 above that there are some arguments by which the assumption of prospective yields and prices independent of the ruling interest rate does not seem acceptable. We may now add that Keynes himself allowed for the effect of the interest rate on prospective yields (e.g. Keynes, 1936, p. 143). We may also observe that the dependence of prospective yields on the ruling interest rate follows from Pasinetti's own analogy between the marginal efficiency of capital and 'Ricardo's ranking of all lands in a decreasing order of fertility' (Pasinetti, 1974, p. 43): the ordering of lands according to fertility must in fact take into account the changes in interest and prices associated with the extension of cultivation.

Now, when we admit that the prospective yields of capital assets and the ruling interest rate can, and sooner or later will, adjust to each other, it does not seem that a generalised inverse relation between the rate of interest and the volume of investment can find a theoretical basis other than the marginalist notion of an increase in the proportion of capital to other factors as the rate of interest falls. In particular, there seems to be no general reason why the construction of new plant for previously unemployed workers (to which Pasinetti refers on p. 43) should be permanently favoured by a fall of the interest rate rather than by its rise (a rise might indeed raise the long-term profitability of investment and thus provide an incentive for it).

inflation, or deflation and unemployment, when the actual rate of interest is not the full employment one; the idea that the market rate of interest tends to gravitate towards its full employment level then acquires plausibility.

It thus seems that the origin of the contrasting meanings attributed to Keynes's theory is to be sought in the doubtful compatibility, from the standpoint of an analysis of long-period tendencies, between the concept of the marginal efficiency of capital and the argument that the level of output plays the leading role in equilibrating planned savings and planned investment. Once the former idea is accepted, it is difficult not to confine the importance of the latter argument to the explanation of the trade cycle and other short-period phenomena. On the other hand, the different conclusions to which Keynes was pointing can be sustained in so far as investment is assumed to be insensitive to the rate of interest, even in the long period. But this assumption is in sharp conflict with the presuppositions of the traditional theory of distribution and cannot find a firm foundation until the critique of that theory has undermined those presuppositions.

If this is so, the conflict between the traditional thesis and that of Keynes, concerning the dependence of investment on the propensity to save, cannot be resolved solely on the terrain of monetary theory, which Keynes chose for his critique. Rather, this conflict leads us back to the questions of 'real' theory discussed in Part I of these Notes. And to the conclusions which were reached there we must now return.

Conclusions

Our argument in Part II has thus brought us to an alternative, the central element of which is the acceptance or the rejection of the traditional representation of capital as a productive factor, employable in the economy in quantities which increase relative to the quantities of the other factors as the rate of interest falls. If one accepts this representation and, consequently, the traditional thesis with respect to the dependence of investment on the rate of interest, it becomes difficult to reject the traditional doctrine concerning the long-period relation between the propensity to save and the level of investment; unless, that is, one assumes either capital saturation or a long-period deflationary policy on the part of the monetary authorities. By contrast, if the validity of that representation of the productive process is found wanting, the doctrine that the community's propensity to save determines the level of investment is thereby deprived of its foundation.

Now, the argument presented in Part I leads us to maintain that the second possibility is that which permits a better understanding of the facts and we may conclude that, in a long-period analysis no less than in a short-period one, the level of investment should be considered as independent of the propensity to save.

It is then necessary to distinguish between two possible situations. The first is that in which the incentive for private investment remains, for long periods of time, at such a level that aggregate demand presses on the limits of available productive capacity, in almost all major sectors of the economy. There will then tend to be a price inflation, one effect of which could be that of reducing consumption, thus making room for the high level of investment. In such conditions, a fall, or a reduced increase, in consumption – especially of those goods which draw on productive equipment which could be used for investment goods[46] – may have the effect of reconciling the high level of investment with greater price stability.

The more usual situation would, however, be a second one, in which private investment does not reach the limit set by available productive capacity. In this case a fall, or a reduced increase, in consumption could not have any *direct* effect in increasing investment, and the indirect effects could well be negative through the contraction of demand for consumer goods and the consequently reduced incentive to invest.[47]

The above conclusions, like any adoption for long-period analysis of the Keynesian thesis concerning the relationship between saving and investment, inevitably implies a rejection of the traditional theory of production and distribution. It thus re-opens the problem of the long-period determination of both the volume of the social product and its distribution between profits and wages. A treatment of these problems is beyond the scope of these Notes, but before concluding we may indicate a few points which directly follow from what we have said so far.

With respect to the long-period determination of the level of social product and labour employment we may return to a question we raised in section 1.1. We there assumed that the productive equipment in the economy was sufficient to employ the entire supply of labour.[48] As will be remembered, this was done in order to follow the Keynesian controversy without having to take care of the dominant explanation of 'structural unemployment' in terms of rigid real wages.

We might now note that rigid *real* wages, entailing as they generally will, rigid *money* wages, could only have strengthened any negative conclusions concerning the long-period dependence of investment on the propensity to save; monetary policy alone would have to be relied on for the necessary ad-

[46] In the short period, the limited adaptability of the existing productive equipment prevents any global alternative between consumption and investment. This alternative becomes increasingly important beyond the period required to set up new plant. Then, however, it applies chiefly to economies without 'structural' unemployment. Where there is unemployment, the labour required to man the new equipment need not be drawn from other production which can accordingly continue with older equipment.

[47] 'The growth of capital depends not at all on a low propensity to consume but is, on the contrary, held back by it; and only in conditions of full employment is a low propensity to consume conducive to the growth of capital' (Keynes, 1936, pp. 372-3).

[48] Keynes's assumption of a decreasing marginal product from the labour employed with *given productive equipment* has generally been interpreted to mean that the marginal product falls very little as long as there is some unused productive equipment and then falls sharply; a reasonably definite limit to the quantity of labour that can be employed with a given productive equipment is accordingly also implied in that notion.

justments in the interest rate. But when the ground for rejecting the idea of an aggregate demand tending to adjust to productive capacity is that advanced in these Notes, the possibility of 'structural' unemployment emerges quite independently of any rigidity of real wages. The critique of the concept of a demand for capital (investible resources) which is elastic with respect to the rate of interest is, in fact, at one and the same time a critique of the 'twin' concept of a demand for labour which is elastic with respect to the real wage rate (cf. p. 41 above). If that critique is well founded, no absorption of 'structural' unemployment could be hoped for from lower real wages and any consequent changes in the physical form of the given 'capital endowment'. This also implies that real wages cannot be relied on to ensure that employment possibilities will increase over time in step with the supply of labour. The factors capable of keeping long-period unemployment within socially tolerable limits are then to be sought not in any spontaneous tendency of the demand for labour to adapt to an autonomous growth of population. They have rather to be sought in the complex economic and demographic phenomena of mutual adjustment between the demand for and the supply of wage labour, which the history of the capitalistic economies has long presented for study.[49]

With respect then to the problem of distribution – which is also opened up by any adoption of the Keynesian thesis for long-period analysis – we may notice the relevance here of that relation, often used in these Notes, between the wage and the rate of profits, which, asserted by Ricardo, has recently been taken up again, overcoming the problems encountered by Ricardo and then by Marx for its exact formulation. This relation may in fact provide a basis for the necessary work of reconstruction. Thus, given such a relation, Keynes's suggestion that the average level of the rate of interest on long-term loans will be determined by conventional factors, ultimately subject to the policy of the monetary authorities (Keynes, 1936, pp. 203-4), would suffice to constitute the nucleus of a theory of distribution. Indeed, it seems reasonable to suppose that, as a result of competition in product markets, the average rate of profit and the average rate of interest on long-term loans will tend, over a sufficiently long period of time, to move in step with one another. If, then, the rate of interest depends on the policy of the monetary authorities, both the long-term movement of the average rate of profit[50] and, through the relation just mentioned, that of real wages are explained by that policy. This does not entail maintaining afresh that the wage bargain has no power to change real wages: the policy of the monetary authorities is not conducted in a vacuum and the movement of prices and of the money wages determined in the wage bargain will be amongst the most important considerations in the formulation of that policy.

[49] The possibility of what is today called structural unemployment is in fact admitted by Keynes. Cf., e.g., the passage '[The rate of interest] may fluctuate for decades about a level which is chronically too high for full employment' (Keynes, 1936, p. 204; see also ibid., p. 217).

[50] Cf. the hint in this direction given by Sraffa (1960), p. 33.

Appendix

This appendix deals with the relationship between the demand for capital as a stock and the demand for investment in the case of fixed capital.

Suppose, for example, that all capital goods last for 10 years, being of constant efficiency throughout their lives and that the initial capital stock is of a uniform age structure. Each year 1/10 of the initially existing set of capital goods will be used up, 'freeing' 1/10 of the workers employed in the economy. Each year, therefore, 1/10 of the initial physical capital can be replaced in the most appropriate form, and in 10 years the replacement cycle will be completed. If the initial prices were equilibrium prices and if conditions remain unchanged, the entrepreneurs will demand each year capital goods identical to those which have been used up during the year. At the interest rate prevailing in the initial situation, there will thus be an annual demand for investment equal in value to a given fraction (lying between 1/10 and 1/5 and depending on the interest rate) of the value shown by the demand for capital function at that interest rate. If the supply of gross savings is equal to that value of investment, the equilibrium will be maintained. Suppose now that – the supplies of the other factors, technical conditions and consumers' tastes all being unchanged – the rate of interest falls and the wage rate and product prices adapt without appreciable delay to the equilibrium compatible with the new rate of interest. The entrepreneurs will then have an incentive to employ the 1/10 of the workers ('freed' each year by the using up of the physical capital) with the techniques and in the industries which are most profitable at the new rate of interest;[51] they will thus demand each year capital goods with a value equal to a given fraction, slightly greater than the previous fraction,[52] of the value shown by the de-

[51] It is assumed here that the increase of wages and the changes in the prices of the products consequent on the decrease in the rate of interest are not so drastic as to drive the gross income from the operation of the not yet fully depreciated initial physical capital to zero. The demand for investment could then no longer be a scale copy of the demand for capital, since the early scrapping of existing physical capital would presumably cause an additional demand for investment. (It should be noted that this additional investment would not result specifically from the *decrease* in the rate of interest, for additional investment due to this cause could equally well result from sufficiently drastic *increases* in the rate of interest.)

[52] At a rate of interest (profits) $r = 0$, the value of a fixed capital of constant efficiency decreases linearly (i.e. by an equal fraction in each year) during its lifetime of n years. For $r>0$, however, the same value traces a step curve which will be the more concave toward the origin the higher the level of r (see for example, Sraffa, 1960, p. 71). The area below the curve constitutes a measure of the value of a stock consisting of a multiple n of pieces of that fixed capital of uniform age distribution between 0 and $n-1$. The vertical intercept will then measure the yearly replacement which will keep the stock intact year after year. The decreasing concavity of the curve as r falls makes it evident that the ratio between the value of the replacement and that of the stock will increase, as was asserted above. (This may be checked from the algebraic value of this ratio which, for $r>0$, will be given by

$$\frac{p(1+r)^n(rn-1)+1}{r(1+r)^n-1}$$

where p is the value of the replacements and n indicates the life of the fixed capital.)

mand for capital function at the new rate of interest. Because of the form which the theory attributes to that function, the demand for investment will thus be greater than it was at the previous level of the rate of interest and will be able to absorb a greater volume of savings. By considering other possible levels of the rate of interest, one could thus define an investment demand schedule. It would no longer be identical to the demand curve for capital as it was in the case of circulating capital; it would nevertheless be a scale copy of it – but for the effect of the rate of interest on the fraction of the value of the total stock which is represented by the value of the yearly replacement – and would indeed reproduce its fundamental property of elasticity with respect to the rate of interest.

Addendum: Heterogeneous capital and the theory of value and distribution[53]

Particular theoretical examples have forced the admission, in recent economic literature, that the switch of systems might operate in a direction contrary to the one traditionally assumed.[54] The tendency however has been to label those cases as 'exceptions': as if the principle about capital intensity had resulted from observed regularities, always liable to exception, and was not a pure deduction from postulates (like Böhm-Bawerk's 'average period of production') now generally admitted to be invalid.

Instead, it must be recognised that the traditional principle, drawn from incorrect premises, is itself incorrect. Moreover, the conditions in which a fall of r results in a relative cheapening of the less capital-intensive productive processes do not seem to be any less plausible than those in which the opposite would be true. This appears to undermine the ground on which rests the explanation of distribution in terms of demand and supply for capital and labour.

To see why that is so, we may begin from the relation between r and the value, in the chosen unit, of the physical capital employed in the economy. This value we shall indicate by K. The relation between r and K – the traditional 'demand function' for capital (saving) – was based on two assumptions: (a) that in the situation defined by each level of r, the labour employed is equal to the supply of it at the corresponding level of w; (b) that the composition of consumption output is that dictated by consumer demand at the prices and incomes[55] defined by the level of r. We shall now grant these assumptions, but we shall restrict the choice of the consumers by supposing,

[53] Reprinted from the *Review of Economic Studies* 1970, pp. 424-8.

[54] Cf. Champernowne, 1953-4, pp. 118-19, 128-9; Hicks, 1965, p. 154; Morishima, 1964, p. 126; Robinson, 1953-4, p. 106, also 1956, pp. 109-10 and 418. Cf. also Levhari, 1965, and the ensuing Symposium, 1966.

[55] In order to determine, simultaneously with the wage and prices, the incomes of consumers and hence the quantities of goods demanded and produced, some hypothesis is necessary regarding the distribution of the ownership of the capital goods in the situation defined by each level of r.

at first, zero net savings (i.e. in each situation, the capital goods are consumed and reproduced in unchanging quantities year by year). From these assumptions, and from what we know about changes in the systems of production and the relative prices of consumption goods, it follows that K may fall or rise, as r falls.

To clear the ground, we must now grant traditional theory two further assumptions in addition to (a) and (b): namely (c) that a tendency to net saving (i.e. a fall in consumption) appearing in the situation defined by a given level of r, brings about a fall of r; (d) as r and w change, with systems of production and relative outputs changing accordingly, net savings realised in the economy can still be meaningfully defined and can be measured – however broadly – by the difference between the K of the final and that of the initial situation.[56]

Let us now imagine that the economy is initially in the situation defined by the level r^* of the rate of interest, with K^* as the amount of capital.[57] Then a tendency to positive net savings appears (i.e. consumption is reduced). We assume that, after a time, the tendency to net saving disappears so that, if a new equilibrium is ever reached, the level of consumption will become that of the situation which corresponds to the new lower equilibrium value of r.

We must now ask whether – as r falls from r^* to some level $\bar{r}$ because of the initial tendency to net saving – a new situation can always be found with an additional quantity of capital ΔK representing the net savings which the community intended to make during the period. The form of the relation between r and K implies that such a new situation cannot always be found: however high r^* is, and however small ΔK, there may well not exist any lower rate of

[56] These assumptions are themselves highly questionable. It is beyond the scope of this article to discuss fully assumption (d). It should however be noted that in order to justify this traditional assumption, we should once more refer to the economy of Samuelson's 'parable', where a single commodity is produced by itself and labour (Samuelson, 1962). In that economy, physical capital and K would be one and the same thing. No change of relative outputs could arise there and changes in the systems of production would not require any qualitative change of the existing physical capital. Then, once we admit, with traditional theory, a tendency to the full utilisation of resources, any change of K could be seen as resulting from an equal opposite change in consumption. But in an economy with heterogeneous capital goods, none of the conditions listed above is verified. The changes in systems of production or in relative outputs will affect the capital stock by changing the *kind* of capital goods or by increasing the quantity of some capital goods and decreasing that of others. The possibility of referring to *physical increments* of the capital stock will fail and with that will fail the possibility of any meaningful notion of 'net saving', not to mention 'net saving' in terms of K. Then, even if we could grant traditional theory the existence of a tendency to the full utilisation of resources, we would have to admit that the changes in total consumption imposed by given changes in the physical capital stock would depend on the *kind* of changes in the stock and on the speed with which they have been accomplished – more than upon the difference between the K of the final and that of the initial situation. As for assumption (c), we may note that Keynes's negative conclusions about the flexibility of r can only be strengthened if, as we shall argue in the text, changes in r provide no mechanism for equalizing 'demand' and 'supply' of capital (saving).

[57] Unless we suppose that the system for the production of each commodity changes 'continuously' with r, K can assume, at any level of r where two systems co-exist, any value between the extremes set by the two systems.

interest $\bar{r}$ at which $\bar{K} = K^* + \Delta K$. Or, to find a situation with an amount $\bar{K}$ of capital just larger than K^*, we may need a fall of r so drastic as to make it clear that, in this case too, it is impossible to determine r by the supply and demand of 'capital' (saving).[58]

This is not all. In traditional theory, our assumption (a) – of a persisting equality between the quantity of labour employed and the supply of it – found its justification in the idea of a demand function for labour. But the fact that, given the quantity of labour employed, K may rise as r rises, implies that the labour employed with a constant K must *fall* with the corresponding fall of w. Thus – even if, by assumption (d), we grant that, in the face of changes in systems of production and relative outputs, we can speak of a constancy of capital and take that to mean constancy of K – there is no reason to suppose a tendency to equality between the demand and supply for labour. Assumption (a) is then unwarranted: the failure of a demand and supply analysis, which we first saw from the viewpoint of the capital market, has its mirror-image in the labour market.

Analogous results would have been reached had we imagined an initial rise in consumption (i.e. a tendency to negative net saving); or an initial change in the 'demand' conditions for capital and labour (i.e. a change in the relation between r and K due to changes in consumer tastes or in the methods of production available).

Thus, after following in the footsteps of traditional theory and attempting an analysis of distribution in terms of 'demand' and 'supply', we are forced to the conclusion that a change, however small, in the 'supply' or 'demand' conditions of labour or capital (saving) may result in drastic changes of r and w. That analysis would even force us to admit that r may fall to zero or rise to its maximum, and hence w rise to its maximum or fall to zero, without bringing to equality the quantities supplied and demanded of the two factors.

Now, no such instability of an economy's wage and interest rates has ever been observed. The natural conclusion is that, in order to explain distribution, we must rely on forces other than 'supply' and 'demand'. The traditional theory of distribution was built, and accepted, in the belief that a fall of r – an increase in w – would always raise the proportion of 'capital' to labour in the economy: the theory becomes implausible once it is admitted

[58] This conclusion would not be affected if we chose to measure capital in the economy by means of the chain-index method proposed by Champernowne (1953-4) and supported by Swan (1956, pp. 348 ff.). It is beyond our scope to discuss this measure of capital or the claim that it permits us to consider as the increase of capital brought about by net saving 'not the change in the value of the stock [in terms of consumption goods], but rather the value of the change' (Swan, 1956, pp. 349 and 356) (cf. however p. 33 above on 'physical increments' of the capital stock). It is sufficient to remark here that when measured in these terms the amount of capital per worker may fall together with r (though it cannot do so in the immediate proximity of $r = 0$). In similar cases, Champernowne (1953-4, p. 118) asserts 'the only way that investment could remain positive ... would be for food wages to leap up and the rate of interest to leap down to levels where capital equipment ... [giving a higher ratio of capital to labour] became competitive'.

that this principle is not always valid.[59]

The idea that demand and supply for factors of production determine distribution has become so deeply ingrained in economic thought that it is almost viewed as an immediate reflection of facts and not as the result of an elaborate theory. For the same reason, it is easily forgotten how comparatively recent that theory is. In the first systematic analysis of value and distribution by the English classical economists up to Ricardo, we would look in vain for the conception that demand and supply for labour and 'capital' achieve 'equilibrium' as the proportions in which those 'factors' are employed in the economy change with the wage and rate of profits. Thus, Ricardo saw no inconsistency between free competition and unemployment of labour. In his view lower wages could eliminate unemployment only by decreasing the growth of population or by favouring accumulation.

What we find in the classical economists is the idea that the wage is ruled by the 'necessaries of the labourer and his family'. Since they regarded these 'necessaries' as determined by social as much as physiological conditions, we may see them as recognising that distribution is governed by social forces, the investigation of which falls largely outside the domain of the pure theory of value. The proper object of value theory was seen to be the study of the *relations* between the wage, the rate of profits and the system of relative prices. These relations would then provide the basis for studying the circumstances on which depends the distribution of the product between classes.

The distinction thus made by the classical economists between the study of value and the study of the forces governing distribution goes together with a separation between the study of value and that of levels of output. Since the inception of the marginal method this separation has been thought no more tenable than that between value and distribution. But the weakness of the marginalist position should now be apparent.

The outputs of commodities and, hence, consumer choice, can influence relative prices, *either* by modifying the technical conditions of production (i.e. the set of methods available for producing each commodity) *or* by affecting the rates of wages and profits.

The first possibility arises because increases in the output of a commodity may, on the one hand, bring about an increase of the division of labour in any

[59] According to Professor Hicks (1965, p. 154), the failure of the principle about capital intensity leaves us in a position which, though not satisfactory, 'has parallels in other parts of economic theory'. He thus seems to suggest that the possible fall, as r falls, in the value of capital per worker does not affect traditional theory any more than do the well-known anomalies of the demand for inferior goods. This seems to ignore that the case of inferior goods did not call into question the general supply-and-demand analysis of prices only because it could be plausibly argued that (a) should those anomalies give rise to a multiplicity of equilibria, the equilibrium position with the highest price would be stable, while that with the lowest price would, in all likelihood, be stable too; and (b) if the latter equilibrium were unstable, the rest of the economic system would not be affected since all we would have is that once the price has fallen below the level of that equilibrium the commodity would not be produced due to a lack of demand willing to pay the supply price. No analogous arguments have been advanced by Professor Hicks with respect to the fall of capital intensity as r falls.

of its possible forms and, on the other hand, where scarce natural resources are used, may force the adoption of methods which increase the output obtained from those resources. But with regard to the changes in the division of labour due to increases in output, the traditional analysis of the firm has in fact restricted the theory of a competitive economy to those technical improvements that are 'external' to the firm. At the same time, the approach in terms of outputs of single commodities has ruled out the technical improvements deriving from the economy's general growth. Consequently, the only 'economies of scale' considered were those 'external to the firm', but 'internal to the industry' – the class which, it has been noted, 'is most seldom to be met with' (Sraffa, 1926, p. 185 of 1953 edn). There remains the case of scarce natural resources. This – as Ricardo showed – can be conveniently treated by first assuming the outputs of the commodities to be given, *then* moving on to inquire about the technical changes associated with changes in outputs, and the consequent changes in the relations between r, w and the prices (including the prices for the use of natural resources). This method would also allow a less restricted treatment of the 'economies of scale'.[60]

The second way in which consumer choice and, hence, outputs can influence relative prices is by affecting the relative scarcity of labour and capital, and thus the wage and rate of interest, given the supply of the two factors and the state of technical knowledge. This link between prices and outputs is one and the same thing as the explanation of distribution by demand and supply of factors of production: and it becomes untenable once that explanation is abandoned.

Thus, the separation of the pure theory of value from the study of the circumstances governing changes in the outputs of commodities does not seem to meet any essential difficulty. On the contrary, it may open the way for a more satisfactory treatment of the relations between outputs and the technical conditions of production. Moreover, by freeing the theory of value from the assumption of consumers' tastes given from outside the economic system, this separation may favour a better understanding of consumption and its dependence on the rest of the system.

With this, the theory of value will lose the all-embracing quality it assumed with the marginal method. But what will be lost in scope will certainly be gained in consistency and, we may hope, in fruitfulness.

[60] This method is apparently the one Sraffa points to, when in the Preface to *Production of Commodities by Means of Commodities* he writes 'no changes in output ... are considered, so that no question arises as to the variation or constancy of returns' and adds: 'This standpoint, which is that of the old classical economists from Adam Smith to Ricardo, has been submerged and forgotten since the advent of the marginal method' (Sraffa, 1960, p. v).

3

Garegnani on effective demand

Joan Robinson

Part I of Garegnani's article (Chapter 2 above) offers a much needed clarification of Keynes's attitude to what he called the classical theory. He put into one box everyone, from Ricardo to Pigou, who neglected effective demand and over-estimated Malthus because he did not, but the main burden of his attack was on the neoclassical marginalists. This Garegnani makes clear and the distinction that he draws between the effects of a change and a difference in static positions is very valuable.

In the second part the discussion of theories of the rate of interest is much less effective.

Murray Milgate (Chapter 5 below) analyses the confusions which have arisen from the concessions that Keynes made to Harrod in drafting chapter 14 of the *General Theory*. Many writers, including Garegnani (see p. 50), have supposed that Keynes advanced 'liquidity preference' as an attack on the theory that the rate of interest is determined by the supply and demand for saving, but his contention was that savings and investment are necessarily equal, whatever the rate of interest may be, because the flow of expenditure on investment creates an excess of income over expenditure on consumption. (There was a long controversy over what now seems obvious, that a reduction in consumption will not cause an increase in investment.) The fact that an increase of income leads to a smaller increase in consumption, and so to an increase in saving, is what makes it possible for the rate of investment to vary from time to time. After Keynes had knocked out the prevailing theory, he had to look around for another account of the rate of interest, as he explained in a passage quoted by Garegnani (p. 50).

Certainly it is true to say that Keynes's theory is in purely short-period terms. This, which Garegnani regards as a weakness, is what gives it clarity. The long-period aspect of investment is the change that it is bringing about in the stock of means of production, often accommodating technical

* Reprinted from *Cambridge Journal of Economics* 1979, **3**, 179-80.

innovations. Keynes for the most part considered investment only as a means of boosting effective demand and thought very little about its long-period effects. However, he made a fatal mistake in offering a quasi-long-period definition of the inducement to invest as the 'marginal efficiency of capital', that is, the profit that will be realised on the increment to the stock of capital that results from current investment and, still worse, identified the profitability of capital with its social utility. This was an element in the old doctrine from which he failed to escape.

He had an alternative concept of the inducement to invest as the expected future return on sums of finance to be devoted to investment. Minsky (1976) points out that he did not seem to recognise the difference between the two formulations. If he had stuck to his short-period brief, he would have used only the second.

In Garegnani's conclusions, the conception of the long period, in particular of the normal rate of profit on capital, is not easy to grasp. Does he mean what the rate of profit on capital will be in the future or what it has been in the past or does it float above historical time as a Platonic Idea? Whichever way we take it, the suggestion that it could be determined by monetary policy seems to be excessively fanciful.

4

A reply to Joan Robinson

Pierangelo Garegnani

There are two basic theses in the article (Chapter 2 above) on which Joan Robinson is commenting (Chapter 3 above). The first is that Keynes's principle of effective demand (i.e. that aggregate demand will not spontaneously adjust to supply) ultimately rests on the refutation of the theory of interest as the equilibrator of saving and investment, and not on the assumed rigidity of money wages. It is accordingly argued that the subsequent rehabilitations of the orthodox long-run relation between saving and investment have been due to weaknesses of Keynes's criticism of that interest theory. The second thesis is that, since the theory in question is the necessary expression of the dominant explanation of distribution in terms of the demand and supply for 'factors of production', the critique of the conception of capital underlying this explanation may provide better support than was provided by Keynes himself for establishing the principle of effective demand in long-period analysis. Associated with this second thesis is the argument that the appropriate theoretical setting for developing effective demand is provided by the surplus approach to distribution found in the classical economists and Marx.

In Chapter 3, Joan Robinson does not refer to either of these two basic theses, and their relationship with the points which she does raise (on liquidity preference and the conception of the long period) needs clarification.

On liquidity preference

Her point on liquidity preference appears to be that Keynes had no need of this concept for his critique of the orthodox theory of interest. In her view the multiplier, i.e. the proposition that

> savings and investment are necessarily equal ... because the flow of

* Reprinted from *Cambridge Journal of Economics* 1979, **3**, 181-7.

> expenditure on investment creates an excess of income over expenditure on consumption,

was all he needed for that purpose.

Here Joan Robinson seems to fall into that oversimplification of orthodox theory against which section 2.2 of my article (Chapter 2 above), devoted to Wicksell's theory of money prices, was intended to caution the reader. The notion that investment '*creates* an excess of income over expenditure on consumption', rather than *being created* by it, is precisely what is under discussion in interest theory, and to use it for a refutation of the orthodox theory of interest comes close to begging the question.

Indeed, the fact that excess decisions to save can be neutralised by a fall in income did not prevent Modigliani from concluding in 1944 that

> As long as wages are flexible, the long run equilibrium rate of interest is determined exclusively by real factors, that is to say, essentially by the propensity to save and the marginal efficiency of investment [i.e. the supply and demand for savings] (Modigliani, 1944, p. 238).

The point is that – as argued in parts of my article which Joan Robinson does not examine (e.g. above, pp. 38, 45-7, 50, 55) – the possibility that decisions to save may be neutralised by a fall in national income will not disprove the orthodox long-run theory of interest, provided that unemployment can bring the rate of interest down to its full employment level through either a decrease in money wages or the operation of monetary policy.

But then – if we leave aside, with the multiplier, the related argument of chapter 14 concerning an indeterminacy of the orthodox theory (cf. p. 52 above) – all that the *General Theory* offers as a critique of that theory of interest is Keynes's alternative to it: liquidity preference.[1]

[1] In the paper by Milgate referred to in Joan Robinson's comment it is argued that 'Keynes did not himself regard [liquidity preference] as part of his *criticism* of the classical theory of interest' (below, p. 80). I can readily agree with Milgate and Joan Robinson on the fact that Keynes himself 'regarded' liquidity preference as part of his 'positive contribution': liquidity preference *is* Keynes's positive theory of interest. The point in my article was a different one: it was whether Keynes had any *effective* criticism of the orthodox theory of interest, other than the accusation that it had overlooked liquidity preference (above p. 52). More relevant against my contention would be the idea that Keynes had a criticism of that theory founded on the deficiency of the underlying concept of capital. But, as Milgate himself appears to realise, the evidence for this idea is not convincing. The passage by Keynes concerning the 'logical error' involved in 'deriving' the rate of interest from the marginal efficiency of capital (quoted by Milgate on p. 84 below), when separated from its implicit reference to liquidity preference and the multiplier, would have no more foundation than claiming that a 'logical error' is involved in deriving the price of a commodity *A* from its demand schedule, because the demand price for *A* depends on the quantity bought, and this in turn on the price. The other references given by Milgate do not then seem to indicate more than a general awareness of difficulties surrounding the notion of capital, such as could have been widely shared, particularly in those years which witnessed a bout of discussion on capital. Keynes's concept of the marginal efficiency of capital is there to show the limits of that awareness.

An implication of my argument on liquidity preference may, however, also have been in Joan Robinson's mind. This is that in the *General Theory* uncertainty and expectations play (through liquidity preference and the volatility of investment decisions) the basically negative role of keeping at bay, so to speak, the demand and supply forces of orthodox theory (above, p. 60 and below, p. 142). Then – since the article also argues that the error of orthodox theory can today be identified at a more fundamental level than simplv the obstacles which uncertainty and expectations might raise for gravitation around the equilibrium of demand and supply for labour – it follows that those two elements may be dispensed with when developing the implications of Keynes's principle of effective demand for long period analysis.

Now, this position, more fully stated in a later article of mine (Chapter 7 below, p. 142), clearly diverges from that of Joan Robinson, who having followed Keynes in basing her critique of marginal theories upon uncertainty and expectations, holds that these elements should be placed at the centre of any work of reconstruction.[2] Concerning this disagreement, I shall here confine myself to noting:

(a) that these concepts have not proved a sufficient basis for establishing the principle of effective demand in long-run analysis;

(b) that, more generally, the procedure by which unobservable, 'expected' quantities are used as determinants of the system runs the risk of depriving the theory of any definite results.[3] These considerations – together with evidence of Keynes's own attitude to liquidity preference as 'something which does not carry us very far', as only an 'intelligible ground from which to proceed' (Keynes, 1973, pp. 213-15) – had led me to argue that

> expectations and even the confinement to the short period of an analysis which Keynes thought had implications going far beyond it, had the main role of providing him with a *provisional* way out of the conflict between [his principle of effective demand] and the dominant theory of distribution (below, p. 142, emphasis added).

On the long period

It seems, however, that for Joan Robinson, the work of theoretical

[2] I may observe that one thing Joan Robinson approves of in my article – namely 'the distinction ... between the effects of a change and a difference in static positions' – is not really there. On the page to which she refers (p. 35 above) I show that the demand for investment (a flow) was often treated in orthodox theory by means of the demand for capital (a stock). This, as far as I can see, bears no relation to the impossibility of analysing changes by comparing equilibria, which Joan Robinson connects with the role of uncertainty and expectations.

[3] On this question cf. below, pp. 139-40. See also Lundberg's remark to the effect that the introduction of expectations as determinants of the system is bound to lead to the 'complete liquidation of economics as a science' (Lundberg, 1937, p. 175): and, further, Schumpeter's view of expectations as 'a mere *deus ex machina* that conceals problems instead of solving them' (Schumpeter, 1936, p. 793n). Similar criticisms of the treatment of expected prices as independent data can be found in Leontief (1966, p. 92n).

reconstruction, besides giving a central role to uncertainty and expectations, should be characterised by concentration on the short period. Thus, in Chapter 3, she points to Keynes's 'fatal' mistake in providing a 'quasi-long-period' definition of the inducement to invest, and writes that Keynes's 'purely short-period terms', regarded as a weakness by me, are rather what gives clarity to his theory.

Let me begin by stating that I do not consider the short-period character of Keynes's theory as any more of a weakness than Joan Robinson herself did when, in 1956, she wrote:

> Keynes's *General Theory* smashed up the glass house of static theory ... But his analysis ... was framed in terms of a short period ... It left a huge area of long-run problems covered with fragments of broken glass from static theory and gave only vague hints as to how the shattered structure could be rebuilt (Robinson, 1956, p. v).

Does Joan Robinson's present stress on the short period mean that she has renounced her early programme of building in that 'huge area', and now thinks that economic theory has little definite to say on problems such as how productive capacity is likely to grow, or how the rates of wages and profits are likely to move relative to one another? Joan Robinson would probably disclaim such a negative attitude to economic theory and argue that long-run problems should be dealt with by an analysis of 'historical processes' based on a sequence of short-period positions (e.g. Robinson, 1974, p. 2), and not by the traditional long-period method used in my article. The fact, however, is that what Joan Robinson has given us concerning these problems has mainly been based on analyses of steady growth which she would freely admit have little to do with accumulation in 'historical time'.

One may wonder at this point whether the source of this contradiction does not lie in Joan Robinson's persistence in that 'provisional way out' (mentioned at the end of the preceding section) which Keynes took when he relied on expectations and the short period in order to establish his principle of effective demand against the dominant theory. This persistence, by entailing the abandonment of the traditional long-period method, has left her treatment of long-run problems with the unhappy choice between, on the one hand, conditions of steady growth which 'are such as never to be found in reality' (Robinson, 1952, p. 92) and, on the other hand, a short-period analysis which is a most unsuitable vehicle for definite conclusions on long-run problems.[4]

[4] One may also wonder whether Joan Robinson's insistence on the short period is not the result of her excessive reliance upon arguments such as that founded on the multiplier (p. 70 above) for her criticism of orthodox theory: adversaries too easily laid to rest have a tendency to revive and maintain their (long-period) ground. Joan Robinson's mention of Keynes's 'fatal' mistake in connection with his concept of marginal efficiency of capital seems to point in that direction: for why should that mistake be 'fatal', if the multiplier were sufficient to dispose of the idea of a long-run, equilibrating function of the interest rate? On the importance of this 'mistake' of Keynes I readily agree with Joan Robinson. In the article under discussion, I had

Joan Robinson argues, however, in her Comment that 'the conception of the long period' in the conclusions of my paper is not 'easy to grasp'. But that conception is no novelty of mine: it is the conception of Smith, Ricardo or Marx, that of Jevons, Marshall or Walras. It is indeed the conception of *every* economic theoretician up to a few decades ago, when it was abandoned as a joint result of the difficulties besetting the notion of capital in the dominant theory[5] and of an incomplete critique of this theory at the hands of Keynes.

This traditional long-period method – which, as such, did not rest on any tendency of the system to the full employment of labour[6] – can perhaps be best made clear today by saying that it analyses those phenomena of Joan Robinson's 'short periods' which are not due to the incongruities between the existing plant, on the one hand, and the relative demand for commodities or the dominant methods of production on the other. This in turn implies that long-period theory analyses what will happen *over an average* of such 'short periods', when, with the possibility of changes in the size of plant, the effects of such incongruities will tend to cancel each other out. As Pareto would have described it, long-period analysis considers the events in these 'short periods' (more generally, the economic phenomena as they are moment by moment) in their 'general form' (Pareto, 1896, para. 37) – so as to explain them in their quality as 'general and average facts' (para. 36).[7]

Now, under competitive conditions, the elimination (averaging out over time) of the incongruities between existing plant and demand for products, or dominant methods of production, is one and the same thing as gravitation around a uniform, 'normal' rate of profits calculated on the supply price of the means of production.[8] This concept of a 'normal' rate of profits is another traditional notion which Joan Robinson finds 'not easy to grasp' and she asks whether this rate 'will be in the future or ... has been in the past or [floats] above historical time as a Platonic Idea'. It is a pity that Joan Robinson's list of possible temporal locations has left out the present: because it is in the

---

indeed argued the 'doubtful compatibility', from the standpoint of long-period analysis, between the marginal efficiency of capital and the principle of effective demand (p. 61 above). But Joan Robinson might perhaps come to see that mistake as less 'fatal' (i.e. as amendable), if instead of withdrawing further into the fortified camp of the short period (as she does with the notion of investment demand suggested in Chapter 3) she advanced into long-period theory to draw the implications of that critique for the marginalist concept of capital, which she has done so much to bring to the forefront of theoretical debate.

[5] On the connection between these difficulties and the abandonment of the 'long-period method', cf. below, in particular pp. 138-9.

[6] This is shown by the fact that this conception was used by Marx and the classical economists who always thought it compatible with permanent unemployment (cf., below, p. 144). On Marx's use of the long-period method, cf. p. 77 below.

[7] Pareto proceeds to observe that a scientific theory can indeed deal only with such 'general and average' facts: this he exemplifies by noting that, whereas it is possible to forecast with a good approximation what the consumption of spirits will be in France next year, it is impossible to forecast the consumption of them by a given individual at a given date (ibid., par. 36).

[8] This applies to the case of competitive conditions, which will however constitute the necessary basis for any treatment of the more complex non-competitive case.

'present' that the 'normal' rate of profits has always been firmly located. It corresponds to the rate which is being realised *on an average* (as between firms and over time) by the entrepreneurs who use the dominant technique. This is so because these firms (like all other firms) will receive, on an average, the normal price for their product and pay, on an average, besides normal wages and rents, normal (supply) prices for the means of production to be replaced. But because this is the rate of profits which is being realised *in the present* under the stated conditions, it is also the rate of profits which that present experience will lead entrepreneurs in general to expect *in the future* from their current investment.

A good description of this traditional notion of the long-period competitive position, and of the attendant uniform rate of profits, may in fact be found in Marx, to whom Joan Robinson often appeals for the kind of analysis in 'historical time' she aims at (cf. e.g., Robinson, 1974, p. 1). After asking himself why political economy always assumes prices of production (and thus a uniform rate of profits), in spite of the fact that these prices (and rate of profits) are never realised except 'by mere accident', Marx answers that such an assumption is made in order

> to be able to study phenomena ... in the form corresponding to their conception, that is ... independent of the appearances caused by the movement of supply and demand' [i.e. independent of the deviations caused by accidental changes in the quantities demanded and supplied].[9]

This he then describes as *the* condition for finding

> the actual tendencies of [the] movements [of the phenomena]

because:

> the result of a deviation in one direction is that it calls forth a deviation in the opposite direction [so] that supply and demand are always equated when the whole is viewed over a certain period, but only as an average of past movements ...
>
> In this way the market-prices which have deviated from the [prices of production] adjust themselves, as viewed from the stand-point of their average ... to equal [the prices of production], in that deviations from the latter cancel each other as *plus* and *minus*.

And this averaging out of market prices he then proceeds to link directly with investment and the corresponding expected rate of profits by writing:

[9] The interpretation appended to Marx's phrase follows when we observe that Marx is using the term 'demand' in Adam Smith's sense of 'effectual demand' – i.e. to indicate the quantity demanded at the price of production of the commodity, and therefore a point and not a curve in the price-quantity space. Equally the term 'supply' is a synonym for what Smith often called the 'quantity brought to market' (Smith, 1964, bk. 1, ch. 7, pp. 48-51).

> And this average is not merely of theoretical, but also of practical importance to capital, whose investment is calculated on the fluctuations and compensations [over the relevant period of time] (Marx, 1974, p. 190).

Finally I come to the suggestion in my paper that the long-run movement of this rate might be affected by monetary policy. Joan Robinson objects to my suggestion, but fails to state her grounds for doing so. In the absence of further clarification, it may perhaps be useful to make my suggestion more explicit, while illustrating some of its precedents. This I shall do by means of a few citations. The first comes from the *General Theory* where, after noting that the long-term money rate of interest is a 'highly conventional phenomenon', Keynes observes that

> precisely because the convention is not rooted in secure knowledge, it will not be unduly resistant to a modest measure of persistence and consistency of purpose by the monetary authority (Keynes, 1936, pp. 203-4).

The second comes from Ricardo and refers to the consequences we should draw if Keynes is correct. Ricardo writes that to suppose that the bank can have the effect of 'permanently lowering the rate of interest' is also to suppose that 'by creating paper money, and lending it at three or two per cent under the present market rate of interest, the Bank would reduce the profits on trade in the same proportion' (Ricardo, 1951, vol. 3, p. 91).

Finally, as long ago as 1844 Thomas Tooke argued:

> Suppose, then, that the reduced rate is general, and the loans for such length of time as to admit of being extensively acted upon by the different dealers of commodities ... [Then] the diminished cost of production hence arising would, by the competition of the producers, inevitably cause a fall of prices of all the articles into the cost of which the interest of money entered as an ingredient (Tooke, 1959, p. 81).

But in considering what Joan Robinson objects to in her comment of 1979 (Chapter 3), I have not only the comfort of Keynes and Sraffa's judgment (cf. Sraffa, 1960, p. 33), Ricardo's logic and Thomas Tooke's fact-finding ability. I also have the company of the Joan Robinson of 1971 who, in at least one passage, drew from Keynes the same conclusions that Ricardo would have drawn:

> a fall in the rate of interest ... may have an important influence in stimulating house building and lowering future rents (Robinson, 1971, p. 31).

Indeed, what is a lowering of house rents if not a lowering of the rate of profits of the house-letting industry? And why should the house-letting industry be an exception in any respect, other than the conspicuousness of the phenomenon?[10]

[10] It should be stressed that – once the basis of the received notion of demand for capital (investment) has been found wanting – an ability of the monetary authorities to control the long-term rate of interest cannot be thought to imply their ability to bring the economy to, or keep it gravitating around, full employment of labour.

5

Keynes on the 'classical' theory of interest

Murray Milgate

I

Keynes's *General Theory* is once again at the centre of theoretical debate. A considerable proportion of the modern 'reconstructions' of Keynes's ideas take the form of the incorporation, in one way or another, of uncertainty into neoclassical general equilibrium models (accompanied by a variety of consequential behavioural hypotheses). These developments derive their credibility as 'Keynesian' analyses from conventional interpretations of the *General Theory* which assign a dual rôle to Keynes's emphasis on expectations and uncertainty. On the one hand Keynes's *positive* contribution is seen to consist of the formulation of a theory of the operation of a market economy in the face of uncertainty. On the other hand his *critique* of the various dimensions of what he called 'classical' theory is seen to consist of an attack on its alleged neglect of the influence of expectations and uncertainty. It follows, as a corollary of this second point, that if 'classical' theory were to be reconstructed by incorporating the effects of expectations and uncertainty then the reconstruction would represent (in some sense) an adequate, more general, 'classical' theory, which circumvents Keynes's criticisms. This is precisely the direction which current 'reconstructions' have taken.

The purpose of this note is to consider one particular aspect of this interpretation: to consider, that is, whether Keynes's *critique* of the 'classical' theory of the determination of the rate of interest is based on its neglect of the implications of uncertainty. This view finds apparent justification in the ambiguity of the critique of the 'classical' theory of interest launched in Book Four of the *General Theory*. It is there that Keynes appears to include the liquidity-preference theory of the rate of interest (based upon individuals' anticipations of an uncertain future) as part of his challenge to the orthodox

* Reprinted from *Cambridge Journal of Economics* 1977, **1**, 307-15. I should like to thank Joan Robinson, a referee and the editors of the *Cambridge Journal of Economics* for valuable comments on earlier drafts of this note.

doctrine. However, it will be argued here that, at least in so far as liquidity preference is concerned, Keynes did not himself regard that theory as part of his *criticism* of the 'classical' theory of interest. Instead his attack suggests a concern with problems of the orthodox theory of capital and interest which arise even in the absence of uncertainty.

Unfortunately, Keynes's position with respect to the criticism of the 'classical' theory of interest has been progressively obscured by conventional interpretations. There is, for example, a large group of writers who agree that the fourteenth chapter of the *General Theory* ('The classical theory of the rate of interest') (*JMK*, vol. 7)[1] is the platform upon which to build an interpretation of Keynes's criticisms of the 'classics', and that Keynes's critique should be sought in the theory of liquidity preference. This places liquidity-preference theory squarely in the *negative* or *critical* part of the *General Theory* (as distinguished from the positive or *constructive* part).[2] Against this view, however, may be set Keynes's subsequent arguments in his 'Alternative theories of the rate of interest' (*JMK*, vol. 14), which clearly assign the theory of liquidity preference to the *positive* part alone. There, Keynes poses once more the question which originally led him to liquidity-preference theory:

> *If* the rate of interest is not determined by saving and investment in the same way in which price is determined by supply and demand, *how* is it determined? (*JMK*, vol. 14, p. 212, italics added).

He goes on to state that it was in the course of providing the 'how' that he 'hit on ... the true explanation' – the theory of liquidity preference. This constructive task is quite distinct from the critical task of substantiating the conjectural 'if'.

Contemporary confusion is due in part to the fact that, in chapter 14, liquidity-preference theory is mixed in with the anti-'classical' arguments. But with the recent publication of the variorum drafts of the *General Theory* and the related Keynes-Harrod correspondence (*JMK*, vols 13 and 14), it is possible to view this chapter and its contents in a new perspective. This evidence suggests an interpretation that has a much closer affinity with Keynes's subsequent statements and casts doubt upon conventional interpretations of Keynes's attack.

The interpretations which fall into this latter class encompass a wide variety of models. Included are all those that might be called the 'special case' interpretations of the *General Theory*, which begin by assigning to liquidity-preference theory the rôle of critique of the 'classical' theory of interest (as, for example, in Professor Hicks's claim that 'it is the liquidity-preference doctrine which is vital', Hicks, 1937b, p. 133) and end by

[1] All references to Keynes's writings are to the appropriate volume and page number of the *Collected Writings* edition (hereafter abbreviated as *JMK*).

[2] This separation was maintained by Keynes and will be amplified in section II below.

concluding that this criticism does not make much impact on the 'classical' theory of interest, either because it only makes a difference 'to a number of short-cut conclusions' (Harrod, 1937, p. 238), or because the question of which of the *n* equations is dropped from the determination of general equilibrium prices (the demand and supply for 'loans' or the demand and supply for money) is 'purely a question of convenience' (Hicks, 1936, p. 246).[3] Included too is a very different variety of interpretation, which derives from Professor Hicks's review of the *General Theory* (Hicks, 1936). The interpretation is based on what Professor Hicks calls the 'method of expectations'; here the negative part of the *General Theory* is held to consist of the argument that 'classical' theory had ignored the fact that the forces of demand and supply might be kept at bay by uncertainty and expectations.[4] Liquidity-preference theory, in which anticipations are vital, is thus associated with the critique.

The one significant group of writers who may be excluded from these classes of interpretations are Keynes's immediate followers in Cambridge, who seem never to have inserted liquidity-preference theory into the negative or critical part of their subsequent descriptions and developments of the *General Theory* (see Joan Robinson, 1960, p. 148, and 1973, p. xi, p. xiv and ch. 8 *passim*; Kahn, 1954; Pasinetti, 1974, p. 47).

With the aid of the evidence provided in vols 13 and 14 of Keynes's *Collected Writings*, it is argued below that there is a clear implication that the theory of liquidity preference plays a rather different part in the *General Theory* than that which has sometimes mistakenly been assigned to it. To substantiate this claim, the evidence will be presented in the following way. In section II the draft version of chapter 14 is examined to show both how it was intended to fit into the schema of the *General Theory* and what criticisms of the 'classical' theory of interest were then offered. In the third section Harrod's reaction to the draft is considered. Harrod's reaction will be shown to have been a decisive factor in moulding the final version of the chapter when, in the last section, attention is focused on the published version, in order to highlight what might be called its 'hybrid' nature.

II

The successive tables of contents which Keynes began to propose for the *General Theory* in 1933[5] indicate that his vision was of a book that would be

[3] It might be noted that Keynes wrote to Hicks over a draft of this paper: 'I am not clear on what you mean by the "demand-and-supply for loans". Do you mean the demand and supply of loans *in terms of money*?' (*JMK*, vol. 14, p. 75, italics in original).

[4] The 'remedy', according to Professor Hicks, is to bring 'people's anticipations of the future' into the determination of a temporary equilibrium (Hicks, 1936, p. 240). But Professor Hicks expressed doubts on the theoretical viability of this approach (Hicks, 1936, p. 241). Moreover, there are other, broader, reasons why this interpretation of Keynes should be treated with caution (see Garegnani, Chapter 7 below, for a further discussion).

[5] The first surviving table of contents dates from December 1933 (see *JMK*, editorial comment, vol. 13, p. 421).

divided into two *mutually exclusive* parts. There was to be a positive part, consisting of the work on the relationship between saving and investment, the principle of effective demand and the multiplier analysis. And there was to be a negative part which would be concerned with the 'flaws' in 'classical' theory.[6] Into this schema, which crystallised in the draft of the *General Theory* that Keynes circulated privately in June 1935, liquidity-preference theory fitted unambiguously into the *positive* part and chapter 14, numbered as chapter 15 in the draft (see *JMK*, vol. 13, p. 526), fitted unambiguously into the *negative* part.[7] This separation is clear from the stylised way in which Keynes chose to structure his argument in the relevant chapters of the draft version. (In referring to the draft we shall adopt the convention of citing its chapters according to their number in the final text, attaching in square brackets their number in the table of contents of the privately circulated version.)

Chapter 13 [14], under the title 'The general theory of the rate of interest', opens as follows:

> To complete our theory ... we need to know what determines the rate of interest. In chapter 14 [15] and its Appendix [16] we shall consider the answers to this question which have been given hitherto ... What, then, is our own answer to this question? (*JMK*, vol. 7, pp. 165-6).[8]

This programme embodies the separation between the positive and negative parts. Already, therefore, one encounters a discrepancy between, on the one hand, the place of liquidity-preference theory in the proposed plan of this part of the *General Theory*, and, on the other, its place as portrayed in the type of interpretation mentioned earlier. Indeed in the draft version of the 'critical' chapter 14 [15], liquidity-preference theory is not mentioned at all.

Although Keynes claimed in both draft and final text to have found it difficult to reconstruct the 'classical' theory of interest (see *JMK*, vol. 7, p. 175), it seems fairly clear that he saw it as a theory which embraced the following postulates. First, that the real rate of profit regulates the money rate of interest. Second, that variations in the rate of interest ensure the equilibrium of the demand and supply for capital (investment and saving). For chapter 14 [15] Keynes reserved the task (the negative task) of demonstrating why 'the notion that the rate of interest is the balancing factor which brings the demand for saving in the shape of new investment

[6] In the correspondence on the drafts Keynes uses this characterisation of his work explicitly. He writes, for instance, of his 'criticism of the classical theory of the rate of interest *as distinguished from* my own theory' (*JMK*, vol. 13, p. 538, italics added), and elsewhere that 'I am still of the opinion that if my constructive sections are correct, my critical sections are more than justified' (*JMK*, vol. 13, pp. 547-8).

[7] This would seem to be further supported by Keynes's references to himself as 'the critic' in the draft of the chapter (see, e.g. *JMK*, vol. 14, p. 477).

[8] This part of the passage remained unchanged from draft to final text (cf. *JMK*, vol. 14, pp. 470-71).

forthcoming at that rate of interest into equality with the supply of saving ... makes no sense' (*JMK*, vol. 14, p. 471).[9]

Some useful additional clues about the intended target of Keynes's attack are provided by the passage from Marshall's *Principles* which Keynes chose to represent the 'classical' argument:

> Interest, being the price paid for the use of capital in any market, tends towards an equilibrium level such that the aggregate demand for capital in that market, at that rate of interest, is equal to the aggregate stock forthcoming at that rate (Marshall, 1961, p. 534; quoted in *JMK*, vol. 7, pp. 175-6).

This is a statement about long-period 'normal' interest. Indeed, Marshall indicates as much in the marginal summary which accompanies the passage (Marshall, 1961, p. 534).[10] The demands and supplies are for 'saving in general' or 'capital in its free form' or 'real capital' (Marshall, 1961, p. 533) and are expressed as quantities forthcoming per unit of time.[11] Although there is a moment in the draft of chapter 14 [15] when Keynes begins to tackle a rather different idea (that interest proper is a monetary phenomenon, not a real phenomenon),[12] in the main his criticisms are directed against the foregoing aspects of the 'classical' theory of interest.

In the draft chapter there are three main lines of attack (though, as will become apparent, the first two may be conveniently reduced to one). The first, which appears only in the draft, is expressed as follows:

> The analogy with the demand and supply for a commodity at a given price is a false analogy. For whereas it is perfectly easy to name a price at which the supply and the demand for a commodity would be unequal, it is impossible to name a rate of interest at which the amount of saving and the amount of investment could be unequal (*JMK*, vol. 14. p. 476).

The second, which appears in both draft and final text, is that:

> The traditional analysis is faulty because it has failed to isolate correctly the

[9] This is at the beginning of chapter 13 [14], where Keynes sets out his ground-plan for what is to follow. The same words appear in a slightly altered paragraph in the final text (*JMK*, vol. 7, p. 165). Keynes reiterates that this is, in fact, the proposition he intends to consider in chapter 14 [15] at the opening of that chapter, when he attempts to spell out what 'classical' theory had maintained (cf. *JMK*, vol. 7, p. 175). The final text differs little from the draft here (the changes are listed in *JMK*, vol. 14, p. 474).

[10] 'The rate of interest is determined *in the long run* by the two sets of forces of supply and demand respectively' (italics added). It is perhaps worth noting here that this was the theory of long-period interest (i.e. of the 'natural rate') to which Keynes had subscribed in the *Treatise* (see, for example, *JMK*, vol. 5, pp. 139, 142, 166, and 170-1). Furthermore, although Keynes does not state explicitly that chapter 14 [15] of the *General Theory* was an intended critique of his *Treatise* views, his references to the theory 'upon which we have all been brought up' (*JMK*, vol. 7, p. 175) lead one naturally back to the *Treatise*.

[11] Thus the 'classical' association between the 'demand and supply of capital' and 'investment and saving' (see Knight, 1915, pp. 301-2 and Eshag, 1963, p. 47).

[12] Keynes relegates this argument to the appendix in the final text (*JMK*, vol. 7, p. 186, n. 1).

independent variables of the system. Saving and investment are the determinates of the system, not the determinants (*JMK*, vol. 7, p. 183).

These criticisms derive from a common position. They both stem from the belief that if the *positive* parts of the *General Theory* are valid (in this case the principle of effective demand) the other theories must, therefore, be invalid.[13]

The third line of attack is of a rather different nature, in that it is levelled against the internal logic of the 'classical' position. As far as the marginal productivity theory of interest was concerned, Keynes argued that

an attempt to derive the rate of interest from the marginal efficiency [productivity[14]] of capital involves a logical error (*JMK*, vol. 14, p. 477),[15]

and this error arises because

the 'marginal efficiency [productivity] of capital' partly depends on the scale of current investment, and we must already know the rate of interest before we can calculate what this scale will be (*JMK*, vol. 7, p. 184).[16]

Although this argument touches on the treatment of capital in 'classical' theory, the degree to which Keynes meant to emphasise the problems associated with this treatment is difficult to judge.[17] He does, however, extend his critique to the demand-and-supply approach of Marshall and of Walras, and once again the treatment of capital is called into question. Three uncharacteristically long footnotes attached to the discussion at this point in the draft concern (either wholly or partly) questions in the theory of capital (cf. *JMK*, vol. 7, p. 176, nn. 2 and 3; vol. 14, pp. 474-5). But Keynes never really specifies *why* the internal consistency of the 'classical' position turns on

[13] Recall Keynes's own statement of this point in the letter to Harrod quoted above, n. 6.

[14] Keynes insisted upon this association (cf. *JMK*, vol. 7, p. 137).

[15] A differently worded statement of the same point appears in the final text (*JMK*, vol. 7, p. 184.

[16] The passage appears in the draft and the final text.

[17] At one point in chapter 11 [12] Keynes does focus directly on these problems. He speaks there of the ambiguity as to 'whether we are concerned with ... one more *physical* unit of capital, or with ... one more *value* unit of capital' (*JMK*, vol. 7, p. 138, italics added). Keynes argues that the problem of the *physical* measure involves difficulties which are both 'insoluble and unnecessary'. The reasons for its insolubility are presumably the same as those which preclude the possibility of measuring aggregate output in physical terms, which Keynes had set out in chapter 4 (*JMK*, vol. 7, p. 38).

However, the reason which Keynes advances for the dependence of the *value* measure on the rate of interest misses the point of the problem of orthodox capital theory. Keynes argues that the problem is that the 'classics' had ignored the increment of value 'expected to obtain *over the whole life* of the additional capital asset; i.e. the distinction between Q_1 and the complete series Q_1, Q_2, ... Q_r' (*JMK*, vol. 7, p. 138). They had instead concentrated their attention only on Q_1. 'Yet this cannot be legitimate except in a static theory, for which all the Q's are equal. The ordinary theory of distribution ... is only valid in a stationary state' (*JMK*, vol. 7, p. 139). But it is clear that this has nothing to do with the problems of traditional capital theory – for these apply (with the exception of one-commodity worlds) even to those versions of traditional theory built within a framework of static assumptions.

its treatment of capital – instead, after suggesting this possibility, he switches to other lines of attack (*JMK*, vol. 14, pp. 474-5).

Two points emerge from the criticisms contained in the draft of chapter 14 [15]. The first is that *liquidity-preference theory is nowhere mentioned in the draft of the chapter* and the second is that *the only criticisms directed at the internal logic of the 'classical' theory show a concern for issues which would today be identified with problems in the theory of capital*. The significance of these two points for any attempt to reconstruct Keynes's critique of the 'classical' theory of interest will become evident in section IV, after the extent of Harrod's influence on this part of the *General Theory* has been examined.

III

The Keynes-Harrod correspondence on the draft version of this chapter (*JMK*, vol. 13, pp. 526-65) indicates that Harrod was highly critical of its content. His criticisms fall broadly into two categories. At one level Harrod questions Keynes's tactics in his rôle as critic of the 'classical' theory of interest, and on another level he challenges Keynes's anti-'classical' arguments on points of substance.

In his biography of Keynes, Harrod remarks that he had objected to the chapter as it stood in draft, because he felt that it was 'pushing criticism too far', that it would 'make too much dust' and hence give rise to 'irrelevant controversies' (Harrod, 1972, p. 534). But it is only now, with the publication of both sides of this correspondence, that it is possible to see the full extent of the impact of Harrod's argument. On the tactical level, Harrod's disquiet over Keynes's attack on the 'classical' position is manifest again and again.

He wrote, for instance, that 'in your [Keynes's] critical part I think you have fallen into what I can only characterise as a confusion ... I feel it has made you quite unnecessarily critical of Marshall and others' (*JMK*, vol. 13., p. 530). And later, in another letter, that 'the effectiveness of your work ... is diminished if you try to eradicate very deep-rooted habits of thought *unnecessarily*. One of these is the supply and demand analysis' (*JMK*, vol. 13, p. 533, italics in original). In another letter Harrod refers to Keynes's criticism of the 'classics' on this point as 'guerilla skirmishing' (*JMK*, vol. 13, p. 534), and in still another Harrod claims that such criticism 'is not essential for your purpose' (*JMK*, vol. 13, p. 546).[18]

All manner of argument was used to try to dissuade Keynes from engaging in what Harrod saw as 'fussy, irrelevant, dubious, hair-splitting and hair-raising' (*JMK*, vol. 13, p. 556) criticism of the 'classical' theory of interest. One variety of argument re-appeared frequently; it was that if Keynes desired to have his positive part accepted he would do well not to make his critical part too harsh. For example, Harrod argued as follows:

> Suppose your reasons in the constructive and critical parts were equally good,

[18] See also the letter from Harrod, 6 August 1935 (*JMK*, vol. 13, p. 537), where the same point is made.

you would have a far greater chance of carrying conviction in the former because your adversaries had not had years of thought in which to prepare an answer (*JMK*, vol. 13, p. 536).

Harrod also argued that Keynes was doing a serious injustice to the younger generation in attacking the demand-and-supply theory of the rate of interest – 'doing great violence to their fundamental groundwork of thought' (*JMK*, vol. 13, p. 533). Yet another argument was that Keynes would not be able to substantiate his arguments against, for instance, Marshall, 'on the basis of short passages torn from their context' (*JMK*, vol. 13, p. 546).

By these polemics Keynes remained profoundly unimpressed,[19] but on the points of substance made by Harrod he tried to come to some accommodation.[20] There were, in the final analysis, only two substantive points. They were directed against the first and third lines of attack which had been adopted by Keynes in the draft of chapter 14 [15]. Against the first line of attack Harrod argued:

This doctrine [demand-and-supply] makes perfectly good sense, but is open to the charge of being incorrect. I find no sense in saying that this doctrine makes no sense *because* in this case supply is always and necessarily equal to demand (*JMK*, vol. 13, p. 530, italics in original).[21]

And further, that

the notion that price is determined by supply and demand always rests on a *cet. par.* assumption ... What you seem to me to have shown is that there are changes in other things which are so relevant and of such overpowering importance, that the old s. and d. analysis had better be put away (*JMK*, vol. 13, p. 531).

Harrod's argument here is clear; the existence of competing theories is not sufficient to demonstrate that one of the alternatives is logically unsound.

On Keynes's suggestion of a lack of internal consistency in the 'classical' theory itself, Harrod mixed tactical arguments with his substantive point. He wrote:

to convict the classical economists of confusion or circularity within the limitations of their own premises ... is not essential for your purpose. And if not essential I should have thought it had much better be left out ... Such a

[19] Keynes replied to Harrod that his purpose in writing the *General Theory* was 'not in order to get read ... [but] in order to get understood' (*JMK*, vol. 13, p. 548) and that what was at stake in their dispute was a 'big question of substance, not of manners or controversial fairness' (*JMK*, vol. 13, p. 547).

[20] This was no doubt due to the clarity of Harrod's précis of the positive structure of the *General Theory* (*JMK*, vol. 13, p. 553; see also Keynes's reply, p. 557).

[21] To this Harrod adds a tactical point: 'in order to give you pause for thought, I should like to add that this was the most criticised part of your address in Oxford ... Frankly it convinced no one' (*JMK*, vol. 13, p. 531).

criticism is bound to seem unfair and I believe it is unfair (*JMK*, vol. 13, p. 546, italics omitted).

In retrospect, this belief is revealed to be unfounded. Keynes had attempted to portray the internal problems of the 'classical' theory of interest as part of the more general problem of orthodox capital theory, and, remarkably, recent work in this field has revealed these problems to be of a far more serious and fundamental character than Keynes (or Harrod) then realised.

Nevertheless, Harrod was led to conclude that it was both possible and desirable to provide a 'reconciliation' of the two theories (cf. Harrod, 1972, p. 534).

I feel that the only way I could possibly be of any assistance is not in the elaboration of your own view, but in endeavouring to restrain you in your criticisms (*JMK*, vol. 13, p. 536).[22]

In this rôle, judging from the change in emphasis Chapter 14 [15] underwent before it reached the printer, Harrod seems to have succeeded only in clouding the issues.

IV

Almost 60 per cent of the published text of chapter 14 had not appeared in the draft version. The added section runs from p. 177, line 32, to p. 183, line 28, in the final text of the *General Theory*.

Harrod's letter of 30 August 1935 contains the following attempted reconciliation of the 'classical' theory of interest with Keynes's theory:

generally when you draw a supply curve $x = f(y)$, it is assumed that you are treating x as a function of a single variable, price, and other things including income were equal. That is the classical supply curve. To relate the classical supply curve to yours, you would have to draw a family of classical supply curves corresponding to different levels of income and to show that the value of each corresponding to a given rate of interest was identical with that of the demand curve (*JMK*, vol. 13, p. 555).

To this passage of the letter Harrod appends the following note:

Let y_1, y_2 etc. be rates of interest and Y_1, Y_2, etc. incomes corresponding to them (Y_1 being derived from y_1 via marginal efficiency of cap. and the multiplier). For each value of Y draw classical supply curves, of which each curve shows the amount of saving corresponding to various values of y at a given level of Y. Then according to you it will be found that the value of y at which the curve appropriate to income Y_r intersects the demand curve is in fact y_r, where y_r represents any given rate of interest whatever (*JMK*, vol. 13, pp. 556-7, italics omitted).

This construct was adopted by Keynes (as a 'very useful ... help to ex-

[22] The same idea is echoed in Harrod (1972), p. 534.

position') in his reply to Harrod of 10 September 1935 (*JMK*, vol. 13, p. 557), and it appears on p. 180 of chapter 14 of the final text of the *General Theory*, where it forms the basis of the six pages of argument that Keynes added during revision. Not surprisingly, a rather new and different thread is thereby woven into the anti-'classical' arguments of the draft. It is this thread which is in large measure the source of the confusion described in section I above.

Gone completely is Keynes's criticism based on the first line of attack which was set out in section II above.[23] More significantly, the criticisms concerning the internal logic of the 'classical' position are considerably watered down. In particular, those which touched on 'capital theory' are much reduced (cf. *JMK*, vol. 14, pp. 476-8 for the changes). Moreover, the adoption of Harrod's reconciliation makes way for the belief that if the level of income were constant then the 'classical' theory of interest would be sound. But more important still is the fact that liquidity-preference theory is now mentioned explicitly in the negative or critical part of the *General Theory* (*JMK*, vol. 7, pp. 180 and 181).

The combined effect of these changes opened the door for the variety of interpretations summarised in section I above. But it has been shown that these interpretations are at odds with the draft of this part of the *General Theory*. They imply that Keynes introduced liquidity-preference theory to show, in some sense, where the traditional theory had gone wrong, whereas, on the contrary, Keynes introduced it to explain the rate of interest. Why the 'classical' theory was false was, for Keynes, an entirely separate question.

Upon which version then should attempts to reconstruct Keynes's critique of the 'classical' theory of interest be based? The evidence seems weighted against an unqualified acceptance of the final text of chapter 14 for the following reasons.

Firstly, although revision wrought important changes in the final content of chapter 14, it was accompanied by no parallel alteration in the groundplan which Keynes had set out in the preceding chapter, which assigned liquidity-preference theory to the positive rather than the negative part of the work. All the passages cited in section II which established this fact appear in the final text. Furthermore, there is no evidence that Keynes had changed his mind about them.

Secondly, even after the publication of the *General Theory*, Keynes again emphasised that liquidity-preference theory was designed as an alternative theory of the rate of interest and that it therefore fell into the positive part of his work. Moreover, a lack of zealous attachment to his theory (see *JMK*, vol. 14, pp. 111, 213, 215) indicates that it was not Keynes's conviction that if liquidity-preference theory was wrong, then the 'classical' theory would be right.

[23] The previously cited statement of the first line of attack is replaced by Keynes's version of Harrod's reconciliation.

Finally, it does not seem that Keynes deflated his one line of attack directed towards the internal logic of the 'classical' theory because he thought it to be unfair, but rather, as Harrod put it, because it was bound to seem unfair.

It may be concluded that, although Keynes was clearly convinced of the necessity of complementing his positive contribution with a logical critique of the 'classical' theory, and he believed that the logical flaws were to be found in the 'classical' theory of capital and interest, the limited scope of his undeveloped criticisms led him to accommodate Harrod's reconciliation so that he might not 'seem unfair'. However, recent debates in the theory of capital have shown Keynes's initial intuition to be well founded. The deficiencies of the neoclassical theory of employment are synonymous with the logical deficiencies of the neoclassical theory of capital. These problems are quite different from the difficulties encountered when attempting to deal with expectations and uncertainty. Indeed, these forces can be incorporated within the orthodox framework, though not without some difficulty and circumlocution.

In adopting Harrod's reconciliation Keynes sacrificed his negative argument on the altar of the immediate success of the positive theory. This has had the unfortunate consequence of appearing to lend support to interpretations of the *General Theory* which distort both the positive and negative parts of Keynes's contribution to the theory of interest.

Postscript: Some comments on the marginal efficiency of capital and liquidity-preference theory

As the preceding note is mentioned in the discussion between Garegnani and Robinson (Chapters 3 and 4 above), some further comments on this particular aspect of that exchange may not be out of place. I will confine myself to a consideration of the connections between the arguments advanced in my own note and the more broadly based conclusions drawn by Garegnani; for here Robinson (p. 70 above) suggests that there is a contradiction between my position and that of Garegnani and so, it seems, does Garegnani (p. 73, n. 1). I will not touch on the issue which seems to me to be at the centre of the Garegnani-Robinson discussion – the validity of the use of long-period 'normal' conditions in theories of value, distribution and employment.

Garegnani argues, in my view correctly, that the adoption of the 'marginal efficiency of capital' as the basis of a theory of investment is equivalent to adopting an orthodox marginalist theory of investment (pp. 22 and 59).[24] He argues that the notion of an interest-elastic investment demand function (the marginal efficiency of capital schedule) is founded upon the conception of a demand schedule for 'free capital' elastic with respect to changes in the

[24] Indeed, Keynes seems to have transplanted the essentials of it from his earlier (orthodox) *Treatise on Money* (see *JMK*, vol. 5, p. 138).

rate of interest (pp. 22 and 64). Both notions are revealed to be inadequate when confronted with reswitching and reverse capital-deepening (p. 39) because these phenomena discredit the notion of a negatively-sloped demand function for 'free capital' and hence the orthodox position with respect to the demand for investment.

Garegnani goes on to indicate that the same (untenable) theoretical position is also at the base of the marginalist school's claim that there exists a long-run 'tendency' towards full employment, (pp. 37-9). I would not wish to dispute any of these arguments. In fact, I was making precisely the same point concerning the connection between the marginalist theories of capital and employment when I wrote in my own note that 'the deficiencies of the neoclassical theory of employment are synonymous with the logical deficiencies of the neoclassical theory of capital' (p. 89 above).

Garegnani proceeds from these results to argue that the positive contribution of the *General Theory* (the principle of effective demand) may be viewed as a *long-period* theory of employment (pp. 21 and 58 above) – a demonstration that the system 'oscillates', as Keynes put it, 'round an intermediate position appreciably below full employment ... determined by "natural" tendencies, namely, by those tendencies which are likely to persist' (*JMK*, vol. 7, p. 254). The possession of this positive theory does not, however, relieve us of our obligation to provide satisfactory arguments for scrapping (by demonstrating an internal inconsistency) the orthodox marginalist theory with which it competes.[25] Thus we arrive at one of Garegnani's fundamental conclusions: Keynes's positive contribution to the theory of employment may be supplemented by invoking the problems of the marginalist theory of capital to complete the negative task (pp. 22-3 above). Here again, the arguments in my own note do not conflict with those of Garegnani; for it was argued there as well that this is the appropriate way of completing the negative task (see especially pp. 84 and 88-9 above).

Garegnani also examines the reasons which explain the absence of a climate of opinion favouring the above course of action (he refers to a degree of 'theoretical uncertainty', p. 21) and why, on the contrary, it has been possible to offer an interpretation of Keynes which amounts to a virtual reaffirmation of the orthodox marginalist theory of the long-run connection between saving and investment. The reasons, as I understand them, are twofold: first, Keynes's adoption of the notion of the marginal efficiency of capital (p. 54 above) and secondly, Keynes's unfortunate reliance on liquidity-preference theory as a *critique* of the conventional wisdom (p. 73). In conjunction, these factors have been responsible for the reassertion of the older orthodoxy by lending support to the argument that an 'inflexibility' in the rate of interest (a 'friction' arising from the presence of uncertainty and expectations) is *all* that prevents the demand for investment and the supply

[25] Confining myself to a discussion of the theory of interest, this is exactly what I had argued (pp. 82 and 86 above). From a wider perspective Garegnani makes the same point (p. 59 above).

of saving from being equated in the traditional fashion at full employment (Garegnani cites Modigliani, 1944b, as having produced just such an interpretation). According to these interpretations, Keynes's theory is relegated to a consideration of that class of circumstances where certain frictions or rigidities prevent the systematic forces outlined by marginalist theory from producing the results that they ultimately have a tendency to produce.

In rejecting such syntheses Garegnani argues (a) that the long-period notion of an 'unemployment equilibrium' is incompatible with the adoption of the marginal efficiency of capital and (b) that the 'ultimate tendencies' of marginalist theory are themselves derived from an internally deficient theory of distribution.[26] In my note, I had to be content to reject the neoclassical synthesis on the grounds that once the negative role of liquidity-preference had been replaced by what we have since learnt about neoclassical capital theory, the rest would follow.

The upshot of Garegnani's argument in Chapter 2 seems therefore to be that we must abandon the marginal efficiency of capital and that if we wish to avail ourselves of an effective criticism of the marginalist theory of interest we should not look to liquidity-preference theory to provide it. In my own note I argued (from a perspective much narrower in scope than that taken by Garegnani) that not only was the second point important but that, once taken, it would be possible to muster an argument to show that it was not a course beyond the 'spirit' of Keynes's own intention.[27] I cannot help but feel that on these points there is nothing in my note which opposes anything that Garegnani has had to say.

On p. 73 n. 1 of Garegnani's 'Reply' (Chapter 4) he seems to me to invent a contradiction between my own position and his when he states that I had suggested that 'Keynes had a criticism [against the orthodox theory of interest] founded on the deficiency of the underlying concept of capital'. I take this to mean that Garegnani feels that I had argued with Keynes actually hit upon reswitching and reverse capital-deepening.[28] Now if this were true then Garegnani would be correct in inferring from it that I held that uncertainty and expectations via their role in liquidity-preference theory were not actually used by Keynes in a criticism of the orthodox theory of saving and investment and so he would be right in seeing a contradiction between my

[26] Thus Garegnani argues that 'one may wonder ... how acceptable these determinations [of the volume of investment] are and, above all, how consistent they are with other parts of Keynes's theory, as soon as problems which are not strictly confined to the short period have to be confronted' (p. 59 above).

[27] This is not the same as saying that such a course of action does not deviate from the *content* of Keynes's eventual position. My whole purpose was to question the orthodox use of the content of chapter 14 as the basis for interpreting the *General Theory*.

[28] The way in which Garegnani examines the evidence produced on p. 84 above appears to indicate this. Garegnani is not convinced (and justifiably so) that this evidence shows Keynes to have been in possession of a critique of the concept of capital as a factor of production. But that evidence was not offered in support of such a strong contention – it shows only that Keynes had a general, yet vague (and, as we can now see, misdirected) idea that something *might* be wrong with the orthodox theory of capital.

position and his own. But this is *not* what I meant to convey.[29]

My argument was that Keynes 'was convinced of the necessity of complementing his positive contribution with a logical critique of the "classical" theory' (p. 89 above) and that in the *early stages* Keynes showed a concern 'for issues which would today be identified with problems in the theory of capital' (p. 85 above, italics omitted). However, 'Keynes never really specifies *why* the internal consistency of the "classical" position turns on its treatment of capital'[30] and, in fact, 'the limited scope of his undeveloped criticism' led him to have recourse to liquidity-preference (p. 89 above). How little Keynes was aware of the 'serious and fundamental character' of the problems of the orthodox theory of capital that have been exposed more recently is shown, I believe, by his using liquidity preference in this way (and, as Garegnani says, the presence of the marginal efficiency of capital only testifies further to this[31]). The inference I drew from this was that if we developed Keynes's 'initial intuition' by completing the negative task with the full-scale critique of the marginalist conception of capital (rather than using liquidity preference as is done in chapter 14 of the *General Theory*) we would have availed ourselves of a criticism of the conventional wisdom that was quite independent of the presence of uncertainty and expectations. It seems to me that this is to reach, by a slightly different route, one of Garegnani's own conclusions (p. 22 and 73-4 above).[32]

[29] In the introduction to my note, when speaking of Keynes's criticism of the traditional theory of interest I wrote, 'Keynes *appears* to include liquidity preference ... as part of his challenge to the orthodox doctrine' (p. 79 above). This may have been an injudicious choice of words, because I say almost immediately afterwards, 'in chapter 14 liquidity preference *is* mixed in with the anti-'classical' arguments' (p. 80 above).

[30] 'The degree to which Keynes meant to emphasise the problems associated with this treatment is difficult to judge' (p. 84 above; see also the footnote that accompanies this statement).

[31] I would not want to go as far as Garegnani does in arguing that this 'general awareness' on Keynes's part owes its origin to the same considerations that motivated Knight and others at that time to dwell upon traditional capital theory. For Keynes saw the issues from a vantage point not enjoyed by his contemporaries – he had an alternative theory. The others, almost to a man, were content to grapple with these questions within the framework of demand and supply.

[32] In my note I chose to examine the implications of the 'hybrid' nature of just one chapter of the *General Theory* prompted by some interesting facts concerning the construction of this chapter contained in *JMK*, vol. 13. In his analysis, Garegnani focusses upon the implications of the 'heterogeneous strands of thought' the *whole book* contains. In aims and conclusions they differ only in the usual way that an analysis limited in scope differs from a more broadly based one – Garegnani goes far beyond the issues which could legitimately have been discussed by me.

6

Theories of value, output and employment

John Eatwell

Theories of value and theories of the general level of output (as opposed to theories of the output of particular commodities) are often treated separately, too little regard being paid to the congruence of the particular theories advanced. The objective of this paper, following the approach initiated by Garegnani (Chapter 2 above) is to examine alternative theories of the determination of the general level of output in the light of the theories of value with which they are associated; our ultimate purposes being a critique of recent attempts to 're-interpret' Keynesian analysis within the framework of neoclassical general equilibrium theory (Clower, 1965; Leijonhufvud, 1968, 1971; Benassy, 1975; and Malinvaud, 1977) and a contribution to the constructive task of relating Keynes's principle of effective demand to the framework of Marxian analysis.

Section I of this paper is devoted to a discussion of the long-period method (Garegnani, Chapter 7 below) in theories of value *and* theories of output. Sections II and III deal with theories of output set within the framework of classical and Marxian analyses – first the classical version of Say's Law, then Marx's rejection of Say's Law and his discussion of the 'possibility of crises'. Section IV presents the neoclassical version of Say's Law, exemplified by Irving Fisher's theory of investment. We then turn in section V to Keynes's theory of output as presented in the *General Theory* and subsequent articles, and in section VI to the interpretation of the *General Theory* generally known as the neoclassical synthesis (Hicks, 1937; Modigliani, 1944). Section VII is devoted to a critique of general-equilibrium analyses of 'rationing' and unemployment. Finally, in sections VIII and IX, it is demonstrated that a more satisfactory critique of neoclassical theories of output than that advanced by Keynes himself may be found in the critique of the neoclassical theory of

* This is a slightly revised version of a paper published in 1979 in *Thames Papers in Political Economy*.

value and distribution based on the analysis of Piero Sraffa's *Production of Commodities by Means of Commodities*; and that the framework of the classical analysis of value and distribution provides a congenial setting for the Keynesian theory of output. Moreover, the characteristics of a capitalist economy, identified by Marx as creating the 'possibility of crises' are, it will be argued, just those characteristics which define the institutional setting for the principle of effective demand.

This is clearly a rather extensive programme for a single paper, and some of the topics will necessarily be treated in a somewhat sketchy fashion. The purpose of this perhaps excessively rapid Grand Tour is to provide an overview of the issues involved, and hence to establish the central theme in an hitherto disparate literature. The reader would do well to keep in mind Garegnani's argument (Chapter 2 above) in which the particular relationship between saving and investment is shown to be the crucial link between a theory of output and a theory of value. Much of our discussion will accordingly focus on the manner in which the saving-investment relationship is formulated in the variety of theoretical structures examined.

I

In relating theories of output to theories of value we must specify the object of the joint analysis with particular care to ensure consistency in the characterisation of the economic circumstances to which the theories refer.

A primary issue in the development of theoretical knowledge in the social sciences (or, indeed, in any science) is the problem of abstraction and the definition of abstract categories. This problem has two dimensions: first, the *object* on which the enquiry is to be focussed must be defined in terms that will permit statements of general validity; secondly, the *theory* which is to explain the magnitude or state of the object must itself be constructed at a particular level of abstraction. Although these two dimensions are not unrelated they are essentially sequential. If they were to be simultaneous (as they are in present day 'intertemporal' models) the object might be defined to fit the theory, and the theory would in consequence reveal little other than its own structure.

In defining the object of the analysis and identifying the forces which determine it, the assumption is made, implicitly, that the forces of which the theory is constituted are the more dominant, systematic and persistent. Transitory and arbitrary phenomena are abstracted from intentionally; as are those forces which are related to specific circumstances as opposed to the general case. The dominant forces are expressed in algebraic form, as functions and constants, and constitute the *data* of the theory. The model may then (if it has been specified correctly) be solved to determine the magnitude of the object. It is known that, except by a fluke, the magnitude determined as a solution will not be exactly that observed in reality. It cannot be, since a variety of transitory forces, known and unknown, have been excluded. None the less, since the theory is constructed on the basis of dominant and persistent forces, the magnitude determined by the analysis is the *centre of gravity* of the actual magnitude of the object. Whether this centre of gravity is a temporal constant, or takes different values through time, does not affect the essence of the method.

The development of abstract categories, in particular the sequential formulation of object and theory, may be traced in the evolution of economic thought.

The seventeenth and eighteenth centuries saw the progressive development of the social division of labour and the emergence of wage labour as the dominant system for the social organisation of production. At this time the idea emerged that prices – the parameters of markets – and hence the entire economic system, might be subject to the influence of systematic 'laws'. On the basis of this insight Adam Smith constructed the abstraction of an economy organised entirely through competitive markets, and isolated the problem of price formation as a necessary element in the search for an understanding of the laws determining the operations of the economy. To distinguish the dominant from the transitory, Smith characterised the competitive market as establishing 'natural or average' rates of wages, profits and rents. When the price of a commodity is just that which provides for the payment of the land, labour and 'stock' used in its production at their natural rates, then the commodity sells at its *natural price* (Smith, 1961, Book 1 ch. 7).

While natural prices were held to be the outcome of the persistent forces in the economy, *market prices*, the prices which actually rule at any one time, are influenced by a variety of transitory or specific phenomena, elements which may be excluded from the analysis of the more permanent forces in the economy.

The natural price is characterised not only as a single price for each commodity, but also by a uniform rate of profit on the value of capital invested in each particular line. Indeed, as Ricardo argued, it is the active role played in the organisation of production by the capitalists seeking the maximum return on the finance they have invested in means of production that is the basis of the tendency toward natural prices (Ricardo, 1951a, p. 91). Marx elaborated this point by emphasising that the tendency toward the equalisation of the general rate of profit and the exchange of commodities at their prices of production (as he called natural prices) 'requires a definite level of capitalist development' (Marx, 1967, p. 177). So the associated categories of natural price and of the general rate of profit were an integral part of the characterisation of a capitalist economy.

The fundamental change in economic theory which occurred in the final quarter of the nineteenth century did not, with respect to prices, lead to any significant change in the definition of the object. The new neoclassical theory was an alternative to the classical theory. As an alternative it necessarily offered a new and different explanation of the same object. This continuity in the object which accompanied the great discontinuity in the theory is particularly evident in Marshall, who devoted considerable attention to the specification of short-period normal prices and long-period normal prices, the concepts he substituted for the market prices and natural prices of Smith and Ricardo (Marshall, 1961, Book 5, chs 3, 5). But the same continuity may be found in the work of Walras (1954, pp. 224, 380), Jevons (1970, pp. 36, 135-6), Böhm-Bawerk (1959, p. 380) and Wicksell (1934, p. 97).

Two important aspects of the specification of this familiar framework for the analysis of capitalist economies should, perhaps, be clarified.

First, the notion of the tendency towards a uniform general rate of profit on the supply price of capital goods derives from the two-fold character of capital in a market system: money-capital and commodity-capital. In a system in which production and distribution are organised by means of a generalised process of exchange money assumes the form of the general equivalent of value, and ownership of money or access to finance endows the ability to own and control the production and distribution processes. Hence the accumulation of monetary wealth becomes, by the nature of the competitive system, the ultimate objective of each individual capitalist, leading him to attempt to maximise the return on the value of the means of production in which he invests his money. But the production of surplus (profits) in the economy as a whole is not a financial phenomenon, it takes place in the process of production. The realisation of a financial return and the organisation of the process of production are two dimensions of the same phenomenon, two phases in the circuit of capital, which find their conceptual unity in the general rate of profit.

Second, the determination of natural prices and the general rate of profit is associated with the 'socially-necessary' or 'dominant' technique of production. At any one time a given commodity may be produced by means of a variety of techniques: some 'fossils' embodying out-of-date methods, which are not being reproduced since at existing prices they would yield a rate of return on their supply price lower than the general rate of profit, but which none the less do yield positive quasi-rents; some 'superior' techniques which are used only by a limited number of producers and yield super-profits. The various theories of value and distribution are not concerned with these, but with 'the conditions of production normal for a given society' (Marx, 1976, p. 129), the 'normality' being defined by dominance throughout the competitive market.

These considerations amount to the proposition that satisfactory analysis of value and distribution in a capitalist economy should endeavour to explain and determine the normal or long-period position of the system – where by long-period is meant not that which occurs in a long period of time, but rather that which is determined by the dominant forces of the system within a period in which those forces are constant or changing but slowly. Hence if we are to present a coherent analysis of the relationship between prices, distribution and the general level of output, then the *object*, the determination of which is to be explained by the theory of output, must be the natural, or normal, level of output, itself the centre of gravity of the transitory forces which affect output at any given time. Thus a long-period analysis of the formation of natural prices must be accompanied by a long-period analysis of output.

This proposition would seem to contradict the popular interpretation of Keynes's theory of effective demand as presented in his *General Theory*. Joan Robinson has argued, for example, that Keynes

> started from a Marshallian short period. Here we are today with whatever stock of capital equipment, training of labour and business organisation that the past has produced; ... (Robinson, 1978, p. 5).

Similarly, Malinvaud (1977) identifies Keynesian analysis with 'short-run equilibrium'.

While there can be no doubt that Keynes developed his theory within what he saw as a short-period setting, it will be argued that it is the long-period implications of his analysis, as a theory of employment, which represent the significant contribution. Indeed, even on its own terms, Keynes's analysis does not warrant the appellation short-period. For example, the fixed composition of the capital stock which defines Marshall's short period plays no role in Keynes's theory of employment – unemployment is, according to Keynes, not due to the shortage of a particular capital good, but to a lack of effective demand. Moreover his assumption that

> We take as given the existing skill and quantity of available labour, the existing quality and quantity of available equipment, the existing technique, the degree of competition, the tastes and habits of the consumer, the disutility of different intensities of labour and of the activities of supervision and organisation, as well as the social structure including the forces ... which determine the distribution of the national income (Keynes, 1936, p. 245)

although it might appear to be intended as a definition of a short period in the Marshallian sense, is really designed to rule out the effect of *accumulation*, for Keynes continues:

> This does not mean that we assume these factors to be constant; but merely that, in this place and context, we are not considering or taking into account the effects and consequences of changes in them ... (ibid.).

Hence Keynes rules out changes in the dominant and persistent forces acting *in a given situation*, changes which Marshall argued would lead to:

> *Secular* movements of normal price, caused by the gradual growth of knowledge, of population and of capital, and the changing conditions of demand and supply from one generation to another (Marshall, 1961, p. 379).

Finally, if Keynes had argued in the *General Theory* merely that the economy might be in a disequilibrium in the short period, then he would have added nothing to the prevailing theory (or indeed to his own argument in the

Treatise on Money). Since a short-period position is *by definition* a disequilibrium, the only novelty of his theory might be the particular form the disequilibrium is presumed to take (as we shall see this is just the approach adopted by modern proponents of 'rationing' theory; see Strøm and Werin, 1978). There would remain the question of what would, in such circumstances, be the level of output toward which the system would tend to gravitate? Would it, for example, be the full-employment level?

Keynes was not concerned with short-period disequilibria. He claimed that the nature of the components of his theory was

> ... adequate to explain the outstanding features of our actual experience; – namely, that we oscillate, avoiding the gravest extremes of fluctuation in employment and in prices in both directions, round an intermediate position appreciably below full employment and appreciably above the minimum employment a decline below which would endanger life.
>
> But we must not conclude that the mean position thus determined by 'natural' tendencies, namely by those tendencies which are likely to persist, failing measures expressly designed to correct them, is, therefore, established by laws of necessity. The unimpeded rule of the above conditions is a fact of observation concerning the world as it is or has been, and not a necessary principle which cannot be changed (Keynes, 1936, p. 254).

The *persistent* forces establish the long-period level of output: it is these forces and that level which Keynes's theory is designed to explain.

In our appraisal of alternative theories of output, and their relationship to theories of value, we should, therefore, bear in mind that

(1) the theories of output should be theories which determine the normal level of output in terms of the dominant and persistent forces comprising the theory:

and in consequence

(2) in relating a theory of output to a theory of value we will be concerned with the effect that prices and the distribution of income may have on the determination of the normal level of output and the tendency towards it;
(3) following Garegnani (Chapter 2) we will look to the saving-investment relationship as the key to the elucidation of (1) and (2); and
(4) an important role will therefore be played by theories of the rate of profit, both because this rate is related (in radically different ways in different theories) to the saving-investment relationship, and because it provides a link between monetary phenomena and the determination of real output.

II

As we are now well aware (Sraffa in Ricardo, 1951a; Garegnani, 1960; Sraffa, 1960), the classical theory of value takes as its *data*

the size and composition of output,
the conditions of reproduction of commodities, and
the real wage;

and these data are sufficient for the determination of relative prices and the general rate of profit. Since output is a *datum* there is no place in the theory of value for functional relationships between quantities and prices, or between saving, investment and the rate of profit. Changes in output will, in general, lead to changes in prices and the rate of profit, but nothing can be said, *a priori*, about the form of such changes, which reflect variations in the conditions of production. So the theory of value and the theory of output are formally *separable* from one another. In Ricardo's case this separability is expressed in the combination of a comprehensive and consistent theory of value with a 'theory' of output, Say's 'Law' of markets, which is no theory at all.

The law of markets proposed by Say in his *Traité d'Economie Politique* (1803) was constructed from two elements: the first, anti-mercantilist, locating the problem in terms of exchanges of commodities, with money being merely a medium of exchange; the second, physiocratic, portraying the interacting forces of demand and supply within the circular flow of commodities in the process of reproduction. Thus to purchase a commodity in the circular flow of production, one must produce a commodity – the supply of one commodity *is* the demand for another. Suppose, for example, that a hat-maker wishes to buy shoes, then he must produce a hat, take it to the market place and attempt to exchange the hat for shoes. If the shoes are available there will be a balance of supply and demand. If, however, the hat is produced but shoes are not, then there will be a 'glut' of hats, and a shortage of shoes. There will be an excess of a particular commodity, but there will not be an excess of all commodities – that, Say argued, is impossible. Ricardo agreed:

> M. Say has, however, most satisfactorily shewn, that there is no amount of capital which may not be employed in a country, because demand is only limited by production. No man produces, but with a view to consume or sell, and he never sells, but with an intention to purchase some other commodity, which may be immediately useful to him, or which may contribute to future production. By producing them, he necessarily becomes either the consumer of his own goods, or the purchaser and consumer of the goods of some other person. It is not to be supposed that he should, for any length of time, be ill-informed of the commodities which he can most advantageously produce, to attain the object which he has in view, namely, the possession of other goods; and, therefore, it is not possible that he will continually produce a commodity for which there is no demand (Ricardo, 1951a, p. 290).

Two elements of this argument should be noted. First, it refers only to the employment of capital, not to the employment of labour. As in all classical analyses it is presumed that there will, in general, be unemployed labour. The level of employment is determined by the current level of accumulation and the social productivity of labour. If there is any tendency toward 'full employment' this must derive either from accumulation having outstripped the growth of the available labour force or by means of some form of the Malthusian population principle. Such forces are quite unrelated to the 'law' which ensures that capacity is fully utilised. Second, since, in this formulation, supply *is* demand, then saving, the production of commodities other than for consumption, *is* investment. This proposition is not based on the ex post identity of saving and investment, but on the characterisation of the motivation of production. 'It therefore seems possible to conclude that in Ricardo "Say's Law" was not the result of an analysis of the investment-saving process, but rather the result of the *lack* of any such analysis' (Garegnani; see Chapter 2, p. 28).

Since full utilisation of capacity is assured by the proposition that decisions to save are decisions to invest, and this proposition was accepted not only by James Mill and Ricardo, but also by Malthus. Malthus's argument for the possibility of a *general* glut is, at first sight, rather puzzling. Malthus's confusion is a reflection of his confusion concerning the theory of value and distribution. He identified the general glut with a fall in the rate of profit brought about by an excess supply of capital:

> ... how is it possible to suppose that the increased quantity of commodities, obtained by the increased number of productive labourers, should find purchasers, without such a fall of price as would probably sink their value below the costs of production or, at least, very greatly diminish both the power and the will to save (Malthus, in Ricardo, 1951b, p. 303).

As Garegnani has shown this is an extension of Adam Smith's argument that accumulation of capital will lead to a decline in the rate of profit, an argument which Ricardo had already refuted by demonstrating that the rate of profit will fall with accumulation only because wages rise due to the increased difficulty of producing wage goods (p. 27 above). As long as Malthus assumed that saving is spending there could be no logical foundation for his argument, for there would be no shortfall in the demand for capital; and to Ricardo the argument that the normal rate of profit might fall with given conditions of reproduction and a given real wage was completely incomprehensible.

The separability of the classical theory of value from the 'theory' of output adopted by Ricardo, leaves the way open for a critique of the tautological status of Say's Law and its replacement by a satisfactory theory of output, while the classical analysis of value and distribution is retained. The foundations for the first task were laid by Marx.

III

Attacks on Say's Law are scattered throughout Marx's works, the most detailed being his critique of Ricardo's theory of accumulation in part two of *Theories of Surplus Value*. There he argues that Say's Law is false because it is based on a false conception of capitalist production; a conception which likens capitalist production to the barter of use values:

> The conception that over production is not possible, or at least that no general glut of the market is possible is based on the proposition that products are exchanged against products ... It must never be forgotten that in capitalist production what matters is not the immediate use-value, but the exchange value and, in particular, the expansion of surplus value. This is the driving force of capitalist production, and it is a pretty conception that – in order to reason away the contradiction of capitalist production – abstracts from its very basis and depicts it as a production aimed at the direct satisfaction of the producers (Marx, 1968, pp. 493 and 495).

Once it is recognised that capitalist production is organised and directed by the necessity of producing commodities, i.e. exchange values, and of transforming those values into the general form of value, money, the barter analysis is revealed as a profoundly deceptive portrayal of 'harmonious' capitalist accumulation:

> ... *money* is an essential aspect of the commodity and ... in the process of metamorphosis it is independent of the original form of the commodity.
>
> Crises are thus reasoned out of existence here by forgetting or denying the first elements of capitalist production: the existence of the product as a commodity, the duplication of commodity in commodity and money, the consequent separation which takes place in the exchange of commodities and finally the relation of money or commodities to wage labour (Marx, 1968, p. 502).

Marx constructs his analysis of output in two stages: first he seeks to establish the *possibility* of crises, those conditions which imply 'that *the framework* for a crisis exists' (p. 509); second, he presents arguments establishing the *actuality* of crises (see Kenway, Chapter 8 below).

The possibility of crises is derived from just those characteristics of capitalistic production which Ricardo has ignored: the commodity and money. The circuits of capital from money to commodity to money and so on, are the necessary form of the production and expansion of surplus value, but the realisation of that surplus is not unproblematical, for the circuit may be broken:

> The difficulty of converting the commodity into money, of selling it, only arises from the fact that the commodity must be turned into money, but the money need not be immediately turned into commodity, and therefore *sale* and *purchase* can be separated (Marx, 1968, p. 509).

Thus Marx's notion of 'the separation of sale and purchase', refers to the separation in a monetary economy between a decision to initiate production and the ability to sell the commodities produced. The possibility of crisis is inherent in this aspect of capitalist production.

Marx's discussion of the *actuality* of crises is less innovative. He falls back on just those conditions of disproportionality and disruption which Ricardo had conceded may occur – the difference being that, given the phenomena which establish the possibility of crises, these conditions lead to 'crisis', which

> is nothing but the forcible assertion of the unity of phases of the production process which have become independent of each other (Marx, 1968, p. 509).

This discussion of the actuality of crises is essentially a short-period analysis, related not to the dominant and persistent forces of the system, but to transitory elements. Marx argued forcefully that the positions of Smith and Malthus whereby an overproduction of capital might lead to a permanent diminution of the rate of profit were wrong both because of their erroneous theories, *and* because they attempted to present long-run analyses of crises:

> When Adam Smith explains the fall in the rate of profit from an over-abundance of capital, an accumulation of capital, he is speaking of a *permanent* effect and this is wrong. As against this, the transitory over-abundance of capital, over-production and crises are something different. Permanent crises do not exist (Marx, 1968, p. 497n).

The character of Marx's discussion is also evident in the contrast between the analysis of the circuits of money capital, in which 'it is ... taken for granted ... that commodities are sold at their values' (Marx, 1967, p. 24) and the discussion of crises in which 'the market prices of commodities ... fall far below their cost prices' (Marx, 1968, p. 494). But a short-period theory must always be related to some centre of gravitation defined by the persistent forces of the system. Transitory disruptions are characteristic of all analyses (including Ricardo's), and though Marx may attempt to argue that such disruptions may be repetitive and severe, it is far from obvious that they can bear the weight which he clearly wishes to place on them unless they are related to a theory of output which contains the possibility of a level of output *permanently* lower than that implied by past levels of accumulation. If a theory of value, based on the conditions of reproduction of a given output, is to encapsulate the dominant and normal forces in a capitalist economy, then that output must also be the outcome of dominant forces. A satisfactory theory of crises must be linked with a theory of output which locates crises as something other than transitory phenomena. Marx failed to provide such a theory because he, like Ricardo, identified saving and investment, proposing no theory of the relationship between them, and relying on time-lags to create transitory disruption:

> If the interval in time between the two complementary phases of the complete metamorphosis of a commodity become too great, if the split between the sale and purchase become too pronounced, the intimate connexion between them, their oneness, asserts itself by producing – a crisis (Marx, 1974, i, 15; see also 1968, p. 495).

So while providing important insights into the possibility of crises, Marx's analysis of the actuality of crises is severely limited by his lack of any theory of the general level of output.

IV

The construction of the neoclassical theory of value involved the provision of a logical foundation for the idea that prices are determined by supply and demand. This required that a method be found of expressing the 'forces' of supply and demand in homogeneous units as functions of prices (Mill, 1945). The requisite homogeneity was constructed by Jevons, Menger and Walras in terms of individual utility maximisation, balancing marginal utility and marginal disutility at the margin of constrained choice. The essential structure of the model involves the relationship between utility maximisation and the constraint provided by a fixed endowment of commodities and/or factors, the process of maximisation being based on the possibility of substitution (either direct or indirect) between the fixed elements. Taking as *data*

utility functions
technology
endowments
distribution of the endowments

demand and offer functions (or the equivalent sets) may be constructed and counterposed to determine the set of prices *and quantities* consistent with competitive market clearing. The necessity of the simultaneous determination of equilibrium prices and quantities means that the theory of value and the theory of output are *the same theory*. In marked contrast to classical analysis the neoclassical theories are completely inseparable. (The peculiar case of the non-substitution theorem in which separability apparently exists, derives from the very basis of neoclassical theory, the possibility of substitution between factors, having been assumed away; Eatwell, 1977).

What we will characterise as the neoclassical version of Say's Law is quite different from the classical version. It consists of two propositions (Garegnani, pp. 29-30 above). First, that there exists a set of market-clearing prices for all commodities and all factors. By definition these prices equalise the supply and demand for all commodities including factors of production; except when commodities are in excess supply at a zero price. It is usually presumed that there is sufficient substitutability in the system to ensure that the price of labour is not zero. Second, that competitive forces will cause prices to tend to their market-clearing levels. Thus the equilibrium set of prices will contain a wage which clears the labour market and a rate of interest which equalises the demand for investible funds to the supply of savings.

Our examination of the neoclassical theory of output will consider the version of the theory proposed by Irving Fisher, but the argument which follows is quite general (see also Garegnani pp. 29-41 above). Fisher's analysis is especially useful for our purposes both because he presents a particularly clear analysis of the relationship between utility maximising consumer choice and saving and investment in the determination of the general level of output, and because it provides a particularly apposite basis of comparison with Keynes's analysis, for Keynes identified part of his theory with that of Fisher:

> Professor Fisher uses his 'rate of return over cost' in the same sense and for precisely the same purpose as I employ 'the marginal efficiency of capital' (Keynes, 1936, p. 141).

Fisher conducts his argument in various stages (which he calls approximations). The first approximation is an analysis of the exchange of immutable consumption streams, the second approximation includes the possibility of altering consumption streams by productive activity. Within each stage the argument proceeds from an examination of an individual's saving and spending decisions to the determination of the rate of interest by the 'market equilibrium' of the economy as a whole. For the individual 'the rate of interest is cause, and his lending and borrowing is effect. For society as a whole, however, the order of cause and effect is reversed' (Fisher, 1930, p. 119).

Intertemporal production possibilities are introduced in Fisher's second approximation in the form of alternative streams of income:

> ... the owner of any item of capital wealth or capital property, including, of course and especially, his own person, is not restricted to a sole use to which he may put it, but has open to his choice several possible or alternative uses, each of which will produce a separate optional income stream. He has, therefore, two kinds of choice: first, the choosing of one from any optional income streams, and secondly, as under the first approximation, the choosing of the most desirable time shape of his income stream by exchanging present income against future (Fisher, 1930, p. 125).

Saving for the economy as a whole may now be defined as taking part of the flow of production and adding it to the pre-existing stock. Production techniques are distinguished by the amount of capital required with a given quantity of land and labour to produce a unit of output.

With the introduction of techniques of production, Fisher needed to postulate a relationship between the stock of capital and the rate of return to investment of capital. He assumes that there are diminishing returns to increased investments of capital, other factors of production being fixed.

The set of available techniques defines the transformation frontier

$$c_2 = f(c_1, x) \tag{1}$$

where c_1, c_2 are consumption per head at time 1 and at time 2, and x is the initial endowment of capital per head at time 1. The rate of return on increased saving at time 1, say from $x - c_1^*$ to $x - c_1^* + h$ is defined as

$$\frac{\text{gain} - \text{sacrifice}}{\text{sacrifice}} \text{ i.e.}$$

$$r = -\frac{f(x - c_1^* + h) - f(x - c_1^*) + (x - c_1^* + h) - (x - c_1^*)}{(x - c_1^* + h) - (x - c_1^*)} \qquad (2)$$

The limit of (2) as $h \to 0$ is $-f' - 1$, the *marginal* rate of return over costs.

The relation between the amount of saving and the marginal rate of return gives the demand for saving as a function of the rate of interest. The assumption of diminishing returns to substitution between capital and labour means that the greater the amount saved the lower is the marginal rate of return or, alternatively, the lower the rate of interest the greater is the demand for saving. By the assumptions made concerning individuals' preferences the supply of saving is lower the lower is the rate of interest. The market rate of interest is that at which the supply of, and demand for, saving are equal. This rate of interest is equal to the marginal rate of return over the cost of the marginal increase in the stock of capital. Equilibrium in the market for saving and investment will be accompanied by equilibrium in the markets for land and labour.

Hence in neoclassical analysis there exists an analysis of the relationship between saving and investment: desire to save and desire to invest are brought into equality by the functioning of the price mechanism. The essential assumption for this to take place is that there should be the possibility of substitution between capital and labour, from which is derived the elastic demand schedule for investment as a function of the rate of interest – or, to be more accurate, the combination of the rate of interest and wage rate which clears the savings-investment market and the labour market.

(It is worth noting at this point that neither the classical economists nor Marx saw any role for the rate of profit, or indeed the rate of interest on money, as an equilibrating mechanism in the market for saving and investment. The rate of interest on money was regarded as a derivative concept 'merely a portion of the profit, i.e., of the surplus value, which the functioning capitalist, industrialist or merchant has to pay to the owner and lender of money-capital whenever he uses loaned capital instead of his own' (Marx, 1967, p. 370). Hence the rate of interest was not susceptible to significant variation other than that due to variation in the social productivity of labour and/or the real wage; see Panico, Chapter 9).

The existence of a market-clearing set of prices does not, of course, mean that such prices will actually be established. Analyses of short-period disruptions, or of trade-cycles and similar disequilibria, by neoclassical economists have therefore assumed the form of particular imperfections which limit the competitive tendency toward market-clearing equilibrium. Such imperfections might be sticky wages and prices, 'disruptive' monetary and financial phenomena, uncertainty or lack of information leading to miscalculation by economic agents, or simply 'imperfect competition'. All of these are, however, defined by their relation to the market-clearing, full-employment level of output implicit within the neoclassical theory of value.

V

The argument of Keynes's *General Theory* is constructed in two essentially distinct parts. In the first section of the book, chapters 1 to 10, Keynes advances the proposition that the equality between desired saving and the volume of investment is maintained by variation in the level of aggregate output and employment. Then in chapters 11 to 18 he attempts to argue that there is no tendency for the level of investment to adjust to a level commensurate with full-employment saving. This involves both the formulation of his own theory of investment and a critique of the neoclassical theory. The structure of the book thus mirrors the intellectual development which led to the formulation of the basic propositions of the *General Theory:*

> ... the initial novelty [of the *General Theory*] lies in my maintaining that it is not the rate of interest, but the level of incomes which ensures equality between saving and investment. *The arguments which lead up to this initial conclusion are independent of my subsequent theory of the rate of interest*, and in fact I reached it before I had reached the latter theory. But the result of it was to leave the rate of interest in the air. If the rate of interest is not determined by saving and investment in the same way in which price is determined by supply and demand, how is it determined? One naturally began by supposing that the rate of interest must be determined in some sense by productivity – that it was, perhaps, simply the monetary equivalent of the marginal efficiency of capital, the latter being independently fixed by physical and technical considerations in conjunction with the expected demand. It was only when this line of approach led repeatedly to what seemed to be circular reasoning, that I hit on what I now think to be the true explanation. The resulting theory, whether right or wrong, is exceedingly simple – namely, that the rate of interest on a loan of given quality and maturity has to be established at the level which, in the opinion of those who have the opportunity of choice – i.e. of wealth holders – equalises the attractions of holding idle cash and of holding the loan. It would be true to say that this by itself does not carry us very far. But it gives us firm and intelligible ground from which to proceed (Keynes, 1937, p. 250, italics added).

The 'initial novelty' is based on the proposition that while saving is dependent on the level of income (output), the volume of investment which entrepreneurs may undertake at any one time is independent of the current level of income. This independence derives from the existence of the monetary system; i.e. of money, credit and finance. The prospective investor can acquire purchasing power, command over real resources, from the financial sector in excess of the current flow of savings:

> If investment is proceeding at a steady rate, the finance (or commitments to finance) required can be supplied from a revolving fund of a more or less constant amount, one entrepreneur having his finance replenished for the purpose of a projected investment as another exhausts his on paying for his completed investment. But if decisions to invest are (e.g.) increasing, the extra finance involved will constitute an additional demand for money ... But 'finance' has nothing to do with saving. At the 'financial' stage of the proceedings no net saving has taken place on anyone's part, just as there has been no net investment. 'Finance' and 'commitments to finance' are mere credit and debit book entries, which allow entrepreneurs to go ahead with assurance ... if the banking system chooses to make the finance available and the investment projected by the new issues actually takes place, the appropriate level of incomes will be generated out of which there will necessarily remain over an amount of saving exactly sufficient to take care of the new investment (Keynes, 1937, pp. 247-8).

It is in this crucial sense that Keynes's theory is a *monetary* theory of employment. The independence with which the monetary system endows the investment decision, combined with the propensity to consume and hence the multiplier, establishes a theory of the determination of the general level of output and hence of employment.

But this particular role of money was not a novel idea. In his analysis of money Wicksell (1935) had pointed out that the banks may provide capitalists with command over resources in excess of the current level of output. The essential difference is that Wicksell was assuming that the real forces established a natural rate of interest and the natural rate of wages at which capital and labour were fully employed (on Wicksell's monetary theory, and its relationship to Keynesian theory see Garegnani, Chapter 2 above). Keynes, however, was advancing a different theory of the relationship between saving and investment, though the task remained of establishing that there were no forces present in the economy which would push the level of investment toward the full employment rate.

This similarity between Keynes and Wicksell should alert us to the fact that Keynes's analysis of output does *not* constitute a critique of the neoclassical theory of output, but simply poses an alternative. A suitably 'neoclassical' theory of investment could, as we shall see, transform his analysis into something remarkably similar to the neoclassical formulation.

Keynes's analysis of the determinants of investment consisted of two elements. First, he argued that the relationship between the volume of investment and the prospective yield on that investment could be represented by the elastic schedule of the marginal efficiency of capital. Second, to determine the volume of investment this schedule was related to the rate of interest which, Keynes argued, was determined not by the relationship between the demand for investible funds and the supply of saving, but by the demand for the stock of monetary assets. This is derived from the demand for money for transactions purposes, and, what is more important with respect to the determination of the rate of interest in any given circumstances, the speculative demand to hold money as a means of holding wealth, a necessary condition for which is uncertainty as to the future rate of interest (Keynes, 1936, p. 168).

This latter proposition was to play a central role in the subsequent development of Keynes's argument. For his formulation of the determinants of investment immediately raises the question: why does not the rate of interest adjust to that level which ensures a full employment rate of investment? Keynes's answer rests squarely on the monetary character of the rate of interest, rather than on any inelasticity of the marginal efficiency schedule:

> Thus in the absence of money and in the absence – we must, of course, also suppose – of any other commodity with the assumed characteristics of money, the rates of interest would only reach equilibrium when there is full employment (Keynes, 1936, p. 235).

So Keynes appears to be resting his case for a less-than-full employment equilibrium *not* on the proposition that a full employment rate of interest does not exist, but on the proposition that monetary phenomena will inhibit (or prohibit?) the tendency of the rate of interest to attain the full employment rate.

The emphasis on the theory of interest is reinforced by Keynes's consideration in chapter 19 of the *General Theory* of the effect of flexibility in money wages on the level of employment. Given the structure of his model wage flexibility can only alter the general level of activity if the propensity to consume, or the marginal efficiency of capital, or the rate of interest are affected. Examining these relations in turn, Keynes argued that the employment effect of a fall in money wages on the propensity to consume and the marginal efficiency of capital would be either neutral or tend to reduce the level of employment. The only manner, therefore, in which a fall in wages could lead to an increase in employment would be through its effects on the real value of the stock of monetary assets and hence on the rate of interest; effects which may be likened to effects of open-market operations designed to increase the quantity of money:

> Just as a moderate increase in the quantity of money may exert an inadequate influence over the long-term rate of interest, whilst an immoderate increase may offset its other advantages by its disturbing effect on confidence; so a moderate reduction in money-wages may prove inadequate, whilst an immoderate reduction might shatter confidence even if it were practicable (Keynes, 1936, pp. 266-7).

Keynes also attempted to lend support to his own theory by criticising the neoclassical theory of output (Keynes, 1936, ch. 14). This critique was based on the propositions that (i) the neoclassical theory of the determination of the rate of interest and of the level of output was false because saving and investment are necessarily equal at any level of employment, and thus there could not be separate schedules of saving and investment the interaction of which would determine the rate of interest; and (ii) that the rate of interest was not determined by the relationship of saving to investment but by the demand for the stock of monetary assets.

The first criticism is related to Keynes's assertion that neoclassical economists *assumed* that the economy operates at full employment, and like that assertion it does not hold water. The full-employment level of output is not assumed by neoclassical economists, it is proved to be the equilibrium output of the economy. Similarly, while it is obvious that in an accounting sense saving and investment are identically equal, this does not mean that the causal relationship between saving and investment may not be characterised by two elastic schedules. If it is supposed that such schedules exist and that wages and the rate of interest are flexible, then as Garegnani has pointed out (p. 31 above) Keynes can argue that the system will not tend toward a full-employment level of activity only by supposing that investment does not react in such a manner as to validate a desire to increase saving. Suppose, for example, that the level of output is below the full-employment level. Wages fall, and individual capitalists decide to hire more labour. The consequent increase in output can be sold only if a fall in the rate of interest leads to increased investment which 'absorbs' the consequent increase in saving. By such a process the system tends towards full employment, with saving always equal to investment (in the accounting sense).

Keynes's second criticism, which relies on the juxtaposition of his theory of the rate of interest and the neoclassical theory is, as Garegnani has also shown (pp. 53-4 above) seriously undermined by the fact that fluctuations in liquidity preference are based on fluctuations of the expected rate of interest around the conventional or normal rate – but no theory is presented for the determination of that conventional rate. It might be argued, for example, that in the long run the normal rate would be determined by the real rate of return on capital, itself determined by the long run relationship of the supply and demand for capital.

So not only does an important element of Keynes's theory of output rest on the monetary analysis of the determination of the rate of interest, but his critique of neoclassical theory does too. But the analysis of interest was just that part of his theory which Keynes was to argue was 'independent' of the initial novelty of his position, and which 'does not carry us far'. The reason for the seemingly peculiar elevation of the analysis of the rate of interest to the centre of the stage has been identified as stemming from the weakness of his critique of neoclassical theory once the very tentative critical remarks made in draft concerning the logical status of the neoclassical theory of capital had been removed following criticism by Harrod (Milgate, Chapter 5 above) and from the necessity of providing an inhibition to the movement of the rate of interest toward the full-employment level once the existence of an elastic demand schedule for investment, the marginal efficiency of capital schedule, had been assumed (Garegnani, Chapter 4 above).

So Keynes was ultimately forced into defending his theory on the rather weak grounds that the effects of uncertainty linked with monetary phenomena would inhibit the tendency of investment to the full-employment level:

> Thus, after giving full weight to the importance of the influence of short-period changes in the state of long-term expectation as distinct from changes in the rate of interest, we are still entitled to return to the latter as exercising, at any rate, in normal circumstances, a great though not a decisive, influence on the rate of investment. Only experience, however, can show how far management of the rate of interest is capable of continuously stimulating the appropriate volume of investment.
>
> For my own part I am now somewhat sceptical of the success of a merely monetary policy directed toward influencing the rate of interest (Keynes, 1936, p. 164).

But scepticism is not enough. The *possibility* of the establishment of a full-employment rate of interest was inherent in Keynes's model:

> It is, therefore, on the effect of a falling wage – and price – level on the demand for money that those who believe in the self-regulating quality of the economic system must rest the weight of their argument; though I am not aware that they have done so (Keynes, 1936, p. 266).

He would not have long to wait!

VI

The characterisation of Keynes's argument as 'Mr Keynes's special theory', and the subsequent integration of apparently Keynesian propositions into the corpus of neoclassical analysis was launched by Hicks (1937). This and the development of what has come to be known as the 'neoclassical synthesis' has been ably surveyed by Garegnani (pp. 54-6 above), and there is no need for us to do anything other than summarise the main points of the argument.

The development of the neoclassical synthesis was based on the limitation of the effects which uncertainty and instability might be expected to have in the longer run, as opposed to their effects on short-run fluctuations of the economy around the long-run position. In the long run it might be argued, for example, that the demand for money would not be dominated by uncertainties concerning the deviation of interest rates from the conventional rate, but would instead be derived from the relative convenience and risk involved in holding wealth in money form:

> The theory of risk-avoiding behaviour has been shown to provide a basis for liquidity preference and for an inverse relationship between the demand for cash and the rate of interest. This theory does not depend on the inelasticity of expectations of future interest rates, but can proceed from the assumption that the expected value of capital gain or loss from holding interest-bearing assets is

> always zero. In this respect, it is a logically more satisfactory foundation for liquidity preference than the Keynesian theory (Tobin, 1958, p. 84).

Tobin prefaced his 'reconstruction' of liquidity theory with the proposition that:

> What needs to be explained is not only the existence of a demand for cash when its yield is less than the yield on alternative assets but an inverse relationship between the aggregate demand for cash and the size of this differential in yields (Tobin, 1958, p. 65).

Having constructed a stable demand function for money one may readily conclude that, other than in the case in which the demand for money is highly elastic with respect to the rate of interest (Mr Keynes's special theory), a fall in money wages or an increase in the quantity of money will lead to a fall in the rate of interest and a tendency of investment to the full-employment level:

> It is the fact that money wages are too high relative to the quantity of money that explains why it is unprofitable to expand employment to the 'full-employment' level (Modigliani, 1944, p. 255).

Employment may be expanded *either* by a decrease in money wages *or* by an increase in the quantity of money, if money wages are constant.

The Keynesian analysis of unemployment is thus confined to the short-period influence of 'rigidities', and of uncertainty and similar 'psychological' effects. The permanent forces in the economy would establish a full-employment equilibrium if it were not for short-period imperfections which cause deviations, of lesser or greater size and length, from the full-employment level of output.

VII

The 'neoclassical synthesis' involves an attempt to derive essentially neoclassical conclusions from a bowdlerised version of Keynesian ideas, focussing in particular on the relationships between the stock of money, measured in wage-units, the rate of interest and the level of investment. An apparently different direction has been taken with the development of theories of 'rationing' in which an attempt is made to derive quasi-Keynesian conclusions from restricted versions of neoclassical general equilibrium models – including models of pure exchange and of non-capitalistic production.

Theories of rationing are descended from Clower's idea of the dual-decision hypothesis relating 'notional' and 'effective' excess demands (Clower, 1965), and similar developments by Leijonhufvud (1968, 1971). The 'rationed' equilibrium does not necessarily satisfy Walras' Law, and thus *in equilibrium* some markets, such as the market for labour, may display negative excess demands, while all other excess demands are equal to zero.

The concept of a ration derives from the idea that the quantity traded in a particular market at a given price is determined by the 'short-side' of the market. So if, for example, the Walrasian notional supply and demand functions for labour are indicated by $S_L(\bar{w})$ and $D_L(\bar{w})$ where $\bar{w} = w/p$ is the real wage, and at $\bar{w} = \bar{w}^*$, $D_L(\bar{w}^*) < S_L(\bar{w}^*)$ then jobs are 'rationed', for workers can only 'supply' an amount of labour equal to $D_L(\bar{w}^*)$. Similarly, entrepreneurs' opportunities to sell goods may be 'rationed' if the demand for goods is less than the quantity they would be willing to sell at the going price; or buyers may be 'rationed' in the quantity of a good they are able to purchase, if the quantity available is less than the notional demand at the going price.

Clower (1965) uses this concept to explain unemployment in a model in which there exists but one good and labour. Suppose that the real wage is at such a level that the notional demand for labour is less than the notional supply, then the demand for the good will be a function of the real wage *and the quantity of labour demanded* which is equal to the effective supply of labour. The money wage and the price level may be such that supply is equal to effective demand in the market for the good. So if D_i, S_i are notional demands for i, and S, D are effective demands for i, then the situation just described may be characterised as

$$D_L(\bar{w}^*) = S_L^e(\bar{w}^*) < S_L(\bar{w}^*) \tag{3}$$

$$D_G^e(\bar{w}^*, D_L) = S_G(\bar{w}^*) \tag{4}$$

As far as the entrepreneur is concerned the market for the good is in equilibrium and there is no incentive to increase output and hence demand more labour; and equally there is no pressure to change the good price. But labour is unemployed. The situation has been characterised by both Clower and Leijonhufvud as peculiar to a monetary economy:

> If the unemployed demanded 'payment' in the form of the products of the individual firms, producers would perceive this as demand for a larger volume of output than is being produced. As long as the unemployed did not demand more in exchange than their marginal physical product, competitive producers would have no reason to turn such barter-bargains down. But, just as workers find that their labour is not a source of direct purchasing power over output, producers find that their output is not a means of payment for the purchase of labour inputs. In offering their services to firms that do not produce a balanced basket of consumer goods, workers ask for *money wages*. From the standpoint of prospective employers, therefore, the offer of labour services is not directly connected with a demand for additional output. Not perceiving that more output is called for, individual firms will, consequently, turn such offers down (a) even if no more than labour's marginal value product (evaluated at going prices) is being asked for, and (b) even if no more than the money wage rate that the system would have in equilibrium is being asked for (Leijonhufvud, 1971, p. 35).

As Hahn has pointed out (1977, p. 31) this is a very limited definition of a monetary economy, and under the conditions postulated the absence of money would lead to greater 'market-failure' than its presence.

But the 'transmission of information' is not really the issue. Suppose, for example, that in a capitalist economy in which all profits are saved unemployed workers guarantee to employers that they will spend all the wages they might earn on the goods they produce. The information is conveyed, but clearly no capitalist would offer employment for there would be no possibility of profit – the total increase in expenditure would be equal to the increased wage bill. If employment is to increase there must be an increase in investment. Here Leijonhufvud's analysis is quite traditional. He argues that the fall in the rate of interest required to stimulate the investment which will absorb increased saving (he must mean increased potential saving) will be inhibited by liquidity preference (1971, p. 38). Thus, the amount of effective saving will be rationed by the 'short-side' of the saving-investment market. The substance of 'rationing' theory comes down to an inhibition on the adjustment of the rate of interest to the market-clearing rate.

A new version of rationing theory which combines the Clower-Leijonhufvud emphasis on relative prices with earlier ideas on the relationship between the average level of wages and prices, the quantity of money and the overall level of spending, has been developed by Malinvaud (1977). In the discussion which follows we will utilise a simplified version of Malinvaud's model developed by Kahn (Chapter 12 below).

Malinvaud assumed that investment expenditure (and hence employment in the investment sector) is autonomously fixed. Variations in the level of output and employment can then be due only to variations in the output of consumption goods. Saving behaviour is determined by a relatively complex analysis in terms of individual utility maximisation in the light of dividends, the wage rate, employment, the price of consumption goods, and the size of money stocks. To simplify the story it may be assumed that all profits are saved, and that the pattern of saving out of wages and the expenditure of money stocks (by the employed and the unemployed) is such that the sum of the two is constant at S_w. This assumption is clearly unrealistic if the average level of wages and prices is very low relative to the size of money stocks, a question I will return to later. If investment sector profits are also fixed at P_I then total profits in the consumption sector, P_c, are determined from the condition that investment equal savings:

$$I = S_w + P_I + P_c \qquad (5)$$

So for any given money wage level, the price of the consumption good must be such as to yield a profit on the total output of consumer goods equal to P_c. This relationship is shown by the curve D in Figure 1, in which a unit of the consumption good is defined as the average amount produced by one unit of

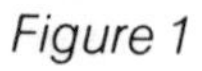
Figure 1

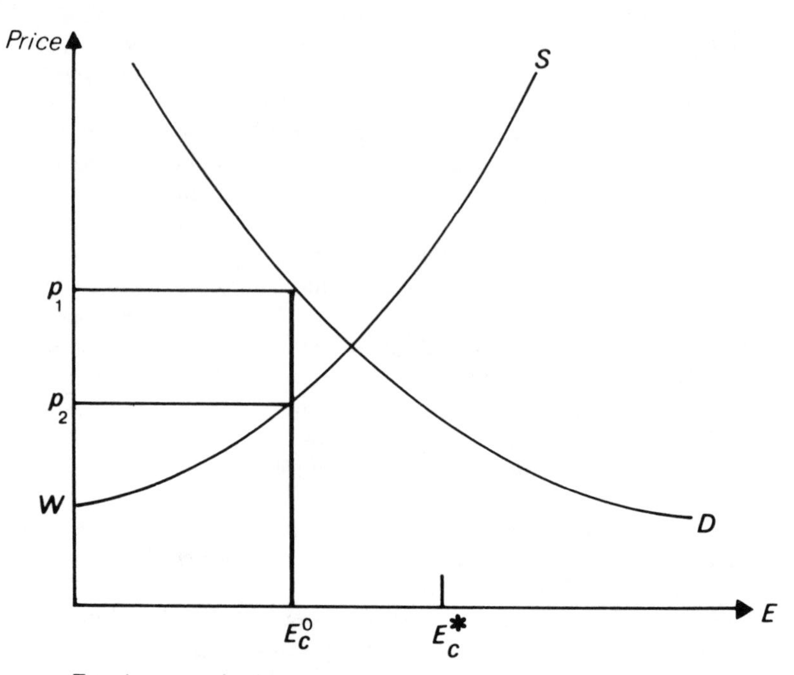

Employment in the consumption sector

labour employed. The curve is a rectangular hyperbola around the y-axis and the level of the money-wage rate.

On the supply side Malinvaud assumes that an arbitrary capital stock embodying many vintages will be used in ascending order of cost per unit output, so that increased output may only be produced at an increased marginal cost. The resultant 'well-behaved' supply function is indicated by the curve *S* in Figure 1.

Finally, Malinvaud argues that the essential characteristic of macroeconomic analysis of 'modern society' is that it should be short run, and hence that on the basis of empirical evidence of administered pricing and the determination of wages in a highly institutionalised environment 'the theory under consideration here is justified in assuming full price rigidity, i.e. in working with models in which prices and wage rates are exogenous' (Malinvaud, 1977, pp. 11-12).

The model may now be used to classify types of unemployment with respect to a given configuration of wage rate and consumption good price. Suppose, for example, that with reference to Figure 1 in which E_c^* indicates the level of consumption sector employment which corresponds to full employment in the economy as a whole, and *W* is the (sticky) money-wage rate, that the price of the consumption good is fixed at p_1. Then the amount of employment is determined by demand, producers are 'rationed' as to the quantity of consumption goods they can sell, and jobs are rationed to the less than full-employment demand for labour. In these circumstances a fall in the price (an increase in the real wage) would lead to increased employment. This situation Malinvaud describes as 'Keynesian unemployment'. Now suppose that the price is set at p_2. Employment is determined by the supply condition, consumers are rationed as to the amount they can buy, and jobs are also rationed. A rise in p (a fall in the real wage) would result in increased employment. This situation Malinvaud refers to as 'classical unemployment'. Finally, if the level of consumption sector employment which would result in full employment in the economy were E_c° then any fixed price level between p_1 and p_2 would result in 'repressed inflation'.

The relationship between these three characterisations of the economy is illustrated in Figure 2. For any given money wage we may find a price which corresponds to full-employment demand, that which corresponds to full employment on the supply side, or that which defines the boundary between 'Keynesian' and 'classical' unemployment. Varying the level of money wages and the price level will trace out loci of such wage-price relations, the shape of the curves being considerably influenced by the change in the real value of the stock of monetary assets. There will be a particular real wage and price level, *WE*, which will correspond to full employment – this point Malinvaud refers to as Walrasian equilibrium.

Figure 2

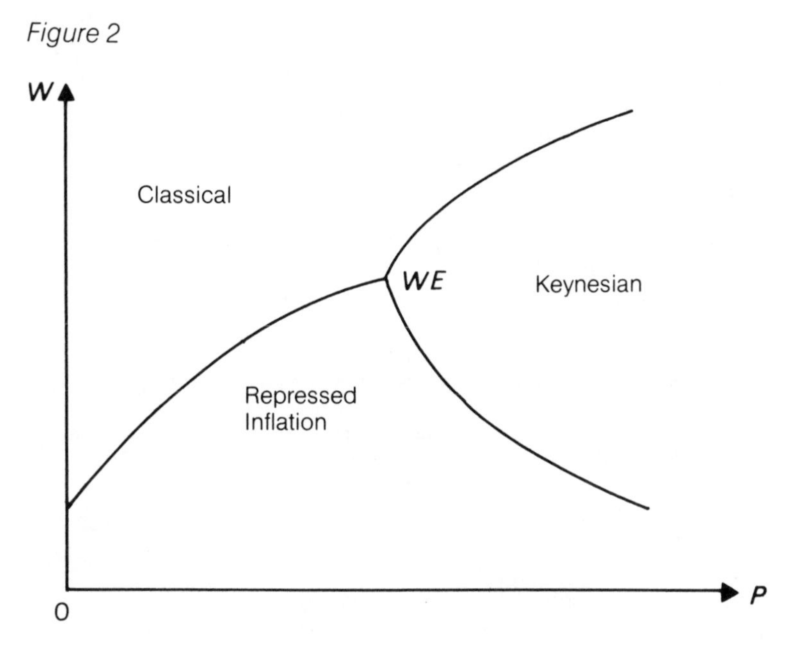

WE – Walrasian equilibrium

Malinvaud asserts that if the data of his model were 'constant through time ... then the long run equilibrium resulting from price theory will be the Walrasian equilibrium'. But 'since prices and wages are sticky, we cannot expect the growth path to coincide permanently with the changing Walrasian equilibrium in our short-term model' (Malinvaud, 1977, p. 93). Institutional factors, which introduce rigidities into the price system are, therefore, to blame for the economy not being at a full-employment equilibrium.

Two major criticisms have been made of the Malinvaud model. Kahn (Chapter 13 below) has argued that the form of the cost curve on which the analysis depends is incompatible with the assumption of administered prices:

> Fixed or 'sticky' prices are found in manufacturing and distribution, where products are not homogeneous and labour costs are constant or decreasing up to the limits of capacity. The result, which has been well confirmed by various empirical studies and is widely known as Okun's Law, is that productivity in industry increases with short run increases in output, while prices are sticky.
>
> Flexible prices are found in those markets for a limited range of primary products where products are homogeneous, demand to the individual producer is almost perfectly elastic, and costs rise with output due to fixed natural resources.
>
> Malinvaud mixes the two ... (Kahn, p. 224 below).

Hahn has argued that the rationing model as formulated by Malinvaud (and indeed by Clower and Leijonhufvud) amounts merely to the proposition that prices and wages are insufficiently flexible for the determination of full-employment output, without any argument being made as to the origin of such flexibility (Hahn, 1977, pp. 32-3). He argues that inflexibility in the face of, say, persistent unemployment, may be explained in terms of 'conjectural equilibria':

> Let us stick for the moment to the labour market and think of money wages as being quoted by the sellers of labour. One now needs to supplement the description of the household by a demand curve conjectured by it ... The household must have some beliefs as to how its ration of labour would respond to a change in the wage it quotes. If there is an equilibrium it is what I call a conjectural equilibrium. That is, it is a state such that actions of agents are compatible and such that, given the conjectures no price can be advantageously changed by any agent ... If an equilibrium is a state where rational actions are compatible and if amongst possible actions one includes changing of price, then there exist non-Walrasian unemployment equilibria. The wage is neither fixed nor arbitrary nor flexible. It is what it is because no agent finds it advantageous to change it. (Hahn, 1977, p. 34).

Hahn has also used the concept of conjectural equilibrium to argue that Malinvaud's identification of a given set of prices with Walrasian full-employment equilibrium is too limited, for rationed conjectural equilibria with unemployment may be associated with the 'Walrasian' prices (Hahn, 1978). Hahn's argument is illustrated in Figure 3. The economy consists of two individuals (or two groups of individuals) a and b, with endowments e_a and e_b of commodities x and y. The competitive equilibrium supported by the prices shown involves a selling $e_a s_a$ of x and buying $s_a t_a$ of y; b sells $e_b s_b$ of y and buys $s_b t_b$ of x. Suppose now that a is rationed (by conjecture) to the sale of $e_a c_a$ of x, then there exists a ration for b, namely the conjecture that b can only sell $e_b c_b$ of y, such that the rationed (conjectural) equilibrium is sustained by the Walrasian equilibrium prices.

Figure 3

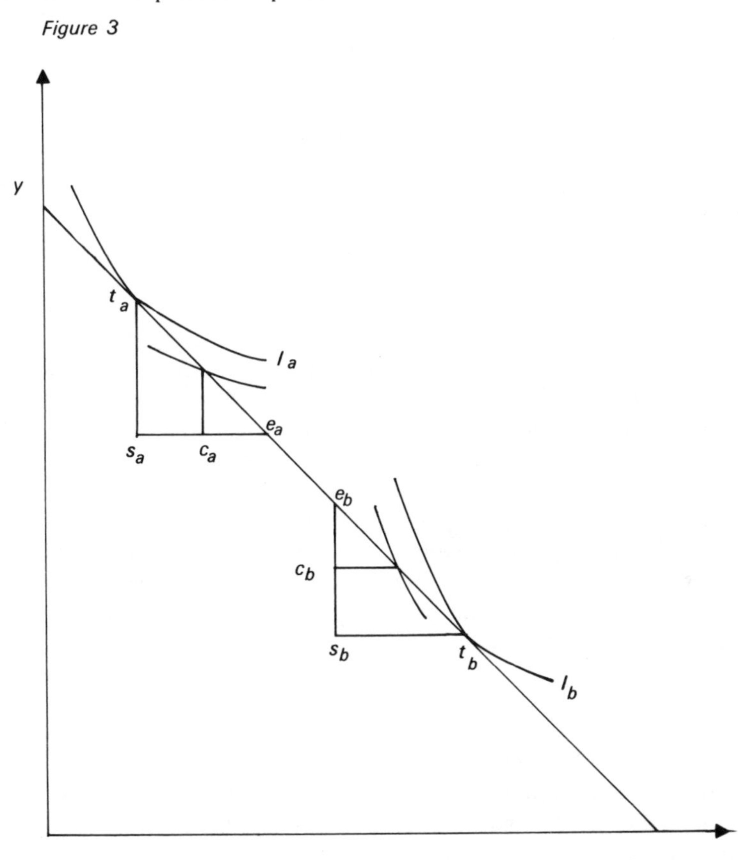

But Hahn's criticism does not take us very far (apart from showing how arbitrary is the fixed price approach). In any disequilibrium position agents act on false information and these actions may, in the short run, exacerbate and perpetuate the disequilibrium. But the crucial question is whether forces endogenous to the system will push it towards a full-employment position. Hahn admits that it seems likely that in competitive economies rationed conjectural equilibria will be unstable and that Walrasian equilibrium will be the only rational conjectural equilibrium possible (Hahn, 1978, p. 3). So his conjectural analysis reduces to an evocation of monopolistic elements as an explanation for sticky prices or 'perceived rations'.

However both Kahn and Hahn seem to miss the main failing of rationing models in general and Malinvaud's model in particular, which is that such models do not address themselves to the fundamental issue in the interpretation of Keynesian analysis – the relationship between saving and investment. In Malinvaud's model, for example, all the weight of adjustment in employment is placed on varying output in the consumption sector, the investment sector output being fixed. The label 'Walrasian' which he attaches to a full-employment position attained primarily through operation of the real balance effect is quite spurious, for no 'Walrasian' analysis of saving and investment is present other than the off-hand remark that:

> It would be still more interesting to introduce into our prototype model a market for bonds with a flexible interest rate and to recognize that 'autonomous' demands depends on the rate of interest (Malinvaud, 1977, p. 114).

In so far as rationing models are constructed on Walrasian lines they amount merely to particular examples of the wide variety of 'imperfections' models: i.e. models upon which particular imperfections are imposed which inhibit the gravitation of prices towards equilibrium. These might even be pure exchange models. They certainly have nothing essential to do with the central issue of Keynes's *General Theory*: the establishment of an under-employment 'equilibrium' by the normal working of the saving-investment relationship through the multiplier. The rationing models hence appear to be a remarkable example of intellectual atavism and spurious sophistication. Under the guise of complex general equilibrium analyses they contrive to produce pre-Keynesian propositions by means of un-Keynesian devices – and triumphantly label the result 'Keynesian'.

VIII

The variety of attempts to generate neoclassical results in a 'Keynesian' framework, and 'Keynesian' results in a neoclassical framework, together point to important failings in the *General Theory*: the inadequacy of Keynes's critique of the neoclassical theory of output and the important ambiguities introduced by Keynes's marginalist treatment of the labour market and by his portrayal of the marginal efficiency of capital as an elastic demand schedule for investment. Garegnani (Chapter 2 above) has argued that these failings may be remedied by application of the results of the debate on the neoclassical theory of capital derived from Sraffa's *Production of Commodities*. I will illustrate this point by reference to the implications of the debate for Fisher's analysis of investment and the rate of interest which, as we saw above, Keynes identified with his own analysis.

But first we will examine Keynes's definition of the marginal efficiency of capital:

> If there is an increased investment in any given type of capital during any period of time, the marginal efficiency of that type of capital will diminish as the investment in it is increased, partly because the prospective yield will fall as the supply of that type of capital is increased, and partly because, as a rule, pressure on the facilities for producing that type of capital will cause its supply price to increase; the second of these factors being usually the more important in producing equilibrium in the short run, but the longer the period in view the more does the first factor take its place. Thus for each type of capital we can build up a schedule, showing by how much investment in it will have to increase within the period, in order that its marginal efficiency should fall to any given figure. We can then aggregate these schedules for all the types of capital, so as to provide a schedule relating the rate of aggregate investment to the corresponding marginal efficiency of capital in general which that rate of investment will establish. We shall call this the investment demand-schedule; or, alternatively, the schedule of the marginal efficiency of capital (Keynes, 1936, p. 136).

Keynes's argument is more complicated than may at first appear, involving as it does assumptions on both the supply and demand conditions for individual capital goods in both short and long run and, finally, at both individual and aggregate levels – the ultimate objective being the derivation of the relationship between the 'rate of aggregate investment' and 'the corresponding marginal efficiency of capital in general', or, to put it another way, the general rate of return.

Taking first the short-period aspect of the argument, Keynes's assumption that increased investment in a given type of capital good will lead to higher cost of production – rising supply price – is quite unfounded. Any short-period situation, and particularly a short-period in which capacity is widely under-utilised, will be characterised by *excess* stocks of materials and machines in some (maybe all) sectors, with (perhaps) shortages in a few sectors too. In such a situation no definite hypothesis may be made as to the likely effect of increased output on cost, though in conditions of widespread excess capacity it seems reasonable to suppose that costs will tend to *fall* as fixed costs are averaged over higher output. 'Pressure on the facilities' for producing a given capital good will only tend to become significant as full employment is approached, and even then the consequences for the cost of production of an increase in supply of any one capital good cannot be predicted with confidence.

The short run influence of the demands for capital goods on 'prospective yield' to be derived from further investment are likewise unpredictable, and as to the aggregate effect of all this – nothing can be said at all. Indeed, there is no short-run 'marginal efficiency of capital *in general*' to say anything about! The relationship which Keynes sought must be a long-run relationship, in the sense that it is sufficiently unambiguous and persistent to allow definite conclusions to be drawn concerning the influence of a given volume of investment on the rate of return.

Now in the longer run Keynes himself suggested that increased output will not result in any increase in cost. Any diminution in return must, therefore, derive from the fall in prospective yield as more capital goods compete to sell their services. What then is the relationship between the volume of investment and the rate of return in the longer run, that is in a situation in which the cost minimising combination of factors is chosen? At the partial level Keynes first considers, the answer seems clear: if all other prices in the economy are taken as given, then *ceteris paribus* it may be argued that there is an inverse relationship between the rate of return and the quantity of capital invested in the production of a given output. But Keynes's argument is on very shaky ground when he attempts to define the relationship for the economy as a whole by simple aggregation of these partial effects, for he can no longer use the *ceteris paribus* condition to keep at bay some fundamental problems.

These fundamental difficulties in Keynes's characterisation of the marginal efficiency of capital may be clarified by returning to Fisher's analysis of the incremental rate of return on investment which Keynes tell us is 'identical with my definition' (Keynes, 1936, p. 140).

Fisher's analysis is based on the substitution of capital for labour in a full-employment equilibrium, and throughout his discussion of the theory of saving, investment and interest, he imposes a major limitation on his argument – he assumes that all prices, wages and rents are fixed, and do not vary with variations in the rate of interest (Fisher, 1930, p. 131n). This 'fixed-price' assumption allows Fisher to express all magnitudes in terms of 'money', and to move between discussion of individual behaviour and that of the economy as a whole without considering the interrelationship between the rate of interest and prices.

An attempt to generalise Fisher's analysis to a many-commodity model, and hence to relate the determination of prices to the determination of the rate of interest, has been made by Solow (1963, 1967). I have analysed Solow's model and the debate it provoked elsewhere (Eatwell, 1976); for our purposes we need only summarise my main conclusions.

It is assumed by Solow that the economy is in a stationary state, producing a consumption good, corn, by means of many reproducible inputs and labour. To enable the definition of limits we may further assume that the technical possibilities of the economy are characterised by a wage-profit frontier which is an envelope to an infinity of wage-profit curves, such that techniques are arrayed continuously along the frontier. Furthermore, consumption and value of capital per head associated with the variation in technique may be described by differentiable functions.

Since the techniques used in the production of corn require inputs of commodities other than corn, the wage-profit line for each technique may assume any negatively sloped curvature. But consumption good output per capita, c, (i.e. net output per head) and the value of produced inputs per capita, k, are continuous differentiable functions of the rate of interest (rate of profit), r, even though the technique in use varies continuously with r:

$$c = z(r) \qquad k = \frac{\text{net output} - \text{wages}}{\text{rate of profit}} = [z(r) - g(r)]/r$$

where $g(r) = w$ is the equation of the wage-profit frontier.

The rate of return over cost of a transition between the technique in use at r and the 'adjacent' technique at $r + h$ is the ratio of the value of the difference in the perpetual consumption streams to the value of the difference in the capital stocks (i.e. the sacrifice required to effect the transition):

$$[z(r+h) - z(r)] \; / \; \left[\frac{z(r+h) - g(r+h)}{r+h} - \frac{z(r) - g(r)}{r} \right] \tag{6}$$

'In the limit, as the number of techniques grows denser', $h \to 0$, and expression (6) becomes,

$$z'(r) \; \frac{r^2}{r[z'(r) - g'(r)] - z(r) + g(r)} \neq r \, ; \tag{7}$$

the marginal rate of return over cost is not equal to the rate of profit. The equality would hold iff:

$$z(r) = g(r) - rg'(r) \tag{8}$$

This would be the case of an economy having the properties of Samuelson's (1962) surrogate production function, and would indicate that, to all intents and purposes, the economy under consideration was set in a one-commodity world. The inequality does not depend on the presence of reswitching or even perversity. So long as the economy contains more than one produced input the rate of profit is not equal to the rate of return over cost. Or, more generally, no demand schedule for investment as a function of the rate of interest may be constructed (Garegnani, pp. 65-7 above).

The lack of any logical foundation for the construction of an elastic demand schedule for investment as a function of the rate of interest is simultaneously a critique of the neoclassical theory of output and of Keynes's concept of the marginal efficiency of capital – which was itself derived from the neoclassical schedule. This follows from the fact that the neoclassical theory of output is synonymous with the neoclassical theory of value and so an effective critique of the latter necessarily constitutes an effective critique of the former. There is no logically consistent foundation to the idea that variation in relative prices, or in the rate of interest, or in money wages, will cause the system to tend to a full-employment level of output. Keynes's utilisation of the notion of a demand schedule for investment may perhaps be explained by the pioneering nature of the *General Theory*, in which the main propositions of a new theory of output are combined with vestiges of the old theory; by the need to present an apparently 'complete' theory; and by the pragmatic ambiguity with which many neoclassical propositions were presented in the then dominant Marshallian formulation. Garegnani has argued that

> ... the origin of the contrasted meanings attributed to Keynes's theory is to be sought in the doubtful compatibility, from the standpoint of an analysis of long-period tendencies, between the concept of the marginal efficiency of capital and the argument that the level of output plays the leading role in equilibrating planned saving and planned investment. Once the former idea is accepted, it is difficult not to confine the importance of the latter argument to the explanation of the trade cycle and other short-period phenomena. On the other hand, the different conclusions to which Keynes was pointing can be sustained in so far as investment is assumed to be insensitive to the rate of interest, even in the long period. But this assumption is in sharp conflict with the presuppositions of the traditional theory of distribution and cannot find a firm foundation until the critique of that theory has undermined those presuppositions (p. 61 above).

In other words, once the corrosive influence of the presence of a marginal efficiency of capital schedule is removed, not only is the neoclassical synthesis seen to be without logical foundation (as is any other version of pseudo-Keynesian theory, such as that of Leijonhufvud or Malinvaud, which assumes a monotonic inverse relationship between the rate of interest and the volume of investment), but also Keynes's positive contribution, the principle of effective demand, is thrown into more dramatic relief.

The issue is still somewhat clouded, however, by the development of a version of neoclassical theory which, its proponents claim, is immune from the criticism of the traditional neoclassical theory of the rate of profit (or interest). The Arrow-Debreu model of intertemporal equilibrium, in which the equilibrium of the economy is defined as a sequence of temporal market-clearing equilibria, is the culmination of a shift in the domain of economic theory dating from the inter-war period. This shift, which began in response to perceived difficulties in the neoclassical theory of capital (Milgate, 1979), was accelerated by the potential challenge of Keynesian theory to neoclassical orthodoxy, and found its most influential expression in the concept of temporary equilibrium in Hicks' *Value and Capital*, involved a change in the fundamental concept of equilibrium which characterises the object of economic analysis (Garegnani, Chapter 7 below). The new concept, of intertemporal equilibrium, does not display a general rate of profit on the supply price of capital goods. But if the intertemporal equilibrium is constrained in such a way that the price of all producible means of production must be equal to their cost of production (a much weaker condition, it should be noted, than the imposition of a stationary price vector) the standard neoclassical analysis is, in general, inconsistent unless the endowment of capital goods is expressed as a quantity of value – the old circularity returns. Since, as I argued in section I above, the notion of a tendency toward a general rate of profit is an essential part of the abstract characterisation of a capitalist economy, the new method of intertemporal equilibrium follows the early versions of Say's Law in assuming away the fundamental aspects of the economic system which it purports to explain; capitalism is assumed away to fit the requirements of the neoclassical theory of value and output.

Yet it is just such 'Walrasian' models which are the typical benchmark for the application of 'rationing' and similar imperfections (including the empirically empty concept of subjective conjecture), and hence for the argument that Keynesian analysis may be interpreted as an analysis of short-period disequilibrium. The apparent pragmatism implied by the definition of 'monopoly', 'lack of information', 'uncertainty', 'rigidities' or 'monetary distortions' as short-period phenomena is a triple deception. First, because these concepts are typically incorporated into models from which the very nature of capitalist production is absent. Secondly, because the short period is only a coherent notion when related to the position towards which the persistent forces of the economy will continuously gravitate. Thirdly, because it is by no means clear that any of these phenomena inhibit the long run forces of capitalist competition (Clifton, 1977).

If then we are to take both methodology and analysis seriously a primary task is to identify those persistent forces which determine the normal, or long-period position of prices and outputs in a capitalist economy. Once logically consistent and congruent theories of the operation of such forces have been established, then it will be possible to proceed to the analysis of the transitory and specific phenomena which may influence the day-to-day working of the system. We have seen in this section that neoclassical analysis has nothing to offer to this programme.

IX

In our search for a satisfactory synthesis of value and output theories we are thus confronted by a logically consistent theory of value and distribution which is 'open' with respect to the determination of output, and a logically consistent theory of output which has not been integrated satisfactorily with a theory of value and distribution. The task of this final section is to enquire into the possible congruence of the surplus approach to value and distribution and Keynes's principle of effective demand.

Before proceeding to more formal elements of this task we will, however, consider the relationship between Marx's 'possibility of crises' and the Keynesian theory of output. It was shown in section III above that Marx argues that the possibility of crises arises from the essential characteristics of a capitalist economy and in particular from the metamorphoses involved in the circuit of capital from money form, to commodity form, to money form, and so on; and the separation which the ability to hold value in money form permits between the decision to produce and the ability to sell.

But there is more to Marx's conception of the possibility of crises than the fact that a capitalist economy is of necessity a monetary economy. Production in a capitalist system is the production of commodities, i.e. of exchange values, and the object of investment is the expansion of the production of exchange values, *not* the production of use values. Thus, as Keynes put it, investment is undertaken for future profit – not for future consumption (Keynes, 1936, pp. 210-12; see also Keynes, 1971, ch. 2). But since Marx advanced no theory of the relationship between saving and investment, his case for the actuality of a general failure to realise the value of output was based on the time-lags induced by disproportionalities and the anarchy of capitalist production (Marx, 1968, p. 529).

In this context 'anarchy' does not mean incoherence, but that what is rational for the individual may be irrational for the system as a whole. In a capitalist economy the individual capitalist may decide to hold his wealth in terms of money rather than commit himself to future production. This may be a rational act in the light of a pessimistic view of future returns. But with Keynes's principle of effective demand it may be seen that the outcome will not be irrational merely in the sense of a 'breakdown', but will lead to a permanently lower level of output from which there is no inherent tendency for the system to move. Permanent 'crises' *do* exist, in the sense of permanently lower output, though they do not necessarily exist as a permanently lower rate of profit.

The Keynesian perception of the working of a capitalist system is not inconsistent with the more comprehensive Marxian characterisation. Indeed if Keynes's principle of effective demand is appended as a theory of the actuality of crises, Marx's conception of crises is expanded from a notion of transitory time-lags and breakdowns into a theory of output, an essential precondition of which is the existence of a monetary commodity economy.

The formal structure of a model combining a surplus theory of value and distribution with the Keynesian theory of output may best be approached through a consideration of Kalecki's version of the theory of output. Kalecki's version of the principle of effective demand (see Kalecki, 1971) is constructed from two relationships: a rather simplistic theory of distribution based on the idea that the mark-up contained in individual commodity prices is determined by the degree of monopoly, and a theory of aggregate profits, determined by the volume of autonomous investment and the propensity to save out of profits (the propensity to save out of wages being set equal to zero). If the mark-up is such that the share of profit is equal to π then from the multiplier condition that

$$s_p P = I \tag{9}$$

where s_p is the saving propensity out of profits, P total net profits and I net investment, we may derive the result that the level of net income, Y, is

$$Y = I \frac{1}{s_p} \frac{1}{\pi} \tag{10}$$

The problem with Kalecki's model is the inadequacy of his theory of distribution (which, as may be seen in Kalecki, 1971, he constantly revised). The mark-up is determined at the level of the individual firm. But the mark-up of one firm is the cost of another, and unless the ramifications of the interdependence of price formation are taken into account the ratio π is simply a definition with no theoretical determination. However, this limitation may be overcome, for the mark-up in any one sector is the outcome of the peculiar circumstances of that sector, *and* the general rate of profit – the latter being the typically preponderant *persistent* element in price formation. In his theory Kalecki does treat the theory of value and distribution and the theory of output *separately*; and it will come as no surprise that the separability condition we have already seen to be characteristic of the classical theory of value allows us to remedy the deficiencies of Kalecki's approach.

Taking the classical data and assuming, for the moment, constant returns to scale, we can solve for the rate of profit and prices from the equations

$$p' A (1+r) + p' b a_0' = p' \tag{11}$$

where A is the matrix of unit input coefficients, a_0 the vector of labour input coefficients, and b the vector of wage-goods per hour of work. Kalecki's equation (9) may now be re-written

$$rp' Ax = p' n_I \frac{1}{s_p} \tag{12}$$

where n_I is the vector of net investments. Thus, the value of net investment, $p'n_I$, determines, via the multiplier, the combinations of levels of gross outputs x appropriate to the rate of profit and prices determined in (11). The level of employment is $a_0'x$, and of net output $[I - A]\ x$. Complications and ramifications, including the abandonment of constant returns to scale, may now be added at will.

Formal manipulation apart, the crucial characteristic which permits the combination of the principle of effective demand with the classical theory of distribution in such a simple way, is that the latter is *not* based on the 'principle' of supply and demand, but on the proposition that the prices of commodities are determined by their conditions of reproduction and the distribution of the surplus as a uniform rate of profit on the value of capital invested. There is, therefore, no tendency for variation in distribution and prices to be an active factor pushing the system toward the full-employment level of output. This is not to say that there will be no relationship between the rate of profit and the level of investment, but this must be located in the more general context of the process of accumulation.

This brings us to the question of the determinants of investment, an issue which is apparently left open with the dissolution of Keynes's investment theory. An understanding of the determinants of investment can only be attained by locating the problem within the context of a general theory of capitalist accumulation adapted to the specific circumstances of any given time and place. The fundamental characteristic of capitalist accumulation is the competitive struggle for markets. The competitive process is shaped by the evolution and utilisation of technology, the cumulative decline of the 'weak' relative to the 'strong', the policies of nation states, the penetration of non-capitalist markets, the structure of industry and competition, relations between capital and labour, and pricing policy. All these factors, plus the institutional setting – financial, political and social – in which they operate, affect the growth of demand and the pattern, scale and rapidity of accumulation in a complex recursive process. The reduction of a theory of investment to two parameters, 'expectations' and the rate of interest, is as empirically vacuous as it is theoretically empty. It could only be taken seriously in a supply-and-demand model.

How then, do we interpret the role of uncertainty in the theory of effective demand, and more generally in the analysis of accumulation?

At the level of the individual capitalist the uncertainties of the competitive process will have a significant influence on investment plans. But, as Keynes pointed out, this does not mean that the long-period position of the economy

> depends on waves of irrational psychology. On the contrary, the state of long-term expectation is often steady ... (Keynes, 1936, p. 162).

Moreover, in a draft of the *General Theory*, Keynes had argued that

> Having ... made clear the part played by *expectation* in the economic nexus and the reaction of realised results on future expectation, it will be safe for us in what follows to discard reference to expectation. It is important to make the logical point clear and to define the terminology precisely ... But when once this has been done, considerations of practical convenience may legitimately take charge, in the light of the fact that in practice the process of revision of expectation is a gradual and continuous one, carried on mainly in the light of realised results; so that expected and realised results run into and overlap one another in their influence. (Keynes, 1973, p. 397; see also Kregel, 1976, pp. 211-14)

and in a lecture following the publication of the *General Theory* he commented:

> I now feel that if I were writing the book again I should begin by setting forth my theory on the assumption that short-period expectations were always fulfilled ... (Keynes, 1973, p. 181).

Thus Keynes is arguing that the effect of expectations and uncertainties is manifest in the form of the real and persistent forces in the system; but the fact of uncertainty is not the fundamental issue in the interpretation of the systematic behaviour of the economy. The issue is a correct understanding of the principle of effective demand – the operation of which is independent of the fact of uncertainty. The prevalence of the idea that uncertainty plays a central determining role in Keynes's contribution (rather than simply defining the environment in which the forces of the theory operate) has been attributed to the incorporation by Keynes of ideas on uncertainty into the corpus of the discussion of the *General Theory* (see also Keynes 1937a) in order to keep at bay the tendency to full employment implicit in the elastic marginal efficiency of capital schedule (Garegnani, Chapters 2 and 7; Milgate, Chapter 5). But once that schedule is abandoned, 'uncertainty' can be treated as, on the one hand, an element in the short-period fluctuations of output around its long-period position, and, on the other hand, as an element, together with 'convention', of the general environment in which the systematic processes of capitalist production and accumulation must operate.

In the construction of our theory of normal output we will come across a difficulty not encountered in the theory of normal price formation. In the latter theory we argued that prices were determined by the dominant technique; in the former case, however, some output is produced using 'fossils' or 'superior' techniques. The problem has two aspects. First, flexibility in the level of output derives both from the excess capacity carried by capitalist firms as a component part of their competitive strategy, and from the fact that if there is a rapid upswing in demand 'fossils' will be more fully utilised. None the less, the normal level of output in a stationary or slow-changing system would be related to the technical and distributional characteristics of the dominant technique. But, secondly, there is no reason to suppose that the pace of accumulation is slow, and hence, in general, equation (12) must be modified to take account of the actual *pattern* of accumulation. This will present greater difficulties when the pace and pattern of accumulation is changing than when the pace of change is fairly steady.

I do not mean to suggest by this remark that we should look to the growth models of recent years, with their emphasis on proportionately growing economies, for any significant insight into the actual process of accumulation. Rather we should ally Keynesian insights to the general theories of the nature of capitalist accumulation which are to be found in Smith and Marx. These theories include the recognition that the commodity composition of output (other than the broad divisions between investment goods and wage goods) is of little general relevance in the accumulation of capital. Although changes in commodity composition, both quantitative and qualitive, may be an important element in competition, the ultimate purpose is the production and accumulation of value in general.

These issues should alert us to the amount of work which needs to be done in order to fully utilise the tools provided by classical, Marxian and

Keynesian theory. The task involves both ridding the particular theories of inconsistences and obfuscations; and elucidating the implications they present for the interpretation of each other. At the core of the resultant analytical schema will stand the surplus theory of value and distribution, supplemented by the Keynesian insight into the theory of output.

7

On a change in the notion of equilibrium in recent work on value and distribution

Pierangelo Garegnani

1. Introduction

In a recent note Samuelson (1975) answers a charge from Robinson (1975b) that he had used relations valid across different 'long-period equilibria' (i.e. equilibria where the prices of products yield a uniform rate of profits on the supply prices of the capital goods)[1] in order to determine the effects of a process of capital accumulation. My concern here will be with the issue on which Robinson and Samuelson seem to agree: the illegitimacy of studying the *permanent* effects of changes in conditions of the economy by means of the comparison between the two 'long-period equilibria' corresponding to conditions before and after the change.

This agreement, which reflects a position increasingly held in theoretical work, constitutes a drastic departure from what had long been the accepted method in the theory of value and distribution. The study of the permanent effects of changes by means of comparisons between positions of the economic system characterised by a uniform rate of profits was in fact the method used by Ricardo and the English classical economists, when they explained profits in terms of the surplus product left after paying wages at the rate determined by independent economic or social circumstances (see Garegnani, above, pp. 68-9). But fundamentally the same method was preserved after Ricardo, across the deep change which the theory underwent in favour of a symmetric explanation of profits and wages in terms of the equilibrium between the forces of demand and supply for labour and capital.

It was only in the last few decades that this method, which was centred on 'long-period positions' of the system – as we may call them in order to cover both the long-period equilibria of the later theories and the analogous notion

* Reprinted from M. Brown, K. Sato and P. Zarembka (eds), *Essays in Modern Capital Theory*, North-Holland Publishing Company (1976).

[1] Samuelson and Robinson refer to the long-period equilibria of economies in 'steady-state growth'.

of the classical theories[2] – was increasingly challenged: be it in favour of short-period equilibria, which do not imply a uniform rate of profits on the supply price of the capital goods, or be it in favour of Robinson's 'analysis of processes'.

What I shall try to suggest is that this departure from tradition has not been due to weaknesses of the method as such, but rather to weaknesses of the dominant theory of distribution and, in particular, of the conception of capital it relies on. The attempt to overcome the deficiencies of the received notion of capital while retaining the basic supply-and-demand approach provides, I shall argue, the main explanation of the move towards short-period equilibria and their sequence in time as the new basis for the theory of value and distribution.

Our concern will here be with this move towards short-period equilibria, but in section 6, after considering the role which Keynes may have had in favouring the move, we shall also advance some remarks about the different ground for Professor Robinson's rejection of the traditional method.

2. The traditional method and the 'long-period positions' of the system

We have been speaking of 'long-period equilibria' or, to cover the similar classical notion, of 'long-period positions' of the system. But the expressions most frequently used today in describing situations with a uniform rate of profits on the supply price of the capital goods, are 'stationary' or 'steady states'. This change in terminology reflects the change in method we are discussing. The abandonment of the method of long-period positions seems indeed to have been generally justified by arguing that, in an economy where the conditions determining the long-period prices are changing through time, the decisions of individuals will be affected by future price changes (whether correctly foreseen, or simply expected); and this will prevent the long-period prices and position from being a guide to the actual prices (and position) of the economy.[3]

This, however, was not the view which the older theorists took of the applicability of their method. Even if we leave aside Ricardo, who did not intend his theory of profits for a 'stationary' or 'steady state' England, it was not for such an economy that Marshall wrote: 'an increase of material capital ... will much increase the national dividend ... and since ... it will have forced down the rate of interest, the joint product of a dose of capital and labour will now be divided more in favour of labour' (Marshall, 1920, VI.11.4,

[2] Since, as just mentioned, the classical economists did not resort to the 'opposite forces of supply and demand' in their explanation of distribution and relative prices, the word 'equilibrium' does not seem appropriate to describe the position of the economic system characterised by 'natural' prices, wages and profits.

[3] Cf., e.g., the passage in Hicks (1946, pp. 116-17), on which we shall comment below, pp. 133-4.

p. 553); and Walras stated: 'In a progressive economy the rate of net income will fall appreciably' (Walras, 1954, lecture 36, par. 334, p. 391). Nor did the older theorists ignore the fact that actual prices change day by day and are expected so to do, whether because of changes in long-period conditions or for other reasons.

As we all know, they understood the long-period position as the 'centre' towards which the competitive economy would gravitate in the given long-period conditions. The basis of the argument had been laid down by Adam Smith with his distinction between the 'market price' and 'natural price' of a commodity. The actual or market price could, at any given moment, be above or below the natural price, i.e. the price just sufficient to cover at their 'natural rates' the wages, profits and rents to be paid in order to produce the commodity. The market price would exceed the natural price when the quantity of the commodity 'brought to market' falls short of the 'effectual demand', i.e. the quantity demanded by those willing to pay the natural price. But just this excess of the market price would cause the quantity supplied to increase towards the effectual demand and thus undo itself. The converse would be true when the market price is below the natural price. As a result, Smith could conclude that: 'the natural price ... is ... the central price to which the prices of all commodities are continually gravitating' (Smith, 1954, bk. 1, ch. 7, pp. 48-51).

It was because of this 'gravitation' that the 'long-period values' of the variables (i.e. their values in the 'long-period positions' of the system) were thought to be those relevant for an analysis of lasting changes in the system. In the words of Ricardo (1951, ch. 4, pp. 91-2):

> Having fully acknowledged the temporary effects which, in particular employments of capital, may be produced on the prices of commodities, as well as on the wages of labour, and the profits of stock, by accidental causes, without influencing the general price of commodities, wages or profits, since these effects are equally operative in all stages of society, we will leave them entirely out of consideration, whilst we are treating of the laws which regulate natural prices, natural wages, and natural profits ...

where the argument for 'leaving entirely out of consideration' the deviations of market from natural values of the variables rests intimately on the 'temporary' nature of these deviations in contrast with Ricardo's concern with lasting changes.

And a similar argument about 'long-period normal' values was still used by Marshall (1920, V.3.7, p. 291) a century later:

> The actual value at any time, the market value as it is often called, is often more influenced by passing events, and by causes whose action is fitful and short lived, than by those which work persistently. But in long periods these fitful and irregular causes in large measure efface one another's influence so that in the long run persistent causes dominate value completely.

The persistent, or non-temporary nature of the causes of long-period values, which was thus stressed by both Ricardo and Marshall, explains why the relevance of these values was not thought to be confined to the analysis of economies which are stationary[4] or in steady growth. That persistence was thought to ensure that changes in the causes, if continuous, would be sufficiently slow as not to endanger the gravitation towards the (slowly moving) long-period values. That same persistence would ensure that, should the changes be rapid, they would be once-for-all changes, and that, after a period of transition, gravitation to the new long-period values would again assert itself.

The forces which Marshall and post-Ricardian theory introduced to determine the normal rates of wages and profits were fundamentally different from those envisaged by Ricardo for his natural rates. Consequently, the gravitation towards such rates (and the corresponding long-period prices) raised very different problems in the two theories. Ricardo and the other classical economists – who considered the real wage as determined *before* profits and relative prices, and not *simultaneously* with them by the 'forces of demand and supply' – were able to separate the determination of outputs from the determination of prices and profits (see Garegnani, above pp. 68-9). When thus separately determining the outputs, they could deal with the interactions between outputs and the effectual demands, both with respect to the system as a whole[5] and with respect to each industry. Accordingly, the adjustment of individual outputs involved in the gravitation towards natural prices could be conceived of as an *adaptation to quantities already fixed, i.e. determined in another part of the theory*. Hence, for example, the notion by Smith referred to above, and so striking to the modern reader, of 'effectual demand' as a single definite point and not as the definite schedule of later theory.

Marshall and the post-Ricardian theorists, on the other hand, who brought demand and supply to determine the division of the product between wages and profits, could only determine outputs simultaneously with relative prices and the rate of profits. Accordingly, the interactions between quantities supplied and demanded became an essential part of the gravitation to the normal rates of wages and profits and the corresponding normal prices. And the difficulties involved in the process of gravitation as conceived in these later theories started to become apparent with Keynes's *General Theory* (1936).

But whatever the differences between the two kinds of theory, and however basic the difficulties raised by gravitation for the later theories, what concerns us here is only to point out that the notion of 'long-period positions' as 'centres' of gravitation was fundamentally the same in the two cases and

[4] Cf. n. 11 below, about a contrary opinion of Hicks on Marshall.

[5] This separation between determination of relative prices and determination of outputs leaves the Ricardian theory of value 'open' with respect to the possibility of deficiencies of effective demand (see n. 33 below).

did not depend for its application on the hypothesis of a stationary (or steady-state) economy.

3. The criticism based on 'price expectations'

What then are the deficiencies of the method based on 'long-period positions' which caused its abandonment in favour of an analysis founded on short-period equilibria of demand and supply?

If we turn to Hicks's *Value and Capital* (1946), the first influential work in which the long-period method was thus abandoned in a general treatment of value and distribution, we find, we shall argue, two distinct lines of criticism against what is there comprehensively named 'static theory', but which the context specifies as being essentially the traditional long-period theory.[6]

'Static theory', Hicks argues in his first line of criticism, would be applicable to the 'real world' only 'if we could say that the system of prices existing *at any moment* depends upon the preferences and resources existing at that moment and upon nothing else'. This, Hicks continues, is not the case because 'the current supply of a commodity depends not so much upon what the current price is as upon what entrepreneurs have expected it to be in the past', and, correspondingly, 'the current position in the factor markets' depends on what the prices of the products are expected to be in the future. In order to have an applicable theory, we must then allow for the fact that 'supplies (and ultimately demands too) are governed by expected prices quite as much as by current prices', and abandon 'static theory' (Hicks, 1946, pp. 116-17, italics added).

Taken literally, this criticism would seem to accuse previous theory of having ignored the fact that since production takes time, the supply of commodities cannot adapt instantaneously to price. This non-instantaneous adaptation was however so little ignored by, for example, Adam Smith that, in discussing the 'market price', he treated the quantity of the commodity 'brought to market' at any given time as fixed independently of the price it would fetch. Incorrect price expectations entertained in the past might indeed be a way of describing some of the factors that make the market prices deviate from the natural prices. But the real point of the method criticised was that there were to be forces capable of eliminating the deviations. It was these forces which gave to the long-period prices their true status: that of

[6] 'Static theory' is there defined simply as that in which the quantities do not have to be 'dated' (Hicks, 1946, p. 115). This definition, however, covers both the long-period theory we have been discussing (which was also that of Hicks (1932)) and the short-period theory where, as in the general equilibrium system of the 'static' part of *Value and Capital*, profits appear as rentals of the capital goods, and will not generally bear a uniform rate to the supply price of such capital goods: Hicks's criticism of static theory on the ground that it ignores the effects of future price changes has evidently very different force in the two cases (cf. p. 138 below). The generality of the criticism of previous theory, and the passages where such theory is charged with 'often' introducing 'a factor of production capital and its price interest' (Hicks, 1946, p. 116n) make it clear, however, that the real target of criticism is long-period theory.

'centres' of gravitation, and not that of 'prices existing at any moment', to which Hicks refers at the beginning of his passage.

Hicks's criticism of previous theory would have been more pointed if he had disputed the gravitation of the market prices towards such centres.[7] This, however, might have raised doubts about the forces of demand and supply which traditional theory had introduced to explain such 'centres': i.e. might have raised doubts about the *theory* and not only about its static *method*. The argument concerning price expectations used here by Hicks has in fact to be read remembering that the *General Theory* had been published not many years before:[8] but Keynes had in fact disputed the gravitation to a demand-and-supply equilibrium in the factor markets and had thus raised, we shall suggest below, as many questions about the theory as he had about its static method. And, as we shall now attempt to show, it is to the theory rather than to its method that Hicks's own second line of criticism in fact points.

4. The criticism relating to the 'quantity of capital'

This second line of criticism appears when it is asserted that 'static theory' is 'quite incompetent to deal properly with capital', a problem, as Hicks continues, where 'the dating of economic quantities is of the first importance'.[9] And for the reader wondering how previous theory, incompetent to deal with capital, could still have dealt with the rates of wages and profits (interest), Hicks adds in a footnote:

> people ... would often introduce into their static theory a 'factor of production', capital and its price, interest, supposing that capital could be treated like the static factors .... That some error was involved in the procedure would not have been denied; but the absence of a general dynamic theory, in which all quantities were properly dated made it easy to underestimate how great the error was.

We are not told exactly what the error was. The fact that this passage is

[7] A few pages after the passage we have quoted Hicks does mention 'stationary-state theorists' who 'regarded reality as "tending" towards stationarity', and adds that 'the existence of such tendency is more than questionable' (Hicks, 1946, p. 119). But, as we shall see below, n. 11, the 'stationary state' there referred to is not 'the long-period equilibrium' of traditional theory and, therefore, the 'tendency' to the former is a different question from a tendency to the latter. In the later (1965) book, Hicks's doubts extend to equilibrium proper and the validity of static theory is there questioned on the two grounds that 'it is by no means inevitable that an equilibrium should exist' and that 'even if the equilibrium exists, it has still to be shown that there is a tendency to it' (Hicks, 1965, pp. 16-18). These drastic statements, however, are only followed by passing references to imperfect competition and the 'cobweb theorem'.

[8] Cf. n. 22 below.

[9] The full passage refers to 'static theory' as 'quite incompetent to deal properly with capital, or interest, or trade fluctuations, or even money, problems where the dating', etc. (Hicks, 1946, p. 116). In an earlier article referred to in n. 21 below, the abandonment of static theory in favour of dynamic theory was motivated only with the need to deal with capital (Hicks, 1935, pp. 268-70).

immediately followed by those concerning the dependence of current on future prices, and by a recognition of the legitimacy of static theory in the case of the stationary state, may lead the reader to think that the error is due to capital accumulation which, while causing changes in the long-period prices, at the same time causes, through investment, a dependence of current prices and outputs on price expectations. And to the older theorists' argument that the changes brought about by accumulation would generally be slow enough to be ignored,[10] the reader will answer by thinking of the difficulties deriving from expectations which Keynes had pointed out not many years before, and which Hicks himself discusses in later parts of *Value and Capital*.

But when, two pages later, Hicks comes back to capital he in fact points in a different direction. After arguing that 'static theory' would only come into its own in the case of a 'stationary state' in which 'it would not be necessary to distinguish between price expectations and current prices', he unexpectedly moves on to quite a different question:

> One thing, however, is evident when we look at this stationary economy. ... This is the dependence of the input-output relations (the production functions) on the quantity of intermediate products carried by the system. How will the quantity of intermediate products – the quantity of capital – be determined?

Hicks's answer is that in a stationary economy the 'quantity of capital' will be determined by the condition of a zero (net) propensity to save (Hicks, 1946, pp. 118-19).

This fortunate coincidence, for which the same stationary state that makes it unnecessary to distinguish between price expectations and current prices also takes care of the separate difficulty about the 'quantity of capital', does not, however, really answer the question which Hicks had asked. As we saw above, previous marginal theorists had not generally assumed the stationary state Hicks refers to.[11] The condition of zero net savings was accordingly not

[10] See p. 131 above.

[11] p. 130 above; Hicks writes (1946, p. 117) that the 'hallmark' of the Austrian economists (Böhm-Bawerk and Wicksell are mentioned) is 'concentration on the stationary state', the stationary state being then defined in the way we saw. This seems misleading: both Böhm-Bawerk and Wicksell assumed the amount of capital in the economy to be a given (value) magnitude and not an unknown determined by the condition of zero net saving (cf. Böhm-Bawerk, 1891, pp. 391, 420; Wicksell, 1954, p. 126; 1934, p. 207). As Robbins (1930), pointed out, two distinct conceptions of the stationary state were present in the literature: in one, the constancy over time of the quantities of factors is *assumed*, while in the other this constancy is one of the results of the equilibrating process. Böhm-Bawerk and Wicksell generally used the expression 'stationary state' for the former conception (e.g. Wicksell, 1954, p. 153; 1934, p. 152) whereas Hicks's description of it unambiguously refers to the latter. On the same subject, Hicks (1965, p. 47) writes about Marshall 'seeing' that 'when it came to capital theory ... all that could be done [by the static method] was the analysis of a stationary state'. This also seems misleading. Hicks quotes the passage where Marshall (1920, V.5.8, p. 315n) says that a 'theoretically perfect' long period would involve 'the supposition of a stationary state of industry'. But in the text to which the passage is appended as part of a footnote, Marshall had

available to them: how, then, did they 'determine' the quantity of capital?

The answer is: in the same way which Hicks himself had adopted in his *Theory of Wages* (1932) not many years before *Value and Capital*, namely by taking it as a magnitude given in some value unit and slowly affected over time by net saving.[12] This procedure, the deficiencies of which Hicks may have become more aware of after Shove's review of his earlier book,[13] was indeed the generally accepted one, having been used with various degrees of explicitness and circumspection by such diverse writers as J.B. Clark, Böhm-Bawerk, Wicksell and Marshall in their determination of long-period equilibria.[14]

The only outstanding exception had been Walras who, in his *Elements* had conceived the capital endowment of the economy as a set of given quantities: as many as there are kinds of 'capital goods proper'.[15] But since Walras, no less than the authors just mentioned, attempted to determine a long-period equilibrium, he was simply incorrect in believing this to be compatible with treating each kind of 'capital good proper' as a separate factor in given supply. With a capital endowment conceived in these terms, the forces of demand and supply can only reach a *short-period equilibrium*, i.e. an equilibrium where the prices of the services of the capital goods will not

---

written that 'the remainder of this volume is chiefly concerned ... with the normal relations of wages, profits, prices etc. for rather long periods', as distinct from the 'very gradual or secular movements of normal price caused by the gradual growth of knowledge, of population *and of capital*': the normal long-period relations are thus held to be compatible with 'the very gradual growth of ... capital'. The passage quoted by Hicks has to be read – it seems – while remembering other passages, where Marshall writes that only in a stationary state would the 'normal price' coincide with an average of the actual prices, and where this 'coincidence' is clearly held to be non-essential for the relevance of 'normal price' (Marshall, 1920, e.g. V.5.5, p. 209; V.3.7, p. 289).

[12] For equilibria where the amount of capital is treated as a given (or independently variable) magnitude see Hicks (1932, pp. 114-15, 127, 187-8, 205-7). For value measurement of such magnitude cf., e.g., the passage in Hicks (1932, p. 20n) where the anticipated scrapping of a machine A to replace it by a machine B having the same original cost, is said to require 'the use of new capital ... to an amount equal to [the] deficiency of the replacement fund'.

[13] Shove pointed out that, contrary to what Hicks had argued (1932, p. 188), a rise of wages not accompanied by a fall in the interest rate cannot render relatively more profitable the more capitalistic methods of production, since the long-period prices of capital goods would then rise in the same proportion as wages have risen (Shove, 1933, pp. 264-5). Shove's argument relies on a peculiarity of interest as the price of a factor measured in value terms: if, for example, the two factors had been labour and land a rise of (money) wages with constant (money) rent, would in fact have rendered relatively more profitable the more land-intensive methods of production, in analogy with Hicks's original contention.

[14] With respect to Böhm-Bawerk and Wicksell, see the references given in n. 11 above. As regards Marshall, see his work (1920, VI.2.4), and the conception of 'the general fund of capital' used there.

[15] Cf. the equations in Walras (1954, para. 238, pp. 271-2) expressing, as Walras writes, the condition that 'in equilibrium [the] selling prices [of capital goods proper] and their costs of production are equal'. (For Walras' error see Garegnani, 1960, part 2, ch. 3. Dr. Nuti mentions the latter book, without giving page reference, as containing 'the accusation that an implicit assumption of malleable capital exists in the multi-commodity multi period model' (Nuti, 1974, p. 353). No such multiperiod model is however considered there.)

generally be compatible with a uniform rate of profit on the (actual or potential) supply prices of the respective capital goods.[16]

It thus emerges that marginal theorists not only generally conceived the capital endowment of the economy as a value magnitude, but also had no alternative to doing so if they were to be consistent with the conditions of long-period equilibrium:[17] that very 'full equilibrium' in which, to paraphrase Hicks (1932), the marginal product of labour is the one resulting when the 'quantity', but not the 'form', of the 'co-operating capital' remains unchanged.[18]

There is no need to say here what difficulties beset this conception of capital. As the emergence of the phenomena of 're-switching' and 'reverse capital deepening' have begun to show, Hicks's question about the 'determination' of the 'quantity of capital' in 'static' (long-period) marginal theory was pointing only, it seems, to the most visible among these difficulties, i.e. that of determining the relative prices of commodities, capital goods included, while taking as a given or independently variable magnitude, the value of the capital endowment of the economy.[19]

What concerns us here is to point out that this difficulty over the determination of the quantity of capital is independent of the divergence between current and expected prices. The same need to measure the quantity of capital would arise if we wanted to determine long-period

[16] This short-period equilibrium was contemplated by Hicks in his *The Theory of Wages* when he contrasted the 'full equilibrium' marginal product of labour with a 'short-period' one. He had then dismissed the latter by saying: 'It is very doubtful if this [short period marginal product of labour] can be given any precise meaning which is capable of useful application' (Hicks, 1932, pp. 20-1).

[17] Cf. n. 22 below, for the case of steady growth.

[18] Hicks (1932, p. 20). In *Capital and Growth* (1965, pp. 40-8) Hicks conjectures that the conception of a 'homogeneous capital substance' was introduced in economic theory in order to avoid the problem of the allocation of saving among diverse capital goods and the consequent need to introduce future prices. This conception of 'capital substance' is then traced back to Ricardo's 'corn-capital' in the *Essay on Profits*, and to the labour-embodied measurements of the *Principles*. Hicks accordingly writes of Ricardo's 'herculean effort' to retain by these means the 'self-containedness of the single period' (1965, p. 47). Here we cannot deal fully with the many perplexing aspects of this interpretation of Ricardo. It may be sufficient to remark that while Hicks's account of the *Essay on Profits* provides evidence of the role played there by the assumption of homogeneity *between capital and output* in one sector of the economy (and not of homogeneity among capital goods in the whole economy, as required in order to support Hicks's interpretation), no evidence is given by Hicks of Ricardo's concern for the allocation of savings, or for 'the self-containedness of the single period'. It would be a surprising coincidence if Ricardo's efforts, quite clearly directed to measuring capital and output independently of the rate of profits (in order to achieve a non-circular determination of the rate of profits as the ratio between surplus product and capital) – should be also directed to the preservation of the 'static method'. The passage from the *Principles* quoted on p. 131 above suggests that Ricardo's 'static' concern for long-period positions of the economy had a different, and better-known, basis than the homogeneity of capital indicated by Hicks.

[19] Thus, the relation between interest and capital stock was there described as follows: 'A fall in the rate of interest would encourage the adoption of longer processes, requiring the use (at any moment) of larger quantities of intermediate products.' We now know that the 'length of processes' or 'quantities of intermediate products' need not increase as the rate of interest falls.

equilibrium while assuming that tastes, techniques and resources are not going to change in the future:[20] a situation in which, as Hicks says, 'actual prices do not need to be distinguished from expected prices'.

It is therefore apparent that this difficulty, unlike that concerning the influence of future prices,[21] regards the *theory*, i.e. the way in which the centres of gravitation of the system are determined, and not the static *method* of analysis based on such 'centres'. Thus, no similar difficulty arises for the classical economists who used the same method but did not determine the centres of gravitation as equilibria between supply and demand, and had accordingly no need to conceive of capital as a single 'quantity' measurable independently of distribution.

5. The 'short-period' general equilibrium

If Hicks's line of criticism concerning the quantity of capital regards theory rather than method, it is none the less true that an abandonment of the method based on long-period positions of the system was entailed in the attempt to overcome the deficiencies of the traditional notion of capital while preserving the basic demand and supply approach.

The way had already been shown by Walras to those willing to take it.[22] All that was needed was to renounce Walras's own inconsistent attempt at determining a long-period equilibrium and accept instead as a basis the short-period general equilibrium of demand and supply compatible with given quantities of the several capital goods.[23]

It is evident, however, that this short-period general equilibrium cannot be determined independently of the changes it will undergo over time (as was done by Walras who was thinking of a long-period general equilibrium). The

[20] i.e. taking the economy to be stationary according to the first of the two conceptions of a stationary state referred to in n. 11 above.

[21] In an article which Hicks published after *The Theory of Wages*, but before Keynes's *General Theory* and in which the dynamic theory of *Value and Capital* was first introduced, Hicks's criticism of previous theories was directed only at their notions of capital, held to be inapplicable outside the 'stationary state' (Hicks, 1935, pp. 268-9). Though price expectations played a key role in that article, no criticism was there raised on the ground of a failure of previous theories to distinguish between price expectations and current prices (cf. also n. 8 above).

[22] We may here leave aside the 'dynamic' analysis based on the hypothesis of steady proportionate growth which would not be defended as a basis for the general theory of value and distribution. We may, however, note that some of the attraction of this kind of demand and supply analysis lies in the fact that the 'quantity' of capital per labourer having a physical composition compatible with a uniform rate of profits, can here be left to be determined by the propensities to save: thus avoiding (as in Hicks's 'stationary state') the dilemma between short-period equilibrium and reliance on a capital endowment given in value terms.

[23] As Hicks prefers to describe it, 'heterogeneity of capital stock can be dealt with by using our formal theory of many factors ... and ... this now makes it unnecessary to insist that the economy is to be taken to be in a state of full equilibrium, in the sense that there is perfect equalization of yields on every sort of capital goods' (Hicks, 1963, p. 346). Accuracy would however require replacing the phrase 'unnecessary to insist that the economy is to be taken to be', by the phrase 'impossible to suppose that the economy is'.

competitive tendency to a uniform rate of profits will be powerful and quick in bringing about changes in the composition of the capital stock and, hence, given the almost complete absence of substitutability in such a system, appreciable changes in the prices of productive services and commodities. The 'persistence' of the governing forces which justified the determination of a long-period equilibrium independently of the changes the latter may be (slowly) undergoing, is clearly absent here.[24]

This analysis had therefore to shed the static method and consider the effect of future conditions on the markets for current commodities and productive services.[25] This it did in one of two ways: by introducing price expectations in the short-period equilibria, as was done by Hicks for his 'temporary equilibria' in *Value and Capital*, or, alternatively, by expanding the analysis into a theory of general intertemporal equilibrium based on the hypothesis of complete futures markets.[26]

We must here leave aside the question of whether these two kinds of analysis have in fact overcome the deficiencies of demand-and-supply theory with respect to capital. We may instead mention two shortcomings which are the direct consequence of the withdrawal from the long-period basis of previous marginal theories. The first regards the meaning we should attach to the short-period equilibrium which forms the basic element of the analysis in both its versions. Even if this equilibrium could be formally shown to be stable,[27] that same impermanence of causes which, as just seen, imposed consideration of its changes over time, would seem to prevent it from being conceived as a centre of gravitation of the economic system: the forces governing it would lack the persistence necessary to distinguish them from those other accidental forces which, at any given time, are likely to keep the economy out of this short-period equilibrium.[28] Thus, before the recurrence

[24] It may also be noted that the above-mentioned competitive tendency considerably narrows the possibility of studying changes by means of comparisons of equilibria. In fact, over any appreciable period of time, the proportions between the several capital stocks will be governed by the tendency to a uniform rate of profits, and consequently the stocks cannot be treated as independent variables as could be done for the quantity of capital in the long-period equilibria. The changes occurring in the economic system must then be studied through sequences and not through comparisons of equilibria, and a second reason emerges why the analysis has to become 'dynamic'.

[25] This need to consider future conditions does not seem to arise, or to arise to the same extent, in the case of Marshall's short-period partial equilibrium. Behind the short-period supply price of the individual industry are the forces which govern the factor prices, or the range in which these vary with the output of the industry. These forces, which are included in the *ceteris paribus* assumption, are, it seems ultimately long-period forces, so that Marshall's short-period equilibrium appears to be a complement to the long-period equilibrium of the system and not an alternative to it.

[26] Cf. e.g. Debreu (1959).

[27] i.e. stable under the assumption of constancy in the forces determining the equilibrium position.

[28] Marshall's short-period analysis, it seems, does not incur this difficulty because of its ultimate reliance on long-period forces (cf. n. 25 above). This seems to have partly remained the case in Keynes's extension of Marshall's short-period analysis to the system as a whole: the

of demand and supply flows has been sufficient to correct, or compensate, previous accidental deviations, the equilibrium position itself will have changed considerably, and the equilibrium can then provide little if any guidance to the behaviour of the economy.[29,30]

The other shortcoming which should be mentioned appears when, in order to avoid the hypothesis of complete futures markets (and its evident lack of basis in reality), price expectations are introduced in their stead and 'temporary' equilibria are preferred to the 'intertemporal' equilibrium. In traditional theory, not only the long-period position, but also the gravitation towards it were generally explained without introducing price expectations. It may be objected that a particular treatment of price expectations was in fact always implied: that, for example, Smith's argument about the tendency of the market price to fall when it exceeds the natural price implies that producers should expect the high market price to last long enough for them to reap an extra profit by acting now in order to produce more of the commodity later. But the important point of Smith's procedure is precisely that this effect upon the minds of people of a market price exceeding the natural price appeared to be so inescapable as to permit proceeding directly to its objective consequence, increased production. This would seem to be the procedure to be aimed at with respect to 'expectations' in the theory of value: to relate them uniquely to objective phenomena, so as to bypass them and relate the facts explaining the expectations directly to the actions of the individuals. The procedure which Hicks (1946) adopted, by which unobservable quantities, the expected prices, are introduced as independent variables, runs the risk of depriving the theory of any definite results, as Hicks himself had earlier come close to admitting.[31] The values which the unknowns assume in a situation which is fully defined in its objective data can be made to vary almost indefinitely by varying the hypotheses about expected prices.

---

wage unit provides the base on which is erected a system of relative prices (implicit in the aggregate supply function) which can only reflect a system of long-period prices with degrees of distortion depending on the relative elasticities of the short-period supply curves of the individual industries, and on the level of the aggregate output.

[29] This difficulty seems to be close to the one which Hicks admits to have been inherent in the temporary equilibrium method he used in *Value and Capital* (1946): namely, the doubtful legitimacy of assuming 'that prices remain unchanged throughout the single period; and that these prices are equilibrium prices' (Hicks, 1965, p. 73).

[30] Moreover, where a sequence of such short-period equilibria is taken into consideration (as is the case, e.g. in the general 'intertemporal' equilibrium) the danger arises of a cumulation of errors due to the uncompensated deviations from equilibrium in preceding periods.

[31] In his review of Keynes's *General Theory* (1936), Hicks had written that 'the method [of expectations] is thus an admirable one for analysing the impact effects of disturbing causes, but it is less reliable for studying the further effects', since, 'it is probable that the change in actual production during the first period will influence the expectations ruling at the end of that period, and there is no means of telling what the influences will be. The more we go into the future the greater this source of error, so that there is the danger, when it is applied to long periods, of the whole method petering out' (Hicks, 1936, p. 241).

These considerations regarding the new notion of equilibrium and the treatment of price expectations may help to explain why the long-period positions remained for so long the undisputed basis of the theory of value and distribution.

6. Keynes's 'short period'

We noticed in section 3 the influence of Keynes in the criticism which Hicks raised against previous theory on the ground that it ignored price expectation. A further indirect role of Keynes in favouring the abandonment of the long-period method may be traced to the fact that the *General Theory* caused attention to be moved on to problems concerning the equilibrium of the system as a whole, away from the partial equilibrium analysis that had long kept the notion of capital and its deficiencies in a dimly perceived background.

In considering now whether the modern withdrawal of value theory from its previous long-period basis might not be traced to some more direct, or more deep-rooted, influence of Keynes's book (rather than, as we have argued so far, chiefly to the problem of capital) it seems necessary to start from one fact. Keynes's primary concern was not a re-examination of the orthodox theory of value from the angle of the short period: it was to establish a single basic proposition, namely that it is the level of incomes which ensures equality between saving and investment.

This basic proposition was, in itself, independent of the 'method of expectations' and was not necessarily confined to the short period. It was, however, in direct conflict with the dominant theory of distribution on its two main fronts – the doctrine that competitive wages gravitate towards a level where the demand for labour is equal to its supply, and the symmetrical notion that the interest rate equilibrates the demand and supply of savings, i.e. the demand and supply of capital in its free form.[32] Owing to his notion of the 'propensity to consume', Keynes succeeded in narrowing the ground of this conflict down to the rate of interest: and it was there, in the critique of

[32] The doctrine symmetrical with that of wages equalising demand and supply of labour is more strictly what we find, when, for example, Marshall writes: 'Interest being the price paid for use of capital in any market tends to an equilibrium level such that the *aggregate demand for capital* in that market at that rate of interest is equal to the *aggregate stock forthcoming* at that rate' (Marshall, 1920, VI.2.4, p. 443, italics added). Keynes (1936, pp. 175, 186-7) quotes this passage and interprets it as *in fact* saying that 'the rate of interest comes to rest under the play of market forces at the point where the *amount of investment* at that rate of interest is equal to the *amount of saving* at that rate'. In effect, what form can an 'aggregate demand for capital' and a 'stock [of it] forthcoming' ever take for the interplay of these two factors to determine the rate of interest – if not that of a sequence over time of demands and supplies of saving in which capital assumes its free form? It was in fact through this sequence over time that the rate of interest was understood to gravitate about the equilibrium level Marshall writes of while, at the same time, the wage gravitated towards its long-period (full-employment) level. Cf., e.g., Marshall (1920, VI.6.6, p. 492).

the orthodox theory of interest, that 'expectations' played an essential role in the *General Theory*, through liquidity preference and the instability of the 'marginal efficiency of capital'.

This distinction between the constructive core in the ideas of the *General Theory*, free from the method of expectations, and the mainly negative, critical part centred on the rate of interest, is thrown into relief in these passages written by Keynes (1937, pp. 250-2, italics added) one year after his book was published:

> The initial novelty [of the ideas in the *General Theory*] lies in my maintaining that it is not the rate of interest, but the level of incomes which ensures equality between saving and investment. The arguments which lead up to this initial conclusion are *independent* of my subsequent theory of the rate of interest, and in fact I reached it before I had reached the latter theory. But the result of it was to leave the rate of interest in the air.

And, after mentioning an initial approach in terms of a rate of interest 'determined in some sense by productivity', he continues:

> It was only when this line of approach [failed] that I hit on what I now think to be the true explanation. ... It would be true to say that [the liquidity-preference theory] does not carry us very far. But it gives us firm and intelligible ground from which to proceed.

Or again, two pages later:

> To speak of the 'Liquidity-preference Theory' of the Rate of Interest is, indeed, to dignify it too much. ... I am simply stating what it is, the *significant Theories on the subject being subsequent*.

These passages are interesting in more than one respect. They stress the independence of the 'initial novelty' in the *General Theory* from the theory of interest advanced there. They also imply that the main role of the latter was to provide an alternative to the orthodox doctrine of interest as the equilibrator of saving and investment. And, above all, they indicate that Keynes tended to regard his 'liquidity preference', with its reliance on expectations, as something 'which does not carry us very far', a provisional basis 'from which to proceed'.

It might then appear that expectations, and even the confinement to the short period of an analysis which Keynes thought had implications going far beyond it, had the main role of providing him with a provisional way out of the conflict between his 'initial novelty' and the dominant theory of distribution. The task of fully facing the conflict – i.e. of pursuing the critique of that theory further, and developing 'the significant theories on the subject' – was to be 'subsequent'.

Looking at Keynes's work in this perspective, it may also be appreciated how the deficiencies of the idea of a substitutability between capital and labour which have since emerged with reswitching and reverse capital deepening, may be relevant to accomplishing the negative part of that task. On the substitutability between labour and capital must in fact rest ultimately – with the demand and supply theory of distribution of which it is a part[33] – any long-run role of the interest rate in adjusting investment to the capacity to save.

If this is so, the *General Theory* does not seem to offer real ground for the contemporary attempt to rework traditional theory in terms of short-period equilibria: though the use of expectations and the short period made in that book may have favoured a climate of professional opinion more ready to accept, or overlook, the peculiar difficulties entailed by a shift of the theory of value to a short-period basis.

This brings us to a few brief comments on Robinson's position on method which we mentioned in section 1. The upshot of her analysis of accumulation lies in the rejection of any general tendency of the economic system to the full employment of labour, in the long run no less than in the Keynesian short period.[34] Her analysis thus clearly implies the impossibility of studying long-run changes by comparing *equilibria of demand and supply*, characterised, as such, by the full employment of labour. It does not however necessarily imply the impossibility of studying changes by comparing *long-period positions* of the economic system. 'Long-period' positions, as we can see in Ricardo,[35] do

[33] Cf. n. 31 above. We may here consider Keynes's (1933) interpretation of the controversy between Ricardo and Malthus about the possibility of a 'general glut of commodities', and the consequent assimilation of Ricardo to later theorists with respect to the theory of the rate of interest (Keynes, 1936, p. 32 and *passim*). Keynes's interpretation – while correct in pointing out the similarity between the *question* raised by Malthus against Ricardo and the one Keynes was raising against his contemporaries – becomes misleading when it also proceeds to suggest a similarity in the *analysis* of such a question. As has been frequently pointed out in the meantime (Meek, 1950-51, p. 156n.; Schumpeter, 1954, p. 641; Robbins, 1958, p. 248; Corry, 1959), both Malthus and Ricardo always took it *as a fact* that any saving would be invested, i.e. used to employ 'productive labourers' (see Malthus, 1836, pp. 322-32): no question could therefore arise between Malthus and Ricardo about interest being the factor which adjusts investment to saving. Ricardo's opinion on the impossibility of 'general gluts' seems thus to have been due to a failure to distinguish between decisions to save and decisions to invest, and not to a theory of the rate of interest similar to that of Keynes's contemporaries.

It may indeed be suggested that Ricardo's theory of distribution and value was 'open' with respect to the possibility of deficiencies of aggregate effective demand. Because of the absence of the idea of a 'substitutability' between labour and capital, his theory did not provide premises for a tendency of investment to adapt to the full-capacity saving. At the same time the theory did not rely on such a tendency for its validity: Ricardo's determination of the wage was compatible with unemployment of labour and this had already been allowed for in his long-period positions of the economy (cf. Garegnani, above, p. 68). Finally, the separation between determination of value and determination of outputs, characteristic of this theory, provided a setting in which the effect of aggregate effective demand on output and employment could be most conveniently studied. (For a fuller discussion of both Ricardo's position with respect to 'general gluts', and Keynes's interpretation of it, cf. Garegnani above, pp. 24-8).

[34] Cf. her distinction between 'unemployment' and 'non-employment' of labour (Robinson, 1962, p. 54).

[35] Cf. n. 33 above.

not as such, imply full employment of labour. And Robinson herself seems in fact often to rely on the method of long-period positions in her analysis of changes,[36] as is shown by the presence there of the method's central feature: the general rate of profits.

What restricts Robinson's use of this method and at the same time prevents it from emerging clearly has to be traced back to the arguments leading to her denial of a tendency to the full employment of labour. These arguments seem to be ultimately reducible to those same factors of 'uncertainty' and 'expectations' which Keynes had used for his critique of the orthodox theory of interest.[37] Given the specificity of physical capital to certain industries and methods of production (i.e. its 'non-malleability'), uncertainty and incorrect expectations would prevent investment from gravitating around the level, and the physical composition, compatible with equilibrium and its preservation over time. Accordingly, the relevance of the notion of equilibrium to the study of the actual behaviour of the economy and, in particular, to the study of capital accumulation is drastically denied. But it is a peculiarity of this line of argument that while the gravitation to equilibrium is denied, the traditional notion of demand and supply forces is not openly disputed. Consequently, equilibrium as a potential centre of gravitation is, so to speak, still there to be reached: in Robinson's view it *would* be reached if uncertainty and incorrect expectations were absent, or made innocuous by a sufficient 'malleability' of capital.[38]

The persistence, in this particular sense, of the traditional notion of a demand-and-supply equilibrium[39] provides, we submit, the main

[36] See, for example, her comparison between the value in terms of consumption goods of a given piece of capital equipment as it is before, and after, a rise in the real wage due to accumulation (1956, p. 144).

[37] Cf., e.g., the passage 'what mechanism ... keeps accumulation going at the right rate? The argument of the *General Theory*, which shows that there is no such mechanism in a private-enterprise economy cannot be true at each moment of time and yet untrue in the long run' (Robinson, 1962, p. 14; cf. also 1956, p. 180). As for the key role attributed to expectations and lack of foresight, cf. Robinson, 1962, p. 133.

[38] Cf., e.g., Robinson (1975a, p. vii), where it is stated that if capital is assumed to be malleable 'putty', then 'there is no role for expectations, because equilibrium is instantly restored after any change. .... Say's law is restored and household saving governs industrial investment. Full employment of the available labour force is always provided. ...' Cf. also the following passage, in Robinson (1974, p. 4): 'In the context of accumulation "putty" is a way of getting rid of differences between the future and the past.'

[39] Until recently Robinson (1962, pp. 31, 132-4) did not dispute the main basis of the traditional theory of distribution: the notion of a technical substitutability between capital and labour. She has, however, since abandoned her former view that 'at any moment there is a range of possible techniques, co-existing in time in the form of blueprints, among which choices are made ...' (Robinson, 1975a, pp. ix-x). The notion of a potential equilibrium which lack of foresight (or the 'non-malleability' of capital) prevents the economy from achieving seems, however, to persist (e.g. 1975b, p. 36; 1974, p. 3), although, once technical substitution is denied, it is difficult to see which are the forces acting on the demand side of the 'equilibrium' in the market for factors (the indirect substitution between factors deriving from substitution between consumer goods plays no prominent role in Robinson's analysis). When, in recent works, equilibrium is exemplified by constructs such as 'putty-capital', alternative techniques are in fact admitted (Robinson, 1974, p. 9).

explanation of Robinson's position regarding the impossibility of studying changes by means of comparisons. The positions to be compared (which can only be conceived of as 'centres' of gravitation of the economy) are implicitly identified with the traditional equilibria still seen as *the* (potential) centres of gravitation, and thus rejected. This leads to ignoring at this methodological level, the possibility of 'long-period positions', which as exemplified in the classical economists, may be determined by forces altogether different from the demand and supply of marginal theory.

PART TWO

History

8

Marx, Keynes and the possibility of crisis

Peter Kenway

Introduction

This paper is the product of two apparently unconnected lines of enquiry. The first is in the nature of a puzzle. In explaining his theory of effective demand, Keynes laid great emphasis on the need for a theory of the demand for output *as a whole*. In this theory, simple manipulations of aggregate variables yield results which appear quite extraordinary compared with those of orthodox economics. Why does a treatment based on aggregate variables produce such different conclusions from the orthodox one, which looks at the component parts of that aggregate? The second is one of exposition. Ricardo was a strong supporter of the argument which sought to show that a capitalist economy would not suffer a general glut of commodities. In *Theories of Surplus Value* Marx challenges Ricardo's argument by showing that it overlooked the very features of a capitalist economy which introduce the possibility of some form of breakdown in the first place. From this is distilled Marx's theory of the 'possibility of crisis' which highlights the elements within a capitalist economy from which a breakdown *could* develop. The paper explains what this theory is about, draws attention to its limitations and traces Marx's argument and the development of 'possibility' theory which underlies it.

The interest of possibility theory is that it provides an answer to the Keynesian puzzle. It shows why the level of aggregate demand is important, though it is itself quite separate from Keynes's theory of effective demand. The sixth section of the paper explains the link. Keynes of course did not need possibility theory to justify a theory of aggregate demand and in the seventh section we seek out his justification. The final section delves a little

* Reprinted from *Cambridge Journal of Economics* 1980, **4**, 23-36. This is a revised version of an essay which won the Adam Smith Prize, 1978, awarded in the Faculty of Economics and Politics, Cambridge. I am grateful to Murray Milgate, Roy Green and the editors of the *Cambridge Journal of Economics* for aid and advice.

further into the writings of Marx and Keynes in an attempt to highlight the problem posed by aggregate demand. It is concluded that Marx and Keynes occupy substantially the same ground on the question of the nature of the problem, though their treatment of it and of the way the system responds is entirely different.

A theory of effective demand: Keynes's claim

There is no doubt about what Keynes saw as the outstanding feature of the *General Theory* which distinguished it from orthodox, neoclassical (he calls it classical) economics.

> Most treatises on the theory of value and production are primarily concerned with the distribution of a *given* volume of employed resources between different uses and with the conditions which, assuming the employment of this quantity of resources, determine their relative rewards and the relative value of their products. The question, also, of the volume of *available* resources, in the sense of the size of the employable population, the extent of natural wealth and the accumulated capital equipment, has often been treated descriptively. But the pure theory of what determined the *actual employment* of the available resources has seldom been examined in any great detail (Keynes, 1973, vol. 7, p. 4).

Keynes's real break with orthodoxy lies not so much in asking this question (which has certainly been asked by general equilibrium theorists), but in the answer he offers. In order to supply an answer, Keynes insists that we need a theory of demand for output as a whole, a theory that according to Keynes, has been neglected since the time of Malthus.

> Will a fluctuation in investment ... have any effect on the demand for output as a whole, and consequently on the scale of output and employment? What answer can traditional theory make to this question? I believe that it makes no answer at all, never having given the matter a single thought: the theory of effective demand, that is the demand for output as a whole, having been entirely neglected for more than a hundred years (Keynes, 1973, vol. 14, p. 119).

Keynes is calling for a theory of the *demand for output as a whole*, the theory of effective demand.

Two important points follow from this. First, in any economy where money acts as means of exchange, demand is a monetary quantity. Of course, in any economy the aggregate demand may be calculated, ex-post, so to speak, after all the exchanges have taken place. Consider, for example, Joan Robinson's example of a prisoner-of-war camp (Robinson, 1971, p. 4). The prisoners are kept alive by monthly deliveries of Red Cross parcels and they exchange the contents of the parcels amongst themselves until an equilibrium is reached (cigarettes are the means of exchange). By keeping an account of all exchanges we could establish the level of aggregate demand in cigarettes. But it would be a variable of little interest and virtually no significance. In complete contradistinction, by insisting on a theory of effective demand Keynes is ascribing considerable operational significance to the magnitude of this monetary variable. Second, and stranger still in the light of the orthodox position, is the theory of effective demand itself (Keynes, 1973b, p. 120). The level of income is determined by the marginal propensity to save and the amount of investment. Expressed symbolically

$$Y = I(1/s). \quad (1)$$

This is not merely an identity; Keynes argues that causality runs firmly from right to left. The consequence of ascribing *operational significance* to aggregate demand and particularly to investment is that the level of output (and income and employment – *real* variables) is dependent on the magnitude of a *monetary* variable. Keynes could hardly be further away from the real-exchange economics of the neoclassical orthodoxy.

How can this be? After all, the base from which the aggregate variables are obtained is precisely the same as that of the orthodoxy. Simply by aggregating one could not obtain a different answer. Moreover, one could always view equation (1) as an identity. Keynes, however, instills it with a very definite one-way causality. Pasinetti (1974, pp. 43-4) has argued that this characteristic of Keynes's analysis is its source of strength. But even so, it is hard to see how Keynes could have obtained results which stand in such total contrast to those obtained from orthodox economics simply through the strength attributed to 'feedback' forces. The difference must lie deeper than that.

The point at which Keynes parts company from the orthodoxy in such a dramatic way is his insistence that demand for output as a whole is of *operational significance* and this is a *monetary* variable. The source of dispute between Keynes and the orthodoxy must stem from this, the role which Keynes attributes to aggregate demand and which the orthodoxy does not. But this role requires justification and my 'opening question' is: why does the aggregate quantity of demand, a monetary variable, matter?

The meaning of 'possibility of crisis'

It may seem odd to seek an answer to this question in the works of Marx. Keynes himself would almost certainly have thought so: Marx warrants only three passing references in the *General Theory*. More importantly, it may be argued that Keynes was not concerned with *crisis* theory at all. It is thus especially necessary to clarify the meaning of 'possibility of crisis' and to highlight its place in the development of a framework within which to analyse the behaviour of a capitalist economy. Clarification is particularly needed to dispel any illusions created by the word *crisis*, which might suggest a far narrower range of impact for possibility theory than is really the case.

Marx's discussion of the possibility of crisis is contained in chapter 17 of the second volume of *Theories of Surplus Value*. This chapter forms part of Marx's critique of Ricardo's *Principles* and is concentrated on Ricardo's denial of the possibility of a general breakdown of the economy, the form of the breakdown in his argument being general overproduction.

The method Marx adopts in mounting this attack is to focus upon the way in which Ricardo understands and represents certain important features of capitalism, in particular the organisation of, and motivation for production. He argues that Ricardo has failed to represent these features at all adequately and this is of great consequence, for it is these very features which introduce the *possibility* that the system could break down. Therefore, Ricardo's model cannot be used to investigate whether the system will suffer a general breakdown because it fails to take account of the very features that make this breakdown possible. Marx's argument does not involve any consideration whatsoever of the *movement* of the system or the interaction between its constituent parts. He is very definitely not confronting Ricardo's arguments with conclusions derived from his crisis theory 'proper' which is a theory of the way in which the capitalist economy actually behaves. It is not a question of challenging conclusions with conclusions. This argument is much closer to basics: Ricardo has a theory, but Marx argues that it is not a theory *of capitalism*.

In his theory of the possibility of crisis, Marx attempts to identify those elements of the system which introduce the possibility that it *could* break down. This theory must precede the development of any model which attempts to investigate how a capitalist economy actually behaves (which, following Marx, we shall call 'actuality' theory). The reason for this is that possibility theory highlights those features of the economy which actuality theory must incorporate and explain. Possibility theory precedes, and is independent of any particular actuality theory.[1]

There is a danger, however, of crediting possibility theory with too much. In the first place, simply by demonstrating that a capitalist economy possesses features which mean that it could break down in no way establishes that it actually will. Moreover, since this theory does not establish that the system *will* suffer breakdowns, it says nothing concerning the nature of any breakdown. It establishes neither that the form of the breakdown will be generalised overproduction, nor, particularly, that the form will be violent, that is, that the breakdown will be a *crisis*. Marx, in a criticism of John Stuart Mill, argues:

[1] Hilferding in his discussion of crises in *Das Finanzkapital* (Hilferding, 1909) draws clearly this distinction between possibility theory ('the general condition for the crisis') and actuality theory ('the causes of crisis') and his development of possibility theory draws on the same parts of *Theories of Surplus Value* as does this discussion. Hilferding's treatment of the subject makes an interesting comparison with this one and on the fundamental issue of the relationship between possibility theory and actuality theory I think there is no important disagreement. On the other hand, there are differences in the substance of possibility theory itself and whilst it is outside the scope of this discussion to elaborate very much on these, I shall refer to one of them.

> These factors which explain the possibility of crises, by no means explain their actual occurence. They do not explain *why* the phases of the process come into such a conflict that their inner unity can only assert itself through a crisis, a violent process (Marx, 1969, p. 502).

Thus possibility theory may in fact be quite consistent with an actuality theory which shows that the form of the breakdown will be, for example, a gradual slide into depression. It is precisely because the form is not established in possibility theory that I prefer to use the term *breakdown* instead of *crisis*.

Marx charges that Ricardo's analysis of the system ignores, or at least overlooks, the very features which introduce the possibility of just such a breakdown in the first place. And we find Keynes making just this charge against Marshall and the neoclassicals:[2]

> ... the conditions required for the 'neutrality' of money, in the sense in which this is assumed in – again to take this book as the leading example – Marshall's 'Principles of Economics', are, I suspect, precisely the same as those which will insure that *crises do not occur*. If this is true, the real-exchange economics on which most of us have been brought up and with the conclusions of which our minds are deeply impregnated, though a valuable abstraction in itself, is a singularly blunt weapon for dealing with the problems of booms and depressions. For it has assumed away the very matter under investigation (Keynes, 1973, vol. 13, p. 410).

If possibility theory can sustain Marx's attack on Ricardo then perhaps it could help to substantiate Keynes's attack on the neoclassicals. If it can do that, then perhaps also it will help to show why the aggregate demand matters in the way Keynes claims it does.

Possibility theory: the commodity

At the basic level, Ricardo's argument rests upon the simple proposition, shared by Say and James Mill, that:

> Productions are always bought by productions, or by services; money is only the medium by which the exchange is effected (Ricardo, 1951, vol. 1, pp. 291-2).

Marx replies:

> Here ... the exchange of commodities is transformed into mere barter of products, of simple use values. This is a return not only to the time before capitalist production, but even to the time before there was simple commodity production: and the most complicated phenomenon of capitalist production – the world market crisis – is flatly denied by denying the first condition of

[2] Although the charge is the same, what each believes their opponents to have omitted is apparently quite different. The question of whether Keynes believed it to be simply a matter of incorporating uncertainty will be discussed below, pp. 160-2.

> capitalist production, namely that the *product* must be a *commodity* and therefore express itself as *money* and undergo the process of *metamorphosis* (Marx, 1969, p. 501).

Ricardo has made two crucial and connected errors. First, he fails to distinguish between, on the one hand, *commodities*, and on the other, *products*, and also to see that capitalist production is production of commodities. He consequently makes the second error which is to overlook the fact that the commodity must undergo the process of *metamorphosis*.

In order to be a product or a commodity, something which has been produced must have *use value*. But a commodity, unlike a product, *must* also have *exchange value*. A commodity is thus necessarily a product but it is also more than that; essentially it is a product produced for exchange. As we have already seen, for Ricardo to confuse products with commodities is to suppose that a capitalist economy is no different, not only from an economy dominated by simple commodity production, but also, even from a barter economy. Thus the distinction can be illustrated by comparing barter with simple commodity production:

> In direct barter, the bulk of production is intended by the producer to satisfy his own needs, or, where the division of labour is more developed, to satisfy the needs of his fellow producers, needs that are known to him. What is exchanged as commodity is the surplus and it is unimportant whether that surplus is exchanged or not. In *commodity production* the conversion of the product into money, the sale is the *conditio sine qua non*. Direct production for personal needs does not take place. Crisis results from the impossibility to sell (Marx, 1969, p. 508).

The life of a commodity has three distinct stages. In the first place it exists in the commodity form (which means no more than its physical form). The commodity is then brought to market and if possible, sold; once sold, it exists in the monetary form. The third stage is reached when the owner of the commodity makes a purchase, thus transforming the commodity on into the physical or commodity form again. This process is called the metamorphosis of the commodity by Marx and is represented

$$C - M - C$$

The first phase, $C - M$, is called the *sale*, and the second, $M - C$, is called the *purchase* (which accords entirely with ordinary usage). Where production is commodity production, for exchange, everything produced must go through this process else the very purpose of production is thwarted. It is this condition that separates an economy based on commodity production from one where production is for the direct satisfaction of producers' needs.

The first reason why the economy might fail to function smoothly, and therefore the first problem for theory to solve, is the 'anarchy of production', under which decisions on what to produce are taken by individual producers without any direct co-ordination. The condition that every commodity has to undergo the metamorphosis process poses the second problem:

> The possibility of a crisis, in so far as it shows itself in the simple form of metamorphosis, thus only arises from the fact that the differences in form – the phases – which it passes through in the course of its progress ... are distinct parts and forms of the process, independent of each other. ... The possibility of crisis therefore lies solely in the separation of sale from purchase (Marx, 1969, p. 508).

Of course, in any one transaction, one commodity passes through its sale phase whilst another passes through its purchase phase. But every commodity has to pass through both phases, and it is the fact that it may succeed in passing through only one, or even neither, that is the problem to be solved: that one commodity being sold is another being purchased contributes nothing to the resolution of this difficulty.

> The difficulty of the seller – on the assumption that his commodity has use value – only stems from the ease with which the buyer can defer the retransformation of money into commodity. The difficulty of converting the commodity into money, of selling it, only arises from the fact that the commodity must be turned into money but the money need not be immediately turned into commodity, and therefore sale and purchase can be separated (Marx, 1969, p. 509).

Thus the particular difficulty might lie in the temporary withholding of commodities in their monetary form. This extension is speculative and Marx is very clear on what possibility theory is able to achieve, and what it is not:

> The general abstract possibility of crisis denotes no more than the *most abstract* form of crisis, without content, without a compelling motive. Sale and purchase may fall apart. They thus represent potential crisis and their coincidence always remains a critical factor for the commodity. The transition from one to the other may, however, proceed smoothly. The factors which turn this possibility of crisis into an actual crisis are not contained in this form itself; it only implies that the framework for a crisis exists (Marx, 1969, p. 509).

Thus far the argument has contributed only a little to the understanding of why the capitalist economy may be subject to periodic breakdown. Once the terminology is understood, then the underlying concepts of commodity and metamorphosis are unremarkable. Neither indeed, has Marx yet defeated Ricardo's argument. For although Ricardo undoubtedly confuses barter and simple commodity production, he would find little to disagree with in Marx's exposition of commodity production. Moreover, as we shall see, much of his efforts are devoted to answering the very problem which Marx shows exists under commodity production, namely, will commodities be withheld for any time in their monetary form?

There is an explanation for this slow progress. So far Marx has developed an argument which shows why an economy where production is commodity production could break down, in contrast to a barter economy which could not. This is as far as we can get simply by concentrating on the commodity and the implications of production being commodity production. Production under capitalism is commodity production and therefore a *mature* possibility theory appropriate for a capitalist economy must be developed from an *immature* theory appropriate to simple commodity production. It is this immature version of the theory which we have at the moment. However, though capitalist production is commodity production, it is more than that: new elements are involved which strengthen and transform possibility theory. Ricardo's argument has remained unscathed so far, precisely because it answers the immature theory. But as that theory is further developed by Marx, Ricardo's arguments are seen to be inadequate to deal with problems of full capitalist production.

Possibility theory: introducing capitalist production

We turn now to Ricardo's main argument:

> No man produces, but with a view to consume or sell, and he never sells but with an intention to purchase some other commodity, which may be immediately useful to him, or which may contribute to future production. By producing, then, he necessarily becomes either the consumer of his own goods, or the purchaser and consumer of the goods of some other person. It is not to be supposed that he should, for any length of time, be ill-informed of the commodities which he can most advantageously produce, to attain the object which he has in view, namely, the possession of other goods; and therefore, it is not probable that he will continuously produce a commodity for which there is no demand (Ricardo, 1951, vol. 1, p. 290).

Against this Marx makes three attacks. First, the claim that 'no man produces but with a view to *consume* or sell' overlooks the social division of labour inherent within capitalism (and indeed essential to it).

> Previously it was forgotten that the product is a commodity. Now, even the social division of labour is forgotten. In a situation where men produce for themselves, there are indeed no crises, but neither is there capitalist production (Marx, 1969, p. 502).

Having dismissed the first alternative, Marx deals swiftly with the second:

> A man who has produced does not have the choice of selling or not selling. He must *sell*. In the crisis there arises the very situation in which he cannot sell or can only sell below the cost price or must even sell at a positive loss. What difference does it make to him or to us that he has produced in order to sell? The very question we want to solve is what has thwarted that good intention of his? (Marx, 1969, p. 503).

The third attack is on the supposed identity of consumers and producers which underlies Ricardo's argument.

> There is nothing more absurd as a means of denying crises, than the assertion that the consumers (buyers) and producers (sellers) are identical in capitalist production. They are entirely distinct categories. In so far as the reproduction process takes place, this identity can be asserted for only one out of three thousand producers, namely the capitalist. On the other hand, it is equally wrong to say that all consumers are producers. The landlord does not produce, and yet he consumes. The same applies to all monied interests (Marx, 1969, p. 519).

The charge is that Ricardo seriously misunderstands the organisation of production under capitalism. For Ricardo it is not really different from simple commodity production. His most serious mistake is his failure to recognise that all the key production decisions are taken by a very small proportion of all those people who are actually involved in the production process. The difference between capitalism and simple commodity production, in so far as the organisation of production is concerned, is that in the former, power to make decisions is concentrated in the hands of a few, whereas in the latter, it is much more evenly diffused throughout all the individuals involved in production. At the level of organisation, this emphasis on the degree of concentration of power and the extent to which capitalism and simple commodity production differ, may seem something of a quibble. But Marx's attack on Ricardo's understanding of the organisation of production develops into an attack on his understanding of the motivation for production.

Marx has a very clear picture of production and the role it plays for the capitalist. His motivation for entering production is the one that matters since he is the decision-maker.

> The circuit of capital comprises three stages:
> *First stage:* The capitalist appears on the commodity and labour markets as a buyer; his money is transformed into commodities, it goes through the act of circulation, $M-C$.
> *Second stage:* Productive consumption by the capitalist of the commodities purchased. His function as capitalist producer of commodities; his capital passes through the production process. The result: commodities of greater value than their elements of production.
> *Third stage:* The capitalist returns to the market as a seller; his commodities are transformed into money, they pass through the act of circulation, $C-M$.
> Thus the formula for the circuit of money capital is
> $$M-C \ldots P \ldots C'-M'.$$
> The dots indicate that the circulation process is interrupted, while C' and M' denote an increase in C and M as a result of surplus value (Marx, 1978, p. 109).

This description illustrates Marx's argument that the producer does not have the choice of selling or not selling; he must sell. The production process will only be completed once the commodity passes through the sale ($C' - M'$)

phase of the process. This much is obvious. But this description also provides support for the argument which is at the very heart of possibility theory. In reply to Ricardo who writes:

> ... he never sells but with an intention to purchase some other commodity, which may be immediately useful to him, or which may contribute to future consumption (Ricardo, 1951, vol. 1, p. 290).

Marx argues:

> What a cosy description of bourgeois conditions! Ricardo even forgets that a person may *sell* in order to *pay* and that these forced sales play a very significant role in the crises. The capitalist's immediate object in selling is to turn his commodity, or rather his commodity capital, back into *money capital*, and thereby to *realise* his profit. ... Everyone *sells* first of all in order to *sell*, that is to say in order to transform commodities into money.
>
> During the crisis, a man may be pleased if he has *sold* his commodities without immediately thinking of a purchase. ... The immediate purpose of capitalist production is not 'possession of other goods' but the appropriation of value, of money, of abstract wealth (Marx, 1969, p. 503).

We can illustrate the contrast between Marx and Ricardo using Marx's symbols. Marx, as we saw above, sees the cycle of production as $M - C \dots P \dots C'$ $- M'$. Ricardo still clings to a pre-capitalist framework and sees the cycles as $P \dots C - M - C$. This contrast helps to explain the meaning of the argument used by Marx on Ricardo's position:

> It must never be forgotten that in capitalist production what matters is not the immediate use-value but the exchange value, and in particular, the expansion of surplus value. This is the driving motive of capitalist production and it is a pretty conception that – in order to reason away the contradictions of capitalist production – abstracts from its very basis and depicts it as a production aiming at the direct satisfaction of the consumption of the producers (Marx, 1969, p. 495).

Consideration of the capitalist's purpose for entering into production shows that this purpose is accomplished as soon as the sale phase of the cycle is completed. Ricardo's arguments were directed toward proving that there was no reason for a break between the sale and purchase phases. By demonstrating that the contrary is true under capitalism Marx succeeds in refuting Ricardo's claims.

Possibility theory: the general achievement

The specific use to which Marx put possibility theory in *Theories of Surplus Value* was to achieve this refutation of Ricardo. However, the mature possibility theory is of wider and more substantial importance. The possibility of breakdown which previously lay only in the anarchy of production and the potential separation of purchase from sale, acquires an entirely new dimension by the introduction of capitalist production.[3]

In Ricardo's perception money acts as the means of exchange only, a convenience but no more than that. Money is of only transient importance; it plays no decisive role and its introduction makes no significant different.

For Marx, however, money is both the beginning and end of the production cycle. In capitalist production, money is indispensable to the cycle. The cycle is not completed until the sale phase is accomplished and neither can the cycle begin afresh until the previous cycle is complete and capital back in its monetary form. Thus the third element of possibility theory is that the production cycle begins and ends with capital in the monetary form. The cycle begins with a purchase and ends with a sale. Any theory which purports to investigate the workings of the capitalist economy has to take that fact into account.

An important question follows. Each capitalist will be interested in whether there will be sufficient demand on the market for him to be able to sell his commodities at a price yielding the 'normal' rate of profit. But will all capitalists be able to sell their entire output, and not merely sell, but sell at prices giving them the customary rate of profit? For this to be achieved, aggregate demand is required to reach some particular level. Will this requirement be met?

If not, then any number of things could happen – an overproduction of commodities; depression; crisis; a sudden fall in the rate of profit – but whatever, this would be the stuff of 'actuality' theory, which investigates the actual behaviour of the capitalist economy. What is of note here is that this requirement exists in the first place, because it is *this* requirement which answers our question. The amount of aggregate demand, a monetary variable, matters for the reason that the smooth and continued operation of the production process requires that this aggregate be at a certain level. Thus we need an explanation of it; we need a theory of what Keynes called effective demand.[4]

[3] In addition to the anarchy of production and the potential separation of the sale phase from the purchase phase of the metamorphosis cycle, Hilferding too introduces an extra dimension to possibility theory. In his interpretation: 'The narrow basis offered by the consumption relation of capitalist production is for that reason the general condition for the crisis because the impossibility to extend it is the general premise for the stagnation of the market. If consumption could be expanded at will, overproduction would not be possible. But under capitalist conditions expansion of consumption means a reduction in the rate of profit. For expansion of consumption of the broad masses is tied to a rise in wages' (Hilferding, 1909, ch. 16). Hilferding is thus arguing that to avoid overproduction, there has to be a shift in distribution from profits to wages. But this shift will only succeed in avoiding overproduction if it increases aggregate demand which implies that Hilferding is making implicit assumptions about the savings behaviour of the two classes. We can see here that what matters is the level of aggregate demand: what is essential is that this reach some particular level. Presenting it as Hilferding does in terms of consumption (and in particular, workers' consumption) obscures this fundamental requirement under distribution and savings considerations.

[4] In his survey of underconsumption theories, Bleaney doubts whether Marx's 'possibility' theory has anything new to contribute to an understanding of the capitalist economy. 'In es-

A theory of effective demand: Keynes's justification

Using some of Marx's insights into capitalist production, we have been able to substantiate the claim that a theory of effective demand is needed to understand the behaviour of the capitalist economy. How does Keynes's justification for a theory compare with this line of argument?

One of the first indications of the way Keynes's ideas were moving after the completion of the *Treatise on Money* is given in an article written in 1933:

> In my opinion the main reason why the problem of crises is unsolved, or at any rate why this theory is so unsatisfactory, is to be found in the lack of what might be termed a *monetary theory of production* (Keynes, 1973, vol. 13, p. 408).

As we have seen, the step in the development of 'possibility' theory which enabled Marx to dispose of Ricardo's argument, was the introduction into that theory of the capitalist form of production. To call Marx's theory of capitalist production a monetary theory of production is to diminish its full extent. But it is at least part of the truth. Money plays the crucial role as the form capital must take at the outset and conclusion of the production process.

Thus Marx and Keynes share one very important view: an adequate analysis of the capitalist economy must be based on a monetary theory of production. Keynes's justification of this view rests upon the belief he is dealing not with a 'real exchange economy' but with a 'monetary economy'.[5] The

---

sence, behind all the flowery language, Marx's general possibility of crises amounts to no more than had been implied by Sismondi in his example of the Leipzig book trade. It relies on the effect that a commodity produced may for some reason or other not be able to find a buyer, and that a producer who has already sold may for some reason or other not want to buy again immediately. In other words it is based on the idea that commodity production is at the same time interdependence and anarchy – interdependence because each producer has to rely on the demand provided by someone else, and anarchy because each producer is left to decide for himself what is best to produce' (Bleaney, 1976, p. 109). This is really a description of the immature version of possibility theory. Bleaney is wrong to argue that Marx makes no fundamental advance on the problems posed by Sismondi. However, to the extent that Bleaney is saying that the *immature* possibility theory is no advance on the example given by Sismondi, he is entirely correct. In this example, merchants produce books and bring them to Leipzig to trade amongst each other. What happens, asks Sismondi, if one merchant offers a book for sale which no other merchant wants? (For a detailed discussion see Bleaney, 1976, p. 75.) This is a description of an economy where the principal problem is one of *exchange* and where production is very much a side issue. An analysis of what might actually happen in this economy – an 'actuality' theory for it – would have to be based on a model designed to treat the exchange of a given quantity and distribution of endowments as the central issue. If immature possibility theory were an adequate theory for capitalism then a general exchange model would be an adequate model on which to develop the corresponding actuality theory. Mature possibility theory advanced beyond the book trade problem. Marx shows that there is an entirely new problem to be reckoned with once production becomes capitalist production. No longer is it only a question of how expenditure is distributed. Instead, it is whether total expenditure is sufficient for all capitalists to sell their output at the customary rate of profit. The level of aggregate demand is important in its own right.

[5] Throughout this section the term 'monetary economy' will be used in the sense defined by Keynes.

former is one which

> uses money but uses it merely as a neutral link between transactions in real things and real assets and does not allow it to enter into motives or decisions

whereas in the latter

> money plays a part of its own and affects motives and decisions and is, in short, one of the operative factors in the situation (Keynes, 1973, vol. 13, pp. 408-9).

Keynes supposedly argues that money plays this operative role because the future is uncertain. But by the time Keynes came to give his 1937 lectures, he had realised that a fundamental change could be made in the way in which uncertainty was to be represented in his theory. Originally, he had thought that the difference between

> the expected and actual income resulting to an entrepreneur from a particular decision

was important, this difference being

> due to a mistake in the short period expectation. ... But eventually I felt it to be of secondary importance, emphasis on it obscuring the real argument. For the theory of effective demand is substantially the same if we assume that short period expectations are always fulfilled. ... I now feel that if I were writing the book again I should begin by setting forth my theory on the assumption that short period expectations were always fulfilled; and then have a subsequent chapter showing what difference it makes when short period expectations are disappointed (Keynes, 1973, vol. 14, pp. 180-1).

In this model, not only are short-period expectations always fulfilled but also long-period expectations are held constant. In adopting this model, Keynes is saying that it is due neither to disappointed short-period expectations nor to changing long-period expectations that money plays an operative role in a 'monetary economy'.

It may be concluded that by this stage Keynes's position was effectively that the operative role played by money and thus the need for a monetary theory of production did not depend upon the existence of an uncertain future.[6] He held, quite correctly, to his original fundamental insight into the special role of money, but his own arguments had developed to a point where he really no

[6] Once Keynes reaches this position his argument becomes much clearer. He needs a possibility theory to explain why, in a monetary economy, money plays an operative role and why, therefore, the level of aggregate demand is important. The insights derived from this theory are then incorporated into an analysis of the way the economy actually behaves to give an explanation of why the level of output is what it is. It is in this actuality theory that uncertainty plays a role. He shows under the assumption of given, unchanging long-period expectations and fulfilled short-period expectations, that the level of output can in principle be anything between zero and full. What is wrong with the general exchange model is not that uncertainty is assumed away, but that the possibility theory underlying the general exchange model is wrong.

longer had any explanation of why it played this operative role, having rejected the original explanation of an uncertain future. There is thus plenty of room for possibility theory to provide that explanation.

Possibility theory: the reproduction schemes

Having understood that capitalism faces the problem of aggregate demand, the question which follows naturally is: will the level of aggregate demand generated by any level of output be sufficient to purchase the whole of that output? This issue is confronted by Marx in the second volume of *Capital* and in particular, in chapter 20. Marx summarises it thus:

> The immediate form in which the problem presents itself is this. How is the capital consumed in production replaced in its value out of the annual product, and how is the movement of this replacement intertwined with the consumption of surplus value by the capitalists and of wages by the workers? (Marx, 1978, p. 469).

The framework used throughout chapter 20 is one of a two-sector economy, operating under conditions of simple reproduction. Department 1 produces means of production; department 2, means of consumption. Marx uses the following schema, which depicts the total annual commodity product.

Department 1

$4000c + 1000v + 1000s = 6000$ means of production

Department 2

$2000c + 500v + 500s = 3000$ means of consumption

The main purpose of chapter 20 is to consider the way commodity flows interact with the monetary flows required to effect the exchanges, thus fulfilling the purpose of production, the realisation of surplus value. Marx comments:

> Two things are always required for commodity circulation: commodities have to be cast into circulation, and so has money (Marx, 1978, p. 469).

Concrete problems are revealed once Marx moves on to consider the situation where part of the total constant capital is not replaced within the one year. A portion of the value of this fixed capital will be transferred to the commodities produced this year, and provided the necessary sales are achieved, the value component will be recovered (that is returned to the money form) by department 2.

> The commodity value of 2000 in which IIc exists contains an element for depreciation which cannot be immediately replaced in kind, but has to be transformed into money, its total sum accumulating bit by bit until the time falls due for the renewal of this fixed capital in its natural form (Marx, 1978, p. 528).

Marx takes this depreciation component of the 2000 to be 200. Thus, if department 2 were able to sell all its output and set aside 200 for depreciation, its income/expenditure account for the year would look like this:

Table 1

Gross income		Gross expenditure	
Sales	3000	Renewal of circulating capital	1800
		Labour	500
		Capitalist consumption	500
	3000		2800
Excess of income over expenditure:	200		

Such a situation is not sustainable, for in setting aside 200 for depreciation department 2's demand for means of production is reduced by 200 from the 2000 worth of demand required by department 1. Department 1 is thus unable to sell all its output and, at the very least, the condition of simple reproduction will have been violated. The point here is that the problem is essentially a monetary one, caused by the excess of income over expenditure – a leakage from demand – in department 2.

Marx is concerned to find what must happen if simple reproduction is to be possible:

> Department 2 consists of capitalists whose fixed capital is at different points in its reproduction. For some, it has reached the point at which it has to be completely replaced in kind. For others, it is more or less distant from this stage: what is common to all members of this latter division is that their fixed capital is not really reproduced, that is, not renewed in kind or replaced by a new item of the same variety, but that its value is successively collected up as money (Marx, 1978, p. 354).

Thus there will be some capitalists in department 2 who have been building up a depreciation fund over a number of years and whose fixed capital is now fully expired. In this year, they will need to purchase fixed capital in excess of the capital consumed in this year alone. If we suppose for illustration, that the fixed capital in question has a life of two years, then dividing department 2 into two and adjusting the accounts of the first half, we reach the following position:

Table 2

Gross income			Gross expenditure		
Sales	1500	1500	Renewal of circulating capital	900	900
			Labour	250	250
			Capitalist consumption	250	250
			Fixed capital	200	0
	1500	1500		1600	1400
Excess of income over expenditure for department as a whole: nil					

Demand for means of production is thus the required 2000. The threat posed by the leakage has been overcome by an injection to demand from other capitalists within the department.

Many comments can be made upon this solution, particularly in the light of Keynes's work and Kahn's multiplier. Assumptions about proportionality required for simple reproduction to continue are noteworthy. For our purpose what is important is the general conclusion reached by Marx: that continued reproduction depends upon monetary flows – leakages, an excess of income over expenditure, and injections, an excess of expenditure over income.

Marx is concerned with finding the conditions which must hold if a particular level and structure of output – in this case simple reproduction – is to be feasible. Keynes, however, is concerned with the slightly different question of what determines the actual level of production. He divides effective demand into two items, investment demand, which he argues is largely independent of the level of current income, and consumption demand, which is taken to be largely dependent on the income level:

> Incomes are partly created by entrepreneurs producing for investment and partly by their producing for consumption. The amount that is consumed depends on the amount of income thus made up. Hence the amount of consumption goods which it will pay entrepreneurs to produce will depend on the amount of investment goods which they are producing. If for example, the public are in the habit of spending nine-tenths of their income on consumption goods, it follows that if entrepreneurs were to produce consumption goods at a cost more than nine-tenths the cost of investment goods they are producing, some part of their output could not be sold at a price which would cover its cost of production. ... Thus entrepreneurs will make a loss until they contract their output of consumption goods down to an amount at which it no longer exceeds nine times their current output of investment goods (Keynes, 1973, vol. 14, p. 120).

The effect of Keynes's assumption that investment is largely independent of the level of the current income, is to make investment the representative of expenditure from sources other than current income generated by the current production. As far as this part of the theory of effective demand is concerned, investment expenditure stands simply for injections to demand. Savings, on the other hand, stand simply for leakages from demand. Looked at this way, we see that the passage from Keynes quoted above, reaches the same conclusion as that reached by Marx: that leakages from demand pose a threat to the successful sale of output at a price yielding the 'customary' rate of profit, while injections present the means to overcoming this threat.

Keynes goes further. In his theory leakages are functions of the level of income, whilst injections are autonomous. He is thus able to show that a level of output exists at which all output can be sold at a price yielding the 'customary' rate of profit. With the additional assumption that production is determined by demand, he produces an explanation of why the level of output is what it is. In so doing, he answers his own question which, as we have seen, is the problem to be solved by the *General Theory*. Then, finally, there is the other part of the theory of effective demand which examines the role of money in an uncertain world and in particular the inducement to invest. Such an investigation of the determinants of injections and leakages is very proper but that is a part of actuality theory. In no way does it affect or explain the role of injections and leakages and their relationship to the level of sustainable output, an understanding of which comes from possibility theory.

However, Mandel in his introduction to the second volume of *Capital* has argued that:

> The technique of aggregation introduced by Keynes has, if anything, made matters worse by dealing with undifferentiated money flows. For it evacuates the problem (not to mention the solution) of whether a given national income has a specific structure of demand (for consumer goods, for producer goods producing producer goods, for producer goods producing consumer goods, for luxury goods, for weapons and other commodities bought only by the state etc.) which correspond exactly to the specific structure of the total commodity value created by the process of production (Mandel, 1978, p. 23).

Whether such a criticism is valid or important is an issue for actuality theory and not for here. But it certainly overlooks the fundamental advance made by Keynes over his contemporaries and predecessors, namely that monetary variables have a decisive influence upon the levels of aggregate real variables such as total output and total employment. It is surprising that Mandel should play down the achievement of Keynes in identifying the role of monetary injections and leakages, for in the identification of their importance, Keynes occupies the very same ground as does Marx.

Conclusion

At the high point of possibility theory, with the significance of monetary injections and leakages uncovered, Marx and Keynes stand in basic agreement and moreover, in opposition to their classical predecessors and contemporaries. This is in spite of the fact that on most other aspects, there are major differences between them.

There is one final point that needs re-emphasis – the central role taken by production. Attention has been focused on a variety of its aspects: its organisation; the motivation for embarking upon it; the conditions which must prevail if its object is to be realised; the determination of the aggregate level of production. Without production Marx would have been quite unable to attack Ricardo, the success of 'possibility' theory turning on the introduction of capitalist production; and the aggregate quantity of demand, though measurable even where it was only a question of exchange, would be of no operational significance without capitalist production. Production, because they are analysing capitalism, lies at the heart of the theories of Marx and Keynes.[7]

[7] It is thus surprising that attempts should have been made to incorporate the essence of Keynesian economics into the neoclassical framework, for the outstanding feature of that approach is that the basic results are obtained without consideration of production, on the basis of exchange alone. Production can of course be introduced, but it is always 'subjugated' to exchange. Benassy (1975) for example, attempts a synthesis within the setting of a general-exchange economy 'à la Debreu'. Production plays no role in this synthesis whatsoever, though Benassy adds that production can be incorporated without difficulty. Such reassurance only serves to underline a profound misunderstanding of Keynes's work, to believe that his contribution can be modelled without production at all. Indeed, all such attempted syntheses must face that charge because of the gulf which separates an approach where production is central and indispensable from an approach where it is basically irrelevant. Attempts to bridge the gap can only be made on a misunderstanding of the true nature of Keynes's theory, and Benassy's attempt is a case in point.

9

Marx's analysis of the relationship between the rate of interest and the rate of profits

Carlo Panico

This essay is a study of the relationship between what Marx called the *general rate of profits*, i.e. that uniform rate established by competition among capitals, and the average or *common rate of interest*, i.e. that rate which tends to prevail in the money market and 'appears in every country over fairly long periods as a constant magnitude' (Marx, 1972a, p. 366). No reference is made to what Marx called the *market rate of interest*, the rate which is continually fluctuating around the average rate of interest.

In the investigation of how the social surplus is distributed, Smith, Ricardo and John Stuart Mill saw the rate of interest as a *portion* of the rate of profits, and attempted to describe the factors which determine this portion and which prevent the rate of profits from falling to the level of the rate of interest. When the classical approach was abandoned at the end of the last century with the development of neoclassical analysis, it was argued that the rate of interest was ultimately determined by the same real forces as the rate of profits. The two rates were considered equal in equilibrium analyses. When differences between them were admitted, they were explained in terms of the unequal levels of risk involved in alternative investment decisions. Analysis of the relationship between these two rates therefore gradually lost its importance.

Interest in the problem was revived by Keynes's approach in the *General Theory* which clearly distinguished the analysis of the rate of interest, considered as a 'purely monetary phenomenon', from that of the rate of profits. Pasinetti (1974, pp. 139-40), for example, has asserted that in equilibrium there may be a difference between the level of the rate of interest and that of the rate of profits. Furthermore, in Sraffa's (1960) representation of classical political economy he suggests that the rate of profits, instead of the wage

* Reprinted from *Cambridge Journal of Economics* 1980, **4**, 363-78. I am grateful to A. Campus, M. D'Antonio, B. Jossa, F. Petri, N. Salvadori and the editors of the *Cambridge Journal of Economics* for comments on previous drafts.

rate, should be taken as an independent variable in the distribution of social surplus thus 'closing' the system:

> The rate of profit, as a ratio, has a significance, which is independent of any prices, and can well be 'given' before the prices are fixed. It is accordingly susceptible of being determined from outside the system of production, in particular by the level of money rates of interest (Sraffa, 1960, p. 33).

Reference is made to Sraffa's suggestion in an essay by Garegnani (Chapter 2 above). Garegnani claims that, if the average rate of profits and the average rate of interest on long-term loans, though different, tend, over a sufficiently long period of time, to move in step with one another, then Keynes's idea that the average level of the rate of interest on long-term loans will be determined by conventional factors, ultimately subject to the policy of the monetary authorities, may provide a new coherent basis for the theory of value and distribution (Garegnani, above, p. 54 n. 34 and pp. 62-3). It is with the aim of exploring this possibility that Marx's writings on the relationship between these two rates are considered below.

Very little attention has been paid to the abundant mass of notes left by Marx on this subject. Major Marxian works, like those of de Brunhoff (1976), Dobb (1973), Mandel (1962, 1971), Rosdolsky (1977) and Sweezy (1942), contain nothing or no more than a couple of pages on these notes.

Marx's analysis, however, turns out to be very interesting. It will be shown that it represents a remarkable advance with respect to Ricardo's analysis of the nature of the rate of interest and of its determination. Moreover, Marx's conclusions on the latter point are clear anticipations of what Keynes argued in the *General Theory* seventy years later. According to Marx the determination of the rate of interest should be based on qualitative descriptions of those economic, conventional and institutional factors which, in a certain country and in specific historical periods, affect the common opinions as to what the future interest rate will be. Moreover, it will be shown that when Marx located his analysis of the credit system within capitalistic reproduction, i.e. when the money-capitalist becomes a financial capitalist, the relationship between the rate of interest and the rate of profits acquires a more systematic form. Some elements of Marx's analysis can then be formalised within a Sraffian price system which explicitly includes the banking sector and establishes links between the rate of interest, the rate of profits and the wage rate. The features of this price-system will, at this stage, simply be outlined. The analysis of its properties will be left for later development.

The role of money-capitalists and the nature of interest

As Engels points out in his Preface to vol. 3 of Marx's *Capital*,

> [As to] Part 5, which dealt with the most complicated subject in the entire volume [i.e. the division of profit into interest and profit of enterprise] ... there

was no finished draft, not even a scheme whose outlines may have been filled out, but only the beginning of an elaboration – often just a disorderly mass of notes, comments and extracts (Marx, 1972a, p. 4).

In spite of this, chapters 21-24, which specifically deal with the role of the money-capitalist in the process of reproduction and the nature of the interest rate, were – as Engels tells us (Marx, 1972a, pp. 4-6) – in an advanced state of elaboration. In these chapters, Marx singled out three categories (classes) of people acting in the process of reproduction: money-capitalists, industrial capitalists and workers.

The money-capitalist owns the interest-bearing capital, which is defined as an independent expression of a certain amount of value, that has a particular use-value consisting of

its being able to serve as capital and, as such, to produce the average rate of profit under average conditions (Marx, 1972a, p. 352).

The form by which the money-capitalist alienates the interest-bearing capital is lending. The revenue he receives is called interest. Having use-value, the interest-bearing capital can be offered on the market as a commodity. As Marx said, it is, however, a 'commodity *sui generis*' (Marx, 1972a, p. 339). On the one hand

what the buyer of an ordinary commodity buys is its use-value; what he pays for is its value. What the borrower of money buys is likewise its use-value as capital; but what does he pay for? Surely not its price, or value, as in the case of ordinary commodities (Marx, 1972a, p. 352).

On the other hand, the commodity, interest-bearing capital, exists only in the sphere of circulation, where, as capital, it is borrowed by the industrial capitalist or by any other borrower. As soon as the industrial capitalist borrows and employs it in the sphere of production to 'exploit labour' and generate surplus-value, which takes the form of profit, the interest-bearing capital is transformed into productive capital. Unlike interest-bearing capital, productive capital never circulates as capital, but as specific commodities or money.[1] That is, while in the process of exchange the money-capitalist alienates his capital, the capital of the industrial capitalist simply changes its form in this process. His capital is not alienated, it is retained (Marx, 1972a, pp. 341-4). The productive capital

exists as capital in the actual movement, not in the process of circulation, but only in the process of production, in the process by which labour-power is exploited (Marx, 1972a, p. 343).

[1] As Marx pointed out, productive capital always appears in the form of commodity-capital and money-capital. The latter differs from interest-bearing capital, which also appears in the form of money, because it is *actually* employed in the process of production.

The industrial capitalist, not working with his own capital, has to pay the interest to the money-capitalist. The revenue left in his hands is called 'profit of enterprise'.

The third class, the workers, is composed of those who sell their labour-power and earn wages.

According to this three-way classification, the process of reproduction is presented as

$$M \rightarrow M \rightarrow C \rightarrow M' \rightarrow M''$$

In the first step, $M \rightarrow M$, the interest-bearing capital flows from the money-capitalist to the industrial capitalist.

In the second step, $M \rightarrow C$, the industrial capitalist employs the interest-bearing capital by buying commodities (means of production and labour-power). Production actually begins.

In the third step $C \rightarrow M'$ (where $M' > M$) surplus-value is extracted in production and is retained by the industrial capitalist as profit.

In the fourth step $M' \rightarrow M''$ (where $M < M'' < M'$) the industrial capitalist pays back the amount borrowed to the money-capitalist and gives him a part of his profit as interest.

From this simple scheme, the role of the money-capitalist and the nature of his earnings can be understood. The surplus-value (or profit) is generated within the sphere of production. It is in the $M \rightarrow C \rightarrow M'$ process that capital increases its original value. But, in order to increase its original value, it must be available. It is the role of the money-capitalist to make this capital available to the industrial capitalist.[2]

In the passage ($M \rightarrow M$), when it flows from the hands of the money-capitalist to those of the industrial capitalist, capital does not increase its value. The money-capitalist does not create, therefore, any value or surplus-value, but he simply earns a part of the surplus-value (profit) generated in the production process. So the role of the money-capitalist and the form in which he shares in distribution is defined on the basis of the capitalist mode of reproduction:

> Loaning money as capital – its alienation on the condition of its being returned after a certain time – presupposes, therefore, that it will be actually employed as capital, and that it actually flows back to its starting point (Marx, 1972a, p. 349).

This, obviously, does not mean that all money lent *must* be actually employed as capital. It may also be spent on consumption. However, the reason why the money-capitalist gets the interest is still to be found in the fact that he alienates a commodity which has the use-value of being potentially capital,

[2] 'B does not expend his own capital but A's; however he cannot expend A's capital without A's consent. There it is really A who originally expends the £100 of capital, albeit his function as capitalist is limited to this outlay of £100 as capital. In respect to these £100, B acts as capitalist only because A lends him the £100, thus expending them as capital' (Marx, 1972a, p. 340).

i.e. the use-value of being employed in the process of production and increasing *in this process* its value:

> Labour-power preserves its property of producing value only so long as it is employed and materialised in the labour process; yet this does not argue against the fact that it is potentially as a power, an activity which creates value, and that as such it does not spring from the process of production, but rather antecedes it. It is bought as such a capacity for creating value. One might also buy it without setting it to work productively; for purely personal ends, for instance, for personal services, etc. The same applies to capital. It is the borrower's affair whether he employs it as capital, hence actually sets in motion its inherent property of producing surplus-value. What he pays for is, in either case, the potential surplus value inherently contained in capital as a commodity (Marx, 1972a, p. 381).

Marx's position was in contrast to the view, held at the time,[3] that the rate of interest was the specific fruit of capital as such, abstracted from the process of production. This view, according to Marx, is generated by the particular form in which the relationship between money-capitalists and industrial capitalists appears. The relation appears as *antagonistic*, because what the industrial capitalist, working on borrowed capital, earns is not the gross profit (surplus-value) generated by means of the capital he has employed in the process of production, but the gross profit *minus* the interest he has to pay to the money-capitalist:

> [His] portion of the profit, therefore, necessarily appears to him to be the product of a capital *as long as it is operative* (Marx, 1972a, p. 373, italics added)

and it is opposed to interest, which appears as that portion of gross profit which is due to the *ownership* of capital as such.

On the other hand, the money-capitalist earns what he is able to get from alienating his own capital. Interest, thus, appears to him as what is earned by remaining *outside* the sphere of production.

> The merely quantitative division of the gross profit between two different persons who both have different legal claims to the same capital, and hence to the profit produced by it, thus turns into a qualitative division for both the industrial capitalist in so far as he is operating on borrowed capital, and for the money-capitalist, in so far as he does not apply himself his capital (Marx, 1972a, 374-5).

This qualitative distinction between interest and profit of enterprise is also applied by those industrial capitalists who spend their own capital.

> Whether the industrial capitalist operates on his own or on borrowed capital,

[3] The opposite view was held by those economists Marx called 'vulgar economists' (see Marx, 1972b, pp. 453 ff.).

> does not alter the fact that the class of money-capitalists confronts him as a special kind of capitalist, money-capital as an independent kind of capital, and interest as an independent form of surplus-value peculiar to this specific capital (Marx, 1972a, pp. 376-7).

The antagonism between the two kinds of capitalists is therefore precisely that which obscures the fact that what both of them earn is a merely quantitative division of the surplus-value. The existence of this antagonism *obliterates* the social antithesis between capital and labour. Both interest and profit of enterprise appear as relationships between two capitalists, not between capitalists and workers.[4]

Determination of the rate of interest

Marx argued that the rate of interest depends on the rate of profits and on the proportion in which the entire profit is divided between the lender and the borrower (Marx, 1972a, p. 358). If the proportion between interest and total profit were *always* constant, the average rate of interest would be completely regulated by the average rate of profits.

It is certainly true, Marx said, that the rate of interest represents a fairly constant proportion of the rate of profits. In some passages, he even suggested that the former can be taken as an empirical indicator of the latter:[5]

> [The] relative constancy [of the rate of profits] is revealed precisely in the more or less constant nature of the average, or common, rate of interest (Marx, 1972a, p. 366).

However, he claimed that there is no reason why the lender should always be given the same percentage of the gross profit, and that this percentage may and does change from one historical period to another. Therefore, changes in the average rate of interest do not always reflect changes in the general rate of profits.

Marx's investigation of the factors determining the portion of profit which is paid as interest presents some analogies with his analysis of the value of labour-power and the length of the working-day. First, he determined the ultimate limits within which these magnitudes can vary within a capitalist system of production, and then he tried to establish the laws regulating their average values.

[4] 'Interest-bearing capital is capital as *property* as distinct from capital as *function*. But so long as capital does not perform its function, it does not exploit labourers and does not come into opposition to labour. On the other hand, profit of enterprise is not related as an opposite to wage-labour, but only to interest' (Marx 1972a, p. 379).

[5] 'It is a fact, therefore, that the general rate of profit appears as an empirical given reality in the average rate of interest, although the latter is not a pure or reliable expression of the former' (Marx, 1972a, p. 365).

Marx defined the maximum limit of the average rate of interest as the general rate of profits. Although he recognised that from the total profit one might deduct that portion which can be considered as 'wage of superintendence'[6] he concluded:

> In any event, the average rate of profit is to be regarded as the ultimate determinant of the maximum limit of interest (Marx, 1972a, p. 360).

On the other hand, the minimum limit of the rate of interest was considered 'altogether indeterminable' (Marx, 1972a, p. 358). In this respect, Marx's analysis of the rate of interest is different from that of the value of labour-power, whose minimum limit is determined by the value of those means of subsistence that are *physically* indispensable to the maintenance and development of labour-power (Marx 1970a, p. 173).

A more fundamental difference between the value of labour-power and the rate of interest can, however, be found in the laws regulating their average values. Competition, Marx argued, affects the division of profit into interest and profit of enterprise, as much as the market prices of all other commodities, including labour-power. But, while for labour-power and all other commodities, competition causes nothing but deviations of market prices from prices of production, in the case of the rate of interest, competition does not determine the deviation from a given level (Marx, 1972a, pp. 355-6). This is because

> there is no good reason why average conditions of competition, the balance between lender and borrower, should give the leader an interest rate of 3, 4, 5%, etc., or else a certain percentage of the gross profits, say 20% or 50%, on his capital. ... The determination [of the average rate of interest] is accidental, purely empirical, and only pedantry or fantasy would seek to represent this accident as a necessity (Marx, 1972a, p. 363).

Indeed,

> The average rate of interest prevailing in a certain country – as distinct from the continually fluctuating market rates – cannot be determined by any law. In this sphere, there is no such a thing as a natural rate of interest in the sense in which economists speak of a natural rate of profit or a natural rate of wage (Marx, 1972a, p. 362).

Marx's conclusion that it is possible to speak of an 'average rate of interest', but not of a 'natural rate of interest', needs further comment.

In the analyses of the classical economists, the natural price of labour and the general rate of interest are to be determined on the basis of the laws of production. Labour-power is a commodity whose natural price

[6] This is the equivalent of the wage to be paid to a manager to control and supervise the activity of the workers (see Marx, 1972a, pp. 383 ff.).

is determined by the labour-time necessary for the production, and consequently also the reproduction, of this special article (Marx, 1970a, pp. 170-1).[7]

Could the process of production also determine the 'natural' level of the interest rate?

According to Marx, interest is the price to be paid for the interest-bearing capital, which is a 'commodity *sui generis*' since it never enters the process of production. It exists as such only in the sphere of circulation, when it passes from the hands of the money-capitalist into those of the industrial capitalist. As soon as the latter employs it in the process of production it is transformed, in the sense that it does not circulate as capital any more, but as money or specific commodities. So there is no such thing as the 'natural' rate of interest, because the material laws of capitalist production cannot, according to Marx, regulate the price of this commodity, which only exists *outside* the sphere of production:

> If we inquire further as to why the limits of a mean rate of interest cannot be deduced from general laws, we find the answer lies simply in the nature of interest. It is merely a portion of the average profit. The same capital appears in two roles, as loanable capital in the lender's hands, and as industrial capital, or commercial capital, in the hands of the functioning capitalist. But it functions just once, and produces profit just once. *In the process of production itself, the nature of capital as loanable capital plays no role* (Marx, 1972a, p. 364, italics added).

The analysis of the determination of the average rate of interest, therefore, rather than being based on any natural or material law,[8] should be 'purely empirical', that is, it should be based on a qualitative description of the factors that, from time to time, affect it.

Marx enumerated some of the factors that can affect the average rate of interest. He noted that Massie was perfectly right when in *An Essay on the Governing Causes of the Natural Rate of Interest* (London, 1750) he claimed:

> The only thing which any man can be in doubt about in this occasion is what proportion of these profits do of right belong to the borrower, and what to the lender; and thus there is no other method of determining than by opinions of borrowers and lenders in general; for, right or wrong, in this respect, are only what common consent makes so (Marx, 1972a, p. 362).

[7] It is the natural price of labour-power, and not the amount of commodities which constitutes the real wage, that is determined by the laws of production. Soon after the passage quoted in the text, Marx argued: 'The value of labour-power is the value of the means of subsistence necessary for the maintenance of the labourer .... On the other hand, the number and the extent of his so-called necessary wants, and also the modes of satisfying them, are themselves the product of historical developlent .... In contradistinction therefore, to the case of other commodities, there enters into the determination of the value of labour-power a historical and moral element. Nevertheless, in a given country, at a certain period, the average quantity of the means of subsistence necessary for the labourer is practically known' (Marx, 1970a, p. 171).

[8] Marx critically reports Karl Arnd's attempt to determine the rate of interest on the basis of some 'natural' law, such as the annual rate of growth of timber in the European forests (Marx, 1972a, p. 363, n. 67).

Here there is a striking similarity with Keynes's analysis of the rate of interest in chapter 15 of the *General Theory of Employment, Interest and Money.* Keynes also argued that any variation in the average rate of interest must occur through changes in the common opinion as to its value.

> [The rate of interest] is largely governed by the prevailing view as to what its value is expected to be. *Any* level of interest which is accepted with sufficient conviction as *likely* to be durable *will* be durable; subject, of course, in a changing society to fluctuations for all kinds of reasons round the expected normal (Keynes, 1973, vol. 7, p. 203).

Marx initially indicated some economic factors which affect this common consent, such as the average conditions of competition between lenders and borrowers. These conditions of competition may change for two reasons. First, as a country becomes richer, an increasing number of people joins the class of money-capitalists, and the amount of interest-bearing capital increases as well. This relative abundance of interest-bearing capital tends to reduce the average rate of interest. Secondly,

> the development of the credit system and the attendant ever-growing control of industrialists and merchants over the money savings of all classes of society, that is affected through the bankers, and the progressive concentration of these savings in amounts which can serve as money-capital, must also depress the rate of interest (Marx, 1972a, p. 362).

Subsequently, Marx added other conventional factors, like custom and legal tradition (Marx, 1972a, pp. 363-4).

Finally, like Keynes, he referred to the role played by institutional factors in affecting the common consent and hence the average rate of interest. By contrast with Keynes, however, Marx conceived the behaviour of monetary institutions as reflecting the distribution of power in the social structure. In vol. 3 of *Theories of Surplus Value*, for example, dealing with the way the antagonistic claims of industrial and of money-capitalists are regulated, he claimed that

> The State is used against interest-bearing capital by means of compulsory reductions of interest rates, so that it is no longer able to dictate terms to industrial capitalists (Marx, 1972b, p. 468).

To sum up, in Marx's analysis of the factors determining the rate of interest, he rejected any attempt to explain the determination of the average rate of interest on the basis of 'laws of necessity'. He proposed instead, to investigate it by means of qualitative description, of those economic, conventional and institutional factors that, from time to time, affect this variable.

The historical development of Marx's analysis

To understand the development of Marx's analysis, and his attempts to extend it to take account of the evolving conditions of the economy, it is useful to place his work in historical perspective. In what follows, we will compare his analysis with that of Ricardo, here representing Marx's classical predecessors, and we will try to point out new lines of investigation which start to appear in his writings.

Marx's debt to Ricardo is immediately apparent once we consider the way in which the analysis of the nature of interest is developed. Ricardo did not consider interest as the specific fruit of capital, but simply as a deduction from the profit obtained in the sphere of production:

> The interest which man agrees to pay for the use of a sum of money is in reality a portion of the profits which he expects to derive from the employment of the capital which the sum of money will enable him to obtain (Ricardo, 1951, vol. 3, pp. 374-5).

However, although he considered as productive capital only that part of the riches of society actually employed in the sphere of production, Ricardo never posed the question why the industrial capitalist has to pay interest to the money-capitalist, and never attempted to develop an analysis of the role of the money-capitalist in a capitalist economy, as Marx did. Ricardo claimed that the average rate of interest was ultimately and permanently governed only by the general rate of profits (Ricardo 1951, vol. 1, p. 297 and 363) and that if the

> rate of interest could be accurately known for any considerable period, we should have a tolerably correct criterion, by which to estimate the progress of profit (Ricardo, 1951, vol. 1, p. 296).

This position was maintained in all his works, independently of the change in his theory of profits – from one based on competition among capitals to one determining profits as the residuum left after paying workers – which occurred during the years 1813-14.

In a letter to the *Morning Chronicle*, dated 18 September 1810, he stated:

> the rate of interest for money is totally independent of the nominal amount of circulating medium. It is regulated solely by competition of capital, not consisting of money (Ricardo 1951, vol. 3, p. 143).

Eight years later, providing evidence before the select committees on the Usury Laws, he answered:

> The rate of interest is regulated by the demand and supply in the same way as any other commodity; but the demand and supply itself is again regulated by the rate of profit to be made on capital (Ricardo 1951, vol. 5, p. 346).

Ricardo's analysis is more narrow than that of Marx, for he stressed only the importance of the rate of profits in the determination of the rate of interest. The former is considered the *only* regulator of the latter.[9] As a consequence, no attempt is made by Ricardo to analyse the factors which affect the portion of the gross profit which has to be paid as interest.

There is reason to believe that Marx, in his later writings, was starting to think of further extending the analysis he inherited from his predecessors. In a letter to Engels, dated 30 April 1868 (Marx-Engels, 1934, letter 109, p. 245), he suggested that the study of the credit system should be a subsequent stage in the investigation of the relation between the rate of interest and the rate of profits. Marx believed that, with the development of capitalist society, the form of organisation and the management of interest-bearing capital changes according to the needs and the laws of capitalist production, and is subjugated to it:

> The real way in which industrial capital subjugates interest-bearing capital is the creation of a procedure specific to itself – the *credit system* ... The *credit system* is its own creation, and is itself a form of industrial capital which begins with manufactures and develops further with large-scale industry (Marx, 1972b, pp. 468-9).[10]

The analysis he had inherited did not take account of this historical element. The money-capitalist had been characterised as a single individual, alienating his own wealth to earn interest. With the development of capitalist society, however, the industrial capitalist, working on borrowed capital, faces the banker, or the financial capitalist, rather than the single money capitalist.

Unfortunately, Marx did not carry on this line of analysis very far. In none of his works is it possible to find a systematic treatment of the credit system. His notes on the subject are scattered in different parts of his writings and can only be considered as first steps. They are sometimes contained in just those chapters of vol. 3 of *Capital* – as, for instance, chapter 25 – that Marx left in the least advanced state of elaboration, and often they only announce further developments which are not worked out in the subsequent text.[11]

These first steps of investigation will be described in the next section, together with possible lines of analytical development stemming from Marx's notes.

[9] From some passages of Ricardo's writings, one may get the impression that he was assuming that these two rates *always* move together (Ricardo 1951, vol. 6, pp. 103, 108 and particularly 110), and that a divergent movement between them can *only* be temporary (Ricardo 1951, vol. 1, pp. 297-8, 363; vol. 7, p. 199).

[10] See also Marx (1972b, p. 518) and Marx (1969, p. 211).

[11] A typical example is given by the announcement of further development of the analysis of bankers' activity given on p. 320 in vol. 3, chapter 19, and the development of this point on p. 402 in vol. 3, chapter 25. But see also the conclusion of chapter 22 in vol. 3.

The role of the financial capitalist and the credit system

In vol. 3 of *Capital* the activity and the role of the bankers is analysed in two stages. In Part 4 Marx considered the activity of the financial capitalist in an economic system without credit in order to analyse his role in the process of equalisation of the rate of profits. In Part 5, Marx started to examine the activity of the banker in a credit system.

In a non-credit system the financial capitalist simply acts as a cashier of the industrial capitalist. To carry on the process of production, the industrial capitalist has to pay out money continually to many persons, and to receive money continually from others:

> This purely technical operation of disbursing and receiving money is in itself labour which, as long as money serves as a means of payment, necessitates drawing up payment balances and acts of balancing accounts ... a definite portion of the capital must be on hand constantly as a hoard ... This [also] entails safekeeping the hoard (Marx, 1972a, p. 316).

It is part of the bankers' activity to perform these purely technical functions, which involve their own labour and expenses.

With the development of the trade in commodities, the quantity and the quality of these technical operations increase. As the credit system develops, the bankers do not only act as cashiers of the industrial capitalist.

> Borrowing and lending money becomes their particular business. They act as middlemen between the actual lender and the borrower of capital ... A bank represents on one hand the centralisation of money-capital of the lenders, and on the other the centralisation of the borrowers. Its profit is generally made by borrowing at a lower rate of interest than it receives in loaning (Marx, 1971a, pp. 402-3).

Two elements, then, characterise the bankers' activity with respect to that of the money-capitalists: (a) the activity of the bankers is organised in such a way as not only to perform the role of the money-capitalist, who advances the capital to be used in the production process, but also to facilitate the circulation of means of payments in the economy; (b) the bankers, as the industrial capitalists, earn profit, and not interest, from their activity.

The financial capitalists participate in the process of reproduction in three ways. First, they provide for that part of monetary circulation which promotes the transactions between individual consumers and retail merchants. Second, they provide for that part of circulation which promotes transactions between merchants and producers, producers and producers, merchants and merchants, by transforming their capital from one form, i.e. bills of exchange or other kinds of credit, into another, i.e. money or other liquid means of payment. Third, they advance capital to those industrial capitalists who require it in industrial activity. Only this third function corresponds to that performed by the money-capitalist in the analysis described above. It is only in this case that the bankers make available new capital to the industrial capitalists. In the other two cases, the bankers only transform revenues or capital already in the hands of the industrial capitalists from a less liquid to a more liquid form. While the money-capitalist appears, in the process of reproduction $M \rightarrow M \rightarrow C \rightarrow M' \rightarrow M''$, only in the first and in the fourth step (i.e. $M \rightarrow M$ and $M' \rightarrow M''$), the banker acts in all four steps.

When they perform the first two functions, the financial capitalists play in the process of production the same role as the commercial capitalists, that is, they facilitate the metamorphosis of commodity-capital into money-capital and vice versa. The activities of the financial and the commercial capitalists are necessary to carry on the process of production. The industrial capitalists could never perform their activity without buying and selling, making and receiving payments.

> In the production of commodities, circulation is as necessary as production itself, so that circulation agents are just as needed as production agents (Marx, 1970b, p. 129).

Being necessary, these acts of circulation would have been performed by the industrial capitalist himself. But, instead, they are assigned by the division of labour to a particular species of capitalists. Without this specialisation,

> the portion of money-reserve in the capital of circulation would always have to be greater in relation to the part employed in the form of productive capital, and the scale of reproduction would have to be restricted accordingly. Instead, however, the manufacturer is enabled to constantly employ a larger portion of his capital in the actual process of production, and a smaller portion as money reserve (Marx, 1972a, p. 275).

To the extent that the financial and the commercial capitalists enable a reduction in the amount of capital to be held as reserve by all industrial capitalists, they enhance the accumulation of capital. However, since their functions only consist of acts of circulation, in the performance of their activity nothing takes place but changes of form of some mass of values. They do not create any surplus value.

To carry on their business, the commercial and the financial capitalists, or as Marx called them, the merchants, advance their own or borrowed money-capital.

> Since the circulating phase of industrial capital is as much a phase of the process of reproduction as production is, the capital performing its function independently in the process of circulation must yield the average annual profit just as well as capital operating in the various branches of production (Marx, 1972a, p. 282).

So, although they do not create any surplus-value, the merchants appropriate the same profit *pro-rata* as the industrial capitalists.

> How does merchant's capital attract its share of surplus value, or profit, produced by the productive capital? (Marx, 1972a, p. 282).

In Part 4, chapter 17, of vol. 3 of *Capital*, Marx tried to answer this question, by producing some numerical examples relating to commercial activity. His answer, however, was meant to hold – and, as we will see, it does hold – for the bankers' activity too.

His examples, where the assumption is made that all productive capital is circulating capital, can be presented as follows. Suppose that the total capital employed in the economy, measured in terms of abstract labour, consists of C units of constant capital and V units of variable capital, and that, given the rate of exploitation, there are S units of surplus-value. The value of the commodities produced, W, is therefore:

$$W = C + V + S. \tag{1}$$

The general rate of profits, r, is

$$r = \frac{S}{C + V} \tag{2}$$

which implies that

$$(C + V)(1 + r) = W. \tag{3}$$

The production of commodities also requires acts of circulation, whose performance involves a further advance of capital. In presenting his examples, Marx initially assumed, for simplicity, that the commercial activity does not require any other advance than the money-capital to be directly advanced in the purchase of the commodities to sell. That is, to carry on the process of buying and selling, no variable capital nor other material inputs are needed (Marx, 1972a, p. 288). In this case, the capital advanced, as Marx pointed out, does not wear out during the process of reproduction, so that it may be considered as fixed capital with a zero rate of depreciation.

As a first step, suppose that the industrial capitalists themselves advance the amount of money capital, measured in terms of abstract labour, say B units, to perform the necessary acts of circulation of the commodities. Equation (1) then becomes

$$B + C + V + S = W + B. \tag{4}$$

The rate of profits earned by the industrial capitalists cannot be calculated by means of equation (2) any more. To obtain the same amount of surplus-value, they have advanced B more units of capital, on which they must receive the same rate of profits as on the other capital advanced. The new rate of profits, r_1, as Marx showed (Marx, 1972a, pp. 284-5) then will be

$$r_1 = \frac{S}{C + V + B} \tag{5}$$

The performance of the acts of circulation, therefore, implies a reduction of the rate of profits of the industrial capitalists. It is clear that for them it would be equally convenient to themselves advance the capital required for the acts of circulation or to let the commercial capitalists advance it, as long as they get the same rate of profits, r_1. In the latter case, the industrial capitalist would advance only $(C+V)$ units of capital, and would sell their commodities to the commercial capitalists at the price W_1 determined as:

$$(C+V)(1 + r_1) = W_1. \tag{6}$$

The commercial capitalists would advance B units of capital to buy the commodities at the price W_1 and sell them at the price W^*, which allows the same rate of profits, r_1 on the capital advanced. Since in this example it happens[12] that W^* is exactly equal to W of equations (1) and (3) we can write the equation relating to the commercial activity as follows:

$$B(1 + r_1) = W - W_1 + B. \tag{7}$$

According to Marx, then, the commercial capital attracts its share of surplus-value produced by the industrial capital because production of commodities necessarily requires acts of circulation, with consequent advance of capital on which the same rate of profits must be paid as in the industrial sector.

The same analysis holds if, instead of the commercial capitalists, we consider the bankers performing the activity relative to the movements of money circulation within the process of production. In Part 4, chapter 19, of vol. 3 of *Capital*, Marx supposed that the only activity of the bankers was that of 'cashiers' of the industrial capitalist.[13] To perform this activity, he supposed, they are paid in the form of fixed charges on the receipts and payments they make on account of the industrial capitalists. They are not paid, therefore, in the form of interest.

As for the commercial capital, Marx also made the simplifying assumption that only one kind of capital is advanced, the money-capital which constitutes the money-reserve of the sector, and that B units of this capital are needed. Assuming that the bankers earn a fixed remuneration, say H, which is paid at the end of the productive cycle, Marx's previous example, applied to the bankers' activity may again be used. Equation (5) still determines r_1,

[12] As Marx showed (Marx, 1972a, pp. 291-2) the selling price W^* would not be equal to the value W if labour-power is employed in the commercial activity. This is clearly stated also in Marx (1973), p. 548.

[13] In this chapter, Marx had not introduced the analysis of credit yet. This is the reason why he postpones the investigation of the interest received and paid to the bankers to Part 5 (see Marx, 1972a, pp. 318 and 320).

the general rate of profits. The bankers' revenue, H, and the selling price of the commodities, W, are determined by the equations:

$$(C+V)(1+r_1)+H=W \tag{8}$$

$$B(1+r_1)=B+H. \tag{9}$$

Equation (8) refers to the industrial sector. For the industrial capitalists H is a cost, paid at the end of the period, added to the capital advanced and to the profit earned on that capital. Equation (9) refers to the banking sector. The revenue of the bankers, H, must be such as to give them the rate of profits, r_1, on the capital advanced, calculated by means of equation (5).

The model of bankers' activity presented in equations (8) and (9) can be further extended to take account both of the fact that other parts of capital have to be advanced by the bankers, and of the fact that their

> profit is generally made by borrowing at a lower rate of interest than they receive in loaning (Marx, 1972a, pp. 402-3).

With reference to the different components of bankers' capital, Marx argued that these consist of three elements.

A certain part – the one we have called B – is that portion of the money-reserve advanced by the banker himself.[14] Another part, which we will call K_b, is advanced to obtain the materials, such as furniture, stationery, and so on, necessary to carry on the banking business. The third part, call it l_b, is used to purchase the labour-power employed in banking activity. The banker must receive the general rate of profits on the whole of his capital $(B+K_b+l_b)$ advanced. K_b and l_b can be considered as that capital technologically necessary to perform the bankers' activity. This means that we can suppose there to exist a technological relationship between them and the level of activity of the bankers.

No such relationship exists between B and the level of activity. No suggestions can be found in Marx's writings on this point. We can try, however, to add something to his notes. We may think of B as the amount of money-capital to be advanced by the bankers, according to institutional rules – laws regulating the access of capitalists to banking activity – or to customary rules, such as the necessity of showing a certain amount of capital as warranty in order to start or expand the collection of deposits. Where no such rules exist, the bankers can perform their activity relying completely on the money-capital borrowed from their depositors. In this case, B could be zero. Moreover, it is in the interest of the bankers to reduce this part of capital to its minimum with respect to a given level of activity, in order to have a higher rate of profits. It seems, therefore, reasonable to suppose that B

[14] The banker may also borrow it from other capitalists or on the stock market. However, it is not composed of deposits collected by the bank itself.

is completely determined by these institutional and customary rules. Although this certainly requires further inquiry, we can take it as a starting point in the analysis of the influence of bankers' activity on the relationship between the rate of interest and the rate of profit.

Marx himself never worked out the analysis of how the model presented in equations (8) and (9) can be extended to take account of the fact that bankers earn their profits by obtaining a higher rate of interest on their loans than on their deposits. In attempting to do this, we will use, instead of Marx's description in terms of abstract labour, the usual Sraffian price system with the modifications necessary to take account of the activity of the banking sector in a credit economy.

To extend the model presented in equations (8) and (9), the first thing to do is to drop Marx's assumption that the bankers only act as 'cashiers' of the industrial capitalists. But at this stage of the argument we suppose that the activity of the bankers consists only of providing for that part of circulation which promotes the transactions between consumers, merchants and producers, by transforming capital from one form (e.g. bills of exchange) into another (e.g. cash). We are, therefore, ruling out the fact that bankers also make available new capital for the industrial capitalists, that is, they also perform the function which was the specific role of the money-capitalists in the analysis Marx inherited from his classical predecessors.

With respect to the analysis contained in equations (8) and (9), we now have that the industrial capitalists, instead of paying a fixed charge to the bankers, pay an interest rate, i, on the loans obtained from them. At the same time, the industrial capitalists receive a lower rate of interest, τ, on their bank deposits. The difference between what they pay and what they receive as interest, represents for the industrial capitalists a cost necessary to carry on production. As such, it must be added to the capital they have advanced to buy the material inputs of production and the labour-power, and to the profit earned on this capital, to determine the prices of production of the commodities.

On the other hand the difference between what the bankers receive and pay as interest represents the bankers' total revenue, and it must be such as to pay the same rate of profits as in the industrial sector on the capital the bankers have advanced.

To present this point in formal terms we make the following assumptions:

(a) the economy produces n commodities;

(b) for simplicity, joint-production is ruled out, and hence durable capital too;

(c) all prices are expressed in terms of wages;

(d) the industrial sector settles its debt with the banking sector at the end of each productive cycle, on the basis of a balance-sheet presented by the banks;

(e) some monetary instrument, e.g. paper-money, is used to make payments.

We can now write the following system of equations in matrix form.

$$(Ap + l)(1 + r) + qi - d\tau = p \qquad (10)$$

$$(K_b p + l_b)(1 + r) + Br + D\tau = Qi \qquad (11)$$

where: A is the input matrix of the industrial sector;
p is the price vector;
l, the labour vector of the industrial sector;
r, the general rate of profits;
q, the credit input vector of the industrial sector, i.e. the amount of loans per unit of product of each industry. This vector shows the amount of paper-money measured in terms of money wages the industrial sector has borrowed from the banking sector;
i, the rate of interest on loans;
d, the deposit vector of the industrial sector, i.e. the amount of deposits per unit of output of each industry. This vector shows the amount of paper money in terms of money-wages the industrial capitalists have deposited in the banks;
τ, the rate of interest on deposits;
K_b the material input vector of the credit sector;
l_b, the amount of labour employed in the credit sector;
B, the portion of money-reserve advanced by the bankers themselves. The amount of paper-money this scalar represents is expressed in terms of money-wages, too;
D, the total amount of deposits. As B, it is a scalar where the amount of paper money is expressed in terms of money-wages.
Q, the total amount of loans. It is a scalar with the same features as B and D.

Since we want to concentrate on the relation between i and r, we fix τ at this first stage of the analysis, assuming that it is not correlated with i. So, we can write another equation

$$\tau = \tau^*, \qquad (12)$$

In the system (10), (11) and (12) we have n+2 equations and n+3 unknowns, that is, p, r, i and τ. There is, therefore, one degree of freedom, which can be eliminated if we consider i as an independent variable, or if we take as given the bundle of commodities which constitutes the real wage. In the latter case, we add the following equation

$$wp = 1 \qquad (13)$$

where w is a row vector showing the commodities contained in the wage bundle.

The solution of this system of equations must always respect the following conditions:

$$r > \tau \tag{14}$$

$$r > i. \tag{15}$$

They express the conditions necessary for the industrial sector and the banking sector to have a positive level of activity. A long-run position with $r \leq \tau$ would be necessarily accompanied by a zero level of industrial production, since it would be convenient to deposit all the industrial capital in the banks. If $r \leq i$, it would be convenient for the bankers to give up their business and become money-capitalists, lending money without organising a bank.

It seems, therefore, that Marx's notes on the credit system and on the role played by the financial capitalist in the process of equalisation of the rate of profit, contain some useful suggestions as to the links between relative prices and distributive shares, including the interest rate. The analytical model obtained from these notes reflects, first of all, Marx's idea that, with the development of capitalist society, the management of interest-bearing capital tends to be based on the same laws as production of commodities (Marx, 1972b, p. 469). Secondly, it links together the analysis of monetary variables and that of real variables. The existence of a monetary economy and the way in which the problems of money circulation are solved are, in fact, directly relevant in the determination of the rate of profits and of the relative prices. Thirdly, it suggests an interesting way in which to develop the analysis of money or, more generally, monetary institutions, which should not be neglected in the formulation of the system of reproduction. Money, that is, should be conceived as a set of institutions performing particular functions and pursuing their own interests.

Conclusions

There appears to be a contradiction between Marx's conclusions that the determination of the average rate of interest cannot be based on any natural or material law (see p. 174 above) and the existence of links between the rate of interest, the rate of profits and the wage rate fixed by the conditions of reproduction (see above). Once the wage rate is taken as an independent variable the rate of interest is determined within the material conditions of reproduction.

Marx obviously could not perceive the existence of such a contradiction, since he did not work out completely his analysis of the credit system and of the role played by the financial capitalists in the process of equalisation of the rate of profits.

Yet as soon as his notes are developed this contradiction becomes evident.

Sraffa's suggestion as to the 'closing' of his system offers us a way out from this situation: the rate of interest could be taken as an independent variable (Sraffa, 1960, p. 33, quoted on p. 168 above). In this case, the analysis outlined in the last section will define the limits of compatibility between the workers' claims and the existing conditions of reproduction, at given rates. At the same time, the analysis of the rate of interest can still be developed along the lines Marx pointed out. That is, it will be based on qualitative descriptions of those economic, conventional and institutional factors which in a certain country and in specific historical periods, affect the common opinion as to what the future interest rate will be.

10

The 'new' Keynes papers

Murray Milgate

Introduction

Late in 1979 the Royal Economic Society published an additional volume containing some of the 'new' Keynes papers that had been discovered at Tilton in 1976 (*JMK*, vol. 29). There is a sense in which the discovery of this material relating to the *Treatise on Money* and *General Theory* parallels the discovery of Ricardo's side of the Ricardo-James Mill correspondence in 1943.[1] Both finds were made largely by accident and both presented the editors of the respective *Collected Works* (Professor Moggridge and Mr Sraffa) with the problem of incorporating 'new' material, unearthed late in the process of compiling their editions, so as to maintain overall continuity. Sraffa's solution was to re-work the whole of the correspondence volumes even though before the discovery of the additional Ricardo letters these had reached the page-proof stage. Moggridge's solution on the other hand, whilst aesthetically less pleasing, was devised under a constraint – the related volumes had already gone to press. But if vol. 29 of Keynes's *Collected Writings* is a compromise in this sense, it is in every other respect equal in quality to its earlier companion volumes.

What then does this 'new' material have to offer the student of Keynes's economic thought? The contents of the first chapter are of little more than anecdotal interest and the bulk of the second chapter (approximately 18 out of 26 pages) is taken up by additions to the already voluminous Keynes-Robertson correspondence over matters arising out of the *Treatise on Money* (see *JMK*, vol. 13, pp. 271-321). It is fairly clear that this correspondence adds little of importance to what was already available (though it certainly fills in some gaps) and that, moreover, to anyone interested in the *General Theory* and the nature of its departure from the orthodox position, the correspondence is best viewed as being between two men differing more on

[1] See Sraffa in Ricardo, 1951, vol. 1, p. ix.

points of detail than on the general tenor of the argument[2] (unlike the issues which so clearly separate Robertson and Keynes in their subsequent disputes over the *General Theory*). However, the third chapter is more interesting. There are Keynes's Easter and Michaelmas lectures of 1932 which are separated by the 'manifesto' delivered to Keynes in response to the first of these by three members of the famous 'circus' that was discussing the *Treatise on Money*. There are the 1933 drafts for the embryonic *General Theory* itself, an exchange with Lindahl, Bryce's survey paper of 'the type of monetary theory held by Research Students in Cambridge' from 1935 (*JMK*, vol. 29, p. 132),[3] and a tantalising, but brief, exchange with Sraffa. These give important clues concerning the process of thought which led Keynes out of the world of the 'classics' to which the *Treatise on Money* had been confined into the light of the *General Theory*. This material will be examined in detail below. The fourth chapter adds more to the Keynes-Robertson exchanges over the *General Theory* and its aftermath, some Keynes-Kuznets correspondence on Keynes's use of Kuznets's statistics on capital formation in the *General Theory*, and other assorted material arising out of matters related to that book.

My purpose is to examine this 'new' material by concentrating on those areas that shed light directly upon the analytical developments in the period 1931-34 that led up to the formulation of the principle of effective demand. In this task, I will address myself not so much to the question of dating the change *per se* but rather to the question of establishing the places in which theoretical propositions are advanced which constitute unambiguously *General Theory*-type arguments (as opposed to those which are merely modifications of the theoretical system embodied in the *Treatise on Money*).

The transition from the Treatise on Money to the General Theory

The first of the important 'new' material in *JMK*, vol. 29, relates to the period between the *Treatise on Money* and the *General Theory*. On all the evidence previously available, it was possible to infer that at this time, and especially in his lectures, Keynes had begun to incorporate changes in the level of output as part of the orthodox *Treatise* analysis of changes in the general level of prices ensuing from an imbalance between planned saving and planned investment (see, for example, the editorial comment in *JMK*, vol. 13, p. 343). According to *Treatise* theory, the disequilibrium between planned saving and investment was itself a reflection of a deviation between the

[2] It must surely have been with the strictures of the 'critics' of the *Treatise on Money* in mind, and not least Dennis Robertson himself, that Keynes was led in the Easter Term lectures of 1932 to draw on a familiar Marshallian analogy and declare that 'it is often impracticable to discuss the most generalised case; ... [an] author selects, therefore, a fairly typical case out of the genus which he is in fact discussing, and talks in terms of this, – satisfied in his own mind that the same argument applies *mutatis mutandis* to other members of the genus, and that the task of mutating the mutands is merely a routine one.' (*JMK*, vol. 29, p. 36).

[3] This material had been published in 1977 as Appendix I of Patinkin and Leith (1977).

natural and market rates of interest (see, for example, *JMK*, vol. 5, pp. 139, 180 and 184). The fragments from which Keynes lectured (and their sequel in the Michaelmas term) which are now published give a somewhat clearer picture of the significance of this development for the process of transition that led up to the *General Theory* and of the role played in it by members of the Cambridge 'circus'. In particular, it seems that it may now be possible to make a definitive judgment as to whether, as Moggridge has suggested, by 'the winter and spring of 1931 the "Circus" had in its hands most of the important ingredients of the system which was ultimately to appear in the *General Theory*' (*JMK*, vol. 13, p. 341). Furthermore, the 'new' material makes it possible to clear away an analytical misunderstanding which has crept into the literature relating to this period of transition; this holds that the move towards the analysis of changes in output *within* the *Treatise* framework provides an 'alternative focus', broadly equivalent to that which was subsequently to appear in the *General Theory* – a view which has been popularised by Moggridge (see, for example, Moggridge, 1980, pp. 93-4). To this end it is essential to bring the picture up to date as of Easter 1932. Three elements are central.

The first element in this picture is, of course, the Fundamental Equations of the *Treatise on Money* which expressed the 'formulae' for determining the price level of consumption goods and the price level of output as a whole:

$$P = \frac{E}{O} + \frac{I' - S}{R}$$

$$\Pi = \frac{E}{O} + \frac{I - S}{O}$$

where

P = price level of consumption goods
Π = price level of output as a whole
E = money income
O = total output
I' = income earned in the production of investment goods
I = amount of current investment
S = amount of saving
R = 'available output' (flow of consumption goods)

The equilibrium of this system (associated with stable prices) occurs when saving and investment balance, and is characterised by the full employment of 'factors of production', including labour (see *JMK*, vol. 5, p. 132). There is nothing here that would have been unacceptable to Marshall. The causes of disequilibrium were those factors which could upset the balance between I (or I') and S. In the *Treatise* Keynes analysed these discrepancies along the wholly orthodox lines of a divergence between the 'natural' and 'market' rates of interest (see, for example, ibid., pp. 139, 165, 180 and 184). It is very important to note that *all* of this analysis, both of equilibrium and disequilibrium, is the standard fare of neoclassical theory: the rate of interest is regarded as the 'balancing factor', variations in which ensure the reconciliation of decisions to save with decisions to invest. Accordingly, it was to the 'real' forces of Marshall's theory that Keynes had to turn for the determination of *long-run* equilibrium variables such as relative prices, the natural rate of interest and the levels of output and employment (see, for example, ibid., p. 161). Only in the short run, in the disequilibrium with which the whole body of the theoretical part of the *Treatise* is concerned, did the interaction of 'monetary' and 'real' forces come into play. The early criticisms of the *Treatise on Money*, as we shall see, were to call into question only the *particular* content of this disequilibrium analysis, not the *general* (and quite traditional) theoretical framework within which that analysis was conducted. Likewise, it will be argued below that the character of the 'revisions' that Keynes had begun to undertake in the Easter and Michaelmas lectures of 1932 provides no evidence of the sort of change in this general theoretical framework that was subsequently to be embodied in the *General Theory*. All the evidence from this period points only to the conclusion that the analysis of particular cases within that framework was undergoing a process of refinement.

The second element of the picture in early 1932 was the so-called Widow's Cruse 'fallacy'. Broadly speaking, this argument ran along the following lines: In the *Treatise*, Keynes had maintained that the impact of the appearance of an excess of investment over saving (referred to by him as 'profits') would be felt through an alteration in the general level of prices (see, for example, *JMK*, vol. 5, p. 125). Apparently, the members of the 'circus' were quick to notice that for this to be the *only* possible effect, an assumption of a constant output has to be added.[4] Keynes conceded the point in a letter to Joan Robinson (vol. 13, p. 270).

The third and final element, though analytically related to the previous point, was the accumulation of ideas from Kahn's 'home investment' paper of 1931 (reprinted in Kahn, 1972) and Joan Robinson's 'parable of savings' paper (Robinson, 1933). Both these papers extended the mechanism already provided in the *Treatise on Money* by incorporating output responses as part of the short run adjustment mechanism between investment and savings (see Milgate, 1982, ch. 6, section A).

This was the state of the art as Keynes walked into the lecture room on April 25th 1932.

These features of the early 1932 landscape stand in marked contrast to the picture embodied in the 1935 drafts of the *General Theory* that Keynes circulated among his colleagues. By that time, the principle of effective demand

[4] Most of the 'critics' of the *Treatise* made this point, Hawtrey apparently being among the first to raise the matter formally with Keynes (*JMK*, vol. 13, p. 152). It is worth mentioning that vol. 29 now makes it clear that Pigou as well, in comments on the proofs of the *Treatise* from the autumn of 1929, had made this point (see p. 5).

had replaced the orthodox marginalist idea that variations in the rate of interest ensured the equilibrium of planned savings and planned investment – the view to which Keynes had subscribed in the *Treatise*. Unlike the theoretical framework of the *Treatise*, where 'equilibrium' and full employment were synonymous, according to the *General Theory* argument the economic system may well tend towards an equilibrium characterised by the unemployment of labour (see, for example, *JMK*, vol. 7, p. 254).

What should be looked for, as far as the transition from a *Treatise* to a *General Theory* position is concerned, is the appearance of the principle of effective demand to explain the mechanism which adjusts intended saving to planned investment – a mechanism which operates not via changes in the rate of interest (or, more generally, relative prices) but rather via changes in the level of output. This requires something more than finding changes in the level of output being incorporated into the Fundamental Equations of the *Treatise* or discovering an argument which held that increased investment implied increased output. Indeed, both these ideas are perfectly compatible with orthodox neoclassical economics, where one would expect, in general, to observe price *and* quantity adjustments in any short-run disequilibrium process. If, in fact, there is some 'flaw' in the *Treatise* analysis by virtue of its focus upon price responses, then that 'flaw' can be eliminated in a perfectly orthodox way by grafting onto the discussion the effects of output responses. That Keynes himself knew this to be the case is evident from his letter to Joan Robinson (14 April 1932) who had raised the issue:

> I think you are a little hard on me as regards the assumption of constant output. It is quite true that I have not followed out the consequences of changes in output in the earlier theoretical part ... Surely one must be allowed ... to make simplifying assumptions of this kind; particularly when ... the assumption in question does not make a very vital difference to the whole character of the argument (*JMK*, vol. 13, p. 270).

While it would be incorrect to deny that the analysis of output variations within, to begin with, the *Treatise* framework was a step along the road to the *General Theory*, it would be equally incorrect to maintain that this step, once taken, was decisive. On the contrary, as long as the *Treatise* framework was maintained, it led to inconsistencies and false assertions about the characteristics of 'equilibrium' in relation to level of employment. Some of these are quite apparent in the 1932 lectures now printed in *JMK*, vol. 29, and they will be returned to below (see also Milgate, 1982, ch. 6 for a discussion of those that are evident in vols 13 and 14 of the *Collected Writings*).

The presence of the principle of effective demand cannot be confirmed without both a statement of what Keynes called his 'fundamental psychological law' – that an increase in income is associated with an increase in consumption of a lesser order of magnitude (*JMK*, vol. 7, p. 96) – and the recognition of its direct incompatibility with the neoclassical (and *Treatise*) rate of interest adjustment mechanism (see, for example, ibid., pp. 93 and 165; vol. 14, p. 212).

The Easter and Michaelmas Term lectures of 1932

In the first of the two Easter Term lectures printed in *JMK* (vol. 29, pp. 35-42) Keynes does little more than urge his 'modern students of short-period economics' to be clear on the distinctions which, at once, separate and unite their analysis with long-period equilibrium economics (ibid., p. 32). Such remarks, and they are repeated in the first Michaelmas Term lecture (ibid., p. 51), would seem to be no more than an echo of Keynes's arguments in the *Treatise on Money* which stressed the importance of short-period problems (like unemployment) despite the fact that in the long run 'it all came out in the wash' (*JMK*, vol. 6, p. 366).

In this regard, it does not seem insignificant that Keynes spent most of this first lecture arguing that different definitions (of S, I, E, etc.) really made no logical inroads into *Treatise* theory. Any definitions, he argued, would lead to 'perfectly accurate Fundamental Equations' (*JMK*, vol. 29, p. 36). In fact, in a section of the lecture Keynes apparently deleted, he had begun to include 'profit' (Q of the *Treatise*) as part of income (now written as E' instead of E), and he admitted that his earlier convention had caused some confusion. There can be little doubt that this is where the Widow's Cruse fallacy had made its impact on Keynes's thinking.

That Keynes did not regard such alterations as being particularly far removed from the *Treatise* theory becomes clearer in the second Easter lecture (2 May 1932). Here Keynes derives the following proposition: changes in the amount of investment and changes in the volume of output (employment) are of the same direction. (Kahn's 'home investment' paper cannot have been incidental in leading Keynes to offer this proposition.) Keynes derives it on the basis of two conditions:

(a) $\left.\begin{matrix}\Delta O \\ \Delta E'\end{matrix}\right\}$ are of the same sign (i.e. as output increases/decreases, income increases/decreases)

(b) $\left.\begin{matrix}\Delta E' - \Delta F \\ \Delta E'\end{matrix}\right\}$ are of the same sign (i.e. an increase/decrease in income implies an increase/decrease in expenditure but by a proportionally lesser amount)

(c) $\Delta I = \Delta E' - \Delta F$ (by definition; F is 'spending')

The right-hand side of (c) is of the same sign as $\Delta E'$ (from (b)) which is, in turn, of the same sign as ΔO (from (a)). So ΔI and ΔO are of the same sign. The proposition is subject only to conditions (a) and (b), since (c) is merely a matter of definition.

Note that from definition (c) we may obtain the following:

$$\Delta I = \Delta E' - \Delta F$$
$$\Delta F + \Delta I = \Delta E' = \Delta E + \Delta Q \text{ (returning to } \textit{Treatise} \text{ notation)}$$

so that

(d) $\Delta Q = \Delta I + \Delta F - \Delta E$

It is important to mention that Keynes regarded equation (d) as merely a 'truism' (albeit an important one) in precisely the same way as the Fundamental Equations of the *Treatise on Money* themselves were 'truisms'. Quite apart from the objections against this method of proof which were raised by Joan Robinson *et al.* (printed in *JMK*, vol. 29), there are two things that must be said about the contents of these Easter lectures which combine in force to indicate that in Easter 1932 Keynes was still only a traveller on the road which was ultimately to lead to the *General Theory*, and that he had by no means reached his destination.

The first point is related to the fact that the expression in (d) above bears a remarkable similarity to a much more modern expression. Were we to rewrite it, we would obtain $\Delta E + \Delta Q = \Delta I + \Delta F$ or $\Delta E' = \Delta I + \Delta F$. Without loss of generality, this becomes $E' = I + F$. This, of course, is nothing but $Y = C + I$ (since E' is income, I is investment and F is 'spending'). Furthermore, expression (b) is very close to Keynes's fundamental psychological law if we chose to write it in a more familiar form:

$C = f(Y)$, with $0 < f' < 1$.

Unfortunately, however, and this is the second point, Keynes does not seem to have realised at this stage that the correct theory of employment involved viewing changes in the level of income as the *mechanism of adjustment* between saving and investment. What Keynes appears to have noticed was rather that the simple disequilibrium adjustment process of the *Treatise* in terms of movement *along* demand (for investment) and supply (of saving) curves might – indeed, in all probability would – be complicated by shifts in the curves themselves induced by the disequilibrium. It is obvious that this does not imply that we have to abandon the traditional neoclassical demand-and-supply theory in the treatment of saving and investment as must be done once the principle of effective demand is embraced; it is just that the exposition of that very familiar theory becomes a little more complicated.

This is not to deny the presence of a wish on Keynes's part to escape from the bounds imposed by *Treatise* theory. Such a desire is especially evident in the second Michaelmas Term lecture of 1932 (*JMK*, vol. 29, pp. 54-7), where Keynes forthrightly challenges the orthodox theory at its citadel: 'There is no reason to suppose that positions of *long-period* equilibrium have ... to be positions of optimum output' (ibid., p. 55, italics added). However, the argument Keynes produces to sustain this conclusion is not entirely consistent, and illustrates the fact that he had not yet fully broken away from the orthodox theory (see also *JMK*, vol. 13, pp. 373-5, for a similar case; this is examined in Milgate, 1982, ch. 6).

Keynes begins with a position of equilibrium 'with saving and investment equal ... and the factors of production fully employed' (ibid., p. 55). He then considers the effect of an increase in the market rate of interest ($i_m > i_n$). Thus according to the *Treatise* argument (to which Keynes explicitly defers), saving exceeds investment, and output, among other things, will fall (ibid., p. 56). This, Keynes argues, will lead to a fall in the (market) rate of interest, retarding saving and stimulating investment, until once again saving and investment balance (output will recover), and the system has returned to its equilibrium position ($i_m = i_n$) by definition a *full-employment* equilibrium of the familiar *Treatise* kind. There is nothing here that is objectionable from the point of view of orthodox neoclassical theory (and, furthermore, changes in output are part and parcel of Keynes's story now).

But then Keynes makes the remarkable assertion that this new *long-period* equilibrium need *not* be a full-employment one (ibid., pp. 56-7). And why? To quote Keynes: 'the [original] decline in output may be itself one of the factors which had, by reason of its retarding effect on saving, produced the new equilibrium' (ibid., p. 57). Unfortunately this conclusion does not follow from the *Treatise*-type analysis Keynes had presented in the same lecture. For if that analysis is appropriate (and Keynes says it is), then the position to which Keynes refers here is not a long-period equilibrium at all. This point is illustrated in Figure 1.

Figure 1

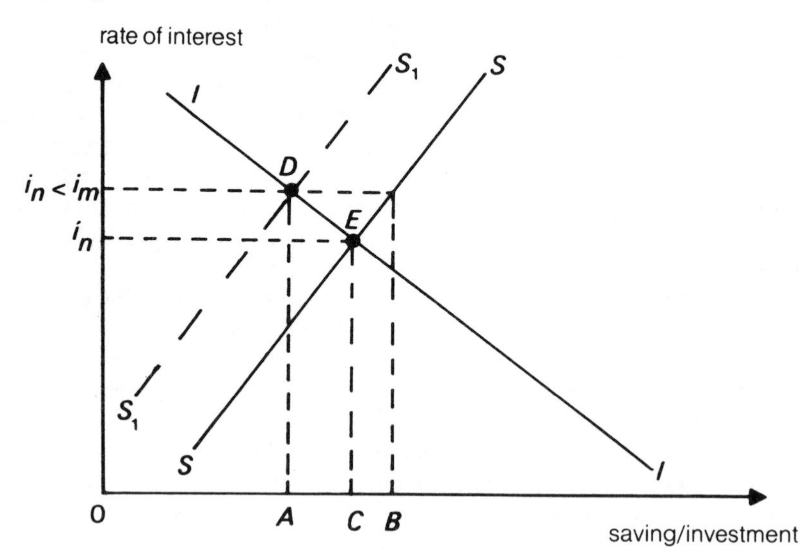

Point E represents the familiar *Treatise* equilibrium with planned investment and planned savings balanced at the full-employment interest rate i_n. Point D represents what Keynes calls the new 'equilibrium' with unemployment. It is evident, however, that so long as there have been no alterations in the conditions of productivity and thrift, and that initial endowments have not changed, D is not an equilibrium at all – there will be an excess supply of saving (measured by the interval AB) at the prevailing rate of interest i_m. This, of course, implies that a tendency exists to push i_m down towards i_n; that is, we have a *disequilibrium* position at D.

This conclusion cannot be avoided by claiming that the SS curve shifts bodily (and fortuitously) to say, S_1S_1 – for this would require a change in the data upon which these demand-and-supply curves rest, and Keynes does not mention any such changes as being relevant to his discussion. Indeed, the fact that Keynes actually analyses the effects of a fall in i_m back to its equilibrium level (ibid., p. 56), *ipso facto* implies that no such change in data has occurred. In any case, even if the data did change in just the right way as to produce a function like S_1S_1, the point D would then be a *full-employment* equilibrium since, given the new configuration of the data, planned saving and planned investment would then balance at D – albeit at a different natural rate of interest.

Nor is it any more satisfactory to argue that S_1S_1 represents savings out of *less than* full-employment income. For in that case all we should have established is that saving and investment balance *ex post*. The *ex ante* inequality between these two magnitudes would persist, D would be a point of *disequilibrium* (or perhaps, even, *short-period* equilibrium if i_m is fixed), and forces would exist the operation of which would tend to push the system back towards full employment *in the long run*. All of the above follows from the *Treatise* framework within which Keynes conducted this lecture.

The above also provides a particularly striking example of the fact that the analysis of changes in the level of output *within* the *Treatise* framework is perfectly compatible with the orthodox doctrine of *laissez-faire* which holds that in the long run market economies will tend towards a position of full employment of 'factors of production'. It was Keynes's subsequent liberation from these orthodox preconceptions, such as those enshrined in the *Treatise on Money* and in the 1932 lectures, that was decisive in the genesis of the principle of effective demand – not the analysis of changes in the level of output.

The early drafts of the General Theory

If I am right in saying that during the 1932 lectures Keynes was still following the orthodox marginalist train of thought, the 1933 drafts of his 'new' book are even more remarkable. For they, too, appear to do very little more than re-express the Fundamental Equations of the *Treatise on Money* in terms of different definitions. They indicate as clearly as the lectures of the previous year that Keynes had not yet broken away completely from the orthodox theory of the equilibrium of saving and investment (*viz*. the orthodox theory of employment). In fact, these drafts seem to be no more than the 'half-forged weapons' of which Keynes had spoken in his letter to Joan Robinson which concluded their debate over the content of the second Easter Term lecture of 1932 (*JMK*, vol. 13, p. 378).

For example, vol. 29 prints two draft tables of contents of a 'new' book which pre-date the two (December 1933 and October 1934, in vol. 13, pp. 421-4) which were previously thought to be the earliest surviving. The contrast between these drafts and those of the following year (which are much closer to the final version) is striking. The first, under the title 'The Monetary Theory of Employment' contains three books, the first six chapters of which are entirely devoted to re-definition of terms. There is no mention in the table of contents of effective demand or anything like the marginal propensity to consume. From this draft table of contents there is already one chapter, 'Historical Retrospect', in *JMK*, vol. 13 (pp. 406-7), and, if not coming directly from it then surely not pre-dating it by very much, the fragments printed in vol. 13, under the title 'The Monetary Theory of Production' (pp. 381-406). Vol. 29 adds only one chapter to this material under the title 'A Summary of the Argument So Far'. In all of this there is no sign of what we are looking for.

Nor does there seem to be any sign of the principle of effective demand in any of the chapters (1, 5, and 8) of the second 1933 table of contents which occupy vol. 29, pp. 66-76 (though the fact that this table of contents bears the title 'The General Theory of Employment' is not without interest).

However, to illustrate further the argument about the resemblance these drafts bear to the 1932 lectures, let us consider chapter 5 (under the title 'Fundamental Equations'). Here, Keynes derives the following expressions from his definitions:

(e) $Y = E + Q = C + I = D$

(f) or, $Q = D - E = I - (E - C)$

It is clear that (f) is an exact replica of (d) of section 3 above. Such an expression is not susceptible to being interpreted as the principle of effective demand.

As for the remainder of the miscellaneous draft chapters in vol. 29, there would seem to be little doubt that all date from a later stage. There are some chapters which can be assigned to the December 1933 table of contents and other fragments which cannot be assigned definitively to any table of contents, but which appear to date from later in 1933. However, when it comes to dating precisely the appearance of the principle of effective demand, the evidence that vol. 29 provides is somewhat indecisive, if not inconsistent. On the one hand, in a fragment from an unspecified date in 1933 Keynes could say:

> ... the theory of Neutral Economics assumes that the banking authority maintains the market rate of interest in a state of continuous equality with the natural rate of interest ...; and it investigates what laws will govern the distribution of the rewards of the community's productive resources subject to this assumption. With this limitation in force the volume of output depends solely on the volume of productive resources ... But without this limitation, the volume of output also depends on the relation of the market rate of interest to the natural rate (vol. 29, pp. 118-19).

Equally, in another place Keynes presents the following scenario for possible policy action in the face of disequilibrium:

> Expenditure might be stimulated or retarded by changes in the rate of interest, because ... a lowering of the rate of interest is calculated to stimulate expenditure both on consumption and on investment.' (ibid., p. 95)

In both of these passages it is quite apparent that the 'classical' mechanism involving variations in the rate of interest to restore a balance between savings and investment is still present.

On the other hand, still, according to the editorial comments, from 1933, we find the following much more familiar *General Theory*-type theoretical argument:

> ... it should not need much reflection to perceive that an increase in individual saving may effect, not an increase, but merely a redistribution, of aggregate wealth. The act of individual saving is entirely distinct from the act of individual investment. The two acts are generally performed, as I pointed out in my *Treatise on Money*, by different persons, and there exists no mechanism to establish a necessary or automatic link between them. What is indubitable, namely the equality between the aggregate of individual acts of saving and of individual acts of investment can be satisfied, not only by an individual act of increased saving being balanced by an individual act of increased investment, but also if it is balanced by another individual act of decreased saving. And unless something occurs to increase investment *pari passu*, this is primarily what must of necessity result. For the direct consequence of an individual act of increased saving is to decrease someone's income and, therefore, that someone's savings unless his consumption is diminished; and if his consumption is diminished, the loss of income is passed on to another; and so on. It is true that there would be no resting place, and consequently no position of equilibrium, if everyone, when his income falls, were to reduce his consumption by an equal amount, keeping his individual savings constant. Thus, it is a necessary condition of equilibrium that, when aggregate income falls, the aggregate expenditure on consumption should fall by a less amount than the fall of income. That this condition is fulfilled in practice is, however, in accordance with what our knowledge of popular psychology leads us to expect ... (ibid., p. 103, italics omitted).

It is almost impossible to accept that this passage, expressing so clearly the *General Theory* position, dates from around the same time as the two that precede it. It is clear, however, that by October 1934 Keynes had put the pieces of the puzzle together and then had only to decide on a mode of exposition best suited to his purpose.[5]

Keynes and the Swedish School

Another area upon which vol. 29 sheds some valuable new light is the contrast between Keynes's economics and that of the Swedish School. Correspondence is published between Keynes and both Lindahl and Myrdal.

Towards the end of 1934 Lindahl sent Keynes a copy of a short paper under the title 'A Note on the Dynamic Pricing Problem', indicating that it was to form part of a book of translations of some of his earlier writings (Lindahl, 1939). Unfortunately, Keynes's reply is brief (see vol. 29, p. 131), and all we have is its tantalising conclusion:

> I am inclined to think ... that your way of dealing with time leads to undue complications and will be very difficult either to apply or to generalise about (*JMK*, vol. 29, p. 133).

Given that successive generations of students have since grown up to believe that Lindahl's chief contribution to orthodox economic analysis lies *precisely* in his treatment of 'time', it may surprise some to find Keynes casting doubts on its 'generality'.

Another exchange (still only of one letter from each) between Keynes and Myrdal also appears in vol. 29. To set the context in which this correspondence took place, a little background detail is essential. On receipt of the first instalment of Ohlin's 'Some Notes on the Stockholm Theory of Savings and Investments' (Ohlin, 1937a and 1937b) Keynes had been particularly struck by one passage (Ohlin, 1937a, p. 55 quoted in Keynes's letter to Myrdal, 16 June 1937, in vol. 29, pp. 262-3). He wrote to Ohlin making a request:

> I am particularly intrigued by your references to Wicksell's views. I should like to follow this up. Could you give me references? Particularly where you attribute to him the view that 'investment purchases are not directly governed by the part of income people want to save' (vol. 14, p. 182).

Ohlin replied (16 March 1937) saying that he had asked 'a Swedish friend' to send the information directly to Keynes (see vol. 14, p. 186 for Ohlin's letter). Myrdal's letter is the result (vol. 29, pp. 259-61).

This request by Keynes must surely have been somewhat tongue-in-cheek.

[5] I would speculate that a decisive move occurred either around the end of 1933 or the beginning of 1934 when, for example, Keynes began seriously to re-examine the 'classical' theory of the rate of interest. In vol. 29 there are a series of fragments all devoted to the question of why the rate of interest should influence 'saving *relative* to investment' (pp. 151-7). It is clear, I think, that Keynes could only have been interested in the flaws in this traditional approach after he had seen the directly opposite nature of the principle of effective demand.

By 1937 both *Lectures* (1935) and *Interest and Prices* (1936) had appeared in English and Keynes could scarcely not have read them. Indeed, what he seems to have been attempting to do was to draw for Ohlin a clear line of distinction between those who had discussed the saving-investment nexus in terms of the rate of interest (the 'classics' of the *General Theory* and the Keynes of the *Treatise*) and those for whom the principle of effective demand (level of income) reconciled the saving-investment question. But Ohlin missed the point, and Myrdal's passages from Wicksell were rejected as not relevant. Keynes wrote:

> I do not doubt that Wicksell held the normal old-fashioned view that saving and investment must be equal and that he investigated the mechanism by which, as he supposed, the rate of interest made them equal. Whether he also investigated, as Ohlin alleged, what happens when they are not equal I am not aware. But in any case this is diametrically opposite from my approach ... (vol. 29, p. 262).

However, this is not all there is to be gleaned from this correspondence. First, it is clear that Keynes is insisting here on the same dividing line between the *General Theory* and the 'classics' as I have already outlined. Secondly, since some of the passages Myrdal quotes are based on the 'different decision' interpretation of saving and investment, it is quite apparent that Keynes is rejecting the *sine qua non* status of this time-honoured distinction. Wicksell had certainly made it in *Interest and Prices* (it is implicit in Marshall also) and Keynes worked with it in the *Treatise*. But all to no avail; because whether one adopted the 'different decisions, different people, different times' distinction or not, one could never reach the principle of effective demand without abandoning the doctrine that the rate of interest influenced, as Keynes had put it in the *Treatise*, 'saving *relative* to investment'.

PART THREE

Criticism

11

The analytical foundations of monetarism

John Eatwell

The nature of the relationship between the general price level and the quantity of money (variously defined) has been a matter of dispute throughout the history of economics. Failure to resolve the debate suggests a failure to define in a precise manner, or even to agree upon, the issues at stake. This failure is evident in the debates surrounding the modern revival of monetarism. Writers who claim that the issues are fundamentally theoretical are opposed by those who argue that it is empirical assumptions which divide the protagonists; and analyses of short-run dynamics – always a fruitful environment for the *ad hoc* – are counterposed to studies of 'long-run equilibrium'. In this chapter I will attempt to elucidate some of the issues by examining the theoretical foundations of monetarism. Paradoxically, these foundations do not lie in the realm of monetary theory, but in theories of the determination of real output.

Beginning from the 'equation of exchange', or 'monetary identity', $MV \equiv PY$, it is evident that even if the velocity of circulation may be assumed to be relatively stable, determined in the longer run by institutional phenomena, a direct behavioural link between M and P alone requires that Y be independently determined. Thus the classical version of Say's Law, in which the level of output was determined by the level of accumulation and the social productivity of labour, given that saving and investment were *assumed* equal, was the basis of classical monetarism (on the classical theory of output, see Garegnani, Chapter 2 above; and on classical monetary theory see Green, 1982). Similarly, the neoclassical version of Say's Law, in which the level of output is determined in the establishment of a market-clearing set of equilibrium prices, is the basis of modern monetarism:

> ... The price level is then the joint outcome of the monetary forces determining nominal income and the real forces determining real income ...
> ... I shall regard long-run equilibrium as determined by the earlier quantity theory model plus the Walrasian equations of general equilibrium (Friedman, 1974a, pp. 27, 48).

The proposition 'that changes in the quantity of money as such *in the long run* have a negligible effect on real income' (Friedman, 1974a, p. 27) is not in itself sufficient to sustain a typically 'monetarist' position, for the causation may as well run from price to money as from money to price – indeed this was the crux of much classical debate[1] – but it is a *necessary* condition for subsequent development of monetarist propositions. Thus examination of the characteristics of the theory of real output espoused in monetarist writings is a *pre-requisite* for consideration of the theoretical status of monetarist propositions.

An important corollary to any such examination must be consideration of the characteristics of the equilibrium level of real output as a position to which the economy tends to gravitate, and hence with respect to which fluctuations in economic variables, both monetary and real, are defined. Thus not only does Friedman argue that the quantity theory will hold in 'long-run equilibrium', but he also constructs his analysis of the short-run dynamics of nominal income in terms of the deviations of particular parameters from their 'permanent' or long-run values (see, for example, Friedman, 1974a, pp. 48-61). The short run is dependent upon, and derived from, the long-run position. The long-run equilibrium is thus the key to the entire system, and Friedman defends ably the long-run conception against the charge that '... a long run constructed to track the ultimate consequences of anything is a never-never land' (Tobin and Buiter, 1976, p. 273):

> The long-run equilibrium in which, as I put it, 'all anticipations are realised' and that is determined by 'the earlier quantity theory plus the Walrasian equations of general equilibrium' is not a state that is assumed to exist in practice. It is a logical construct that defines the norm or trend from which the actual world is always deviating but to which it is tending to return or about which it tends to fluctuate. The hypothesis that the logical construct does specify the norm or trend in this sense is entirely compatible with the existence of uncertainty, just as the hypothesis that $s = 1/2\, gt^2$ specifies the law of falling bodies is entirely compatible with the existence of air (Friedman, 1974b, p. 150).

Friedman nowhere spells out what he means by 'long-run equilibrium', but it is evident from his writings that he is referring to the Marshallian conception (Marshall, 1920, Book V, chapters 3 and 5). Nor does he attempt to justify this characterisation of the 'norm or trend' of the economy as a persistent centre of gravitation; being apparently content to rest on the arguments built up throughout the development of economic theory from Smith's conception of 'natural price' (Smith, 1776, Book 1, chapter 7) to Marshall's long-run normal equilibrium. But in the past forty years the notion of equilibrium used in economic analysis has undergone a fundamental, though little noticed, change (Garegnani, Chapter 7 above; Milgate, 1979), and confusion

[1] Kaldor's argument (1970) that the money supply is 'endogenous', not 'exogenous', is a revival of the classical controversy.

over the specification of equilibrium may, at least in part, contribute to the confusion of monetary debate.

The theoretical foundations of monetarism consist of both a theory of real output *and* a clearly specified conception of equilibrium. It will be argued below that much confusion has been created by the fact that many of the protagonists in the monetary debates, while sharing the same theory of real output, have adopted different conceptions of equilibrium, and that mutual criticism based on various aspects of the same theory has been erroneously interpreted as being derived from different theoretical bases. In the light of these fundamentals, some other disputed issues, such as the proposition that the real equilibrium of the economy is homogeneous of degree zero in money stock and prices, become of secondary importance.[2]

Theory

In arguing that many[3] of those involved in the current debate share the same *theory* I do not mean that they characterise the economy in terms of the same 'model'. What they share is the broad view that prices and quantities in a market economy are determined by the balance of the forces of supply and demand, expressed more or less formally as the market resolution of individual utility maximisation subject to the constraints of endowment and technology. Let us label this broad view 'neoclassical'. Particular neoclassical models may take either aggregative or disaggregative forms, may comprise different specifications of the endowment or of arguments of the utility functions, or may include a wide range of 'auxiliary constraints' (Samuelson, 1947, pp. 30-9) such as sticky prices, probabilistic adjustment or search speeds, uncertainty, misinformation, and so on.

Such differing formulations of the same base theory seem to have been responsible for some of the 'non-communication' in monetary debates. An example is the comparison of, on the one hand, a variety of models in which normal output is 'given' by real forces, and, on the other hand, models in which output is determined by a 'Keynesian' *IS-LM* mechanism. Yet these models are essentially the same. Modigliani (1944) has shown that by defining the liquidity preference schedule as a demand curve for money,

[2] The role of the 'homogeneity postulate' in the debates is most ambiguous. While Friedman appears generally to ignore the problem, he relies heavily on the Pigou effect to refute Keynesian propositions on the long-run level of employment. Hahn (1971) and Tobin (1974) both cite the failure of the homogeneity postulate as important theoretical evidence against Friedman, and yet attempt to contest his analysis on other grounds. The ambiguity seems to derive from a feeling that the effects of non-homogeneity do not significantly alter the results of the standard neoclassical model in which homogeneity is presumed and equilibrium prices and outputs are determined by real forces.

[3] Kaldor (1970) and Cripps (1977) are exceptions to this generalisation. It should, however, be noted that neither Kaldor nor Cripps present a critique of the theory of real output used by Friedman. Instead they either contrast Friedman's monetary theory with their own, or attempt to refute his propositions on institutional and empirical grounds.

and the marginal efficiency of capital schedule as the demand function for investment, the Keynesian system may, in the absence of sticky wages, be split into real and monetary parts. The real equations determine the equilibrium output, real wage and interest rate, and the monetary equation determines the level of nominal wages and prices – resurrecting the Wicksellian image of an equilibrium determined by the interaction of real forces mediated through monetary flows. Since the real forces determine a market-clearing equilibrium, factors of production will be fully employed (or free goods). This conclusion may be modified in those models in which information is transmitted by 'search' as well as prices, and the natural rate of unemployment may not be zero (Phelps, 1970).

So the independence of the determinants of real output from monetary phenomena depends upon the absence of 'stickiness' of prices; a plausible assumption in a long-run context.[4] But it is only this stickiness which differentiates monetarist and *IS-LM* models.

A somewhat different confusion has been introduced into the debate by Hahn (1980), who refers to the 'Friedmanite' class of models in which price-determined market clearing occurs, and a class of models of the Clower (1956) or conjectural equilibrium variety (Hahn, 1978), as *different* theories:

> ... the proposition that monetary policy that is systematic cannot affect the natural values of real variables is essentially related to the Walrasian model. ... But the Walrasian model does not capture any of the market failures macroeconomists have been concerned with for forty-five years. The argument must thus be about appropriate models of the whole economy, and that strikes me as largely a theoretical problem. (Hahn, 1980, p. 6).

But Hahn does not propose a new *theory* in the sense that the apparatus characterising the behaviour of a market economy in terms of maximisation subject to constraint is to be abandoned. Instead a number of imperfections are incorporated into the Walrasian framework, and the same type of equilibrium is then sought. This equilibrium may not be market-clearing in the sense that for a variety of reasons agents offer or demand quantities other than those which would correspond to equilibrium in a system in which the imperfections were not present. And an economy in such an 'imperfect' equilibrium *might* respond to a variety of policy measures, fiscal or monetary, in quite a different manner than would an economy without 'auxiliary constraints'.

From the catalogue of 'imperfect' equilibria Hahn proposes a 'conjectural equilibrium' as an alternative to 'Walrasian equilibrium', and argues that what the

[4] Tobin and Buiter (1976) present a model in which the flexible-price, full-employment equilibrium position of the economy is altered by a change in the state's fiscal policy financed without any change in the money supply. By so doing they demonstrate that the equilibrium is not independent of the structure of spending decisions by one of the economic agents. They do *not* demonstrate that the real equilibrium is dependent on the supply of money *given* the spending preferences of all agents, including the state.

> ... monetarist view depends on is a unique Walrasian equilibrium and denial of the possibility of rational expectations conjectural non-Walrasian equilibria. It seems to me I have now made the case for the view that quite fundamental theoretical matters are at stake. If further study should show that the notion of rational non-Walrasian equilibrium is not viable, then there would be a great strengthening of the view that systematic monetary policy is ineffective. If, on the other hand, it survives the detailed study it is now rather widely receiving, rather more old-fashioned Keynesian views will survive without violating the axiom of rationality and greed (Hahn, 1980, p. 10).

But to refer to these models as differing in theoretical fundamentals is profoundly misleading. The theoretical apparatus is essentially unchanged. What is changed is the method by which price signals communicate adequate information concerning demands and offers, and, indeed, how they are interpreted. Hence the equilibrium will depend on the *degree* to which one level of communication/interpretation predominates rather than another; i.e. the *empirical* specification of the model.

So the underlying model of real output adopted by both Friedman and most of his critics is based on the orthodox neoclassical theory of value, output and employment and variants thereof. Differing conclusions are reached by incorporating a variety of essentially arbitrary imperfections and assumptions about speeds of adjustment. But consideration of the relative importance of different versions takes the argument 'out of the realm of those questions that can be considered by *a priori* considerations of internal consistency and logical validity, and into the realm of those questions that can be decided only by empirical considerations of the actual magnitudes of the relevant economic parameters' (Patinkin, 1974, pp. 130-1).

Equilibrium

> I suspect that our difference is a by product of my Marshallian approach to theory ... versus Tobin's Walrasian approach (Friedman, 1976, p. 311).

The context in which Friedman expressed his suspicion was in arguing that a fundamental issue in the evaluation of monetarist propositions is whether a failure to satisfy theoretical conditions *perfectly* is of any practical importance. His identification of his own position as 'Marshallian' refers to the general method of long-period equilibrium, in which the determinants of long-period positions are the dominant and persistent forces of the economy, and specific imperfections or chance events are the causes of short-run fluctuations around the long-run position.

The origins of this method are to be found in the *Wealth of Nations*. Smith was faced with the dual task of characterising a market economy at such a level of abstraction that statements of general validity might be made about its behaviour, *and* of building a theory to provide the material for such statements.

The former task required the identification of the objective force in a market economy which endows its operations with systematic character – the force of competition. Competition creates the tendency toward a uniform wage for each category of labour, a uniform rent for each quality of land, and a uniform rate of profit on the value of capital invested in each particular line as capitalists adjust the composition of the capital stock in search of maximum profits. If these uniformities were established then commodities would sell at their natural prices. Since in reality the full effects of competition are disrupted by chance events or specific (as opposed to general) circumstances, commodities will sell at their market prices, which competition will always push toward natural prices. Market prices are concrete phenomena and not susceptible to theoretical generalisation.

Theoretical generalisation involves the abstraction from the complexity of reality of those forces which are believed to be dominant, and the combination of these forces into a formal model. It is obvious that except by a fluke the solution of the model will not determine the actual magnitudes of the variables under consideration since, by definition, so many concrete forces have been excluded by abstraction. But the implicit assumption is that these forces are not dominant, and hence the determined magnitudes will be centres of gravitation to fluctuations of the actual magnitudes.

Thus Smith's conception of natural price linked the empirical characteristics of a competitive market to the necessity of theoretical abstraction.

Smith's concepts of natural and market price were refined by Ricardo and Marx, and then adopted by the early neoclassicals. Natural prices were redefined as long-run equilibrium prices. A significant modification made at this time was that between the abstract long-period and the concrete market price was introduced a further abstract notion, that of short-period equilibrium. However, this new notion was generally confined to partial equilibrium analyses where its dubious status as a centre of gravitation was of relatively little significance and where it might be assumed, *ceteris paribus*, that the rest of the economy is in long-run equilibrium. Thus the short run was defined as a specific deviation from the long run; i.e. had no independent existence other than as a deviation from the long-run normal position.

It is to the long-run normal equilibrium that Friedman consistently refers in expositions of his theory. In this context it is quite reasonable for him to regard imperfections as being essentially short-run phenomena which will be overcome by the long-run force of competition, and the effects of which will be confined to fluctations around the long-run position. Hence although perfect conditions are never fully attained 'as a practical matter sufficiently correct results will be obtained by treating them *as if* they were perfectly satisfied ... I continue to believe that the fundamental differences between us are empirical, not theoretical; that what we really differ on are precisely what effects are and are not "minor", not on whether an effect is precisely zero' (Friedman, 1976, pp. 310, 312).

However, Friedman has failed to notice that the differences between himself and his Walrasian critics possess a further dimension, for the Walrasians are basing their critique on a quite different conception of equilibrium.[5] As Garegnani (Chapter 7 above) has demonstrated, a change in the concept of equilibrium used in economics took place in the 1930s. Under the pressure of Keynes's theoretical critique of the foundations of orthodox theory, and of some partially perceived difficulties in the theory of capital, the notion of long-run equilibrium and the associated normal prices and general rate of profit were abandoned, and replaced by an equilibrium characterised as a temporal sequence of general short-period equilibria, displaying, consequentially, no general rate of profit. Originated by Hayek and Lindahl (see Milgate, 1979) the new notion of equilibrium was introduced into the English language literature by Hicks (1939). The simplest form of this intertemporal equilibrium is that incorporating perfect foresight and complete futures markets presented by Debreu (1959).

No longer confined to partial equilibrium analysis under the protective umbrella of the *ceteris paribus* assumption the new short period, defined purely in terms of market clearing without reference to any long period, purportedly defines the temporal path the economy will actually adopt. The basic characteristic of a short-period equilibrium is that it contains all the information (auxiliary constraints) which define it as a short period *within* the determination of the equilibrium. Since the intertemporal equilibrium is in this sense 'all-enveloping', the idea of imperfections causing fluctuations around a short-period equilibrium does not make any sense – the equilibrium is fully defined, warts and all.

Thus the new neoclassical economics of intertemporal equilibrium does not contain the vocabulary of the old, which specified centres of gravitation and fluctuations around them. A short-period equilibrium is something from which the economy moves away, not toward. So Tobin and Buiter refer to a long-period position as a never-never land, and Hahn wishes to incorporate all the imperfections of his conjectural analysis into the specification of the equilibrium rather than having them determine short-period fluctuations around the long-period normal position. In these circumstances Friedman's old-fashioned notions of approximation, and 'not quite perfect' models make no sense. Models and equilibria are completely specified.

Evaluation

We have, therefore, established two distinct, though interrelated, sources of confusion in contemporary monetary debates:

(1) The belief of particular writers that they are advancing different theories

[5] As will be evident from what follows, the term 'Walrasian' refers to modern (post-1939) general equilibrium theorists, *not* to Walras himself, whose concept of equilibrium was the traditional long-period position characterised by a uniform 'rate of net income'.

of the economy when, in fact, their theories are fundamentally the same. This has led not only to failure to communicate but also has severely diminished the effectiveness of critiques of the monetarist position.

(2) Writers have used different conceptions of equilibrium, which in turn led to quite different interpretations of the role of imperfections in short-run and long-run analyses.

As has already been noted, Friedman argues that the theory of real output underlying his monetary theory is that in the long run output and employment will be at their natural level, i.e. at 'the level that would be ground out by the Walrasian system of general equilibrium equations, provided there is embedded in them the actual characteristics of labour and commodity markets, including market imperfections ...' (Friedman, 1968, p. 8). An immediate neo-Walrasian reaction to this argument would be to point out that it is well known that no proof of the existence of equilibrium in an economy with imperfect markets is available (Hahn and Neild, 1980; Roberts and Sonnenschein, 1977). But this would miss the point.

To avoid confusion and provide the strongest ground for Friedman's propositions, let us suppose the economy to be perfectly competitive with fully flexible wages and prices manipulated by a Walrasian auctioneer. Friedman could then argue that the long-run Walrasian equilibrium with associated outputs, prices and general rate of profit would be established by the real forces of individual utility maximisation subject to the constraints of endowment and technology. Given this real equilibrium then he could with confidence set about building models of the short-run dynamics of nominal income and of the relationship between the quantity of money, the value of nominal income, and the long-run price level.

But he would be wrong.

For as a result of the work on the theory of capital done in the last two decades, we now know that it is not logically possible to solve a neoclassical system for the determination of long-run equilibrium (Robinson, 1953; Garegnani, 1960; Sraffa, 1960; Symposium, 1966; Garegnani, 1970). Put more generally, outside a one-commodity world, there exists no logical foundation for the proposition that long-period quantities, prices and rate of profit are determined by the forces of supply and demand. This logical failure applies to all versions of neoclassical theory, Austrian, Marshallian, Walrasian and Wicksellian (Garegnani, 1960, Part 2).

Since this point is less familiar in the context of Walrasian systems it may prove useful to express it in modern terms. We begin with the specification of a private enterprise economy by Debreu (1959, p. 79) in terms of preferences, endowments and technology – the endowments of capital goods being each specified in terms of their own physical units. Since the work of Wald (1936) it has been known that the system can only be solved for economically meaningful values of quantities and prices if it is expressed in terms of inequalities. In particular, the price of any producible commodity will, in equilibrium, be *less than* or equal to, its cost of production. If the price of a capital good is, in equilibrium, less than its cost of production, the rate of return over cost on that good will be less than the general rate of return ruling in that time period on the capital goods for which the equality holds. There is no general rate of profit and changes in the composition of the capital stock would lead to higher profits – a typical short-period situation.

Expressed in terms of inequalities the system solves. Now impose the condition that in each elementary time period there be a uniform general rate of profit (not necessarily the same rate in different periods), i.e. that the demand prices of all capital goods be equal to their costs of production. This amounts to adding a new set of constraints to an already determinate system. The model will be overdetermined and will not solve.

This general failure of neoclassical long-period models may be expressed in a variety of different ways. In the early stages of the capital theory debate attention was focussed on the successful demonstration that no logical foundation can be provided for the existence of an elastic, well-behaved demand schedule for capital as a function of the general rate of interest. Since such a schedule provided the logical foundation for the marginal efficiency of capital schedule, the critique removes all logical status from the *IS-LM* models (Garegnani, Chapter 2 above). Similarly, it is not possible to construct a consistent analysis of the labour market in terms of supply and demand, i.e. it cannot be shown that real wages and a long-run natural rate of employment (and unemployment) are determined by supply and demand. In orthodox neoclassical analysis the demand curve for labour was derived from the possibility of substitution of labour with other factors of production, including capital. The inadequacies of the neoclassical theory of capital are thus replicated in the inadequacies of the neoclassical theory of the labour market.

It may be concluded that there is no logically consistent neoclassical model of long-period employment, real output, relative prices and the general rate of profit.

The logical failure of neoclassical long-run analysis provided a major impulse to the abandonment of the notion of long-run equilibrium and its replacement by intertemporal equilibrium. The proof of the existence of intertemporal equilibrium is, on its own terms, logically sound.

This raises the question of whether Friedman's analysis may be based on intertemporal equilibrium rather than long-period equilibrium. Unfortunately, it cannot. A central aspect of Friedman's analysis is that the real output determined independently of monetary forces should be the centre of gravitation to any fluctuation of the economy brought about by unanticipated changes in the quantity of money. The intertemporal equilibrium is not satisfactory on this count. First, as Hahn and Neild (1980) point out, with respect to the stability of the mathematical functions defining the equilibrium 'absolutely no satisfactory theoretical answer is available' (see also Arrow and Hahn, 1971, chapter 12). Secondly, and more important, quite apart from the characterisation of the mathematical functions, the intertemporal equilibrium is not a centre of gravitation toward which the economy would tend and around which it would fluctuate. Any chance fluctuation away from a given sequence of short-period equilibria will establish a new sequence; it will not set up pressures pushing the system back to the old sequence. The old long-period notion derived coherence from the fact that it defined a centre of gravitation in terms of the general outcome of capitalistic competition. The new intertemporal equilibrium lacks coherence because while, on the one hand, it purports to define the equilibrium of a competitive economy, on the other hand it is a point from which any chance deviation will be reinforced, not counteracted, by competitive forces. Thus despite its logical rigour, the Arrow-Debreu general equilibrium model cannot serve as a basis for Friedman's monetary analysis, or, for that matter, of any analysis of a competitive market economy (for a full discussion of this point see Eatwell, 1982).

Conclusion

I have concentrated on Friedman's monetary analysis not only because he is the most prominent proponent of monetarist ideas, but also because he clearly regards his work as a serious foundation for the analysis of economic policy and hence the issue of the concept of equilibrium as a centre of gravitation is important to him. It would be quite possible to erect formally consistent monetarist models on the basis of Arrow-Debreu determination of real output, but such models could not be advanced as the basis for analysis of the short and long-run dynamics of market economies. I should perhaps emphasise that the issue is not simply one of formal mathematical stability. It is true that even in an economy with a single capital good and many other non-reproducible factors in which long-run (uniform rate of profit) and Arrow-Debreu equilibria are identical, no general proof of stability is available (as Tobin and Buiter, 1976, show), and that this severely weakens all neoclassical analysis. But my point is more general. Given the objective and omnipresent force of competition, the long-run position characterises the centre of gravitation established by that force. The same competitive forces ensure that the intertemporal equilibrium cannot be a centre of gravitation.

Friedman is left, therefore, with two unpalatable options: either to adopt the Arrow-Debreu framework and hence eschew any pretence of policy relevance; or to locate his analyses overtly in single-produced-means-of-production worlds, such as that of Solow (1970), from which they cannot escape, and within which it is extremely difficult to provide any rationale for the existence of money and of monetary policy.

Some final comment should perhaps be made on the 'wealth of empirical evidence', which, it is argued, supports monetarist hypotheses. Those who wish to appeal to such evidence should take suitable warning from the 'production function fiasco'. Despite the fact that the theoretical foundations of the aggregate production function were known to be extremely weak (the one-commodity world once again) literally thousands of studies produced the 'empirical evidence' that such functions 'fitted' the characteristics of a variety of economies. It took Fisher's (1969, 1971) demonstration that the studies were based on a statistical artifact to call a halt to the production of nonsense. Shaikh (1975) later demonstrated that the statistical specification created the 'good fits' as an *algebraic* necessity.

Economists should learn to take their theory seriously before attempting to sustain logically inconsistent theories with empirical evidence. As Friedman himself argued in his Nobel Prize Lecture (quoting Pierre S. du Pont):

> Bad logicians have committed more involuntary crimes than bad men have done intentionally. (Friedman, 1977, p. 471).

12

Malinvaud on Keynes

Richard Kahn

Malinvaud's book, *The Theory of Unemployment Reconsidered,* is likely to have a great success. There is something in it to please everyone – Walrasian equilibrium, unemployment that can be reduced by cutting real wages, unemployment that can be reduced by raising real wages, workers who prefer leisure to earnings, savings equal to investment and prices equal to marginal cost – all presented in an ostensibly precise and elegant model.[1] But the reader needs to keep his wits about him to follow the intricacies of the argument.

1. Introduction

The conundrum that Edmond Malinvaud sets himself is to see what modifications to Walrasian theory (which he calls classical) have to be made in order for it to deal with the Keynesian problem of unemployment:

> The classical teaching, according to which prices quickly react to excess supplies or demands, is more and more inadequate for short-run macroeconomic analysis as we move into ever-higher degrees of organisation of society (p. 9).

A number of economists have been working on these lines in recent years. Malinvaud gives them full credit. Perhaps the most important article is 'Neo-Keynesian disequilibrium theory' by Jean-Pascal Benassy (*Review of Economic Studies*, October 1975) which also contains a useful bibliography. But Malin-

* A review of Edmond Malinvaud, *The Theory of Unemployment Reconsidered*, 1977 (3 lectures delivered for the Yrjö Jahnsson Foundation, Helsinki). Reprinted from *Cambridge Journal of Economics*, 1977, **1**, 375-88. I would like to express my gratitude to the editors of the *Cambridge Journal of Economics* for their generous help, and also to Robert Neild and Dick Goodwin.

[1] The problem of inflation is not faced: 'It is well understood that static equilibrium analysis has limited scope for a theory of inflation. But I do not claim to discuss here mainly the theory of inflation' (p. 32, n. 27).

vaud's book is a highly original presentation – far more than a synthesis of earlier contributions.

Malinvaud's proposal is to deal with the problem by assuming fixed prices and rationing:

> Hence, the proper theoretical framework is one in which supplies are rationed both on the labour market and on the goods market. Moreover the two types of rationing are so tightly interdependent that, in order to study policies against involuntary unemployment, one feels justified in concentrating attention exclusively on the formation of demand on the goods market (p. 4).

This is quite inadequate, for there are many differences between a Walrasian model and a Keynesian one besides the speed of reaction of prices.

First of all, the modern version of the Walrasian model is set up to deal with instantaneous equilibrium in an economy where there are given 'endowments' of 'factors', while Keynes's theory deals with a world where production and accumulation are going on through time. Secondly, in the Walrasian model, individuals are free to decide how much work it is worth their while to do. The return per unit of work (corresponding to the real-wage rate) is determined by the demand for commodities and the amount of work offered, while, in the Keynesian world, the number of men to be employed is decided by industrial firms in the light of the state of demand. Moreover, the amount of work per man is fixed by collective agreements, say an eight hour day and a 300 day year. This may be changed from time to time. But, at any one moment, one agreement is in force and when there is a good deal of unemployment, a man who takes more leisure than is provided in the collective agreement will soon be sacked. Thirdly, and most important of all, in the Walrasian world the equality of saving and investment is attained by variation in the rate of interest (and other appropriate prices), whereas in Keynes's analysis the equality is attained by variation in the level of income. Investment, which determines saving, is itself determined by a process quite different from the Walrasian notion of utility maximisation subject to constraint.

Malinvaud's conception of 'rationing' runs through the whole argument, but it is used in a sense all his own. When industry is working up to capacity, consumers are said to be rationed:

> The immediate impact of changes in demand or supply is to be found in order-books, waiting lines, inventories, delivery dates, output, hours of work, employment. ... Such quantitative adjustments are the first signals of changes in the demand-supply relationship. Shifts in relative prices come later and in a less apparent way (p. 9).

Where there is less than full employment, workers are said to be rationed. It is true that employers can often pick and choose whom to employ. This might be described as rationing jobs. But here the workers are all alike, the 'ration' of employment is simply the number of workers employed. When 'firms do not produce more because of lack of effective demand' (p. 31), they are said to be 'rationed in the goods market':

> In business surveys, firms are regularly asked whether they would produce more if demand was higher, i.e. whether they are rationed in the market for output (p. 33).

This unnatural use of language clouds the whole argument, but with care and patience the reader can work out a commonsense interpretation of what it all means.

2. The basic model

In a non-Walrasian economy, with firms employing labour for money wages, the real wage is governed by the price of consumer goods. Malinvaud distinguishes two cases, one *Keynesian*, where a higher level of real wages brings about a higher level of employment, and one, which he calls *classical*, where higher real wages are associated with less employment. He regards the Keynesian case as the most prevalent and it is the less incomprehensible. I therefore start by examining this case in terms of his model.

He states:

> It concerns the operations during one given period, which is analysed independently of past and future periods (p. 38).

But this is not accurate. At the beginning of the period there is a stock of plant and of wealth which must have been inherited from the past, and investment and savings are going on during the period, which are affected by expectations of the future and will, in turn, affect the future.

The economy is capitalist. But little attention is paid to the organisation of production or of society. There are capitalists who seem rather amorphous. They produce goods; they make profits; but they do not appear to consume. There are no rentiers as such. The only other class consists of workers, who are sometimes called consumers. Each worker owns a certain amount of wealth at the beginning of the period. Employed workers may save. The unemployed live on their accumulated wealth.

> This neglects the public transfer payment to the unemployed, which will not be considered in the present prototype (p. 45, n. 5).

Wealth is held in the form of money, on which no interest is received. Some of the wealth takes the form of shares, but the references to shares are cryptic: they play no active role in the analysis.

> This suggests that consumers have no other income than wages. But I do not really mean this: the implicit assumption is rather that non-labour incomes are exogenous, i.e. independent of the employment level; this is certainly an ad-

missible hypothesis to make in a first approximation of short-run income distribution (p. 39).

There is a government and an investment sector, the expenditures of which are aggregated in the exposition. The firms in the investment sub-sector are free to employ as much labour as they please. The government can make what expenditure it pleases. There is no taxation. All profits are saved. Net savings of the workers are equal to the excess of government expenditure and investment over profits, in accordance with the Keynesian principle that, given the propensity to save, the level of income is such that the flow of saving is equal to the budget deficit and the rate of investment.

It is convenient to suppose that money takes the exclusive form of bank deposits (although Malinvaud does not adopt that use of language). The firms deposit their profits and the workers their savings. The banks' deposits are equal to their loans to the government and the producers of capital goods. The treatment is based on the assumption that government expenditure has

> no utility for individuals; this is of course a simplification, but it is admissible for the study of short-term equilibrium. In any case removing it is not likely to change the conclusions reached here (p. 64, n. 15).

As utility plays an important role in Malinvaud's analysis, the removal of this assumption would make a great deal of difference.

3. The determination of employment

I now turn to the main topic – the determination of employment in the consumption-good sector. Malinvaud treats employment in the government and investment sectors as exogenously given.

It is convenient to take the money wage per worker as given. Malinvaud prefers to take both money wages and the price of the commodity as variable. But diagrams are more perspicuous if the money wage is taken as given, with the price of the commodity on the y axis and the level of employment in the consumer-good sector on the x axis. A lower price represents a higher real wage rate.

Since there are no other variable inputs, the prime cost of the output of the consumer-good sector is equal to its wage bill.

The flow of expenditure on consumer goods is the wage bill of both sectors *minus* saving by employed workers *plus* expenditure out of wealth of the unemployed. Since prime cost is equal to wages in the consumption-good sector, it follows that the flow of profit on the sale of the consumer good is equal to the wage bill of the government and investment sector, *minus* saving out of wages in both sectors *plus* expenditure by the unemployed.

The higher the price of the commodity, the lower the real wage and the lower the real value of workers' wealth held in money. The lower wealth, taken by itself, means a higher rate of saving. The lower real wage means a lower rate of saving. The lower level of employment means, taken by itself, a lower rate of saving. The higher level of unemployment which goes with it means more spending out of wealth. Purely in order to simplify the argument, I assume that these four influences on the rate of saving – one in the positive direction and three in the negative – cancel out. The object is to represent in a two-dimensional diagram the relationship between the real wage and employment in the consumption-good sector with a given money wage bill and given employment in the government and investment sectors. Otherwise it would be necessary in order to allow for the relationship between employment and saving in the consumption sector to use a third dimension.

Since the amount of saving by workers is independent of the level of employment, the flow of profits in the consumption-good sector is independent of the level of employment in that sector. The relationship between the real wage and employment in the consumption-good sector can then be represented by a rectangular hyperbola between the y axis and a horizontal line running above the x axis at the level of the money wage. At each point on the curve the area of the rectangle represents the flow of profits, which is the same at all prices. The profit per man employed is determined by the price of the commodity.

Figure 1

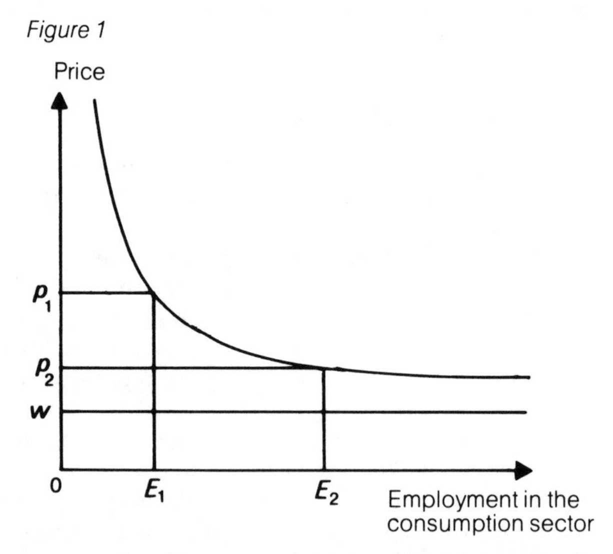

There are no overhead costs, no interest charges, no taxation, no uncertainty about future sales, and Malinvaud admits to being quite vague about the constitution and policy of firms. There is no theory here to account for the level of profit margins. We must follow Malinvaud in taking the price of the commodity (relatively to the money wage) to be arbitrarily given.

However, we can compare different prices. The higher is the price, the lower is the real wage and the lower the level of employment. This is shown in Figure 1. The level of employment, E_1, corresponding to the higher price, p_1, is less than E_2, corresponding to the lower price. This model illustrates some Keynesian arguments. The greater is the propensity to save, the lower is the level of employment at a given price (the curve is shifted to the left). The higher is the level of government expenditure and investment, the greater is the amount of employment in the consumption-good sector (the curve is shifted to the right).

But this is a very thin representation of Keynes's theory. There is no mention of liquidity preference, no effect of uncertainty or of expectations about the future. The level of investment is arbitrarily fixed without any discussion of how it is determined. The only scope for policy is to vary government expenditure. However, the model brings out one clear point: in a given state of effective demand, a reduction in profit margins would raise real wages and increase employment. It is not clear whether this is really the moral which Malinvaud intended to draw.

4. Marginal costs

Malinvaud includes another element in his story that is incompatible both with Walras and with Keynes – an aggregate marginal cost curve, based in effect, on the assumption of perfect competition.[2]

> A theory aiming at explaining the short-term determination of unemployment must take as given the equipment of firms. For each producer there is then a strict functional relationship between labour input and output; this assumption has indeed been made in section 8 of the first lecture. More precisely, we may say that the different types of available equipment differ with respect to the labour productivity achieved when they are used; they differ within each firm as well as between firms ...
>
> The easy hypothesis to make is that the allocation of labour and the distribution of sales among firms are efficient, i.e. do result in an overall efficient use of available equipment as they would if the price system was working under ideal conditions ...
>
> To go from this principle to a definite mathematical representation, one needs only to define the existing stock of equipment with its distribution according to productive capacity and labour requirements. A precise identification of firms is no longer necessary, since the most productive equipment will be used first irrespective of which firms use it (pp. 49-51).

Evidently, Malinvaud assumes a rising supply curve determined by marginal cost as in an old-fashioned textbook.

To follow his story we require a different diagram. With given money-wage rates, there is a supply curve of output in the consumer-good sector

[2] There was an element of 'rising supply price' in Keynes's aggregate supply function, but it is not essential to the main argument. It was criticised on empirical grounds as soon as the *General Theory* was published.

with marginal costs rising with employment, starting from the level of average prime costs with the most efficient plant. The amount of labour taken on is now governed by the price of the commodity, the real-wage rate being equal to output per man on the plant which is marginal at a particular level of demand. This relationship is depicted by the supply curve *S* in Figure 2. The 'demand curve' *D* relates the price level and the level of effective demand. For ease of exposition I assume (as Malinvaud does in the Appendix in his book) that the labour of each worker is fixed. The level of consumption compatible with full employment is indicated by OE^*.

With any given flow of money expenditure on the commodity, there is a price (and real wage) at which supply and demand are equal. There is then no 'rationing' in the goods market (see Figure 2). This amount of employment in the consumer-good sector is governed by the plant available and the flow of expenditure, being such that the price of the commodity is equal to its marginal cost. Profits, or rather quasi-rents, in the consumer-good sector, are determined by the excess of marginal cost over average cost at the corresponding level of output. Malinvaud notes that a rise in the flow of expenditure (a shift of *D* to the right), which increases employment and lowers real wages, involves a conflict of interest. Workers already employed have a lower income, while there is a gain to the unemployed who now get jobs (p. 64).

Figure 2

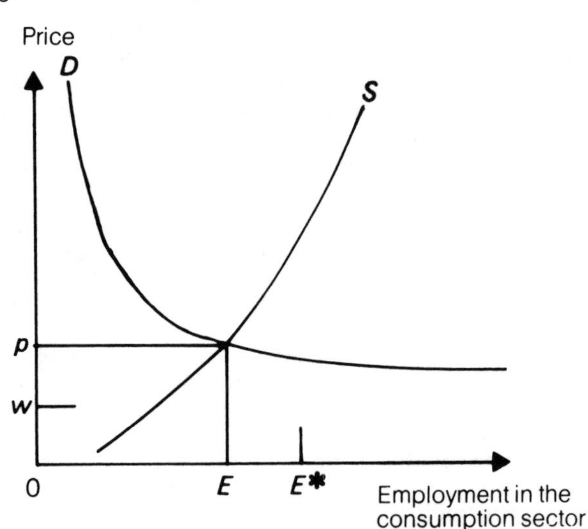

Malinvaud devotes little attention to the possibility of equilibrium with the price equal to marginal cost. For him, the real wage is an arbitrary independent variable:

Given the short-run price rigidities that actually exist, the theory under con-

> sideration here is justified in assuming full price rigidity, i.e. in working with models in which prices and wage-rates are exogenous (pp. 11 and 12).

He considers a number of cases. In his first case, the price is fixed above (and the real wage below) the level at which supply and demand would be in equilibrium; see p_1 in Figure 3. This case is described by Malinvaud as Keynesian, in which a higher real wage would result in a higher level of employment.

Malinvaud's second case is what he calls the classical position. This is not classical in the sense of being a Walrasian equilibrium. It is a case in which the real wage has been set above the level that equates demand to supply (the price is too low). Now employment, and therefore output, in the consumer-good sector is restricted by the high real-wage rate – see p_2 in Figure 3. There is a violent excess of demand for the commodity.

> In order to know whether a classical equilibrium holds, we must check that there is an excess of supply of labour and an excess demand for goods (p. 79).

Malinvaud regards this position as rare, but it should rather be described as impossible. Anyone who could succeed in buying some goods at the fixed price would resell them at a higher price and take a profit for himself. Workers would have to buy the commodity at black-market prices. The real wage could not be kept at the high fixed level.

There is also a case (which Malinvaud calls Walrasian equilibrium) in which both demand and supply just happen to be sufficient to maintain full employment. The level of effective demand is such that the plant which is marginal when the whole labour force is employed gives an output per man

Figure 3

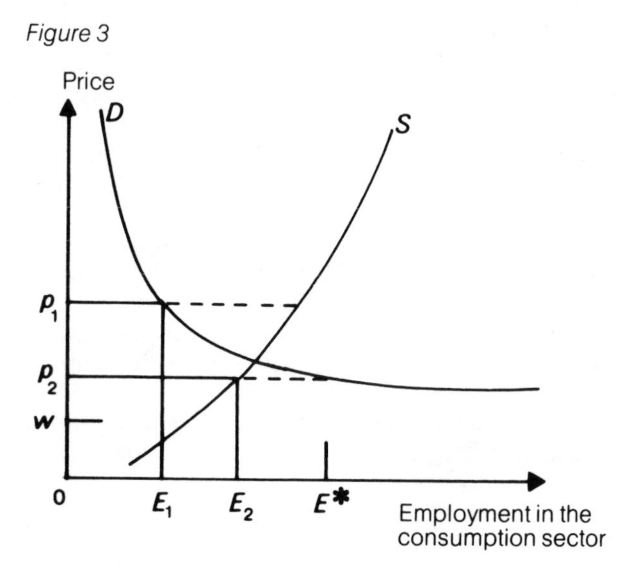

Figure 4

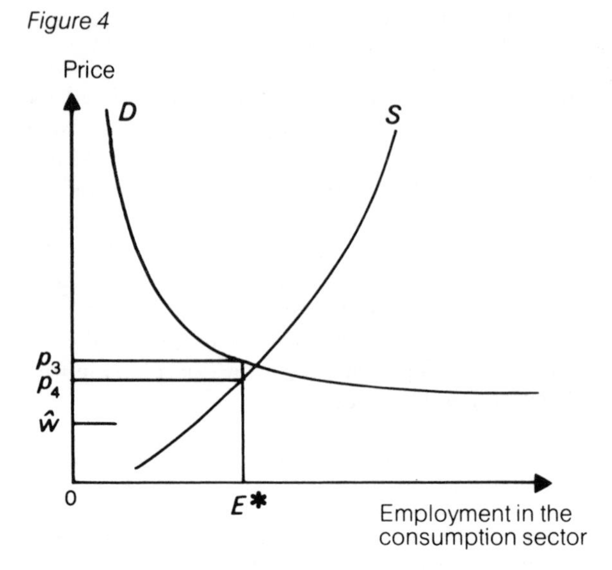

At price levels between p_3 and p_4 there is repressed inflation

which determines the real wage rate. Marginal cost is equal to the demand price for the corresponding level of output. In terms of Figure 2 above, the intersection would be at the level of full employment.

A final case is that in which the real wage is forced up higher than is consistent with full employment. There is a shortage of labour in the consumption sector and money wages would tend to be forced up by competition between employers. This is Malinvaud's case of 'repressed inflation' (see Figure 4).

Malinvaud depicts these various cases in a kind of map, drawn in the space of the money wage and the price of the commodity (p. 85). As he draws the map, it is rather obscure. It is more perspicuous if it is interpreted as in Figures 5 and 6. The real wage shown by the slope of the *FE* line is that which, on Malinvaud's assumptions, will be consistent with full employment demand for labour, being the product per man on the plant that is marginal when the whole labour force is employed. The line *FD* represents the flow of demand in real terms which would purchase the output produced at full employment. Effective demand for consumption goods is equal to consumption expenditure out of wages (cwE), where c is the propensity to consume, *plus* consumption expenditure out of wealth (A). The relationship between the wage level and the price level at full-employment output of the consumer good (Y^*) is then

$$A + cwE^* = pY^*.$$

The line FG, which Malinvaud describes as the frontier between Keynesian and classical situations, represents positions at which supply is equal to demand.

The various cases can now be placed on Malinvaud's map.

Figure 5

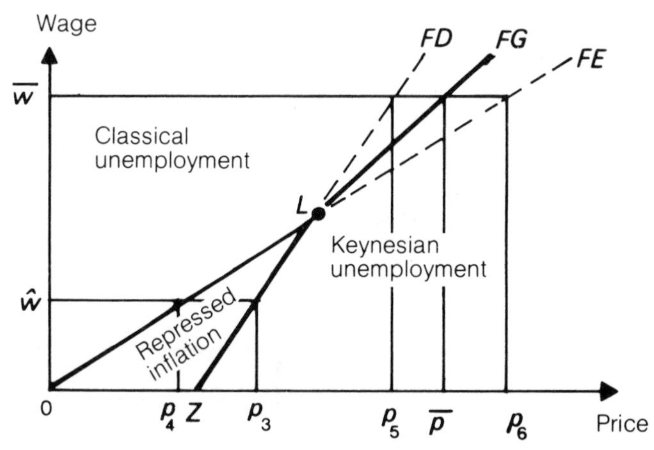

At the money wage rate $\overline{w}$, demand at p_5 is sufficient for full employment, but the real wage is higher than the output per man on plant which is marginal at full employment, p_6 covers marginal cost at full employment but gives a large deficiency of demand; at $\overline{p}$ marginal cost is equal to price at less than full employment. At $\hat{w}$ (cf. Figure 4) prices corresponding to repressed inflation lie between p_4 and p_3. $Z = A/Y^*$

In the upper triangle between the lines FD and FE, the real wage is higher than that corresponding to full-employment demand for labour, and expenditure in real terms is less than that required to purchase the full-employment output. Our first case, in which the price (relatively to the money wage) is such that supply and demand are equal at less than full employment lies on FG.

At the point of intersection of the lines, L, there is full employment and sufficient outlay to purchase the corresponding output. It is the case in which both demand and supply happen to be sufficient to establish full employment.

In the lower triangle the real wage is higher than corresponds to full employment and so is expenditure. This is the case of repressed inflation (compare with Figure 4).

In the area below the lines ZL and FG, expenditure is too low to permit full employment. Although in the triangle between FE and FG real wages are too high as well as expenditure being too low, it is the expenditure constraint which is binding. This is what Malinvaud treats as the Keynesian case (his first case).

In the area above the lines OL and FG, the real wage rate is too high to correspond to full employment. Although in the triangle between FD and FG

Figure 6

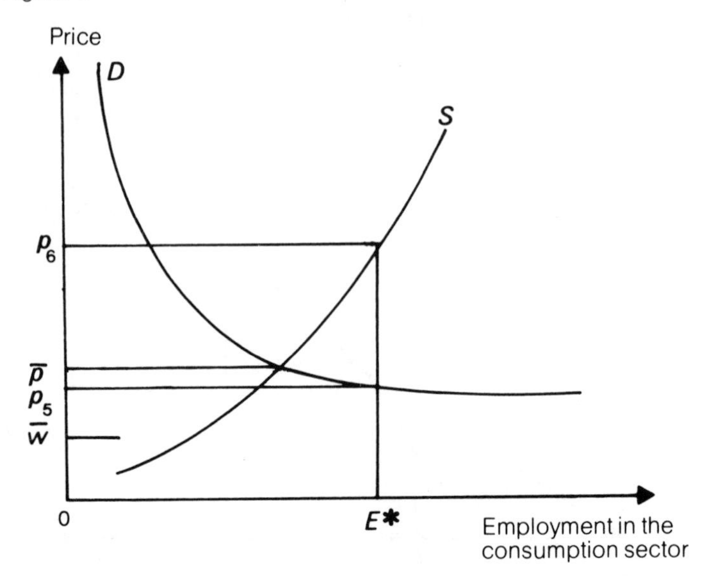

expenditure is too low as well as real wages too high, the real wage rate is the binding constraint. This is Malinvaud's second case – his classical case.

As I indicated above, I regard this case as impossible. It is the consequence of mixing assumptions about the shape of the cost curves and the degree of price flexibility which are inconsistent with one another.

Fixed or 'sticky' prices are found in manufacturing and distribution, where products are not homogeneous and labour costs are constant or decreasing up to the limits of capacity. The result, which has been well confirmed by various empirical studies and is widely known as Okun's Law, is that productivity in industry increases with short-run increases in output, while prices are sticky.

Flexible prices are found in those markets for a limited range of primary products where products are homogeneous, demand to the individual producer is almost perfectly elastic, and costs rise with output due to fixed natural resources.

Malinvaud mixes the two, assuming a single homogeneous commodity, many producers with rising cost curves, and yet prices which stay fixed in the face of excess demand. It is this that is impossible. For, on these assumptions, producers who are profit maximisers would not keep their prices fixed. The whole notion of sticky prices, based on the studies of the real manufacturing world to which Malinvaud refers early in his lectures, cannot be squeezed into the textbook notion of homogeneous products and rising cost curves. If, on the other hand, one wishes to justify the assumption of sticky prices by returning to reality, then one must assume constant or falling variable costs.

Even if one ignores overheads, it follows that, if the real wage is at a level at which it pays a firm to produce, it will increase, not reduce, its profits by increasing output in response to extra demand. There will be no rationing of goods in Malinvaud's sense.

Ironically, 'rationing' can only be introduced into this setting, interpreted either way, if one gives the word its normal meaning and introduces a government which overrules the market forces.

5. Leisure

There is an elaborate treatment of the determination of the amount of work done (and of leisure) under the influence of a worker's psychology, and the amount of his wealth.

All this evidently belongs to the Walrasian world, in which the individual can decide how much work he wants to do. In a Keynesian world, the preference for leisure of the typical worker may influence collective agreements about hours and conditions in relation to the real wage and the average amount of wealth. But, under any given agreement, there is little choice for the individual about the amount of effort he can offer. The only effect of Malinvaud's psychological theory is to blur the distinction between unemployment and leisure. The number of men employed (for standard hours of work), and the number not employed, are objective facts. But, amongst those who are not employed, some may be in distress and very anxious to find a job while others, who have plenty of wealth, may not be particularly reluctant, for the time being, to remain out of work.

Malinvaud's picture of the social system, in which there is no spending out of profits, every worker has an arbitrary amount of wealth in the form of money, which yields no income, and the unemployed are provided with no means of support and are forced to live on their wealth, is too remote from reality to be of interest, though perhaps it will appeal to those who regard unemployment as being due to idleness.

6. Present-day economic problems

In the third lecture Malinvaud wanders around present-day economic problems, trying to illuminate them by reference to his three models, Walrasian, Keynesian and what he claims is classical; as though it were possible to move from one set of institutions and technical conditions to another merely by altering the real wage rate.

> One may first wonder how the short-term equilibrium would progressively shift if its environment did not change, i.e. if behaviour as well as policy were to remain unchanged for some time. A number of economists argue that a strong tendency towards a long-term full employment equilibrium does exist. According to them, policy measures, which may look favourable in the short run,

> actually disturb the spontaneous tendency toward full employment. Theory should permit an examination of such views (p. 77).

The problem of introducing accumulation through time into the market economy is much more complicated than Malinvaud seems to realise. In a Keynesian world, investment is going on, and the most important concomitants of the passage of time are changes in the amount of productive capacity. Also saving and dis-saving are going on so that the amount and distribution of private wealth is altering. Perhaps a number of economists are objecting to the rise in the national debt that results from continuous government borrowing, but they would have hard work to show that there is a spontaneous tendency to full employment under a regime of 'sound finance'.

This Malinvaud seems (partially) to recognise:

> Individual assets, autonomous demand and technical possibilities change through time for many reasons including capital accumulation, technical progress and frequent changes in the economic or non-economic environment. Since prices and wages are sticky, we cannot expect the growth path to coincide permanently with the changing Walrasian equilibrium of our short-term model (p. 93).

There is a curious passage in which he contrasts Keynesian with Walrasian accumulation:

> In each period, whether it experiences repressed inflation or Keynesian unemployment, aggregate savings are equal to investment, i.e. to autonomous demand in our model. The short-run equilibrium always fulfils this basic requirement; moreover, the demand for investment being exogenous in the short run, the supply of savings must adapt to it, as it does in Keynesian economics (this is forced saving under repressed inflation). Hence, it cannot be said that the need for capital accumulation requires a shift of the income distribution in favour of those types of income that are most saved. The same amount of capital accumulation that is considered to be made in a stationary Walrasian equilibrium will also be made on average in a sequence of non-Walrasian short-run equilibria as long as the demand for investment is on average the same in both cases. Any argument in favour of a different price-wage constellation must involve the demand for investment rather than the supply of savings (p. 99).

This last sentence seems to indicate that he wishes to take off from Walras altogether and sail with Keynes, to a world where accumulation depends upon investment, not upon the desire of individuals to save. But he can never quite bring himself to cut the hawser.

He attempts to relax the assumption of a single market and allow for a multiplicity of goods. He suggests that there may then be Keynesian unemployment with 'classical contamination' (p. 110). This would mean that, while prices are in general too high to permit full employment, for some commodities prices are too low (real wages are too high) to secure full capacity operation. But if there is a demand for these commodities why should not prices be raised? At the same time, there may be a few industries working up to capacity, enjoying a seller's market, while most are suffering from slack demand.

Malinvaud's curious system of analysis leads him to make some excellent points, for instance that technical progress, which raises output per man employed, should be accompanied by rising real wages (p. 90).

The most important and sensational of his statements is that the nature of unemployment in the 1960s and early 1970s was classical.

> Among the many conceivable combinations of events, the one most favourable to classical unemployment occurs when there is a sudden decrease in the quantity of final output per unit of labour, and when anticipations or social tensions lead to an abnormal increase in real wages (p. 107).

This combination of events would reduce the share of profit in the proceeds of industry and this is likely to lead to a reduction in plans for investment. Here is a highly important and completely Keynesian cause of recession. It is all very sad, but not at all 'classical'.[3]

Malinvaud towards the very end of his book states:

> There is no doubt that the main features of the 1975 unemployment are again Keynesian (p. 109).

However he adds:

> There are signs that the [substitution effect of the deterioration of the terms of trade] will soon again emerge (p. 109).

7. Conclusion

Ultimately Malinvaud's argument rests on two pillars: an elaborate utility analysis of the determination of the workers' propensities to consume and to supply labour; and the combination of a rising marginal cost curve of the textbook type with fixed prices. The first seems unnecessarily mystical, and the second has nothing to do either with Keynes or with the real world. On the fundamental difference between Keynesian and classical theory – the relationship between saving and investment – he has nothing to say. His faith in the Walrasian long run (p. 93) is simply wishful thinking.

Malinvaud evidently feels that he has seen a great light.

> At the end of these lectures, we realise that a great many questions require

[3] Malinvaud cites a paper by H. den Hartog and H.S. Tjan as providing evidence for the existence of classical unemployment. This paper was discussed by R.A. de Klerk, H.B.M. van der Laan and K.B.T. Thio in their paper 'Unemployment in the Netherlands: a criticism of the den Hartog-Tjan vintage model', *Cambridge Journal of Economics*, September 1977, pp. 291-306.

> further theoretical and econometric studies. The general equilibrium approach, in a world where prices are sticky in the short run, is not only highly relevant but also highly challenging. I do hope that economists will devote some of their best efforts to developing this approach and that, as a consequence, these lectures will soon be out-dated (pp. 115-16).

Actually, Malinvaud's commonsense observations, which are often acute, have been distorted by this approach and further development of it would distort them all the more. *The Theory of Unemployment Reconsidered* is a sad example of the effect which the study of orthodox economic theory can have upon a powerful mind.

13

Kahn on Malinvaud

Bertram Schefold

The object of this chapter is to clarify the main argument in Richard Kahn's review (Chapter 12, above) of Malinvaud's *The Theory of Unemployment Reconsidered* (1977) by simplifying it and by removing an inconsistency in Kahn's diagram, and to extend the argument to include the case of diminishing average costs. Malinvaud's mystifying concept of 'classical unemployment' will then disappear.

I will present three variations of Kahn's model. The first is a simplification to explain the concepts; exogenous demand is fixed in terms of employment and a neoclassical production function is used (section 2). The second is Kahn's own version with a change of units to make it consistent, and with exogenous demand fixed in monetary terms (section 3). The third introduces production functions with increasing returns (section 4).

The models will be used to discuss Kahn's critique of Malinvaud's interpretation of Keynes's theory of unemployment. The dangers of confusions arising from iterated critiques (BS on RK on EM on JMK) are obvious, particularly if the interpretations are based on different points of view. Keynes was, at the time of writing the *General Theory*, still a Marshallian, Malinvaud is a Walrasian, and Kahn is, in so far as he represents a later development of Cambridge economics, close to the classical theory of value and distribution.

Although the determination of relative prices will be irrelevant for our discussion, which is essentially confined to a one-commodity model, the different methodologies of the schools do come into play. They are contrasted by way of introduction (section 1), but the true methodological alternatives for the analysis of historical change (classical and old neoclassical method of comparing long-period positions *versus* 'modern' method of stringing together short-period equilibria) will become clear only at the end (section 5) as a by-product of the formal consideration of the three models.

* I should like to thank V. Caspari, J. Eatwell, G. Winckler and others for helpful suggestions.

1. Questions of method

According to the simplest pre-Keynesian explanation of unemployment in the short period with a given stock of equipment, one draws a demand curve D for labour L as a function of the real wage rate w/p, derived from the marginal productivity condition $F'(L) = w/p$, $D = D(w/p)$, where $F(L)$ is the production function with its usual properties of diminishing returns, and where D is the inverse function of F'. This may be confronted with a fixed labour supply $S = L^*$. Unemployment then arises if the real wage rate is given and is too high.

Unemployment thus appears as a disequilibrium; it seems that the real wage rate has to be lowered to restore equilibrium. However, lower real wages are associated with a lesser purchasing power of the workers. Moreover, if production takes place under conditions of falling average costs, lower levels of employment may be associated with higher prices. This leads to a view which is the opposite of the pre-Keynesian explanation of unemployment: the lower the level of prices relative to the money wage, i.e. the higher the real wage, the higher is the level of employment at which the sum of the demand of workers spending their money wage *plus* other demand (regarded as fixed exogenously) is equal to the supply forthcoming at that level of employment. Hence demand for labour, as determined through the equilibrium condition on the product market, may rise with the real wage.

The same method of analysing unemployment in terms of a deviation of sticky prices from their equilibrium value in the short period can therefore lead to opposite conclusions as to the causes of unemployment according to (1) whether demand is derived from a marginal productivity condition or from the equilibrium condition in the product market and (2) whether increasing or diminishing returns in the short run are assumed.

Keynes's own views were ambiguous in several respects. He – but not his followers in Cambridge – had retained the marginal productivity theory of the real wage (Keynes, 1936, p. 5). But demand for labour also depends on expected proceeds:

> Let D be the proceeds which entrepreneurs expect to receive from the employment of N men, the relationship between D and N being written $D = f(N)$, which can be called the *aggregate demand function* (Keynes, 1936, p. 25).

The demand function together with 'an aggregate supply curve' $Z(N)$, derived from the marginal productivity condition, defines a point of intersection, called 'the effective demand' which is regarded as stable:

> Now if for a given value of N the expected proceeds are greater than the aggregate supply price, i.e. if D is greater than Z, there will be an incentive to entrepreneurs to increase employment beyond N and, if necessary, to raise costs by competing with one another for the factors of production, up to the

> value of N for which Z has become equal to D. Thus the volume of employment is given by the point of intersection between the aggregate demand function and the aggregate supply function; for it is at this point that the entrepreneurs' expectation of profits will be maximised. The value of D at the point of the aggregate demand function, where it is intersected by the aggregate supply function, will be called *the effective demand* (Keynes, 1936, p. 25).

This is then declared to be the 'substance of the General Theory'. It consists in having it both ways. The point of effective demand is at the intersection of two curves: one determines the demand for labour through the marginal productivity condition, the other determines the demand for labour through the equilibrium between the flows of expenditure and sales. Unemployment may arise because of shifts of the curves engendered by several causes, but in particular by a reduction of investment which causes a shift of the aggregate demand curve and hence a reduction of the effective demand.

So Keynes derives demand simultaneously from the marginal productivity condition and from the equilibrium in the product market, yet his method of analysis is not based on the assumption of fixed prices. In the above quotation, Keynes is clearly not concerned with a disequilibrium due to prices being sticky. If there are surplus profits because the demand price exceeds the aggregate supply price, employment is increased until demand price and supply price coincide. This is not, however, a 'Walrasian' model with given factor endowments. It is a world where 'production and accumulation are going on through time' (Kahn, 1977, p. 376). Keynes is concerned with a process of accumulation, for investment depends on an uncertain future.

The methodological shift in the treatment of equilibrium is the primary concern of Kahn's critique of Malinvaud, although his main argument is of a more formal nature.

In order to confront the issues, Kahn has constructed a model which is sufficiently close to Malinvaud's to explain his method, but which is also original in that it brings in aspects of the modern Cambridge interpretation of Keynes. I start with my own variation of Kahn's model which allows a relatively easy exposition of the key concepts.

2. A simple two-sector model

> There is a government and an investment sector, the expenditures of which are aggregated in the exposition ... The main topic ... [is] the determination of employment in the consumption-good sector (Kahn, 1977, p. 377).

We may take the distinction between 'sectors' literally and simplify matters drastically by assuming that there is no investment and that the government sector employs a fixed number L_a of workers who are paid wages W_a at the ruling wage rate to provide free services (schooling, say) to the community. L is the number of the remaining workers who offer their labour inelastically to the firms of the consumption good sector. The workers in the consumption good sector (which produces bread) and the workers of the government spend all their income, W_c and W_a respectively, and the unemployed live on gifts of the employed. The profits P_c of the consumption good sector (with net output of value $W_c + P_c$) are taxed away to pay for the wages of the government sector, hence $P_c = W_a = G$, where G is government expenditure.

The marginal productivity condition in the consumption sector defines a demand for labour (given the real wage). In order to take the effect of the level of wages on the demand for commodities and hence labour producing them into account, followers of Clower (1965) distinguish different kinds of demand and define a new type of equilibrium.

Notional demand and supply are demand and supply as formulated by agents on the basis of their perception of prices of factors and goods. Notional demand for labour in the consumption good sector depends on the decisions of profit-maximising entrepreneurs who perceive a money wage rate w and a price p; they maximise profits $p \cdot f(L_c) - wL_c$ so that

$$\frac{w}{p} = f'(L_c) \tag{I}$$

where $f(L)$ is the production function of the sector producing the consumption good and L_c labour employed in that sector.

But Keynes pointed out that the demand of entrepreneurs for workers is limited by their expectations as to the proceeds of the output which can be sold to the consumers. There has to be a balance between expenditure and the proceeds $p \cdot f(L_c)$ which result if the production of L_c workers is sold at price p. This leads to Clower's concept of *effective* demand. The demand for consumption goods emanates from the workers L_c in the consumption good sector itself and the workers in the other sector who together consume $W_a + W_c = wL_a + wL_c = p f(L_c)$ or

$$\frac{w}{p} = \frac{f(L_c)}{L_c + L_a} \tag{II}$$

We call relationship (II) the effective demand curve.

The notional demand curve (I) and the effective demand curve (II) are shown in Figure 1. The shapes of the curves derive from the properties of a production function with diminishing returns. In particular it can be shown[1] that curve (I) crosses curve (II) at the maximum of the latter: it turns out that the highest value of output that can just be sold to the government and the workers in the consumption goods sector satisfies the condition of profit maximisation at the corresponding level of the real wage. We call this point of intersection the Point of Effective Demand (PED). It corresponds to the 'effective demand' in the quotation from Keynes cited above, although the specification of the curves and the concept of equilibrium differ in several respects.

[1] By putting the derivative of (II) equal to zero.

Figure 1

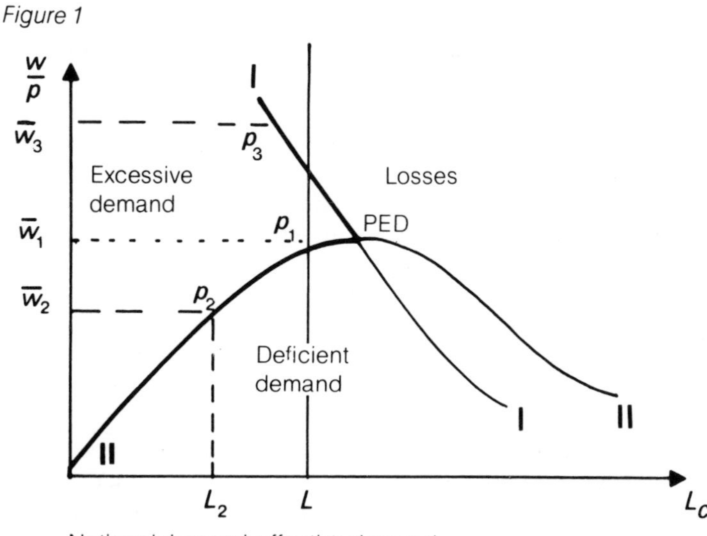

Notional demand, effective demand and point of effective demand

Entrepreneurs incur losses for levels of the real wage and of employment above the notional demand curve (I). This area may therefore be ruled out. The effective demand curve (II) divides the plane into an area of excessive demand (where the demand emanating from the workers in the consumption good sector and the government is, given the corresponding levels of employment and the real wage, in excess of the value of the output of consumption goods) and an area of deficient demand.

If the actual labour supply to the consumption good sector L happened to be equal to that at the point of effective demand, the corresponding level of the real wage would represent an equilibrium in the traditional sense. However, suppose that the labour supply L is smaller than this equilibrium value. The Malinvaud school then considers alternative levels of the real wage and regards as a new type of equilibrium, or as a specific disequilibrium (equilibrium with rationing), a situation in which there results *either* a seller's *or* a buyer's market. The (dis-)equilibrium in this sense is unique in our model for any level of real wage in the relevant range:

1. At the level of the real wage $\bar{w}_1$ there is excessive demand so that full employment will be reached. The labour market is a seller's market and so is the market for consumption goods. The workers are said to be rationed in the market for consumption goods and the firms in the markets for labour. This is what Malinvaud calls 'repressed inflation'.
2. If the real wage is lowered to the level $\bar{w}_2$, demand for consumption goods is reduced. Since output is limited by demand, effective demand for labour and employment is limited to L_2; this is what Malinvaud calls

'Keynesian unemployment'. The introduction of the demand curve has demonstrated what happens if the real wage is lowered: employment is not increased but diminished.

3. There is also 'classical unemployment'. If the real wage is raised to the level $\bar{w}_3$, profit-maximising firms will employ fewer workers than correspond to full employment. The real wage is here so high that the demand for consumption goods exceeds the production of consumption goods at all levels of employment. Malinvaud believes that notional demand then limits employment; profit-maximising firms employ fewer workers than correspond to full employment because of diminishing marginal productivity. The labour market is a buyer's market, the market for consumption goods a seller's market.

The distinction between Keynesian and classical unemployment may also be expressed by saying that workers receive less than their marginal product in the Keynesian case because of price rigidity. Thus firms will be willing to employ more workers at the current real wage rate provided demand is increased. Moreover, an increase in the real wage rate under these conditions will generate more demand and hence will lead to more employment, the reason being that firms are demand-constrained and not cost-constrained. However, if real wages are already equal to the marginal product of labour (assumed to fall with increasing employment), then firms are cost-constrained (classical case). They will therefore only employ more workers if the real wage rate is reduced. Thus the crucial distinction is between a demand-constrained situation (real wage rate less than marginal product), and a cost-constrained situation (real wage rate equal to a marginal product which falls as employment rises).

The concept of classical unemployment is one of the main targets of Kahn's attack on Malinvaud. The construction is first tied to a production function with diminishing returns which comes up in Malinvaud and Kahn in the shape of a rising supply curve of the firms producing consumption goods. This does not fit in with fixed 'administered' prices, which only make sense in a world of imperfect competition and falling cost curves. Other explanations of price rigidity are neither convincing nor relevant (cf., however, Malinvaud, 1977, pp. 9-12).

Kahn objects, secondly, that prices could not be kept constant anyway in conditions of classical unemployment (Kahn 1977, p. 381). Money prices would rise because of excessive demand while money wages would be checked by unemployment so that the real wage would fall until full employment with repressed inflation, or 'Keynesian' unemployment, was reached. Indexation of money wages by strong trade unions supporting the high level of real wages seems to give more credibility to classical unemployment, but the inflationary process would make it impossible to maintain government expenditure in real terms so that unemployment would again soon be associated with deficient demand.[2]

The model illustrates two points: Keynesian unemployment is mitigated (1) if the real wage is increased, because of the counter-intuitive slope of the demand curve and (2), for each level of the real wage, if 'autonomous demand', i.e. wL_a, is increased, because the effective demand curve then shifts to the lower right.

3. Kahn's model

The first model, although drastically simplified, has allowed the introduction of some key concepts of the Malinvaud school and preparation of the ground for an easier understanding of Kahn's critique. The first model differs from Malinvaud's approach – among other things – in that he uses a one-good model, even though there are two sources of demand for total output (consumption expenditure on the one hand, government and investment expenditure on the other). Kahn's exposition is ambiguous, since he talks of the determination of employment in a consumption good sector while employment in the other 'sector' is regarded as given (p. 217 above) but then he does not discuss the influence of changes of the wage level on government expenditure. Later he seems to include government expenditure (fixed in monetary terms) in 'expenditure out of wealth' (denoted by A), and identifies total employment with employment in the consumption good sector (p. 223 above). We shall assume from now on that there is only one good for consumption and investment, and that the government is a pure consumer and spends a fixed amount of money.

Malinvaud's model is complicated mainly because he introduces utility functions to determine how much work the workers are willing to offer, how much of their income is to be saved (added to money holdings of consumers) and what proportion of their money holdings is to be spent (dis-saving) by the unemployed. The unemployed do not live on welfare (government expenditure).

If this were to be taken seriously, expectations about the future of employment would have to be taken into account which would break up Malinvaud's division of time into periods with everything happening in a given period on the basis of given utility functions and a given stock of capital (which is here assumed to be large enough to accommodate the fluctuations of employment of labour under consideration). Malinvaud believes that the

[2] It should be noted that the uniqueness of the 'equilibria' is due to a particular assumption of Malinvaud's: at low levels of the real wage ($\overline{w}_2$), full employment could also be compatible with the definitions which have been given so far. Full employment would be reached because notional demand for labour would be high at low levels of the real wage. The entrepreneurs might try to employ workers as long as their marginal product was higher than the given real wage. They would then find that the output produced could not be sold completely to the government and to the workers, and an accumulation of stocks would result. Malinvaud quite reasonably regards this 'fourth' case as implausible (Malinvaud, 1977, pp. 30-1) and excludes it by assumption.

expectations can be summarised in functions for desired money holdings in the given period.

Kahn cuts the Gordian knot by assuming that the various influences on the rate of saving of workers (employed and unemployed) cancel out (p. 218 above). The money market is dropped from the argument.

We then have three identities. The value of output $pf(L_c)$ is on the one hand equal to the sum of profits and wages $pf(L_c) = P_c + W_c$. On the other, it is equal to the sum of consumption of employed consumption sector workers C_E plus consumption of unemployed workers C_U plus investment and government expenditure G, since profits are saved (or absorbed by taxation): $pf(L_c) = C_U + C_E + G$. Thirdly, consumption of employed workers C_E equals the difference of wages and savings of employed consumption sector workers $C_E = W_c - S_E$. Hence we obtain the equation

$$P_c = G + C_U - S_E = X.$$

Profits P_c may be regarded as given and equal to an exogenously given X because government expenditure G (including investment) is exogenous while the difference $C_U - S_E$ is subject to opposing tendencies which Kahn assumes – and this is his point – to cancel out for analytical convenience. In fact, if the price of the consumption good rises, C_U is likely to go down but so is S_E, and if employment falls, S_E is likely to rise but so is C_U. It is clear that this reasoning holds only within limits which ought to be kept in mind in the analysis of the following diagrams.

Kahn sometimes speaks of employment, not monetary expenditure, in the investment and government sector as being exogenously given (p. 218 above) as in our first model. But in the first part of the review he also assumes a given money wage, which implies that autonomous expenditure from that source is fixed in money terms, while he later directly assumes a fixed government outlay in money terms. Malinvaud varies his assumptions in this respect (Malinvaud, 1977, p. 53) but he is mainly interested in government consumption in real terms (as we shall be in the third model) when he discusses 'budgetary measures' as 'policy measures' (ibid., p. 54).

The purchasing power of autonomous demand X is invariant if X is fixed in real terms; it rises with the real wage if X is fixed in terms of employment; and it varies inversely with the price level if X is fixed in monetary terms. Since Kahn assumes $C_U - S_E$ to be given, it is appropriate to assume at this point that G and hence X are also fixed in monetary terms.

Here we may suppose that monetary government expenditure is financed not through taxation of profits (as in section 2) but through deficit spending. G includes investment. Net saving consists of profits P_c which are all saved and the difference between the saving of employed and the dissaving of unemployed workers $C_U - S_E$. Net savings of workers $S_E - C_U$ are assumed to be given independently of employment.

Kahn thus succeeds in bringing in a Cambridge-type theory of income distribution: profits are determined by expenditure. The influence on employment remains to be examined. This is now slightly more difficult than in the model of Figure 1 because autonomous expenditure X is given in monetary terms, so that it is not possible to treat employment only as a function of the real wage. Kahn takes the money wage w as given, and he reckons in Keynesian units of employment. If we write $pf(L_c) = P_c + W_c = C_E + C_U + G = X + S_E + C_E$, we have $S_E + C_E = wL_c$ and

$$X + wL_c = pf(L_c) = \frac{pf(L_c)}{L_c} . L_c = \pi L_c.$$

Here $\pi = (f/L_c)p$ is the price of the good in units of employment, i.e. the *money price of the average product per worker employed in the consumption sector*. So

$$\pi = w + X/L_c.$$

This is the *only* way which makes it possible for Kahn in his first diagram to draw employment on the abscissa and the price in terms of units of employment together with the money wage on the ordinate *because price and money wage rate can be drawn on the same axis only if they are of the same dimension, i.e. money per worker*. 'The profit per man employed is determined by the price of the commodity' (Kahn, p. 218 above).

The resulting curve is a hyperbola between the y-axis and the horizontal line representing the money wage rate w. Kahn matches this hyperbola (which he calls the demand curve) with a marginal cost curve. The latter is the reverse of the notional demand curve which we have considered above.

But here we run into a formal difficulty. We can write the marginal cost curve in the form

$$p = w/f'(L_c) \qquad (\mathrm{I}')$$

This curve is rising because the marginal product of labour is falling. But, since he has chosen 'money per man' as his dimension on the y-axis, Kahn needs a supply function in terms of units of employment, therefore, using (I′),

$$\pi = \frac{p \cdot f(L_c)}{L_c} = w \frac{f(L_c)}{f'(L_c) \cdot L_c}$$

This curve is rather odd for two reasons. First, it is not necessarily the rising curve drawn by Kahn (e.g. it is horizontal if $f(L_c)$ is Cobb-Douglas). Secondly, employment cannot be analysed by taking the price π in terms of employment as given, because it is the *money price in physical units* (money per unit of output), p, which is administered by firms or, if one prefers, 'rigid', and *not* π (money per unit of labour).

Kahn's analysis is easily rescued. Notional demand for labour as defined

Figure 2

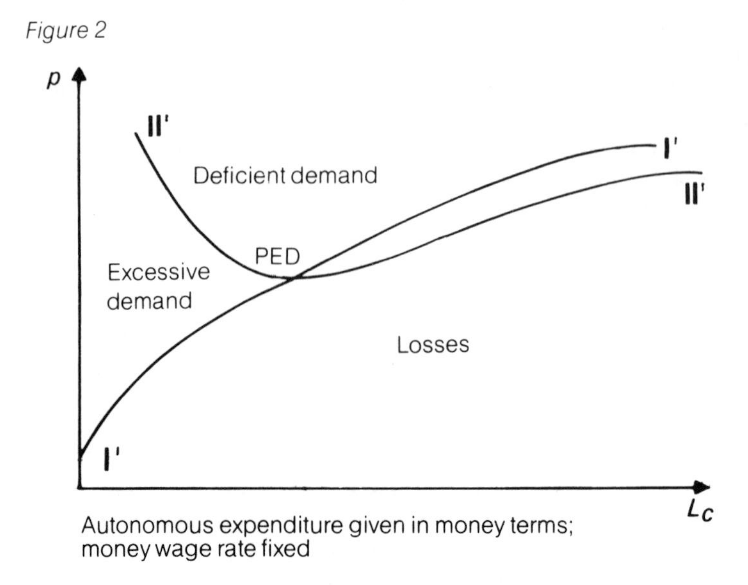

by marginal cost is represented by (I′). The curve may now be viewed as a curve of notional supply of the single good. Effective demand for labour is represented by

$$p = w\frac{L_c}{f(L_c)} + \frac{X}{f(L_c)} \qquad \text{(II}')$$

For any given level of the money wage, the curves (I′) and (II′) have the shape shown in Figure 2; (II′) is not a hyperbola but rather like (II) in Figure 1 turned upside down.[3] Losses are incurred below curve (I′). Demand is deficient above curve (II′) and excessive below. The point of effective demand PED, with similar properties as in Figure 1, is here not fixed any more if the money wage changes *ceteris paribus*. The point of effective demand shifts to the upper left if w is increased and to the lower right if w is diminished, as can be seen by inspecting the formulae of the curves or by calculating the co-ordinates of PED from (I′) and (II′). What this means is that a reduction of the money wage increases employment from the point of view of profit maximisation, but this increased employment is compatible with a balance of output and demand only if the real wage is not reduced to the same extent as the money wage, hence the money price must fall and PED shifts to the lower right.

[3] It must be U-shaped. Demand consists mainly of autonomous demand at low levels of employment and production so that the price must be high. The price will fall as employment, production and demand of employed workers increase, but it must rise again eventually, since demand will continue to rise linearly with employment, whereas production rises only with diminishing returns, so that the price must go up to compensate for the fall of the average product.

Figure 3a

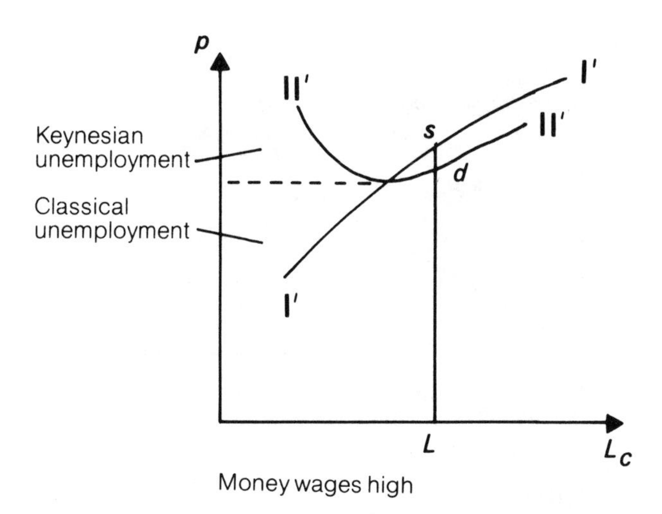

Figure 3b

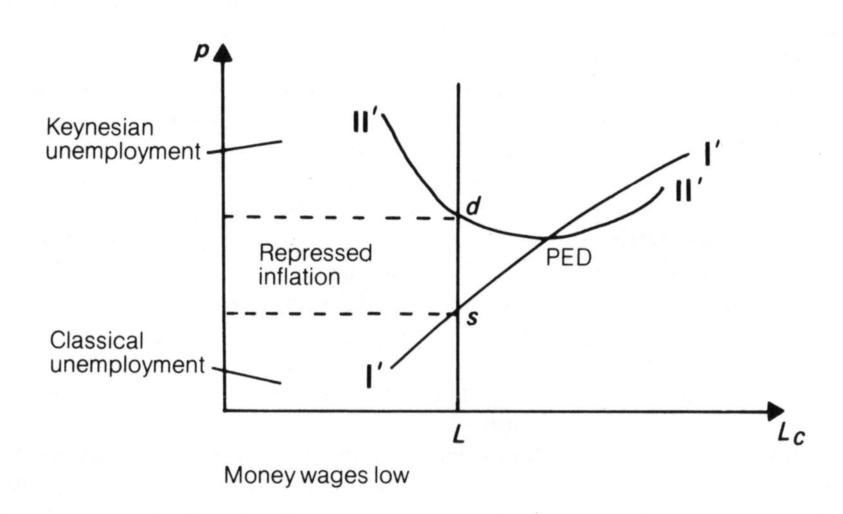

The main Keynesian argument was that an increase of autonomous expenditure shifts the curve of effective demand for labour, (II′), to the right so that employment increases. The same effect is reached with a reduction in the money price, given the money wage; employment then increases as one moves down the descending part of curve (II′). Both arguments could be presented in our first model, but we now have another effect. Since autonomous expenditure is given in monetary terms, a mere

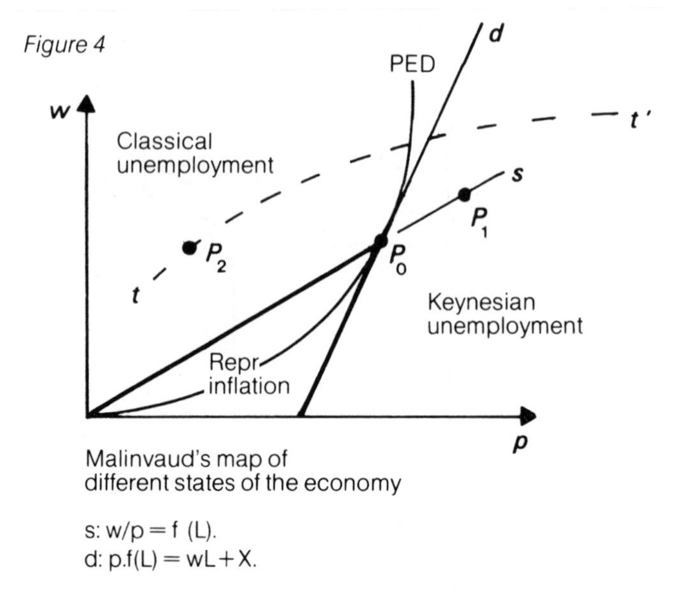

Malinvaud's map of different states of the economy

s: $w/p = f(L)$.
d: $p.f(L) = wL + X$.

deflation, the simultaneous reduction of the money wage and the money price, may increase employment. This follow from the shift of the point of effective demand to the lower right with a reduction of the money wage rate.

We again assume the labour supply to be given. Figures 3a and 3b show the picture which emerges from the same fixed labour supply, L, if money wages are high (Figure 3a) or low (Figure 3b). A high money price implies a low real wage and therefore Keynesian unemployment; *vice versa* for classical unemployment. The case of repressed inflation is in between and is possible only if money wages are sufficiently low (Figure 3b). It is therefore clear that an appropriate setting of the money wage will ensure that the point of effective demand lies on the vertical line expressing the labour supply L; this is then the point of so-called 'Walrasian' equilibrium. The point of effective demand could have been made to shift to the point of full employment in the first model only by changing government expenditure so as to increase L_a. Here it can be reached because deflation or inflation alters the purchasing power of autonomous expenditure X.

Malinvaud's celebrated 'map' for the different states of the economy is shown in Figure 4. For a high level of the money wage there are only two states, Keynesian unemployment or classical unemployment. For a low level there is repressed inflation in between.[4]

[4] The states depend in each case on the level of the money price, given the money wage. The map is obtained by drawing the three curves for the price as a function of the money wage defined by the intersections of (I′) with L (point *s* in Figure 3), (II′) with L (point d in Figure 3) and of (I′) and (II′) (point PED in Figure 3). The formula for the last of these three curves cannot be given explicitly without specifying the production function, but it can be shown to have the shape of Figure 4 for all production functions with the usual properties. One can then play games on the map, e.g. by considering effects of deflation and inflation (comparing two positions

4. Increasing returns

We now turn to a modification of the model by introducing increasing returns. The view that money prices and money wages are sticky is at the heart of the disequilibrium school. But administered prices prevail in industries which have, at normal capacity utilisation, falling average cost curves, and which therefore set prices according to a variant of full cost pricing or target return pricing. In order to simplify matters, we assume that the conditions of production lead to constant marginal costs and that average costs are equal to marginal costs plus overheads due to the existence of a minimum core of employed workers L_0 who cannot be dismissed. The corresponding production function is of the form

$$f(L_c) = \gamma\,(L_c - L_0), \quad L_c \geq L_0,$$

with γ constant. All firms are alike and have the same share of the market. We assume further that full employment of labour is reached before the limits of capacity utilisation, which does not therefore have to be treated explicitly.

Notional demand for labour is infinite as soon as the marginal product of labour, γ, is greater than the real wage rate w/p; it is zero otherwise. For profit maximising firms will want to produce and sell without limit if prices are above costs and if they are constrained neither in the product market nor in the labour market. The marginal productivity condition thus becomes trivial.

But firms are constrained if only an amount L of labour is available to them. So workers will only be employed if their number is sufficient to reach

---

on a straight line through the origin) or by comparing different maps engendered by modifications of X (cf. Malinvaud, 1977, pp. 88f. an Kahn, p. 223 above). The former exercise concerns real balance effects (effects of changes in the price level, given X in monetary terms), the latter concerns the multiplier.

As it stands, the model seems to lend support to those who believe that unemployment may be rectified by changing prices and wages. There is a level of the money wage rate and the money price such that the unique Walrasian equilibrium is reached. However, it would be careless to argue, e.g., that a deflation would be appropriate to cure Keynesian unemployment simply because this is what Figure 4 suggests (along the straight line s). The model is incapable of dealing with expectations affecting the volume of investment which would follow from deflation and which would shift the curve of effective demand. So it is questionable whether the comparison of two points (e.g. P_0 and P_1 on s) can be used to argue that the real balance effect of deflation will turn unemployment at P_1 into full employment at P_0 and leave X unaffected. Similarly for classical unemployment and an increase of the money price at a given money wage so that the real wage is reduced in a movement from P_2 to P_0: here I should turn the argument round. Since the coexistence of excessive demand with unemployment at P_2 will inevitably trigger off open inflation, classical unemployment will tend to be transformed into Keynesian unemployment along a trajectory such as $t\,t'$ in Figure 4, as long as X is kept constant. Finally, the emergence of open inflation with the level of money wages, money prices and government expenditure all rising at the same rate is best analysed in the first model of Figure 1; classical unemployment will then – as is rather obvious – remain unchanged, since the real wage stays the same while government expenditure wL_a rises with the wage rate of government and investment workers L_a.

Figure 5

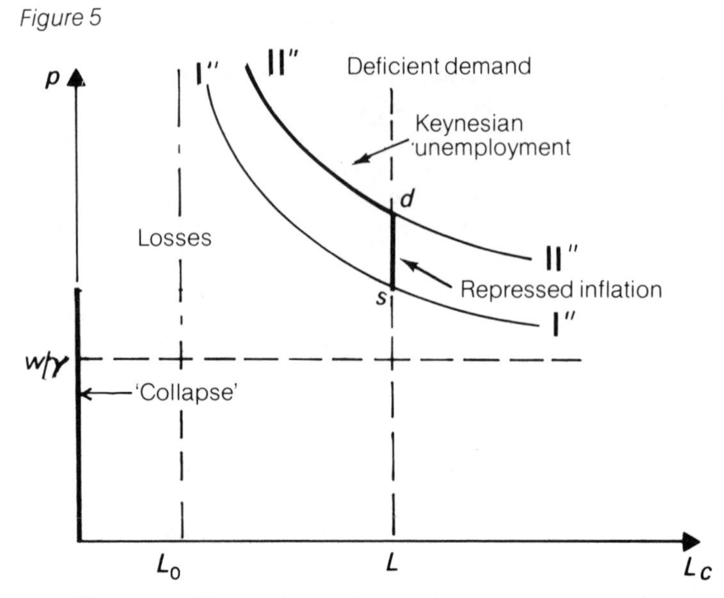

The case of increasing returns

a level of capacity utilisation at which production is profitable, given the real wage, i.e. if, and only if

$$p \cdot f(L) - wL = p\gamma(L - L_o) - wL > 0.$$

The curve corresponding to zero profits (I'') is shown in Figure 5 for a given level of the money wage rate.

But firms may also be constrained in the market for products. We assume that autonomous demand, in particular expenditure emanating from the government and investment sector on consumption goods, is fixed in monetary terms and equal to X. This, *plus* wages in the consumption sector, buys the output of consumption goods. The relationship

$$p \cdot f(L) = p\gamma(L - L_o) = X + wL$$

is also shown in Figure 5 (II'').

The picture is now clear. With the labour supply L given, there is Keynesian unemployment at high prices, given the money wage rate, and employment increases as the real wage rises until repressed inflation is reached. What happens with a further increase in the real wage might more accurately be described as a collapse rather than as classical unemployment. For if the real wage rises to the point where profitable production is not even possible at full employment, the consumption goods sector starts making losses which cannot be eliminated by reducing employment before production has ended altogether. In effect, the state of classical unemployment has become impossible.[5]

Classical unemployment could never take place, for it would be turned into unemployment characterised by deficient demand, therefore into what we have called Keynesian unemployment. A rise in the real wage in an initial situation of repressed inflation would normally be prevented by open inflation. This would settle the matter if money wages did not follow suit. The increase of real wages could only take place if money wages rose faster than the index of the cost of living. If the open inflation led to the firms loosing money, they would have to stop investment. Autonomous expenditure would be reduced (the curve (II″) would shift to the left in Figure 5), and this would rapidly lead to Keynesian unemployment.

It is the threat of this outcome rather than the possibility of the 'collapse' actually taking place which is relevant in the discussion. All that the concept of classical unemployment amounts to is the obvious point that the increase in the real wage is limited by maximum output per worker. Then the unemployment which results eventually is not classical but Keynesian.[6]

According to Kahn (p. 227 above), Malinvaud's argument 'rests on two pillars: an elaborate utility analysis of the determination of the workers' propensities to consume and to supply labour; and the combination of rising marginal cost curve of the textbook type with fixed prices'. Both pillars have now been removed. The model which has been derived from what remains may help to clarify the (at least from the old neoclassical point of view) counterintuitive slope of the demand and supply curves for labour. If we now combine the assumption of autonomous expenditure given not in money, but in terms of the numbers of workers in the government and in the investment sector as in the first model (Figure 1) with that of increasing returns of the third model (Figure 5), we obtain a *rising* demand curve D for labour as a function of the real wage rate which may be combined with a *falling* supply curve S for labour as in Figure 6, since it is well known that the elasticity of the supply of labour is often negative in the relevant range because people prefer more leisure with rising wages.

In order to show this as succinctly as possible and to demonstrate that the assumptions can be varied without affecting the conclusions, let us suppose that government and investment expenditure is simply given in real terms, g, and that the production function shows constant returns. The condition that

[5] The map of the three states of the economy looks formally like the map of the previous model of Figure 4 with the point of Walrasian equilibrium pushed out to infinity so that line d becomes parallel to s.

[6] The old Keynesian view according to which full employment (possibly with inflationary tendencies) and unemployment with deficient demand are the only equilibria of the economy has then been vindicated even within Malinvaud's own framework, on the assumption of increasing returns. 'Classical unemployment' is not a third kind of equilibrium but rather a phase of transition which will, if it obtains, at once be transformed into a different state, much in the same way as Malinvaud's own 'fourth' case of accumulation of stocks at full employment and deficient demand.

prices must exceed average cost is then given by $p\gamma L_c > wL_c$ so that the border-line between the areas of profits and losses is given by

$$\frac{w}{p} = \gamma, \qquad \text{(I''')}$$

while the balance between proceeds and expenditure is given by $p\gamma L_c = wL_c + pg$, therefore simply

$$\frac{w}{p} = \gamma - \frac{g}{L_c} \qquad \text{(II''')}$$

This is how Figure 6 has been drawn. The demand for labour may exceed the supply (repressed inflation) or *vice versa* (Keynesian case) at low levels of the real wage; the real wage cannot rise beyond γ, i.e. beyond output per worker.

Figure 6

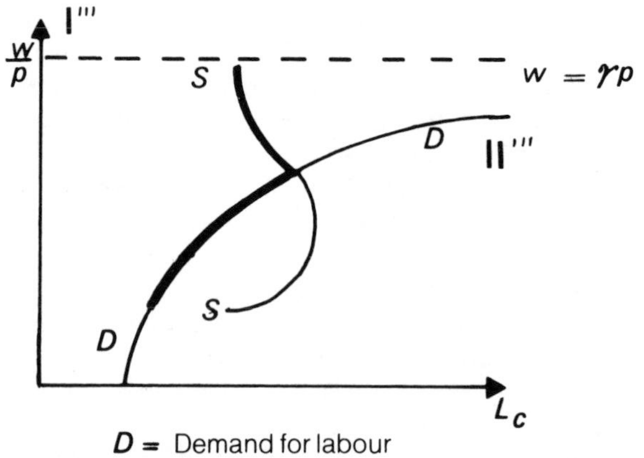

D = Demand for labour
S = Supply of labour

One might wish to introduce a capacity constraint in this context, as Malinvaud does in his later book (Malinvaud, 1980). Here it could be expressed in terms of a maximum number of workers who can be employed. If this is less than labour supply and labour demand, there is again a kind of unemployment which is not Keynesian. Its analysis is clearly of interest, but it would be misleading to call it 'classical' as Malinvaud does in the later book; this has nothing to do with his original concept of classical unemployment, which was regulated by marginal productivity and the real wage, not by capacity.

If we continue to assume that the capacity constraint exceeds the labour supply, the picture suggests that one way to cure unemployment is to raise the real wage. This policy conclusion is correct to the extent that the total of government and investment expenditure can be kept constant in real terms and that international competitiveness does not suffer.

5. Conclusions

Looking back at our three variations on the theme of 'Kahn on Malinvaud on Keynes' one might think that the method of analysis used in these models represents an instructive extension of the multiplier, but Kahn is not happy with Malinvaud's approach even after having added a post-Keynesian flavour of his own. What is missing?

> ... there is no effect of uncertainty or of expectations about the future ... (Kahn, p. 219 above).

But the effects of the past and of expectations concerning the future are represented in Malinvaud (even if perhaps not quite adequately), in the shape of stocks, utility functions and – in particular – desired money holdings, which have been removed in Kahn's simplified account. Malinvaud's second book shows that from this starting point he is able to go forward effortlessly to an analysis of his system in terms of processes going on through time as a sequence of connected short-term equilibria. Should we conclude that the critique can be reduced to one of detail, style and exposition?

> Malinvaud admits to being quite vague about the constitution and policy of firms ... There is no mention of liquidity preference .... The level of investment is arbitrarily fixed without any discussion of how it is determined ... (Kahn, pp. 218-19 above).

Now these objections are not irrelevant, but they clearly concern abstractions which are standard in models of the multiplier (cf., e.g., Robinson and Eatwell, 1973, Book 2, ch. 3).

The one substantial point of disagreement concerns the analysis of price formation, in this case the method of neo-Walrasian equilibrium with rigid prices. Leijonhufvud proposes to follow Marshall and to take quantities rather than prices as given in disequilibrium (Leijonhufvud, 1974) but Keynes obviously considered some process of adaption of both quantities and prices so this suggestion could not satisfy Kahn.

Kahn does not say explicitly how he would like to replace the Marshallian theory of value in the *General Theory*. Keynes himself made a tentative step towards a model with full cost pricing in reaction to articles by Kalecki (1938) and others:

> Most businessmen are surprised by the suggestion that it is a close calculation of short-period marginal cost or of marginal revenue which should dominate their price policies. They maintain that such a policy would rapidly land in bankruptcy anyone who practised it. And if it is true that they are producing more often than not on a scale at which marginal cost is falling with an increase in output, they would clearly be right; for it would only be on rare occasions that they would be collecting anything whatever towards their overhead (Keynes, 1939, p. 407).

The model of section 4 is constructed on such Kaleckian lines with constant marginal costs and falling average costs, and it may therefore be asked whether this approach, by taking up ideas which Keynes reluctantly came to accept after writing the *General Theory*, overcomes the limitation of the neoclassical concept of equilibrium which is the real target of Kahn's critique.

I believe that the answer is no. It is true that, although there is in general no stable Walrasian equilibrium with diminishing costs, we have here a disequilibrium at a rigidly given price which explains the relationship between employment and the real wage in conditions of increasing returns. The concept of rationing has therefore apparently overcome an important limitation of neoclassical theory.

But this means that, in the course of achieving more 'realism' starting from the Walrasian world, we have bit by bit emptied the Walrasian universe of its theoretical content. Malinvaud and his school took away the flexibility of prices and the auctioneer to get closer to Keynes, Kahn eliminated utility, we have removed the rising supply curve, and the resulting model is a hybrid which may be of use in a discussion, but which cannot serve as the basis of a unifying theory.

In fact, full cost pricing itself is not a theory but a description of business practice in need of a theoretical explanation. Only the classical theory of prices, which does not require an assumption about returns to scale, can provide it by treating fixed capital as a joint product[7] so that gross profit margins on direct costs cover net profits and amortisation calculated according to a general rate of profit. The mark-up therefore represents not an arbitrary monopolistic charge but the result of a competitive process in which the fluctuations in the market show up – mainly for technological reasons – as fluctuations of capacity utilisation rather than as deviations of market prices from prices of production.

This has never been worked out completely. Nevertheless, it appears that, if we pursue the line of Kahn's methodological critique, we end up with the alternatives of either analysing processes of change in an ever more complex anecdotal chain of disequilibria, as in Malinvaud (1980), or of returning to the unifying principles of classical economics.

[7] One obtains the mark-ups from a fixed capital system of the Sraffa type with a uniform rate of profit by forming the 'centre' (Schefold, 1980, p. 163) of the system to eliminate old machines. The centre is like a single product system but with some coefficients which are functions of the rate of profit and represent the amortisation of the machine. The direct costs of full cost pricing are equal to the raw material costs and labour, the mark-up is equal to amortisation (depreciation *plus* financial charge) and net profits. The rate of the mark-up to prime costs is then seen to vary from industry to industry, although the rate of profit is uniform.

14

'Keynesian Fundamentalism': a critique

Marco Magnani

The central theme of what has come to be called 'Keynesian Fundamentalism' (Coddington, 1976, p. 1259) is fairly obvious; it attempts to stress the incompatibility of Keynes's major insights with neoclassical interpretations of the *General Theory* by offering an interpretation of Keynes that emphasises the importance of 'historical time' (and therefore of uncertainty and expectations) as opposed to the 'logical time' of orthodox neoclassical theory. Of course, while there is general agreement on this central theme, there are differences between the approaches of individual 'Fundamentalists'. For example, on the one hand there is the group of writers who focus mainly on the works of Keynes *per se* to erect their interpretation. The leading exponents of this approach are Davidson and Wells. On the other hand, there is the group of writers who erect a 'Fundamentalist' interpretation of Keynes's contribution not only on the basis of Keynes's own work but also in conjunction with arguments derived from what might be called the Kaleckian tradition. This second approach is followed explicitly by Eichner, Kregel and S. Weintraub. Indeed, what Eichner and Kregel call the 'Post-Keynesian Paradigm' or 'Post-Keynesian Economics' (Eichner and Kregel, 1975, Eichner, 1979a, b) adds to the central theme of reconstructing 'economic methodology in the face of uncertainty' the subsidiary ideas of incorporating into this approach the so-called Post-Keynesian theory of economic growth[1] and a theory of full cost pricing in an oligopolistic setting.

The purpose of this paper is to consider, from a theoretical point of view, whether these Fundamentalist interpretations are capable of sustaining the claim made on their behalf; namely that they mark a clean break from neoclassical attempts to deal with Keynes's contribution. In what follows I will refer mainly to the first group of writers mentioned above; the questions

[1] This 'theory' is derived from the contributions of Harrod, Joan Robinson, Kaldor and Pasinetti.

related more directly to the integration of the Kaleckian tradition with the Keynesian core of the Fundamentalist approach will be discussed very briefly, in order to focus better on 'historical time', uncertainty and expectations.

However, the neoclassical interpretations to which the Fundamentalists see themselves opposed are not all of one kind. First, there are those that are widely referred to under the heading 'Neoclassical Synthesis'. This approach was developed originally by Hicks (1937) and Modigliani (1944), and holds that Keynes's work is best seen as a particular case of traditional neoclassical theory modified by the presence of exogenous rigidities in some prices – usually the money wage rate or the rate of interest. Secondly, there is the more recent approach to Keynesian economics which uses the temporary equilibrium model (see, e.g., Grandmont, 1977) and tries at the same time to provide new microfoundations for neoclassical theory. For brevity, I will refer to this interpretation as the 'Post-Walrasian' approach.[2] It will be necessary for us to examine the analytical basis of the Fundamentalists' critique of each of these two types of neoclassical interpretation in order to assess both the extent to which these critiques are viable and whether it is possible (Fundamentalist assertions notwithstanding) to find a common ground between the Fundamentalist position and the two more orthodox ones. To this end, three questions will be considered.

First, the position of Fundamentalist and Post-Walrasian theory with respect to the traditional long-period method will be examined. It will become clear from this discussion that the long-period method is rejected by Fundamentalists as well as by Post-Walrasians. Secondly, we will examine Davidson's attempts to erect an explicit critique of the Post-Walrasian approach. On the one hand, it will be argued that Davidson misunderstands the essence of that part of Post-Walrasian theory he criticises; on the other hand, it will be argued that, on the central point concerning the role of expectations, Davidson's analysis overlaps in substance with the Post-Walrasian one. Thirdly, the 'Fundamentalist' attack against the explanation of involuntary unemployment given by the Neoclassical Synthesis will be examined. From this discussion we will see that the interpretation of Keynes given on this point by Fundamentalists does not diverge from the more orthodox one; in particular, it does not provide a satisfactory basis for a critique of the latter.

1. Keynesian Fundamentalism and the traditional long-period method

The general features of Fundamentalist views on the role played by uncertainty and expectations appear most forthrightly in the works of Joan Robin-

[2] Such labels are always to a certain extent matters of convention. Some of those writers I call Post-Walrasians would prefer to call themselves Non-Walrasians. In my view, the first label is more enlightening since it highlights the common ground they share with orthodox neoclassical theory concerning the idea of the role of scarcity as the basis of value.

son and Shackle. Indeed, Shackle's contributions seem to provide the most complete, unabridged statement of 'Fundamentalist philosophy'. The analysis of uncertainty and time is the central theme around which Shackle develops his arguments. In *Epistemics and Economics*, he argues that economics, being a discipline concerning human conduct, cannot be directed towards providing a general set of principles, comparable, say, to the law of gravity in physics. Neoclassical theory is accused by Shackle of attempting to do precisely this. By contrast, he stresses that the basic contradiction which *every* economic theory should recognise is that between reason and time. This contradiction is supposed to stem from the fact that the application of reason by means of formal tools *must* exclude uncertainty and 'novelty bearing time'.[3] This, according to Shackle, is also the very message of Keynes, '(who) pronounces the dissolution of the view of business conduct as *rational*, as the application to men's affairs of fully informed reason' (Shackle, 1974, p. 35, italics added).

It is not difficult to understand why this approach must reject the traditional long-period method of economic analysis which was based on the idea that the object of economics was to isolate the more persistent and systematic forces operating in the real world by abstracting from transitory, short-lived phenomena (see, e.g., Garegnani, 1976, and Milgate, 1979). It is precisely the abstraction from transitory forces that is *not* justified in Shackle's framework. Shackle's critique of neoclassical theory amounts also to an attack against the long-period method. In fact, by rejecting the very possibility of formulating *general* statements about the working of the economy, he must also abandon the possibility of building a theory based on the isolation of persistent forces which define the centres of gravity of the system. Instead, he puts forward a rather vague 'scientific' procedure which is supposed to acknowledge

> the fluorescence of mankind, the manifoldness, the richness and the detailed particular variants and individual facets of humanity, rather than dismissing them as the contingent outcomes of some original and essential principles which it is the real purpose of science to identify (Shackle, 1972, p. 29).

Even without ascribing to all Fundamentalists Shackle's extreme hostility to every kind of 'abstract' economic argument,[4] the rejection of the long-period method is common to Fundamentalists. Joan Robinson, for ex-

[3] This approach is retained also by Eichner: 'The change in investment or whatever else has produced the income effects is likely to initiate a process (or more accurately, modify a process already under way) *without a determinable end state*. In other words, the analysis shifts from logical time to historical time in which the future cannot be predicted because of the complex nature of the interaction among the different subsystems that comprise the larger system' (1979a, pp. 170-1, italics added).

[4] Shackle's attack on neoclassical economics seems in fact to fall into the trap of criticising it because of its lack of realism; a result which emerges from his indiscriminate critique of any procedure of abstraction. The sterility of this line of criticism has been neatly shown by Hahn (1973a, 1973b).

ample, has described long-run equilibrium (and the associated general rate of profit) as 'floating above historical time as a Platonic idea' (Robinson, 1979, p. 180). Minsky is equally explicit in rejecting it when he contrasts what he calls a 'Keynesian transitional equilibrium' with Marshall's long-period normal equilibrium:

> Every reference to an equilibrium is best interpreted as a reference to a *transitory* set of system variables, towards which the system is tending: but, in contrast to Marshall, as the economy moves toward such a set of system variables, endogenously determined changes occur which affect the set of system variables towards which the economy tends (Minsky, 1975, p. 71, italics added).

In other words, according to Minsky as well, no distinction can be drawn between changes, or the speeds of changes, in the data and in the dependent variables: *any* notion of equilibrium – a state reached by variables given a set of data – is eliminated. Thus, *a fortiori*, Minsky rejects the concept of long-run equilibrium. Furthermore, Eichner and Kregel do not seem to be clear about the concept of the long-period method. In fact, they identify it ultimately with steady-state growth paths where relative magnitudes do not change; therefore, according to these two writers, the only correct reference under these conditions is the Robinsonian Golden Age (see, e.g., Eichner and Kregel, 1975, p. 1296; Eichner, 1979a, p. 13).

The similarity with the current Post-Walrasian interpretations of the notion of long run equilibrium is straightforward, for the rejection of the traditional long-period method is not a prerogative of Fundamentalists; *it is the very essence of modern orthodox theory*. In *Value and Capital* Hicks provided the analytical foundations of the concept of temporary equilibrium, where uncertainty and expectations *have* to be taken into account as part of the data given at the beginning of the week. Indeed, the crucial role of expectations, and more generally of the way expectations are generated, is the hallmark of temporary equilibrium theory and therefore also of Post-Walrasian analysis:

> the current supply of commodities depends not so much upon what the current price is as upon what entrepreneurs have expected it to be in the past ... *This is the first main crux of dynamic theory* (Hicks, 1946, p. 117, italics added).

It is therefore not surprising to find that uncertainty and expectations are considered by Post-Walrasians as one of the most important features of Keynes's theory. Thus, for example, Grandmont can write:

> The idea that economic units have imperfect knowledge of their future environment and that, consequently, the future overshadows the present through the agents' expectations is at the heart of Keynesian thinking (Grandmont, 1977, p. 536).

The idea that the outcome of a market process depends on expectational factors provides the explicit foundation for the rejection of the traditional long-period method by the Post-Walrasians.[5]

Thus, Fundamentalists as well as Post-Walrasians argue that the attempt at building a theory on the basis of entirely objective and observable data, the goal of the traditional long-period method, must be dismissed.[6] It is clear therefore that the Fundamentalists' rejection of the traditional long-period method is not enough to separate them from the Post-Walrasians (or, indeed, from orthodox theory from *Value and Capital* onwards), since the latter advocate positively this course of action (see Milgate, 1979). It is necessary to look elsewhere for a difference.

2. Davidson's critique of Post-Walrasian reformulations of Keynes's theory

In an article entitled 'Money and General Equilibrium' (1977), Davidson attempts to erect an explicit critique of what we have referred to as the Post-Walrasian interpretations of Keynes. This section will consider the arguments that Davidson mounts in this and subsequent papers, to see if these provide the grounds necessary for us to distinguish between the two approaches.

As far as the controversy with Post-Walrasians is concerned, Davidson makes three 'fundamental' points. First, in a Keynesian context, money has two basic properties: it is the means of contractual settlement, and also a 'one way (present to future) time machine' (Davidson, 1977, p. 542), i.e. it is the most liquid asset in the economy. This property of liquidity requires that money must possess two well known characteristics analysed by Keynes in chapter 17 of the *General Theory*: a zero or negligible elasticity of production and a zero or negligible elasticity of substitution (see Davidson, 1977, p. 543). In a slightly more recent paper, Davidson argues that these are the essential features of a monetary economy, since in an uncertain world people

> feel queasy about undertaking any actions which will commit their current claims on resources on to a path which can be altered, if future events require, only at a very high cost (Davidson, 1978a, p. 222).

Money is therefore an asset which is not (either directly or indirectly) 'employment inducing'; its presence *explains* the existence of unemployment.[7]

[5] With respect to the role played by these latter in temporary equilibrium analysis, Garegnani has argued that 'the procedure which Hicks adopted, by which unobservable quantities, the expected prices, are introduced as independent variables, runs the risk of depriving the theory of any definite result' (Garegnani, above, p. 140).

[6] Note that in this context the term 'objective' does not bear any relation to the meaning usually attached to it in the debate 'subjective versus objective theories of value'. It means simply that the long-period method aims at a science founded on the possibility of identifying laws which work by abstracting from erratic and subjective factors like expectations – Garegnani's 'unobservable quantities' (n. 5 above).

[7] On this point see Davidson, 1977, pp. 551-3; 1978b, p. 66.

Davidson goes on to argue that the existence of an asset which is not resource-consuming destroys the universality of Walras's law, i.e. the equality between expected production earnings and intended expenditure. Thus, according to Davidson,

> it is the peculiar properties of money in a world where the future is uncertain that is the fundamental cause of unemployment (Davidson, 1977, p. 555).

Davidson's logic on this first point seems to run as follows. Uncertainty implies the existence of an asset with negligible elasticities of substitution and of production which prevents the economy from reaching full employment. Moreover, the stability over time of the unemployment position so determined depends, given these premises, on well-behaved expectations, i.e. an elasticity of expectations not greater than unity (see Davidson, 1978, ch. 16). These, in turn, are generated by a belief in the stability of monetary magnitudes. Davidson stresses that in a monetary economy, where 'money comes into existence, along with debts, which are contracts for deferred payments, and price lists, which are offers and contracts for sale or purchase' (Davidson, 1978a, p. 147), money-denominated forward contracts play a crucial role in controlling the uncertain future.

It is interesting to note that among these 'money-denominated' contracts the money wage emerges as the most important one; for the 'stickiness' of money wages (so that, given productivity, prices remain stable) is a *necessary* condition for the belief in the stability of monetary magnitudes.[8]

Davidson's second point concerns the criticism of Grandmont and Laroque (1976), which is based on the fact that they would restore the standard explanation of involuntary unemployment provided by the Neoclassical Synthesis, i.e. the rigidity of money wages due to market imperfections and monopolistic factors. We will return to this point in the next section.

Thirdly, on the basis of these first two points, Davidson concludes that Post-Walrasian theory – once the necessity of abandoning the neat Arrow-Debreu model is recognised – becomes a hopeless attempt to generate new ideas by means of a theory which is by its nature unable to provide them.

Obviously several points need to be clarified in order to evaluate Davidson's critique. The first is straightforward. Davidson's analysis of the necessity that the elasticity of price expectations be less than unity in order to have a definitely stable system overlaps entirely with the Hicksian one (see Hicks, 1946, p. 255). In Hicks's framework expectations play a crucial role in defining the temporal paths of the system. Indeed, the subsequent 'Post-Walrasian' analysis made the properties of the expectation function one of the necessary conditions for the existence of a temporary equilibrium with a positive price of money.[9]

[8] This is the same interpretation of Keynes's view – on this point – as provided by Hicks, 1946, p. 246; see Davidson, 1978a, pp. 388-92, and Davidson, 1978b, p. 66.

[9] Grandmont (1971) introduced the condition that expectations should not, loosely speaking, depend 'too much' on current prices. This property was called 'uniform tightness' by Radner

The other points relating to Davidson's article concern the role of money and the money wage in determining an unemployment equilibrium. The most striking paradox is the fact that Davidson, while arguing that Grandmont and Laroque's model is not a model of a monetary economy because there are no contracts in money terms, is actually forced to admit that Grandmont and Laroque 'introduce into the system (without acknowledgment) Keynes's essential properties of money' (Davidson, 1977, p. 558). In fact, in the first part of their article Grandmont and Laroque analyse a short-run Walrasian model with fiat money, the latter being also the only store of value available to agents. All prices except the money wage, which is bounded from below, are perfectly flexible. Under standard assumptions they show that an equilibrium with rationed labour supply exists. But the existence of money with both the properties mentioned above is not sufficient to determine an unemployment (rationed) equilibrium; the rigidity of money wages is, in this framework, a *sine qua non* condition. In fact, the two French authors show also that in the absence of a downward rigid money wage a temporary *competitive* equilibrium (i.e. market clearing, given uniform tight expectations) does exist in spite of the presence of 'Keynesian' money (Grandmont and Laroque, 1976, p. 58). Davidson is obviously right in underlining the insufficiency of a picture which relates Keynesian economics to a short-run framework with exogenous price rigidities. But Grandmont and Laroque, in the second and more relevant part of their article, do not simply *postulate* the rigidity of money wages, they actually attempt to explain it by invoking the idea that prices (wages) are fixed by firms (workers). This second line of argument pertains to the monopolistic competition approach, where the wage is not *assumed* to be fixed but is rather *determined* in a particular way (albeit at a level which exhibits involuntary unemployment):

> the wage is neither fixed nor arbitrary nor flexible. It is what it is because no agent finds it advantageous to change it (Hahn, 1977, p. 34).

Negishi follows the same line with respect to the 'rejection' of *exogenous* wage rigidity:

> the assumption of wage rigidity is not necessary. The wage rigidity is not a cause of underemployment equilibrium (Negishi, 1977, p. 497).

These (and other) developments of Post-Walrasian theory are completely neglected by Davidson; his only reference to Walrasian models plus exogenous rigidities is really not important. This, of course, is not to deny that inflexibility of money wages is at the heart of this approach to Keynes – but it is clear, though Davidson does not seem to notice, that this inflexiblity is not

---

(1974, p. 65) and is inconsistent with an elasticity of expectations equal to unity. Davidson, himself, seems in one place to connect Keynesian unemployment equilibrium with a zero or negligible elasticity of expectations (1977, p. 549).

a *postulate*, it is explained by a particular theory.

It is therefore not surprising to find that, in reality, this stream of Post-Walrasian theory *agrees* with Davidson about the unnecessary assumption of an exogenous rigid money wage in order to define the features of a Keynesian economy. Indeed, the only basic difference between the two approaches is that whereas Post-Walrasians work on the basis of microfoundations, Davidson rejects these foundations without apparently knowing what they are. He is therefore bound to reconstruct *de facto* Keynesian unemployment by means of exogenous rigidities of wages in spite of his critique of orthodox Keynesianism (we will return to this point in the next section). Furthermore, it has been shown that there is no substantial incompatibility between Davidson's approach to the role of expectations and that of Post-Walrasian theorists.

It is difficult to understand how it is possible to reject the Post-Walrasian approach, which tries to interpret Keynesian economics by invoking uncertainty, expectations and money, and to state at the same time that the main issue of Keynesian economics is this very triad of uncertainty-money-expectations.[10] This, of course, is not to deny that there are many ways of modelling expectations which will lead to very different results on the stability properties of the system. The point is rather that in their emphasis on expectations, the role of money and the rejection of the long-period method, the Post-Walrasians and the Fundamentalists are of one mind.

3. Keynesian unemployment, money wage rigidity and the Fundamentalist interpretation of the theory of effective demand

At this stage, it will be instructive to develop a point already dealt with partially in the previous section. It concerns the role of wage and price rigidities in the explanation of involuntary unemployment.

Patinkin's *Money, Interest and Prices* seems the most useful basis on which to tackle the problem at hand, since it provides one of the clearest versions of the so-called 'Bastard Keynesianism', the major theoretical enemy of Fundamentalists. In Patinkin's model the aggregate demand for labour is identified *tout court* with the marginal productivity schedule. Equilibrium can mean only full employment:

> by definition the extent of involuntary unemployment is identified with the ex-

[10] Davidson mentions a 'Marshallian microeconomics' which is supposed to be considered as different – because of the possibility of inserting into it historical time – from the Walrasian one. The only sense one could make of this claim is the Hicksian one: in *Value and Capital* Hicks argues that Marshall faces up to the fact that 'supplies and (ultimately demands too) are governed by expected prices quite as much as by current prices' (p. 117). But this is also the Post-Walrasian position. It is interesting to note that Davidson's critique of the procedure adopted by Hicks in *Value and Capital* is directed at the idea that spot prices lead to market clearing at the beginning of the 'week' (auctioneer hypothesis) and *not* at the role played by expectations (see Davidson, 1978b, pp. 59-60).

> tent of the excess supply of labour which exists at the prevailing wage rate. It follows that ... the coexistence of involuntary unemployment and flexible wage rates precludes the existence of equilibrium (Patinkin, 1965, p. 315).

At the same time Patinkin is aware that his tautological definition does not bring us – as it stands – very far. The real problem is whether a market system with flexible prices is able to eliminate involuntary unemployment. As is well known, Patinkin's analysis of this question is centred on departures from the supply and demand curves of labour; involuntary unemployment becomes a dynamic disequilibrium process. Once the system happens to have been brought out of equilibrium, the perfect flexibility of money wages and prices assures, through the real balance effect, the convergence to full employment. This interpretation of Keynesian unemployment has been challenged by Fundamentalists.

It is fairly evident that once unemployment has been discarded as a possible permanent 'resting place' of the system – as in Patinkin, where the notion of equilibrium implies both clearing of markets and no tendency for the variables to change over time – the rationale for a fundamentally different 'Keynesian economics' must fall (see, on this point, Davidson, 1967 and 1977, pp. 546-50). A very different view is therefore necessary to the Fundamentalists in order to show the inadequacy of Patinkin's interpretation. This supposedly 'different' view is often referred to as the 'aggregate supply' approach. The first step is to reject the idea according to which the labour market is the bargaining place of the real wage – a course which leads Patinkin to define only one equilibrium level of income, i.e. that which corresponds to full employment. By contrast, the Fundamentalists purpose is to provide the rationale for the existence of a multiplicity of levels of income (and hence of employment) at which the system presents no tendency to change over time.

In their analysis, all the possible equilibrium levels of employment are determined by the intersections of aggregate demand and supply curves. *Given money wages*, the real wage is determined by the firms' profit-maximising condition, i.e. price equals marginal cost. Once the levels of output and employment have been determined by the 'point of effective demand', the resulting marginal productivity of labour is equalised to the real wage through variations of the price level. Moreover, the hypothesis of a decreasing marginal product of labour (made by Keynes in the *General Theory* and retained by some Fundamentalists; see Wells 1974, Davidson and Smolensky, 1964, pp. 119-20) ensures that the curve relating real wage and employment is downward sloping. The aggregate demand for labour therefore depicts a *market equilibrium curve*: every point on this curve corresponds to an equilibrium level of income.[11] Wells, for example, writes:

[11] The distinction between individual demand curves and market equilibrium curves had been introduced by Patinkin and is accepted by Davidson (1967) who, however, argues that on the point concerning the aggregate demand for labour Patinkin confused them.

In direct opposition to the classical line of thought which made the level of employment depend upon the real wage rate, Keynes finds in chapter 20 that in fact it is the level of employment that determines the real wage rate (Wells, 1974, p. 160).[12]

Of course, in this framework the assumption of a rigid money wage is necessary in order to derive the relation between real wage and employment; involuntary unemployment is therefore explained by assuming an infinitely elastic supply of labour curve:[13]

Involuntary unemployment can exist because the supply curve for labour (in money units) has a perfectly elastic floor which is set by institutional factors (Davidson and Smolensky, 1964, p. 172).

Roberts (1978), E.R. Weintraub (1979) and Tuchscherer (1979) slightly modify this analysis by emphasising that the profit-maximising condition entrepreneurs adopt has to be considered as an *expected* equality, which does not have to be realised *ex post*. However, the substance of the picture does not change at all, since the disappointment of short-run expectations is by no means the essence of the theory of effective demand – as Keynes pointed out in a now famous passage (Keynes, 1973, vol. 14, p. 181). The analysis can therefore be carried out under the simplifying hypothesis that short-run expectations *are always met*; i.e. expected prices coincide with the realised ones.

In any event, the following question naturally arises. To what extent does the hypothesis of rigid money wages – necessary in order to derive the Fundamentalists' employment function – differ from the explanation of Keynesian unemployment provided by the Neoclassical Synthesis? The answer is that it does not. E.R. and S. Weintraub, in their critique of Patinkin's labour market analysis, state explicitly that:

on this [their] interpretation ... we are back to Lange-Klein representation of 'involuntary' unemployment or underemployment equilibrium (E.R. and S. Weintraub, 1972, p. 95).

In fact, by means of the 'Lange-Klein representation' Modigliani was able to define an equilibrium which is not normally a full-employment one, since once the money wage is given there is no mechanism that assures automatically the attainment of full employment (see Modigliani, 1944, 1963). On this point, there is no substantial difference with the Fundamentalists' position. It would seem, in fact, that Fundamentalists, in order to escape from Patinkin's analysis, find themselves in the company of another prestigious orthodox Keynesian!

Here we reach the heart of the problem. The fact that the neoclassical

[12] For the same kind of analysis, see Wells, 1979; Davidson, 1967; Minsky, 1975, p. 40.

[13] A rationale for this particular shape of the supply curve of labour is provided by Davidson (1967) in order to separate the notion of equilibrium over time from the clearing of markets.

system with exogenous rigid money wages displays an under-employment equilibrium was recognised long ago and has since been rigorously demonstrated (see, for example, Glustoff, 1968). Once one accepts the hypothesis that the money wage is exogenously given, unemployment follows as a straightforward consequence. This is true, so to speak, by definition. If we take as reference framework a neoclassical system with perfectly flexible prices, unemployment can result *only* as a consequence of rigidities in some prices. Fundamentalists cannot escape this conclusion; the explicit reference made by some of them to a 'flat form' of the supply curve of labour reveals their need to translate into an orthodox language the existence of involuntary unemployment.

As we noticed above, Davidson tries to find a rationale for this exogenous rigidity by postulating that a rigid money wage rate is a necessary condition for the viability of a monetary economy. This might be true, *but it does not contradict the view that it is by means of this rigidity that unemployment is to be explained.* On the contrary, it merely explains *why* the money wage must be rigid; once this has been clarified he can use the rigidity assumption in a *different* part of his analysis (i.e. effective demand) in order to derive unemployment equilibrium. Davidson's attempt to demonstrate unemployment equilibrium within a framework *based on supply and demand functions* (even if Marshallian ones) without wage rigidity, however motivated, is an impossible task, quite independently of the existence of money with the two Keynesian properties.[14]

However, several Fundamentalists claim that their approach denies the existence of a labour market in the neoclassical sense (S. Weintraub, 1978; Tuchscherer, 1979; Eichner, 1979a; Appelbaum 1979). Thus to assume a horizontal supply function of labour amounts for them to an empty exercise in neoclassical economics. But from an analytical point of view, this argument is not sufficient to remove, on this issue, the similarity in explanations of involuntary unemployment between this approach and that of the Neoclassical Synthesis. One can easily maintain the general framework of the latter, yet argue (as the Fundamentalists seem to do) that the money wage is not determined by the market, but by bargains which reflect the relative strengths of the two monopolies (trade unions and entrepreneurs' organisations). In fact, these Fundamentalists feel the need to go further, by stating that prices are determined in the industrial sector by a mark-up over costs. The competitive world of orthodox neoclassical theory is thus abandoned in favour of an analysis based on oligopoly. Unfortunately, if this choice is made only in the name of a closer contact with reality the results it can achieve are not very far reaching. As a matter of fact, Modigliani (1963) introduced as 'a more realistic case' oligopolistic competition (full-cost pric-

[14] This does not mean that the theory of effective demand is not based on monetary magnitudes. Those authors who try to relate Keynes's contribution to the Marxian theory of crisis consider this point as central to this relation (see, e.g., Kenway, ch. 8, above). But the zero elasticities of money do not play any role within the latter approach.

ing) without invalidating his general approach at all (see Modigliani, 1963, pp. 91-3).

Moreover, in order to analyse the role of the hypothesis of given money wage in the Fundamentalist approach we can neglect full-cost pricing, since this does not alter the logic of the aggregate supply approach; the determination of unemployment equilibrium via intersection of aggregate supply and aggregate demand runs along the same tracks with only minor amendments (see, for example, S. Weintraub, 1978, ch. 10).

Let us now return to the main theme of this section, i.e. the Fundamentalists' critique of the Neoclassical Synthesis, in order to make a final point. It has been shown that the hypothesis of rigid money wages is crucial as far as the existence of unemployment is concerned. Another *separate* and important problem concerns the *effects of a change in the rigid money* wage. The two issues should not be confused. Davidson's (1977) critique of the hypothesis of rigid money wages made by Grandmont and Laroque (1976) reveals precisely this confusion. Davidson writes – considering this point as the separation line with respect to orthodox theory – that Keynes argued that:

> a reduction in money wages (or prices) would not, *ceteris paribus*, have a direct tendency to increase employment (Davidson, 1977, p. 558).

The distinction between the two problems can be seen most clearly in the fixed-price model of Malinvaud (1977) where the hypothesis of given money wages and prices allows for the existence of rationing equilibria. Once the different types of rationing have been determined in the wage-price space (which contains the Walrasian equilibrium) Malinvaud discovers that in the 'Keynesian region', i.e. where excess supply prevails in the labour market and the goods market, an increase in money wages at constant prices reduces unemployment.[15] A very 'Keynesian' result, *perfectly in line with Davidson's claim*.

This already casts serious doubt on Fundamentalist statements about correlation between wage changes and employment as *the* crucial difference between Keynes and orthodox theory. However, the weakness of the claim will become yet more apparent if we examine another example, taken this time from the criticism of writers belonging to the Neoclassical Synthesis. Davidson and Smolensky (1964a, 1964b) argue that a change in the exogenous money wage does not influence the equilibrium of the system via the effects on the real money supply, as in the 'strict Keynesian version' of Modigliani (1963). It has (they claim) an effect that works through changes in the real spending functions. In order to reach this conclusion they abandon the hypothesis of an unitary elasticity of expectations and of the absence of redistributional effects,

[15] See, however, the *caveat* of K. and W. Hildenbrand (1978). I ignore here other aspects of Malinvaud's model, like the hypothesis of autonomous investment, which might be sources of serious discussion, in order to concentrate only on the positive correlation between the wage rate and employment, which is the point raised by Fundamentalists.

both made by Modigliani in his model. In this way, consumption and investment depend directly on the level of prices. At the same time, the real balance effect – which indeed *states* this dependence – is weakened because of the abandonment of the hypothesis mentioned above. This means that, if wages and prices fall, there is no sure tendency to push the system towards full employment because of the existence of opposite tendencies. The crux of the matter is obviously the *relative weight* of expectational and redistributional factors (which have *negative* effects in the case of a fall of prices) with respect to the real balance and the Keynes effect – which have *positive* effects (see Davidson and Smolensky, 1964a, pp. 199-205; E.R. and S. Weintraub, 1972, pp. 95-6). This conclusion is, however, quite familiar to orthodox Keynesians. Modigliani (1963, p. 88) stressed that the importance of the real balance effect is empirically questionable because of the existence of other effects. Furthermore, Patinkin points out that the working of the real balance effect may be impeded by the existence of adverse expectations. Of course, the field is open for different opinions about the importance in the real world of the effects mentioned above. However, these disagreements on the relationship between money wage and employment pertain to the empirical field; *they do not concern the analytical framework, which is the same.*

4. Conclusion

Thus, in the last analysis, on the question of involuntary unemployment most of the theoretical differences between Fundamentalist and mainstream interpretations of Keynes disappear. Moreover, as we have seen, the elevation of uncertainty and expectations to the centre of the Fundamentalist stage has not generated conclusions significantly different from those derived from recent neoclassical interpretations of Keynes. Of course, there does exist another line of argument that links Keynes's contribution and the principle of effective demand to the classical theory of value and distribution without making expectations and uncertainty the lynch-pin of the argument (see Garegnani, Chapter 7 above; Milgate, 1982; Eatwell, Chapter 6 above). But even leaving this approach aside, it is clear that a prior problem is to clear the ground of theoretical misunderstandings. The controversy between Fundamentalists and Neoclassicists seems to be founded largely on such a misunderstanding.

15

Unemployment and the market mechanism

Murray Milgate and John Eatwell

> There are ..., I should admit, forces which one might fairly well call 'automatic' which operate under any normal monetary system in the direction of restoring a long-period equilibrium between saving and investment. The point upon which I cast doubt – though the contrary is generally believed – is whether these 'automatic forces' will ... tend to bring about not only an equilibrium between saving and investment but also an optimum level of production (Keynes, 1973, vol. 13, p. 395).

An analysis of the determination of the level of unemployment in a market economy requires some characterisation of the relationship between unemployment and the operation of the market mechanism. The aim of this chapter is to provide a classification of the various positions adopted towards the problem of unemployment according to the role differing schools of economic thought ascribe to the market mechanism. It will be possible in this way to reveal the structure of ideas which underlies the differing positions.

Two main groups of writers will dominate the discussion. On the one hand, there are those authors who argue that in the long run the forces of demand and supply will tend to push the economic system towards a full-employment level of activity (or, in certain more recent expositions, towards a 'natural' rate of unemployment). These we shall refer to as the 'market mechanism group'. On the other hand, there are those who, while accepting the characterisation of a market mechanism which operates under the influence of the forces of demand and supply, maintain that this mechanism is inhibited (or perhaps even totally obstructed) by the presence of a variety of market imperfections, social and institutional, such as sticky wages and prices, sticky interest rates or the disruptive impact of uncertainty and disap-

* An earlier version of this chapter was presented at the *Cambridge Journal of Economics* conference on 'The New Orthodoxy', held in July 1981. It has since been substantially revised.

pointed expectations. This latter group, which we shall refer to as the 'imperfectionists', encompasses a whole variety of writers who often have little in common other than the fact that their support for employment policies based on the direct manipulation of the level of effective demand derives from the characterisation of unemployment as arising from an obstruction of the market mechanism.

The major theme of this chapter will be that the position of the imperfectionists is, in the final analysis, untenable. For not only is the determining role of imperfections more difficult to sustain the longer the period of time that is taken into account, but also the argument that the operation of the market mechanism is inhibited by, say, the role of trade unions or the influence of uncertainty, involves *a priori* the acceptance of the underlying theoretical model of the operation of that mechanism which is provided by the market mechanism group. It all becomes a matter of degree.

It is important to realise that the issue at stake here is not simply one of theoretical interpretation or empirical verification. It is a matter of the utmost practical importance. The formulation and justification of economic policy is rendered arbitrary by the imperfectionist position. The ultimate superiority of a policy of fiscal expansion *vis-à-vis* a policy of social legislation to, say, 'unstick' the wage, is not self-evident. Indeed, if the powerful mechanism of market adjustment via demand and supply *is* present in the economy, then it seems almost perverse not to attempt to harness these (ultimately) beneficial forces. Of course, many of these issues are partially obscured by the distinction between long-run and short-run situations. However, just as short-run movements in the economy are regulated by the more persistent forces governing its long-run tendencies, so short-run policy measures to remedy the consequences of disequilibrium are conditional upon long-run policy prescriptions.

Thus it can be said that the theoretical position of the orthodox market mechanism school (whether in monetarist, rational expectations or supply-side guise) is perfectly secure – for its imperfectionist critics share its characterisation of the operation of the market mechanism; albeit with some lack of conviction.

In marked contrast to both of these positions, there is the view presented in the *General Theory*, which is particularly clearly stated in the passage from the drafts of that book reproduced at the beginning of this chapter (see also Keynes, 1973, vol. 7, p. 254). Here, the novel idea which emerges is not that the market mechanism is obstructed or inhibited ('there are ... automatic [forces] which operate ... in the direction of restoring long-period equilibrium') but rather that the way in which this mechanism functions is not such as to establish full employment by 'clearing the labour market' – i.e. the market mechanism will not even 'tend to bring about ... an optimum level of production'. However, this chapter will not dwell on the implications which follow from this more radical idea (which is fully discussed in Milgate, 1982). Instead, our aim will be to elucidate the theoretical underpinnings of the members of the orthodox market mechanism group, and thence to analyse their debates with various imperfectionists – examining as we proceed the extent to which the imperfectionist position in any sense reflects Keynes's contribution.

In section 1 of this chapter we examine the various interpretations which may be placed on the notion of a 'self-adjusting market', particularly with respect to Keynes's own view of the market mechanism and the imperfectionist view. In section 2, one of the most prominent and influential of imperfectionist arguments (that unemployment may be attributed to rigid or sticky money wages) is exposed to Keynes's own arguments on the movement of money wages. Finally, in section 3, we examine the debate over the natural rate/rational expectations hypothesis; a debate in which the theoretical poverty of the imperfectionist position has been starkly revealed.

1. Self-adjustment and the market mechanism

The notion that the study of the economic system presupposes an autonomous, law-governed market mechanism is as old as economics itself. From Adam Smith to the present day, economists have been trying to reveal the forces which regulate the operation of the market mechanism and, consequently, to provide an account of the results which those forces tend to produce in the economic system. Indeed, it can be said with some confidence that all the most important doctrinal disputes in the history of the discipline have been conducted not over whether there *are* systematic and persistent forces at work in the economy, but rather over what these forces may be. The decline of the classical surplus theory of value and distribution and its replacement by the marginalist theory of demand and supply is, of course, the most prominent example of a change in the characterisation of the operation of the market mechanism. But the really interesting question in the context of the analysis of unemployment concerns the interpretation of Keynes's challenge to the orthodox position on the market mechanism.

It is well known that Keynes not infrequently couched general statements of his opposition to the orthodox conception of the market mechanism and the notion of self-adjustment in terms that were, at best, somewhat ambiguous. Very early on in the *General Theory*, for example, one reads that the traditional doctrine is 'equivalent to the proposition that there is no *obstacle* to full employment' (Keynes, 1973, vol. 7, p. 26, italics added; but see also vol. 14, p. 26). Just one year before the publication of the *General Theory*, Keynes told a radio audience that he disputed the idea that 'the economic system is, in any significant sense, self-adjusting' (Keynes, 1973, vol. 13, p. 487). It is obviously crucial to understand correctly the meaning of such statements. Broadly speaking, two views have prevailed. The first of these holds that the statements should be taken to imply that there are no automatic, self-adjusting forces at work in the economy at all: 'A theory of unemployment is necessarily, inescapably, a theory of disorder' (Shackle,

1967, p. 133). The second holds that while there are underlying forces promoting self-adjustment *towards full employment*, the operation of these forces is disturbed by the presence of certain frictions or rigidities. Neither view is satisfactory.

The first reading can be eliminated readily enough. The strange supposition that Keynes's analysis of unemployment embodies the idea that there are *no* systematic forces at work in the economic system (i.e. that the notion of the very existence of a systematic market mechanism, however defined, was itself rejected by Keynes) is contradicted again and again throughout the course of the *General Theory*. One can only wonder at what nonsense, according to this reading, Keynes must have been thinking when he wrote of 'the economic machine' (Keynes, 1973, vol. 7, p. 50) and of unemployment being the outcome of 'natural tendencies' (ibid., p. 254), or when, having drawn attention to the innumerable cross-currents at work in the economic system at any given moment, he held that the components of effective demand were 'useful and convenient to isolate' because 'if we examine any actual problem along the lines of ... [that] schematism, we shall find it more manageable; and our practical intuition ... will be offered a less intractable material upon which to work' (ibid., p. 249). Indeed, the passage quoted at the beginning of this paper, though coming from the drafts of the *General Theory*, makes it perfectly clear that Keynes was never in any doubt about the presence of automatic forces in a market economy.[1]

If, therefore, we must conclude that Keynes did not reject the notion of the market mechanism and the related idea of self-adjustment in its most general setting, then there would seem to be a *prima facie* case for the second interpretation of the remarks cited above: namely, that since under the normal operation of the market mechanism self-adjustment promotes the *full* employment of labour, the essence of Keynes's position was to focus attention upon the consequences of interferences or 'obstacles' to this process. This is, of course, the view which has dominated the literature, and it is the basis of all imperfectionist analyses of unemployment. However, this reading of Keynes on the notion of self-adjustment, though more widely accepted, is no more firmly grounded than the first.

Let us consider, to begin with, the point in the *General Theory* where Keynes states that orthodox theory pre-supposes that there is no 'obstacle' to full employment – for at first sight this appears to provide some textual evidence upon which to base an imperfectionist reading. Now, if this is to be taken as

[1] The fact that Keynes was dealing with 'statements of tendency', as such a stance implies, is clearly revealed in a passage from one of the earliest drafts of the material that was later to become the *General Theory*: 'the orthodox equilibrium theory of economics has assumed ... that there are natural forces tending to bring the volume of ... output ... back to the optimum level whenever temporary forces have led it to depart from this level. But ... the equilibrium level towards which output tends to return after temporary disturbances is not necessarily the optimum level' (Keynes, 1973, vol. 13, p. 406). Indeed, the market mechanism and the isolation of determining circumstances are those 'formal principles of thought' without which, Keynes noted, 'we shall be lost in the wood' (ibid., vol. 7, p. 297).

an accurate reading of Keynes, then one would expect to find immediately following it a catalogue of such 'obstacles' – frictions and rigidities which, on this reading, would disturb the underlying tendency towards full employment. Unfortunately, in the very next sentence one finds Keynes drawing an entirely different implication from his statement than any that would be required to substantiate an imperfectionist reading. For instead of deferring to 'obstacles', Keynes states forthrightly: 'this is not the true law' (Keynes, 1973, vol. 7, p. 26).[2] This can be read in only one way; that the orthodox doctrine that there is an underlying tendency towards full employment is not a true statement of the general tendencies inherent in the operation of the market mechanism. Indeed, this conclusion is highlighted a few pages further on when Keynes observes that 'it may well be that the classical theory represents the way in which we should like our Economy to behave ... but to assume that it actually does so is to assume our difficulties away.' (ibid., p. 34; see also p. 16).

In those passages where Keynes mentions explicitly the notion of self-adjustment, the textual evidence to support an imperfectionist reading is no more convincing. The customary circumstances in which Keynes raises this issue concern the self-adjustment of wages and the self-adjustment of the rate of interest. Since the former case (wage flexibility) will be examined in detail in the next section of the paper, we may concentrate here on the latter case – self-adjustment of the rate of interest.[3]

It is essential at the outset to define precisely the proposition to which Keynes objected. On this matter the *General Theory* is perfectly clear: 'the weight of my criticism', Keynes writes, 'is directed ... against the notion that the rate of interest and the volume of investment are self-adjusting *at the optimum level*' (Keynes, 1973, vol. 7, p. 339, italics added). A little later, he observes:

> for several millenniums, enlightened opinion held for certain and obvious a doctrine which the classical school has repudiated as childish, but which deserves rehabilitation and honour. I mean the doctrine that the rate of interest is not self-adjusting *at a level best suited to the social advantage* ... (ibid., p. 351, italics added).

There is ample evidence here to suggest that when Keynes rejected the idea that economy is 'self-adjusting' he was rejecting a much more specific

[2] It is worth remembering, in this context, that whenever Keynes outlined the basis of the orthodox view that there was a tendency towards full employment (the 'law' to which this passage refers) he invariably *included* as part of that statement the possibility of temporary deviations and interferences (see, e.g., Keynes, 1973, vol. 7, pp. 6, 8, 9, 16, 257, 279; vol. 13, pp. 486-7; vol. 14, pp. 363-4; vol. 29, pp. 97, 102). In this light, it is all the more difficult to understand how imperfectionist interpretations have gained such credibility as accurate readings of the text.

[3] On this issue we are concerned exclusively with Keynes's views on self-adjustment. We will not here refer to the weaknesses of Keynes's theory, which derive from the presence of a traditional, interest elastic, investment demand function – which, once admitted, re-introduces the requirement of a 'sticky' interest rate.

doctrine than the general idea that the normal operation of the market mechanism tends to produce definite outcomes. For it is evident that Keynes was attacking the idea that there is a tendency for self-adjustment *towards full employment* (as the italicised sections of the passages quoted above confirm).[4] In short, we must distinguish carefully, as Keynes sometimes failed to do, between two quite distinct propositions which, in the present context, we keep strictly separate:

(1) that the economy is a self-adjusting mechanism in the general sense, i.e. it produces definite outcomes;

(2) that the process of self-adjustment is explained by having recourse to the orthodox demand-and-supply theory of the market mechanism which attempts to specify *which* outcomes will be forthcoming.

Keynes's quarrel was with the second of these propositions, not the first. Indeed, the second proposition is just another way of stating the orthodox doctrine that in the long run there is a tendency for the market mechanism to produce full employment.

Returning to Keynes's remark that he rejected the idea that the 'economic system is, in any significant sense, self-adjusting' (quoted on p. 262 above), the key to its correct interpretation lies in that qualifying clause, 'in any significant sense'. For the 'significant sense' refers to full employment. What is being rejected here is not the general notion of self-adjustment but the orthodox theory of employment.[5] The imperfectionists might wish to argue that Keynes should not have made such a claim (as Schumpeter, 1954, p. 624 and Leijonhufvud, 1971, p. 22, n. 1 have done), but the fact that he did so bears out our argument that the market mechanism and self-adjustment were basic to Keynes's alternative theory of unemployment.

Keynes's adherence to the general notion of self-adjustment is, perhaps, nowhere more clearly evident than in his discussion of the process through which planned saving and investment are brought into equilibrium.[6] For here, although the theory of effective demand indicates that this self-adjusting process (i.e. the operation of the market mechanism as it affects employment) does not tend to produce those desirable outcomes that it was asserted to produce according to the orthodox demand-and-supply characterisation of the market mechanism, it is not to frictions and rigidities (or 'obstacles' to the normal operation of the market mechanism) that Keynes appeals for his results.

[4] See also Keynes, 1973, vol. 14, p. 26 and vol. 29, p. 97. This conclusion is further supported by Keynes's frequent substitution of the term 'self-righting' for that of 'self-adjusting' (see, e.g., ibid., vol. 14, p. 118).

[5] Thus, towards the end of the *General Theory* Keynes states that his objection is against 'the theoretical foundations' of the orthodox school (Keynes, 1973, vol. 7, p. 339). See also the passage quoted in Chapter 1, p. 17 above.

[6] See, e.g., Keynes, 1973, vol. 14, p. 211 and vol. 29, pp. 262-3.

Given these facts, the development of an imperfectionist interpretation of the *General Theory* was doubly fortuitous from the point of view of orthodox neoclassical analysis. In the first place, it provided the grounds for a rapid absorption of 'Keynesian' economics into what could be held up to be a more 'practical' and 'relevant' version of the older orthodoxy.[7] Secondly, and probably most important, it eliminated the necessity of scrapping the entire corpus of neoclassical theory; a course that would have been required had the central message of the *General Theory* – that the normal operation of the market mechanism will ensure neither the maintenance of, nor a tendency towards the full employment of labour – been taken seriously. Of course, this does not mean that the famous 'neoclassical synthesis' was entirely without textual foundation. By skilfully focussing on the crucial weaknesses of the *General Theory*, most notably the marginal efficiency of capital theory of investment and Keynes's unsatisfactory attempts to criticise the internal logic of the classical theory of interest by means of liquidity-preference theory, it was possible to present Keynes's results as special cases, albeit empirically relevant ones, of a more general theory.[8]

However, despite the apparent rigour and striking popularity of imperfectionist approaches to 'Keynesian' economics in the immediate post-war years, their ultimate reliance upon arbitrary inhibitions has proved to be a central flaw. Once their prestige as the accredited theoretical foundation for economic policy formulation began to falter with the manifest failure of the policies they suggested in the late 1960s and early 1970s, authors who advocated a more explicit long-run equilibrium approach to the study of macroeconomic phenomena came to the forefront (see pp. 272-7 below). This apparent turn-around in the climate of economic opinion, which has left 'Keynesian' economists confused and searching for ever more complicated explanations, is, in fact, not at all surprising. For in truth there has been no turn around at all. The only thing that has happened is that the underlying orthodox theoretical foundations of the imperfectionist position have been re-asserted; this has re-established the dominance of analytical coherence over arbitrary 'realism'. Once the imperfectionist position, whose only attraction was the fact that it somehow seemed to be talking about well-defined and easily observable economic phenomena, ceased to reflect the behaviour of the economic system, the underlying orthodox analysis of the relationship between employment and the operation of the market mechanism was bound

[7] Indeed, Hicks made just such a claim in his 1937 'Mr Keynes and the Classics' paper, where he incorrectly attributed to Keynes's analysis of unemployment the postulate of money-wage rigidity. In that paper Hicks argued that 'this is the kind of change ... we ought to be making all the time in response to changing facts' (Hicks, 1937, p. 147). It is difficult to know exactly what 'facts' had changed, since institutional wage determination had evolved in Britain from at least the second half of the nineteenth century; an attempt to rescue a demand-and-supply explanation of wages on the grounds that once-upon-a-time this was so, is rather dubious.

[8] Thereby implicitly, and somewhat disingenuously, accusing Keynes of exaggeration in the choice of title for his book (*cf.* Pigou, 1936, who makes the charge explicit).

to re-surface – if only by virtue of its greater theoretical consistency (see, for example, Friedman, 1974, for a cogent claim to this effect).

In the remainder of this paper we will consider in detail the failings of the imperfectionist argument, both as an interpretation of the *General Theory*[9] and as a critique of and alternative to the orthodox theory of employment itself. In order to make the discussion manageable, we will focus on two examples of imperfectionist analysis: the hypothesis that 'sticky' wages cause unemployment and the hypothesis that 'incorrect expectations' are the culprits.

2. Wages and the market mechanism

The *IS-LM* system, as well as some other interpretations of the *General Theory*,[10] is built around the idea that with a fixed money supply, inflexible money wages prevent the attainment of full-employment equilibrium. For a closed economy, the system can be summed up in three equations:

$$Y = i(r) + G \tag{2.1}$$

$$\frac{M}{P} = l(r) + k(Y) \tag{2.2}$$

$$Y = f(P) \tag{2.3}$$

Equation 2.1 is the *IS* curve, income (Y) being determined by investment, itself a function of the rate of interest (r), and autonomous expenditures (G).[11] Equation 2.2 is the *LM* curve, M being the nominal value of the money stock, and P the price level. The demand for the real money stock (M/P) is the sum of the demands for money arising from speculative motives ($l(r)$), and from transactions and precautionary motives combined in $k(Y)$. Equation 2.3 is the aggregate supply curve. This is derived from the condition of labour market equilibrium and an aggregate production function determining the relationship between employment and output.

Labour market equilibrium is defined by:

$$S(P, N) = W = P \cdot D(N) \tag{2.4}$$

where W is the money wage rate, S the labour supply function, D the labour demand function and N the amount of labour. If we define

$$S(P, N) \text{ as } P \cdot L(N) \tag{2.5}$$

[9] Clearly, the *General Theory* itself should not be regarded as definitive in all respects. Yet the imperfectionists have used it to give respectability to their arguments, and it seems worthwhile to check the accuracy of their claims against the original.

[10] See, e.g., those discussed by Magnani in Chapter 14 above.

[11] Government deficit spending would be included here.

(i.e. the price level enters the labour supply function as a multiplicative factor, and money wages are fully flexible in response to price changes) then the labour market clears at an equilibrium real wage:

$$D(N) = W/P = L(N) \tag{2.6}$$

If, on the other hand, the money wage (W) is fixed

$$(\delta S/\delta P = 0) \text{ or sticky } (D(N) > \delta S/\delta P > 0),$$

labour market 'equilibrium' does not necessarily imply full employment. The latter depends on the demand conditions expressed in equations 2.1 and 2.2.

Combining the labour market equilibrium condition (equation 2.4) with an aggregate production function

$$Y = g(N, K) \tag{2.7}$$

where K is the quantity of capital, permits the derivation of the aggregate supply function (equation 2.3). As long as the money wage is 'sticky' this will have a positive slope ($\delta f/\delta P > 0$); the elasticity of the function being dependent not only upon the characteristics of the aggregate production function, but also upon just how 'sticky' the money wage might be. For example, if the money wage is perfectly flexible then equation 2.3 can be replaced by $Y = Y_F$; where Y_F is the full-employment level of output associated with the market-clearing real wage.

Leaving aside the manifest analytical weaknesses of this straightforward modification of orthodox demand and supply theory (not the least of which is its use of the discredited marginal productivity theory of distribution in the description of the labour market), a question which arises immediately relates to the extent to which this model faithfully represents Keynes's explicit discussion in the *General Theory* of the relationship between money wages and the level of employment. This question is rendered all the more interesting given the fact that Keynes's orthodox predecessors had not failed to notice that money wage rigidity would act as an obstacle to the tendency they believed the market mechanism possessed to promote full employment (see, for example, Marshall, 1920a, pp. 709-10, and Pigou, 1933, pp. 252-6).

There are two closely related aspects of this question that call for attention. The first concerns Keynes's views on the role of any hypothesis about money-wage rigidity in his own explanation of unemployment, and the second the role that such an hypothesis would play in what he termed 'classical' theory.

The rationale for the attribution of an assumption of money-wage rigidity to Keynes (see, for example, Hicks, 1937; Modigliani, 1944; Haberler, 1958, p. 242; Barker, 1980) derives from two rather different sources. On the one hand, the trend towards interpreting the *General Theory* along wholly orthodox lines imposed the theoretical necessity of watering down, at least as far as short-run analysis was concerned, the central conclusion of neoclassical economics: that the operation of the price system might tend to establish, *relatively swiftly*, the full employment of 'factors of production'.[12] On the other hand, some of Keynes's remarks on the subject of money wages in the *General Theory*, when taken out of context and coupled with the erroneous conviction that Keynes's analysis of employment 'must' have been a modification of orthodox neoclassical theory designed to bring it into closer conformity with reality, have been used to bolster this reading.

Unfortunately (at least from the point of view of the proponents of this reading), Keynes is perfectly clear in the *General Theory* that his analysis of unemployment *does not* depend upon any assumption of wage rigidity. For although when Keynes conducts his reader through a summary of the essentials of his own theory (in chapter 3) he does assume that 'money wage[s] ... are constant per unit of labour employed', he immediately adds a crucial warning: 'this simplification ... is introduced solely to facilitate the exposition ... the argument is *precisely the same* whether or not money wages ... are liable to change' (Keynes, 1973, vol. 7, p. 27, italics added). Indeed, chapter 19 of the *General Theory* is concerned exclusively with the case of money-wage flexibility – and Keynes *does not* reach there the conclusion that this flexibility tends to establish the full employment of labour (see, for example, ibid., pp. 260-1, 262, 265 and 278) as he would have done had it been the case that his analysis was an imperfectionist one based on the hypothesis of money-wage rigidity.[13]

What is more, Keynes's celebrated remark to the effect that 'we must have some factor, the value of which in terms of money is, if not fixed, at least sticky' (ibid., p. 304, italics omitted), which follows hard on the heels of a statement that workers are 'disposed to resist a reduction in their money-rewards' (ibid., p. 303), is no more supportive of the money-wage rigidity interpretation than is the analysis discussed in the previous paragraph. For the requirement of 'stickiness' to which Keynes alludes here is adduced not to provide an explanation of unemployment, but to ensure stability in the general level of prices – it is required, writes Keynes, 'to give us ... stability of values in a monetary system' (ibid., p. 304). The argument leading up to this conclusion is sketched by Keynes in chapter 21 of the *General Theory*. It warrants careful consideration.

Starting from the proposition (ibid., p. 294; see also p. 302) that the general level of prices depends essentially upon two *independent* variables – the volume of output (i.e. employment) and 'costs' (under appropriate

[12] Indeed, a number of imperfectionists, alerted by Leijonhufvud's warning that attributing a money-wage rigidity hypothesis to Keynes was more than a little questionable (see, e.g., Leijonhufvud, 1971) have searched out other rigidities. Leijonhufvud himself seems to have chosen the rate of interest (Leijonhufvud, 1971, p. 38).

[13] This point is elaborated in Milgate, 1982, ch. 7.

assumptions, the wage-unit)[14] – Keynes enunciates what he somewhat jestingly calls a 'Quantity Theory of Money':

> So long as there is unemployment, *employment* will change in the same proportion as the quantity of money; and when there is full employment, *prices* will change in the same proportion as the quantity of money (ibid., p. 296, italics in original).

There are, however, a number of important qualifications to this statement[15] – one of which is relevant here for it leads up to Keynes's remark on the connection between price stability and the behaviour of money wages. This concerns the possibility that money wages may tend to rise with increases in the quantity of effective demand (the change in which, for simplicity, we shall assume is proportionate with a change in the quantity of money) *below* full employment (ibid., pp. 295 and 301-2).

The latter possibility implies that there may exist positions of less than full employment where increases in effective demand (i.e. the quantity of money under our assumption) give rise to an increase in money wages, and hence the price level, as well as to an increase in output. Keynes then draws a distinction between these situations – he calls them 'positions of semi-inflation' (ibid., p. 301) – and situations of full employment where every increase in effective demand is translated into an effect on prices, he calls this 'absolute inflation' (ibid., p. 301). Thus:

> when a further increase in the quantity of effective demand produces no further increase in output and entirely spends itself on an increase in the cost-unit fully proportionate to the increase in effective demand, we have reached a position which might be appropriately designated as one of true inflation (ibid., p. 303).

Now, it is around this critical level that there exists the asymmetry between inflation and deflation of which Keynes often spoke,[16] and in relation to which his remark about 'stickiness' was made. For if money wages were to rise and fall with every expansion or contraction of effective demand, the price level would be violently unstable. In particular, every contraction of effective demand would so disturb the price-level (and note that the process is a cumulative downward spiral in this case) that there would be no point of price stability 'until either the rate of interest was incapable of falling further or wages were zero' (ibid., p. 304). The predisposition of workers not to accept reductions in money wages, the 'stickiness' to which Keynes refers,

[14] This will be the case when, taking technique and equipment as given, all elements of cost change in the same proportion as the wage-unit (see Keynes, 1973, vol. 7, p. 295).

[15] The most significant here is that the level of effective demand changes in proportion to the quantity of money. This assumption will be retained through the rest of our discussion of this point (see Keynes, 1973, vol. 7, pp. 298-9 for a discussion of the effects of relaxing it).

[16] Where expansions in the quantity of money above this critical level affect money wages and hence prices, whereas contractions below it reduce output and employment and need not necessarily alter the price-level.

thus explains the asymmetric behaviour, in terms of price versus output responses, above and below this 'critical level' (ibid., pp. 291 and 304) in reaction to changes in the quantity of money (which are to be associated with proportional changes in effective demand):

> the long-run stability or instability of prices will depend on the strength ... of the wage-unit (or, more precisely, the cost-unit) ... (ibid., p. 309).

The 'stickiness' is *not* used to explain the level of unemployment, but rather is an explanation (however limited) of the relative stability of the value of money in an economy in which output is not normally at the full-employment level.

We should not leave this subject without also noting that Keynes was alert to the proposition we have already stated in this section of the paper. Namely, that far from being an alternative to the neoclassical theory of employment, the money-wage rigidity hypothesis is part and parcel of that very theory. 'Classical theory', wrote Keynes, 'rest[s] the supposedly self-adjusting character of the economic system on an assumed fluidity of money wages; and, when there is rigidity ... lay[s] on this rigidity the blame for maladjustment' (ibid., p. 257; see also pp. 7-8 and 16). This theory of unemployment is, according to Keynes, the orthodox one (see also Keynes, 1973, vol. 14, pp. 26 and 43; vol. 29, p. 97, for further confirmation of this point). Unsuspecting generations of students have been asked to accept that the very author who claimed to have made such a radical break with the 'classical' school and its 'habitual modes of thought' actually fell back on what he knew to be the orthodox explanation of unemployment.[17] This fraud is all the more clearly exposed now that we can appreciate that Keynes's analysis of unemployment does not depend upon any such imperfectionist arguments (see Chapters 1,2 and 6 above).

Thus we arrive at the central conclusion of this section. It was not Keynes's view that his explanation of employment (based on the operation of the principle of effective demand) required an hypothesis of money-wage rigidity. Indeed, far from being 'Keynesian', such an explanation was, according to Keynes himself, completely 'classical'.

3. Expectations and the market mechanism

The analysis of the co-existence of inflation and unemployment posed a serious problem for *IS-LM* analysis. In a situation in which money wages, the price level and the quantity of money are increasing, differential

[17] One cannot help but imagine that Keynes was contemplating his earlier self, so to speak, when he remarked in the *General Theory* that: 'a classical economist may sympathise with labour in refusing to accept a cut in its money wage, and he will admit that it may not be wise to make it in conditions which are temporary; but scientific integrity forces him to declare that this refusal is, nevertheless, at the bottom of the trouble' (Keynes, 1973, vol. 7, p. 16).

variations in the respective rates of increase of these variables will be sufficient to precipitate the changes in the real wage and the real value of the quantity of money required for the establishment of a full-employment equilibrium in the labour market (a fact noted by Keynes himself; 1973, vol. 7, pp. 9 and 15). Thus the popular inhibition to the operation of the market mechanism, sticky wages, upon which much imperfectionist analysis of unemployment was grounded, is no longer operative. However, instead of alerting the proponents of such models to the inherent weakness in the imperfectionist position – a weakness derived from sharing the same view of the market mechanism as the orthodox demand-and-supply school – the imperfectionists have side-stepped the problem. Not unexpectedly, 'new' inhibitions to the operation of the market mechanism have been 'discovered': real wage resistance (Hicks, 1974, ch. 3), interest rate inflexibility (Leijonhufvud, 1971, p. 38), and mark-up pricing behaviour (Tobin, 1980, p. 35).

The opening created by such *ad hoc* theorising was exploited to great effect by Friedman (1968) and Phelps (1967 and 1968). These authors were able correctly to point out (given that so-called 'Keynesians' and 'monetarists' accepted the same characterisation of the market mechanism) that the flexibility present in an inflationary environment could not only restore the power of the market mechanism to generate full employment, but also that the uncertainty engendered by that same inflationary experience was sufficient to explain a trade-off between inflation and unemployment in the form of a *short-run* Phillips curve. Of course, the *long-run* Phillips curve is vertical at the point where involuntary unemployment is zero – i.e. either at full employment or at the natural rate of unemployment (its modern analogue).

The argument is straightforward. Given that relative prices and quantities are determined by the mutual interaction of the forces of demand and supply, then if the general level of future prices is perfectly anticipated the economy will settle down in a steady-state equilibrium with no involuntary unemployment. Unexpected deviations of actual prices from their expected levels will, however, disrupt equilibrium in, according to Friedman, a predictable way. If nominal prices were higher than expected, unemployment would be lower than the natural rate. If nominal prices were lower than expected, unemployment would be higher than the natural rate. Both effects are, of course, 'temporary'. They give the classic Phillips curve form to the *short-run* relation between unemployment and the rate of change of the general level of prices. It is important to note that the part of the argument which holds that, in the *long run*, the Phillips curve is vertical has been overwhelmingly successful. For example, Modigliani was forced to concede that

> a specific implication of that model, namely that the long-run Phillips' curve is vertical, or, in substance, that in the long-run money is neutral ... by now does not meet serious objection from non-monetarists, at least as a first approximation (1976, p. 119).

Of course, this measure of agreement is not surprising. It confirms the fact that the imperfectionist and orthodox analyses of unemployment are, ultimately, the same.

All scope for a thorough-going theoretical critique of the orthodox pre-Keynesian position having thus vanished, the only path that was left open for the imperfectionist critics was to dispute the central policy conclusion Friedman drew from his analysis – *viz.* an efficient government policy to promote stable prices was all that was required to ensure that the market mechanism would move the economy to a position corresponding to the natural rate of unemployment (see, for example, Friedman, 1968 and 1980). This path, to the credit of their practical intuition rather than their logical consistency, most imperfectionists were swift to follow. Modigliani, for example, felt the policy conclusion to be 'of little practical relevance' because it was based on too optimistic a view of the empirical evidence (Modigliani, 1976, p. 119).

The adequacy of the defences erected against Friedman's initial challenge to the imperfectionist position will be returned to later. It is first necessary to consider some more recent arguments which add a further dimension to the orthodox attack on the imperfectionist position. The arguments in question revolve around the hypothesis that the formulation of expectations is 'rational'. The significance of this challenge is not difficult to grasp: it attempts to remove 'uncertainty and expectations' from the catalogue of imperfections upon which the neoclassical analysis of unemployment is based.

The issues at stake in this debate may be revealed by applying a simple extension of the model set out in the previous section so as to include anticipations. In this case, the level of output must be expressed as a deviation from that level associated with the natural rate of unemployment; a deviation which will be minimised when expectations are perfectly fulfilled. Any residual deviation from this position arises solely from random shocks. The following model is adapted from the analyses developed by Sargent (1973) and Sargent and Wallace (1976):

$$y_t - \bar{y}_t = a(p_t - p_t^e) + \varepsilon_1 \quad (3.1)$$

$$y_t = b_0 [r_t - (p_t^e - p_{t-1})] + b_1 g_t + \varepsilon_2 \quad (3.2)$$

$$m_t - p_t = c_0 y_t + c_1 r_t + \varepsilon_3 \quad (3.3)$$

where y, p and m are the natural logarithms of real national income, the general level of prices, and the (exogenously given) money supply respectively. The nominal interest rate (not a logarithm) is denoted by r; g is a vector of exogenous demand variables (say, government expenditures). The parameters a, b_0, c_0 and c_1 are assumed to be scalars, while b_1 is a vector conformable to g. The variables ε_1, ε_2 and ε_3 are mutually uncorrelated, normally distributed random variables. The variable p_t^e is the public's expectation of p_t at $t-1$; $\bar{y}$ is the level of output associated with the natural rate of unemployment.

Equation 3.1 is the aggregate supply schedule in the form associated with the natural rate hypothesis. Equation 3.2 is the *IS* curve, relating income to the expected real interest rate and to exogenous expenditures. Equation 3.3 is the *LM* curve, or portfolio balance condition, relating the real value of the stock of money to the transactions and portfolio demands for real money balances.

Other than the random variables, the model contains four unknowns, y_t, p_t, r_t and p_t^e. To complete the system some hypothesis must be advanced on the formation of expectations.

For example, the model might be closed with the supposition that price expectations are formed by the simple adaptive or extrapolative scheme:

$$p_t^e = \lambda p_{t-1} \tag{3.4}$$

It may then be shown (see appendix for derivation) that:

$$y_t - \bar{y}_t = a\left[(m_t - \lambda m_{t-1}) + d_1 (g_t - \lambda g_{t-1}) + d_2 (y_t - \lambda y_{t-1}) + d_3 \left\{(\lambda - 1)(p_{t-1} - \lambda p_{t-2})\right\}\right] + \mu \tag{3.5}$$

where d_1, d_2 and d_3 are simply redefined parameters, and μ is a combination of error terms.

It is evident from equation 3.5 that despite the aggregate supply function being based on the natural rate hypothesis, an important role for a discretionary monetary and fiscal policy remains. By selecting appropriate values for m and g the authorities can attempt to minimise the fluctuation of actual output around its full-employment level (or, more strictly, its natural rate of unemployment). Active policies are on the agenda because of the manner in which expectations have been supposed to be formed (equation 3.4). The adaptive expectations hypothesis implies that past mistakes are only slowly corrected, and it is the need to overcome the unfortunate consequences of this 'stickiness' in the process of correction that provides the rationale for government intervention – a very familiar theme indeed in imperfectionist arguments.

But what is the rationale for the adaptive rule on the formation of expectations (equation 3.4) which has led to this conclusion? If individuals blindly followed this rule, then they would soon discover that they were systematically wrong. 'Wrong', in the sense of making systematic expectational errors. This conflicts with the underlying proposition that individuals attempt to make rational utility-maximising and profit-maximising decisions, albeit (typically) with only a limited amount of information available to them. Of course, predictions can only possibly be improved if the economic variables under consideration are subject to determination by systematic forces; i.e. if the market mechanism operates according to systematic and persistent 'laws'. As we have seen, the imperfectionists agree that this is the case by deferring to the forces of demand and supply.

The hypothesis of rational expectations, unlike that of adaptive expectations which provides the basis for an imperfectionist position, takes these (shared) underlying propositions seriously. The rational expectations school identifies the forces at work in the market mechanism with those outlined in Walrasian general equilibrium theory – i.e. the forces of demand and supply. Notice how a *theory* has simply been taken to *be* 'objective reality'. As Muth, in the case of predictions by firms, argued:

> The hypothesis can be re-phrased a little more precisely as follows: that expectations of firms (or, more generally, the subjective probability distribution of outcomes) tend to be distributed, for the same information set, about the prediction of the theory (or the 'objective' probability distribution of outcomes) (Muth, 1961, p. 316).

The consequence of making this supposition about expectation formation is that for any given prediction of, say, the price level,

$$p_t^e = E\,(p_t | \varphi_{t-1}) \tag{3.6}$$

where E is the expected value operator and φ_{t-1} is the set of information concerning p_t^e at t–1, the expected value of the difference between prediction and event is zero. That is

$$E\,(p_t - p_t^e | \varphi_{t-1}) = 0 \tag{3.7}$$

When this hypothesis is introduced into the discussion of unemployment, money and inflation (see, for example, Walters, 1971; Lucas, 1972a and 1972b; Sargent, 1973), the consequences are dramatic. They can be seen if, following the procedure adopted by Pesaran (1982), we replace equation 3.4 with equation 3.6 and complete the model by assuming that expectations are formed rationally (in the sense of equation 3.7). Then, remembering that the random variables have a zero mean, taking expectations of equations 3.1, 3.2 and 3.3, gives:

$$y_t^e = \bar{y}_t \tag{3.1a}$$

$$y_t^e = b_0\,[r_t^e - (p_t^e - p_{t-1})] + b_1 g_t^e \tag{3.2b}$$

$$m_t^e - p_t^e = c_0 y_t^e + c_1 r_t^e \tag{3.3a}$$

where $y_t^e = E\,(y_t | \varphi_{t-1})$, $r_t^e = E\,(r_t | \varphi_{t-1})$ and so on.

By subtracting these equations from 3.1, 3.2 and 3.3 respectively, the *unanticipated* change in endogenous variables may be found. For example, subtracting equation 3.1a from 3.1 gives:

$$y_t - y_t^e = a\,(p_t - p_t^e) + \varepsilon_1$$

and so on. Now, since $\bar{y}_t = y_t^e$ (equation 3.1a) and $E\,(p_t - p_t^e \mid \varphi_{t-1}) = 0$, the deviation of actual income from its natural level may be shown (see appendix) to be:

$$y_t - \bar{y}_t = z_1\,(m_t - m_t^e) + z_2\,(g_t - g_t^e) + \eta \tag{3.8}$$

where the z_i's are combinations of parameters and η is a combination of error terms.

The extent of the influence of monetary and fiscal policy upon the level of activity is revealed in equation 3.8 to be dependent upon the deviation of the actual policy from the policy which was expected to rule. If government policies follow an unpredictable course then they can continue to influence the levels of output and employment. But if the government pursues *any* consistent monetary and fiscal policy, all effects on activity disappear (since individuals can predict policies in the same way as they an predict other economic variables).

Suppose, for example, that current monetary and fiscal policy is based upon last year's money supply, fiscal stance and level of output, plus a normally distributed random element. That is, suppose:

$$m_t = f_m\,(m_{t-1}, g_{t-1}, y_{t-1}) + \varepsilon_m \tag{3.9}$$

and

$$g_t = f_g\,(m_{t-1}, g_{t-1}, y_{t-1}) + \varepsilon_g \tag{3.10}$$

Since individuals and firms can form rational expectations of government policies:

$$m_t^e = E\,(m_t \mid \varphi_{t-1}) = f_m \tag{3.11}$$

$$g_t^e = E\,(g_t \mid \varphi_{t-1}) = f_g \tag{3.12}$$

Substituting equations 3.11 and 3.12 into equation 3.8 gives:

$$y_t - \bar{y}_t = z_1\,\varepsilon_m + z_2\,\varepsilon_g + \eta \tag{3.13}$$

That is, the deviation of actual output from its full-employment level (natural rate) is simply a sum of random events. Only random elements in government policy can have any impact – and precisely what effect cannot be known in advance. There is no role for systematic monetary and fiscal policies. The imperfectionist position which relied on the influence of uncertainty and expectations to provide a rationale for interventionist policies has disappeared.

The striking re-affirmation of the *laissez-faire* position that the above argument entails should have come as no surprise to the imperfectionists. It arises simply from following through in a clear and consistent manner the logic of the presupposition of imperfectionist analysis: that the market mechanism is ultimately governed by the 'laws' of demand and supply. However, the rational expectations hypothesis has been widely criticised in imperfectionist circles. Such criticisms fall into two broad groups. First, criticisms of the conclusions drawn with respect to monetary policy by the rational expectations variant of the orthodox market mechanism school; and second, criticisms of the hypothesis that expectations are formed rationally. Each may be taken in turn.

The rational expectations position has been associated with propositions concerning the neutrality of money – in the sense that the real equilibrium of the system is independent of monetary policy which serves only to determine nominal magnitudes (Lucas, 1972a). However, as was pointed out by Samuelson (1958), different monetary policies, even if fully anticipated, will have consequences for real variables; primarily through portfolio balance and substitution effects. Buiter (1980) advances these considerations as a critique of the rational expectations school, but it is a critique of limited significance. Samuelson's argument amounts to saying nothing more than that different monetary policies will result in the economy being at different *full-employment* equilibria. Since there is no criterion for choosing between one full-employment equilibrium and another, the fact that strict monetary neutrality does not hold is of very little importance. Indeed, it is no more significant than noticing that multiple equilibria are entirely possible anyway.

The second set of objections to the rational expectations model involves primarily a resurrection of familiar imperfectionist themes:

> prices are determined in non-competitive markets by a mark-up process (Modigliani, 1977, p. 120; Tobin, 1980, p. 35; Buiter, 1980, p. 41);
>
> the adjustment of wages and relative prices to their equilibrium levels is sluggish (Tobin, 1980, pp. 25-7; Buiter, 1980, p. 41);
>
> neither labour markets nor individuals are sufficiently homogeneous to permit the simple derivation of rational expectations results (Modigliani, 1977, p. 121; Tobin, 1980, p. 26);
>
> empirical evidence suggests that the economy is not typically in a natural rate equilibrium (Modigliani, 1977, pp. 119 and 121; Buiter, 1980, p. 41).

Once again, the pragmatic appeal of these observations should not be permitted to disguise the fact that they in no way constitute an alternative explanation of the underlying relationship between the operation of the market mechanism and the determination of the level of employment. Rather they are additional considerations to be incorporated into the old orthodox theory to give it a more plausible empirical content. Indeed, if it really is the case that prices and quantities are not determined in accordance with the generally accepted principles of demand and supply, then it is that very theory of the operation of the market mechanism which should be abandoned. However, the unquestioning acceptance of this conception of the market mechanism as applicable to long-run (or equilibrium) analysis, and the discussion of all relevant considerations in terms of deviations from that long-run analysis not only involve the acceptance of the orthodox model of the market mechanism but also consign the analysis of unemployment to an underworld of *ad hoc* hypotheses. The end of the doctrine of *laissez-faire*, of which Keynes himself spoke so optimistically over fifty years ago, will not occur until economists realise that the market mechanism is not explained by demand-and-supply theory. And this will not be easy; this homely but inadequate theory has so dominated the discipline that whole generations of economists, industrialists, bankers, politicians and journalists have grown up believing it to be not just a theory about the real world, but the real world itself. Unfortunately, however, no such ultimate truth was discovered when the familiar demand-and-supply curves were first drawn on the back of an envelope.

4. Conclusion

We can now draw together the central themes of this paper. The orthodox neoclassical theory of value, distribution and output characterises the market mechanism as *tending* always to ensure the full utilisation of 'factors of production', including labour. Therefore the orthodox neoclassical theory of unemployment is based on the imposition of arbitrary imperfections onto the general equilibrium theory of demand and supply. The arguments contained in the present paper suggest that this analysis of the relationship between unemployment and the market mechanism is unsatisfactory on four main counts:

1. The attempt to relegate empirical *regularities* into the secondary class of imperfections (of frictions and rigidities) completely ignores the fact that such regularities should be part and parcel of the characterisation of the *normal* operation of the market mechanism (not of its abnormal operation as the imperfectionist position requires).
2. There exists a perfectly satisfactory explanation of the relationship between unemployment and the market mechanism, in the form of Keynes's principle of effective demand, which does not invoke arbitrary imperfections to explain unemployment.

3. The appeal to unknowable imperfections – uncertainty, disappointed expectations, 'conjectures' and the like – serves to deprive economic analysis of all definite content, thus reducing the discussion of economic policy to the status of guesswork and negating the single most important achievement of economic theory during the past two hundred years – namely that the market mechanism is governed by systematic, objective forces.
4. There are fundamental analytical shortcomings to neoclassical theory even when applied to the analysis of equilibrium (see, for example, Garegnani, 1970 and Chapter 7, above; Eatwell, 1982) which suggest that the imperfectionist superstructure is in any case erected on crumbling foundations.

The two examples from the multitude of imperfectionist arguments upon which we have focused, the hypothesis that money wages are inflexible and the debate over the natural rate of unemployment/rational expectations position, illustrate clearly the foundations which are common to both the orthodox market mechanism school and the imperfectionists.

The abandonment of these common foundations sweeps away both the theory of employment of the market mechanism school and the theories of unemployment conjured up by the imperfectionists. This does not mean that some of the 'empirical regularities' utilised by the imperfectionists are now to be ignored. Rather their importance should be assessed in the context of the more satisfactory theory of employment which is to be found in the characterisation of the market mechanism provided by Keynes's theory of effective demand and the surplus approach to the analysis of value and distribution.

Appendix

Combining 3.2 and 3.3:

$$p_t = m_t + d_1 g_t + d_2 y_t + d_3 (p_t^e - p_{t-1}) + \frac{c_1}{b_o}\varepsilon_2 - \varepsilon_3 \qquad \text{(A.1)}$$

$$\text{where } d_1 = \frac{c_1 b_1}{b_o},$$

$$d_2 = -\frac{(b_o c_o + c_1)}{b_o},$$

$$\text{and } d_3 = -c_1.$$

Using 3.4 and substituting A.1 into 3.1
results in 3.5, with

$$\mu = \varepsilon_1 - \frac{a \lambda c_1 \varepsilon_2}{b_o} + a(\lambda - 1) \varepsilon_3$$

3.8 is derived by subtracting 3.1a, from 3.1, 3.2a from 3.2, and 3.3a from 3.3; and then solving the resultant equations for $y_t - \bar{y}_t$ (remember that the rational expectation of y_t is $\bar{y}_t$). Terms have been collected as follows:

$$z_1 = \frac{a b_o}{b_o + a(b_o c_o + c_1)}$$

$$z_2 = \frac{a c_1 b_1}{b_o + a(b_o c_o + c_1)}$$

$$\eta = \frac{b_o \varepsilon_1 + a c_1 \varepsilon_2 - a b_o \varepsilon_3}{b_o + a(b_o c_o + c_1)}$$

References

Entries marked with an asterisk are included in this volume.

Andrews, P.S. 1938. Summary of replies to questions on effects of interest rates, *Oxford Economic Papers*

Appelbaum, E. 1979. The labour market, in *A Guide to Post-Keynesian Economics* (ed. A.S. Eichner), London, Macmillan

Arrow, K. and Hahn, F.H. 1971. *General Competitive Analysis*, Edinburgh, Oliver and Boyd

Barker, T. 1980. The economic consequences of monetarism: a Keynesian view of the British economy, 1980-1990, *Cambridge Journal of Economics*

Benassy, J.P. 1975. Neo-Keynesian disequilibrium theory, *Review of Economic Studies*

Bhaduri, A. 1966. The concept of the marginal productivity of capital and the Wicksell effect, *Oxford Economic Papers*

Böhm-Bawerk, E. 1891. *The Positive Theory of Capital*, Macmillan, London

Böhm-Bawerk, E. 1930. *The Positive Theory of Capital*, New York, Stechert

Bortkievicz, L. von. 1906-7. Wertrechnung und Preisrechnung im Marxschen System, *Archiv fur Sozialwissenschaft und Sozialpolitik*. Translated in *International Economic Papers*, 1952

Bortkievicz, L. von. 1907. Zur Berichtigung der Grundlegenden Theoretischen Konstruction von Marx in Dritten Bande des 'Kapital', *Jahrbucher fur Nationalokonomie*, Translated in Böhm-Bawerk, E. *Karl Marx and the Close of his System* (ed. P.M. Sweezy), New York, Kelley, 1949

Brockie, M.D. and Grey, A. 1956. The marginal efficiency of capital and investment programming, *Economic Journal*

Brown, M. *et al.* (eds). 1976. *Essays in Modern Capital Theory*, Amsterdam, North Holland

de Brunhoff, S. 1976. *Marx on Money*, New York, Urizen Books

Buiter, W. 1980. The macroeconomics of Dr. Pangloss: a critical survey of the new classical macroeconomics. *Economic Journal*

Champernowne, D.G. 1953-4. The production function and the theory of capital: a comment, *Review of Economic Studies*

Clark, J.B. 1907. *Essentials of Economic Theory*, New York, Macmillan

Clifton, J.A. 1977. Competition and the evolution of the capitalist mode of production, *Cambridge Journal of Economics*

Clower, R. 1965. The Keynesian counter-revolution: a theoretical appraisal, in Hahn and Brechling, 1965

Coddington, A. 1976. Keynesian economics: the search for first principles, *Journal of Economic Literature*

Corry, B.A. 1959. Malthus and Keynes, *Economic Journal*

Cripps, F. 1977. The money supply, wages and inflation, *Cambridge Journal of Economics*

Davidson, P. 1967. A Keynesian view of Patinkin's theory of employment, *Economic Journal*
Davidson, P. 1977. Money and general equilibrium, *Economie Appliquée*
Davidson, P. 1978a. *Money and the Real World*, London, Macmillan
Davidson, P. 1978b. Why money matters: lessons from a half-century of monetary theory, *Journal of Post-Keynesian Economics*
Davidson, P. 1979. The dual-faceted nature of the Keynesian revolution: money and money wages in unemployment and flow prices, *Journal of Post-Keynesian Economics*.
Davidson, P. and Smolensky, E. 1964a. *Aggregate Supply and Demand Analysis*, New York, Harper Row
Davidson, P. and Smolensky, E. 1964b. Modigliani on the interaction of monetary and real phenomena, *Review of Economics and Statistics*
Debreu, G. 1959. *Theory of Value*, New Haven, Yale University Press
Dixit, A. 1977. The accumulation of capital theory, *Oxford Economic Papers*
Dobb, M. 1973. *Theories of Value and Distribution since Adam Smith*, Cambridge, CUP
Eatwell, J. 1976. Irving Fisher's 'rate of return over cost' and the rate of profit in a capitalistic economy, in Brown *et al.*, 1976
Eatwell, J. 1977. The irrelevance of returns to scale in Sraffa's analysis, *Journal of Economic Literature*
*Eatwell, J. 1979. *Theories of Value, Output and Employment*, London, Thames Papers in Political Economy
Eatwell, J. 1982. Competition, in *Classical and Marxian Political Economy* (ed. Bradley and Howard), London, Macmillan
Ebersole, J.F. 1938-39. The influence of interest rates upon entrepreneurial decisions in business, *Harvard Business Review*
Eichner, A.S. 1979a. Introduction, in *A Guide to Post-Keynesian Economics* (ed. A.S. Eichner), London, Macmillan
Eichner, A.S. 1979b. A look ahead, in *A Guide to Post-Keynesian Economics* (ed. A.S. Eichner), London, Macmillan
Eichner, A.S. and Kregel, J.A. 1975. An essay on post-Keynesian theory: a new paradigm in economics, *Journal of Economic Literature*
Eshag, E. 1963. *From Marshall to Keynes*, Oxford, Blackwell
Feinstein, C. (ed.) 1967. *Socialism, Capitalism and Economic Growth*, Cambridge, CUP
Fisher, F. 1969. The existence of aggregate production functions, *Econometrica*
Fisher, F. 1971. Aggregate production functions and the explanation of wages: a simulation experiment, *Review of Economics and Statistics*
Fisher, I. 1930. *The Theory of Interest*, New York, Macmillan
Friedman, M. 1968. The role of monetary policy, *American Economic Review*
Friedman, M. 1974a. A theoretical framework for monetary analysis, in Gordon (ed), 1974
Friedman, M. 1974b. Comments on the critics, in Gordon (ed.), 1974
Friedman, M. 1976. Comment on Tobin and Buiter, in Stein (ed.), 1976
Friedman, M. 1977. Inflation and unemployment, *Journal of Political Economy*
Friedman, M. 1980. Memorandum of evidence, in Treasury and Civil Service Committee (1980)
Garegnani, P. 1960. *Il Capitale nelle Teorie della Distribuzione*, Milan, Giuffre
Garegnani, P. 1964-65. Note su consumi, investimenti, e domanda effettiva, *Economia Internazionale*
Garegnani, P. 1966. Switching of techniques, *Quarterly Journal of Economics*
*Garegnani, P. 1970. Heterogeneous capital, the production function and the theory of distribution, *Review of Economic Studies*

*Garegnani, P. 1976. On a change in the notion of equilibrium in recent work on value and distribution, in M. Brown, K. Sato and P. Zarembka (eds.), *Essays in Modern Capital Theory*, Amsterdam, North Holland
*Garegnani, P. 1978. Notes on consumption, investment and effective demand: I, *Cambridge Journal of Economics*
*Garegnani, P. 1979. Notes on consumption, investment and effective demand: II, *Cambridge Journal of Economics*
Glustoff, E. 1968. On the existence of a Keynesian equilibrium, *Review of Economic Studies*
Godley, W.A.H. and Nordhaus, W.D. 1972. Pricing in the trade cycle, *Economic Journal*
Gordon, R.J. (ed.) 1974. *Milton Friedman's Monetary Framework*, Chicago, University of Chicago Press
Grandmont, J.M. 1971. On the short-run equilibrium in a monetary economy, in *Allocation under Uncertainty: Equilibrium and Optimality* (ed. J. Dreze), London, Macmillan, 1973
Grandmont, J.M. 1977. Temporary equilibrium theory, *Econometrica*
Grandmont, J.M. and Laroque, G. 1976. On temporary Keynesian equilibrium, *Review of Economic Studies*
Green, R. 1982. Money, output and inflation in classical economics, *Contributions to Political Economy*
Haberler, G. 1939. *Prosperity and Depression* (2nd edn), Geneva, League of Nations
Haberler, G. 1958. *Prosperity and Depression* (4th edn), London, Allen and Unwin
Haberler, G. 1964. *Prosperity and Depression* (4th edn), London, Allen and Unwin
Hahn, F.H. 1971. Professor Friedman's views on money, *Economica*
Hahn, F.H. 1973a. *On the Notion of Equilibrium in Economics*, Cambridge, CUP
Hahn, F.H. 1973b. The winter of our discontent, *Economica*
Hahn, F.H. 1977. Keynesian economics and general equilibrium theory: reflections on some current debates, in *The Microfoundations of Macroeconomics* (ed. G. Harcourt), London, Macmillan
Hahn, F.H. 1978. On non-Walrasian equilibria, *Review of Economic Studies*
Hahn, F.H. 1978. Unsatisfactory equilibria, mimeo, Cambridge
Hahn, F.H. 1980. Monetarism and economic theory, *Economica*
Hahn, F.H. and Brechling, F. 1965. *The Theory of Interest Rates*, London, Macmillan
Hahn, F.H. and Neild, R.R. 1980. Monetarism: why Mrs Thatcher should beware. *The Times*, London, 25th February
Harcourt, G. (ed.). 1977. *The Microeconomic Foundations of Macroeconomics*, London, Macmillan
Harrod, R. 1937. Mr Keynes and traditional theory, *Econometrica*, as reprinted in Harrod, R. 1972. *Economic Essays* (2nd edn), London, Macmillan
Harrod, R. 1972. *The Life of John Maynard Keynes*, Harmondsworth, Penguin (1st edn 1951)
Hicks, J.R. 1932. *The Theory of Wages*, London, Macmillan; 2nd edn, New York, St Martin's Press (1964)
Hicks, J.R. 1935. Wages and interest: the dynamic problem, *Economic Journal*, reprinted in Hicks (1932)
Hicks, J.R. 1936. Mr Keynes' theory of employment, *Economic Journal*
Hicks, J.R. 1937a. Mr Keynes and the 'Classics': a suggested interpretation, *Econometrica* as reprinted in *Readings in the Theory of Income Distribution*, Toronto (1946)
Hicks, J.R. 1937b. Mr Keynes and the 'Classics', *Econometrica*, as reprinted in J.R. Hicks, *Critical Essays in Monetary Theory*, Oxford, Clarendon Press (1967)

Hicks, J.R. 1939. *Value and Capital* (1st edn), Oxford, Clarendon Press
Hicks, J.R. 1946. *Value and Capital* (2nd edn), Oxford, Clarendon Press
Hicks, J.R. 1963. Commentary, in Section III of Hicks (1932)
Hicks, J.R. 1965. *Capital and Growth*, Oxford, Clarendon Press
Hicks, J.R. 1974. *The Crisis in Keynesian Economics*, Oxford, Blackwell
Hildenbrand, K. and Hildenbrand, W. 1978. On Keynesian equilibria with unemployment and quantity rationing, *Journal of Economic Theory*
Jevons, W.S. 1970. *Theory of Political Economy*, London, Penguin, (1st edn 1871)
Kahn, R.F. 1954. Some notes on liquidity-preference, *Manchester School*
Kahn, R.F. 1972. *Selected Essays on Employment and Growth*, Cambridge, CUP
*Kahn, R.F. 1977. Malinvaud on Keynes, *Cambridge Journal of Economics*
Kaldor, N. 1955-56. Alternative theories of distribution, *Review of Economic Studies*
Kaldor, N. 1970. The new monetarism, *Lloyds Bank Review*
Kalecki, M. 1938. Distribution of national income, revised version in Kalecki (1971)
Kalecki, M. 1939. *Essays in the Theory of Economic Fluctuations*, London, Allen and Unwin
Kalecki, M. 1971. *Essays on the Dynamics of the Capitalist Economy*, Cambridge, CUP
*Kenway, P. 1980. Marx, Keynes and the possibility of crisis, *Cambridge Journal of Economics*
Keynes, J.M. 1933, Thomas Robert Malthus: the first of the Cambridge economists, in Keynes, J.M. 1951
Keynes, J.M. 1936. *The General Theory of Employment, Interest and Money*, London, Macmillan
Keynes, J.M. 1937. Alternative theories of the rate of interest, *Economic Journal*
Keynes, J.M. 1937a. The general theory of employment, *Quarterly Journal of Economics*
Keynes, J.M. 1939. Relative movements of real wages and output, *Economic Journal*, as reprinted in Keynes (1973), vol. 7
Keynes, J.M. 1951. *Essays in Biography*, London, Hart-Davis (1st edn 1933)
Keynes, J.M. 1971. *Economic Consequences of the Peace*, London, Macmillan (1st edn 1919)
Keynes, J.M. 1973. *The Collected Writings of J.M. Keynes*, London, Macmillan (all references to Keynes (1973) and to *JMK* are to the appropriate volume and page number of this edition)
Klein, L.R. 1950. *The Keynesian Revolution*, London, Macmillan
Knight, F. 1915. Neglected factors in the problem of normal interest, *Quarterly Journal of Economics*
Kregel, J. 1976. Economic methodology in the face of uncertainty, *Economic Journal*
Leijonhufvud, A. 1968. *On Keynesian Economics and the Economics of Keynes*, New York, OUP
Leijonhufvud, A. 1971. *Keynes and the Classics*, London, IEA
Leijonhufvud, A. 1974. Keynes' employment function, *History of Political Economy*
Leijonhufvud, A. 1981. *Information and Coordination: Essays in Macroeconomic Theory*, Oxford, OUP
Leontief, W. 1936. The fundamental assumptions of Mr Keynes, *Quarterly Journal of Economics*, as reprinted in W. Leontief, *Economic Essays*, vol. 1, Oxford, OUP (1966)
Levhari, D. 1965. A non-substitution theorem and switching of techniques, *Quarterly Journal of Economics*
Lindahl, E. 1939. *Studies in the Theory of Money and Capital*, London, Allen and Unwin
Lucas, R. 1972a. Expectations and the neutrality of money, *Journal of Economic Theory*
Lucas, R. 1972b. Econometric testing of the natural rate hypothesis, in *The Econometrics of Price Determination Conference* (ed. Eckstein), Washington, Federal Reserve System

Lundberg, E. 1954. *Studies in the Theory of Economic Expansion*, New York, Kelley (first published in Swedish, 1937)
Malinvaud, E. 1977. *The Theory of Unemployment Reconsidered*, Oxford, Blackwell
Malinvaud, E. 1980. *Profitability and Unemployment*, Cambridge, CUP
Malthus, T.R. 1836. *Principles of Political Economy* (2nd edn), reprinted, London, Pickering (1951)
Malthus, T.R. 1958. *Principles of Political Economy* (2nd edn), New York, Kelley (first printed 1836)
Mandel, E. 1962. *Marxist Economic Theory*, London, Merlin Press
Mandel, E. 1971. *The Formation of the Economic Thought of Karl Marx*, London, New Left Books
Marshall, A. 1920. *Principles of Economics* (8th edn), London, Macmillan
Marshall, A. 1920a. *Industry and Trade*, London, Macmillan (3rd edn)
Marshall, A. 1961. *Principles of Economics* (9th (variorum) edn; ed. C.W. Guillebaud), London, Macmillan (1st edn 1890)
Marshall, A. 1965. *Money, Credit and Commerce*, New York, Kelley (first published 1923)
Marx, K. 1967. *Capital*, vol. 3, New York, International Publishers
Marx, K. 1968. *Theories of Surplus Value*, part 2, London, Lawrence and Wishart
Marx, K. 1969. *Theories of Surplus Value*, part 2, London, Lawrence and Wishart
Marx, K. 1970a. *Capital*, vol. 1, London, Lawrence and Wishart
Marx, K. 1970b. *Capital*, vol. 2, London, Lawrence and Wishart
Marx, K. 1972a. *Capital*, vol. 3, London, Lawrence and Wishart
Marx, K. 1972b. *Theories of Surplus Value*, part 3, London, Lawrence and Wishart
Marx, K. 1973. *Grundrisse. Foundations of the Critique of Political Economy*, Harmondsworth, Pelican Books
Marx, K. 1974. *Capital*, vol. 3, London, Lawrence and Wishart
Marx, K. and Engels, F. 1934. *Selected Correspondence 1846-1895*, London, Lawrence and Wishart
Meade, J. 1961. *A Neo-Classical Theory of Economic Growth*, London, Allen and Unwin
Meek, R.L. 1950-51. Thomas Joplin and the theory of interest, *Review of Economic Studies*
*Milgate, M. 1977. Keynes on the 'classical' theory of interest, *Cambridge Journal of Economics*
Milgate, M. 1979. On the origin of the notion of 'intertemporal equilibrium', *Economica*
Milgate, M. 1982. *Capital and Employment*, London, Academic Press
Mill, J.S. 1945. Notes on N.W. Senior's Political Economy, *Economica*
Minsky, H. 1976. *John Maynard Keynes*, New York, Columbia UP
Modigliani, F. 1944a. Liquidity preference and the theory of interest and money, *Econometrica*, as reprinted in *Readings in Monetary Theory*, London, Unwin (1952)
Modigliani, F. 1944b. Liquidity preference and the theory of interest and money, *Econometrica*
Modigliani, F. 1963. The monetary mechanism and its interaction with real phenomena, *Review of Economics and Statistics*
Modigliani, F. 1977. The monetarist controversy, or should we forsake stabilization policies? *American Economic Review*; reprinted in *Modern Macroeconomics* (ed. Konliras and Thorn), New York, Harper and Row (1979)
Moggridge, D. 1980. *Keynes* (2nd edn), London, Macmillan
Morishima, M. 1964. *Equilibrium, Stability and Growth*, Oxford, OUP
Muth, J. 1961. Rational expectations and the theory of price movements. *Econometrica*
Negishi, T. 1977. Existence of an underemployment equilibrium, in *Equilibrium and*

Disequilibrium in Economic Theory (ed. G. Schwoediauer), Dordrecht, Reidel Publishing Company

Neild, R.R. 1963. *Pricing and Employment in the Trade Cycle*, Cambridge, CUP

Nuti, D.M. 1974. On the rates of return on investment, *Kyklos*

Ohlin, B. 1937a. Some notes on the Stockholm theory of savings & investments: Part I, *Economic Journal*

Ohlin, B. 1937b. Some notes on the Stockholm theory of savings & investments: Part II, *Economic Journal*

Pareto, V. 1961. *Corso di economia politica*, Turin, Boringhieri (first published in French, 1896-97)

Pasinetti, L. 1960. A mathematical formulation of the Ricardian system, *Review of Economic Studies*

Pasinetti, L. 1969. Switches of technique and the 'rate of return in capital theory', *Economic Journal*

Pasinetti, L. 1974. *Growth and Income Distribution: Essays in Economic Theory*, Cambridge, CUP

Patinkin, D. 1948. Price flexibility and full-employment, *American Economic Review*, as reprinted in *Readings in Monetary Theory*, London, Unwin (1952)

Patinkin, D. 1965. *Money, Interest and Prices*, New York, Harper Row

Patinkin, D. 1974. Friedman on the quantity theory and Keynesian economics, in Gordon (ed.) 1974

Patinkin, D. and Leith, J.C. (eds). 1977. *Keynes, Cambridge and the General Theory*, London, Macmillan

Pesaran, M.H. 1982. A critique of the proposed tests of the natural rate – rational expectations hypothesis, *Economic Journal*

Phelps, E. 1967. Phillips curves, inflationary expectations, and optimal employment over time, *Economica*

Phelps, E. 1968. Money wage dynamics and labor-market equilibrium, *Journal of Political Economy*

Phelps, E. 1970. Money wage dynamics and labour market equilibrium, in Phelps (ed.), *Microeconomic Foundations of Employment and Inflation Theory*, Norton, New York

Pigou, A.C. 1933. *Theory of Unemployment*, London, Macmillan

Pigou, A.C. 1936. Mr. J.M. Keynes' General Theory of Employment, Interest and Money, *Economica*

Pigou, A.C. 1947. Economic progress in a stable environment, *Economica*, as reprinted in *Readings in Monetary Theory*, London, Unwin (1952)

Radner, R. 1974. Market equilibrium and uncertainty: concepts and problems, in *Frontiers of Quantitative Economics*, vol. 2 (ed. M.O. Intriligator and D.A. Kendrick) New York, Elsevier

Ricardo, D. 1951. *The Works and Correspondence of David Ricardo* (ed. P. Sraffa), Cambridge, CUP (all references to Ricardo (1951) are to the appropriate volume and page number of this edition).

Ricardo, D. 1951a. *Principles of Political Economy and Taxation*, vol. 1 of *Works and Correspondence of David Ricardo* (ed. P. Sraffa), Cambridge, CUP

Ricardo, D. 1951b. *Notes on Malthus*, vol. 2 of *Works and Correspondence of David Ricardo* (ed. P. Sraffa), Cambridge, CUP

Robbins, L. 1930. On a certain ambiguity in the conception of stationary equilibrium, *Economic Journal*

Robbins, L. 1958. *Robert Torrens and the Evolution of Classical Economics*, London, Macmillan

Roberts, D.L. 1978. Patinkin, Keynes and aggregate supply and demand analysis, *History of Political Economy*

Roberts, J. and Sonnenschein, H. 1977. On the foundations of the theory of monopolistic competition, *Econometrica*
Robertson, D.H. 1963. *Lectures on Economic Principles*, London, Fontana (first published in three volumes, 1957-59)
Robinson, J. 1933. The theory of money and the analysis of output, *Review of Economic Studies*
Robinson, J. 1952. *The Rate of Interest and Other Essays*, London, Macmillan
Robinson, J. 1953-54. The production function and the theory of capital, *Review of Economic Studies*
Robinson, J. 1956. *The Accumulation of Capital*, London, Macmillan
Robinson, J. 1960. *Collected Economic Papers*, vol. 2, Oxford, Blackwell
Robinson, J. 1962. *Essays in The Theory of Economic Growth*, New York, St Martin's Press
Robinson, J. 1971. *Economic Heresies*, London, Macmillan
Robinson, J. 1973. *Introduction to the Theory of Employment* (2nd edn), London, Macmillan, (1st edn 1937)
Robinson, J. 1974. *History versus Equilibrium*, London, Thames Polytechnic
Robinson, J. 1975a. Introduction, *Collected Economic Papers*, vol. 2 (2nd edn), Oxford, Blackwell
Robinson, J. 1975b. The unimportance of reswitching, *Quarterly Journal of Economics*
Robinson, J. 1978. *Contributions to Modern Economics*, Oxford, Blackwell
*Robinson, J. 1979. Garegnani on effective demand, *Cambridge Journal of Economics*
Robinson, J and Eatwell, J. 1973. *Introduction to Modern Economics*, London, McGraw-Hill
Rosdolsky, R. 1977. *The Making of Marx's Capital*, London, Pluto Press
Samuelson, P.A. 1947. *Foundations of Economic Analysis*, Cambridge, Mass, Harvard UP
Samuelson, P.A. 1958. What the classical theory of money really was, *Canadian Journal of Economics*
Samuelson, P.A. 1962. Parable and realism in capital theory: the surrogate production function, *Review of Economic Studies*
Samuelson, P.A. 1966. A summing-up, *Quarterly Journal of Economics*
Samuelson, P.A. 1975. The unimportance of reswitching: comment, *Quarterly Journal of Economics*
Sargent, T.J. 1973. Rational expectations, the real rate of interest and the natural rate of unemployment, *Brookings Papers on Economic Activity*
Sargent, T.J. and Wallace, N. 1978. Rational expectations and the theory of economic policy, *Journal of Monetary Economics*
Sayers, R.S. 1940. Business men and the terms of borrowing, *Oxford Economic Papers*
Schefold, B. 1980. Fixed capital as a joint product and the analysis of accumulation with different forms of technical progress, in *Essays in the Theory of Joint Production* (ed. L. Pasinetti), London, Macmillan
Schumpeter, J.A. 1936. Review of the *General Theory of Employment, Interest and Money*, by John Maynard Keynes, *Journal of the American Statistical Association*
Schumpeter, J.A. 1954. *History of Economic Analysis*, New York, OUP
Shackle, G.L.S. 1967. *The Years of High Theory: Invention and Tradition in Economic Thought, 1926-1939*, Cambridge, CUP
Shackle, G.L.S. 1972. *Epistemics and Economics: A Critique of Economic Doctrines*, Cambridge, CUP
Shackle, G.L.S. 1974. *Keynesian Kaleidics*, Edinburgh, Edinburgh University Press
Shaikh, A. 1975. Laws of production and laws of algebra: the humbug production function, *Review of Economics and Statistics*
Shove, G.F. 1933. Review of Hicks' 'The Theory of Wages', *Economic Journal*, reprinted

in Hicks (1932)
Smith, A. 1904. *An Inquiry into the Nature and Causes of the Wealth of Nations*, London, Methuen (1st edn 1776)
Smith, A. 1954. *The Wealth of Nations*, London, Irwin (1st edn 1776)
Solow, R. 1956. A contribution to the theory of economic growth, *Quarterly Journal of Economics*
Solow, R. 1963. *Capital Theory and the Rate of Return*, Amsterdam, North Holland
Solow, R. 1967. The interest rate and the transition between techniques, in Feinstein, ed. (1967)
Solow, R. 1970. *Growth Theory*, Oxford, OUP
Spaventa, L. 1968. Realism without parable in capital theory, in Ceruna, *Recherches recentes sur la fonction de production*, Universitaire de Namur
Sraffa, P. 1926. The laws of returns under competitive conditions, *Economic Journal*, reprinted in *Readings in Price Theory* (ed. G.J. Stigler and K.E. Boulding), American Economic Association, 1953
Sraffa, P. 1960. *Production of Commodities by Means of Commodities*, Cambridge, CUP
Sraffa, P. (ed.) with Dobb, M. 1950-55. *The Works and Correspondence of David Ricardo* (10 vols), CUP
Stein, J.L. (ed.) 1970. *Monetarism*, Amsterdam, North Holland
Strøm, S. and Werin, L. 1978. *Topics in Disequilibrium Economics*, London, Macmillan
Swan, T. 1956. Economic growth and capital accumulation, *Economic Record*
Sweezy, P.M. 1942. *The Theory of Capitalist Development*, New York, OUP
Symposium. 1966. Symposium on paradoxes in capital theory, *Quarterly Journal of Economics*
Tobin, J. 1955. A dynamic aggregative model, *Journal of Political Economy*
Tobin, J. 1958. Liquidity preference as behaviour toward risk, *Review of Economic Studies*
Tobin, J. 1974. Is Friedman a monetarist?, in Gordon (1974)
Tobin, J. 1980. *Asset Accumulation and Economic Activity: Reflections on Contemporary Economic Theory*, Oxford, Blackwell
Tobin, J. and Buiter, W. 1976. Long-run effects of fiscal and monetary policy on aggregate demand, in Stein (1976)
Tooke, T. 1959. *An Inquiry into the Currency Principle*, London, London School of Economics (first printed in 1844)
Treasury and Civil Service Committee. 1980. *Memoranda on Monetary Policy*, London, HMSO
Tuchscherer, T. 1979. Keynes' model and the Keynesians, *Journal of Post-Keynesian Economics*
Wald, A. 1936. On some systems of equations in mathematical economics, in *Econometrica* (1951)
Walras, L. 1954. *Elements of Pure Economics* (translated W. Jaffe), Illinois, Irwin
Walters, A. 1971. Consistent expectations, distributed lags, and the quantity theory, *Economic Journal*
Weintraub, E.R. 1979. *Microfoundations; the Compatibility of Microeconomics and Macroeconomics*, Cambridge, CUP
Weintraub, E.R. and Weintraub, S. 1972. The full employment model, a critique, *Kyklos*
Weintraub, S. 1978. *Capitalism's Inflation and Unemployment Crisis: Beyond Monetarism and Keynesianism*, New York, Addison Wesley
Wells, P. 1974. Keynes' employment function, *History of Political Economy*
Wells, P. 1979. Modigliani on flexible wages and prices, *Journal of Post-Keynesian Economics*

Wicksell, K. 1901. *Lectures on Political Economy*, vol. 1 (translated from 3rd edn by E. Classen, Routledge and Kegan Paul, 1934-35)
Wicksell, K. 1907. The enigma of the business cycle, as reprinted in Wicksell, *Interest and Prices*, New York, Kelley (1965)
Wicksell, K. 1934. *Lectures on Political Economy*, vol. 1, London, Routledge and Kegan Paul
Wicksell, K. 1935. *Lectures on Political Economy*, vol. 2, London, Routledge and Kegan Paul
Wicksell, K. 1936. *Interest and Prices* (translated by R.F. Kahn), London, Royal Economic Society
Wicksell, K. 1954. *Value, Capital and Rent*, London, Allen and Unwin
Wicksell, K. 1965. *Interest and Prices*, New York, Kelley (first published 1898)

Index